WITHDRAWN

Contemporary Political Ideologies

A Comparative Analysis

Fourteenth Edition

WADSWORTH
CENGAGE Learning

Korea • Mexico • Singapore • Spain • United Kingdom • United States

WADSWORTH
CENGAGE Learning™

Contemporary Political Ideologies: A Comparative Analysis, Fourteenth Edition
Lyman Tower Sargent

Publisher: Suzanne Jeans

Executive Editor: Carolyn Merril

Assistant Editor: Katherine Hayes

Editorial Assistant: Nathan Gamache

Technology Project Manager: Caitlin Holroyd

Marketing Manager: Amy Whitaker

Marketing Communications Manager: Heather Baxley

Art Director: Linda Helcher

Print Buyer: Linda Hsu

Permissions Editor: Mardell Glinski Schultz

Production Service: Pre-Press PMG

Photo Researcher: Pre-PressPMG

Cover Designer: C Miller

Cover Image: Jason Reed/Photodisc/©Getty Images

Cover Printer: Webcom

Compositor: Pre-Press PMG

Printer: Webcom

For product information and technology assistance, contact us at **Cengage Learning Customer & Sales Support, 1-800-354-9706**

For permission to use material from this text or product, submit all requests online at **cengage.com/permissions**
Further permissions questions can be emailed to **permissionrequest@cengage.com**

Library of Congress Control Number: 2008935799

ISBN-13: 978-0-495-56939-8

ISBN-10: 0-495-56939-9

Wadsworth
10 Davis Drive
Belmont, CA 94002-3098
USA

Cengage Learning is a leading provider of customized learning solutions with office locations around the globe, including Singapore, the United Kingdom, Australia, Mexico, Brazil, and Japan. Locate your local office at: **international.cengage.com/region**

Cengage Learning products are represented in Canada by Nelson Education, Ltd.

For your course and learning solutions, visit **academic.cengage.com**

Purchase any of our products at your local college store or at our preferred online store **www.ichapters.com**

Printed in Canada
1 2 3 4 5 6 7 11 10 09 08

To Evan

Contents

II NATIONALISM AND GLOBALIZATION

V MARXISM AND ANARCHISM

About the Author

Lyman Tower Sargent is professor emeritus of political science at the University of Missouri–St. Louis and a fellow of the Stout Research Centre, Victoria University of Wellington, New Zealand. He has been a fellow at the Institute for Advanced Study, Princeton; a Visiting Fellow at Mansfield College, University of Oxford; a Research Fellow in the Centre for Political Ideologies in the Department of Politics and International Relations, University of Oxford; a visiting professor at the University of Exeter, England; the University of East Anglia, England; and Victoria University of Wellington, New Zealand; and an academic visitor at the London School of Economics and Political Science.

Sargent is the author of *New Left Thought: An Introduction* (Dorsey, 1972); *Techniques of Political Analysis* (with Thomas A. Zant, Wadsworth, 1970); *British and American Utopian Literature, 1516–1985: An Annotated, Chronological Bibliography* (Garland, 1988); *New Zealand Utopian Literature: An Annotated Bibliography* (Stout Research Centre, 1997); *New Zealand Intentional Communities: A Research Guide* (Stout Research Centre, 1997); *Living in Utopia: Intentional Communities in New Zealand* (with Lucy Sargisson, Ashgate, 2004); and numerous articles on political theory. He is the editor of *Consent: Concept, Capacity, Conditions, Constraints* (Franz Steiner Verlag, 1979); *Extremism in America: A Reader* (New York University Press, 1995); *Political Thought in the United States: A Documentary History* (New York University Press, 1997); *The Utopia Reader* (with Gregory Claeys, New York University Press, 1999); and *Utopia: The Quest for the Ideal Society in the Western World* (with Roland Schaer and Gregory Claeys, Oxford University Press, 2000), which was also published as *Utopie: La quête de la société idéale en Occident* (Fayard, 2000).

Preface

In this book, the essential features of a wide range of ideologies—such as nationalism, democracy, and feminism—are presented so they can be easily understood. To the extent possible, they are described as they are understood by their believers, together with some of the criticism by their opponents. In addition, each ideology is shown in the context of contemporary political and social issues and institutions. My goal is to help readers draw their own conclusions about each ideology based on a reasonably balanced presentation of that ideology and how it functions today.

This book was first published in the period known as the Sixties (in the United States, roughly 1965 to 1975), when Americans were first becoming aware of ideological debate in the United States. Americans had taken pride in being free of ideological conflicts, and compromise was thought to be the essential component of U.S. politics. Many outside the United States saw this very belief as identifying a dominant U.S. ideology, and few Americans today would argue that political debate in the United States is free from ideology. But it is still quite striking that as the confirmation hearings for Judge John G. Roberts, Jr. (b. 1955) for Chief Justice of the Supreme Court were being planned, it was explicitly stated that his ideology would need to be examined, and a poll showed that well over half those polled wanted to know his "beliefs" on key issues.

Therefore, to understand what is happening both in the United States and the rest of the world, it is important to understand the ideologies that inform the thought and actions of both politicians and average citizens. Today it is clearly essential that we understand how others think, and this book is designed to facilitate that understanding.

Understanding ideologies can also help us understand ourselves and what we believe. Self-identity—who we are and how we came to be who we are—is a question that most of us face at various times in our lives. When we are students we are finding out who we are, or creating ourselves, and part of that process of identity building is achieved through identification with like-minded others. Along with that identification often comes a set of beliefs, which sometimes constitutes an ideology. Later in life, we may reaffirm or change whom we identify with, and that change may bring a change in beliefs.

At the same time, many people are unaware of what different groups of people believe. I have heard many women say, "I am not a feminist, but…," finishing the sentence with a statement that comes straight from feminism. The person is rejecting the stereotype of feminism, but not understanding the actual beliefs. When I have asked women who have used the phrase "I am not a feminist" about specific positions taken by most feminists, they have most often agreed with the feminist position. Because stereotypes are used as part of political debate to distort the position of an opponent, it is important to know the actual positions.

Ideologies are reflected in political institutions and policies and are often used as tools, both consciously and unconsciously, by political actors. Ideologies change over time, reflecting both reconsideration of the principles or core beliefs found in the ideologies and how practical political issues influence these beliefs. Thus the reader will find here much discussion of current political debates throughout the world to illustrate how ideologies affect politics and are affected by it.

Since the first edition of *Contemporary Political Ideologies: A Comparative Analysis* was published 40 years ago, it has been the leading text in the field. But the book has undergone dramatic changes over the years as ideologies have changed, emerged, and faded. The changes in this edition are the result of the fact that ideologies, and our understanding of them, appear to be going through some significant changes that some would argue are revolutionary. Four changes are being noted, three of which I have allowed for in previous editions of this book. The fourth I have discussed previously and have expanded on considerably here in the new chapter, "Globalization: An Emerging Ideology?" But I am not convinced that globalization reflects as revolutionary a change in the nature of ideologies as some contend. For example, Manfred B. Steger argues that all ideologies are in the process of changing from a national basis to a globalized one, and his position is presented in the new chapter.[1]

One question Steger raises that suggests a possibly far-reaching change in ideologies is why we have so many variants of ideologies that require us to add

---

[1] Steger made this argument in a lecture he gave November 6, 2007, at the Centre for Political Ideologies, University of Oxford, entitled "Political Ideologies and Social Imaginaries in the Global Age." He also refers to the question in the Preface to his *The Rise of the Global Imaginary: Political Ideologies from the French Revolution to the Global War on Terror* (Oxford, England: Oxford University Press, 2008: ix).

a prefix like *post* or *neo*. We now even have post-postmodernism. At the least this suggests a growing flux in ideological thinking and an uncertainty about the validity of some of our labels. Steger argues that the change is much more basic than this and that it is part of the process of changing from a nationally based way of thinking to a globalized way.

Of the other three changes in the way the text is presented, one has brought about a slight adjustment to the structure of the text. Some editions ago, I added Liberation Theology as an ideology, and then I added the ideological aspects of Islam. Now it is clear that the influence of religion on ideologies has become much more important. This has led to the addition of a discussion of the relationship between ideology and religion.

Many argue that we are entering a post-secular age, following a long period of secularism in which political thinking and religious thinking were perceived by most people as separate spheres belonging in separate compartments. While important overlaps have always been acknowledged, generally we talked about political thinkers or religious thinkers; we did not refer to thinkers as "politico-religious," nor did we employ some other awkward word. This apparent shift has to be approached with care. It is still the official position of many Christian churches that a deep division between church and state should be maintained, largely due to the fear—based on historical experience—that to avoid control by the state it is best for churches to keep their distance from the state. It is also true that many people feel that their political positions and their religious beliefs have little to do with one another. But a number of political ideologies exist in which religion and politics are not separate but intertwined, and this appears to be growing for individual believers in many ideologies. Still, some secularists strongly believe that maintaining secularism is essential. This position is based on the fear, again founded on historical experience, that to avoid religious control of political thinking, the two modes of thinking must be kept completely separate from each other. Therefore, given the importance of these developments, I have made the connections more explicit in this edition.

This relates to another change in the nature of ideologies: ideological thinking is in a transition from very clear-cut ideologies, with only a few core principles, to ideologies with a number of variants built on those core principles. While the cores remain roughly the same, the ways those cores are developed by different sets of believers may differ dramatically. And the growth in importance of two ideologies that were not in the first editions of this book, feminism and environmentalism, means that all the other ideologies have had to change to incorporate a position on them.

Finally, ever since Karl Mannheim published the first version of his *Ideology and Utopia* in 1929, ideology and utopia have been treated as two totally different ways of thinking. But it is clear that there is a utopia at the heart of, or in the core of, every ideology; and although I have only suggested the connection between utopia and ideology in the past, here I make it explicit. In doing so, I point out that even Mannheim said something of the sort.

I have maintained the essential character of the book as a comparative introduction to the dominant and some minor ideologies found in the world today. As always, I have included extensive lists of suggested reading so that readers can explore further questions that interest them. These lists include scholarly studies of the ideologies as well as statements for and against the beliefs expressed in the ideologies. They have been updated, and I have appended brief notes to some of the items indicating the subject or argument.

I have revised the list of websites in the suggested readings, and all were live and recently updated in early 2008; but anyone familiar with the Web will know that some of these addresses will not be valid throughout the life of the book. As with the lists of suggested readings, these sites include both those designed to present information and those designed to advocate a position.

ACKNOWLEDGMENTS

Obviously I have accumulated a near-infinite number of debts in writing 14 editions, debts much too numerous to mention specifically. This edition was begun while I was a Visiting Fellow at Mansfield College, University of Oxford, and a Research Fellow in the Centre for Political Ideologies in the Department of Politics and International Relations, University of Oxford. I wish to thank both institutions and particularly Professor Michael Freeden, Director of the Centre, for the opportunity to work in such congenial surroundings. This edition was completed while I was a Fellow at the Stout Research Centre for New Zealand Studies at Victoria University of Wellington, New Zealand. I wish to thank Professor Lydia Wevers, Director of the Centre, for giving me the opportunity to return to the Stout's congenial surroundings. In addition, I want to specifically thank Professor Manfred B. Steger for a discussion of his position and for allowing me to see page proofs of parts of his *The Rise of the Global Imaginary* (Oxford University Press, 2008) prior to publication.

Wadsworth and I would also like to thank the reviewers of the fourteenth edition: Leda Barnett, Our Lady of the Lake University; John Korsmo, Western Washington University; Jean Marie Makang, Frostburg State University; JoAnne Myers, Marist College; and Guy Poitras, Trinity University.

Contemporary
Political Ideologies

1

Ideologies

What Are They and Why Study Them?

Today all over the world, people are killing in each other in the name of ideology. Although ideology is often a disguise for a lust for power or economic gain, it is used to justify such killing. At a different level, in political campaigns, each side insists that they have the only right answers to economic and social problems, and they use ideological language to support their position. To understand the world today, it is essential to understand the conflicting ideologies that are at the heart of many conflicts and so much political debate, and it is the purpose of this book to provide a comparative introduction to these ideologies.

Of course ideology is not the only thing that divides or unites people; race, ethnicity, religion, gender, class, national and regional identification, and many other things both pull people together and push them apart. But ideology is one of those things, and it is important to understand how ideology works and the content of ideologies. In addition, because we are influenced by ideology whether we are aware of it or not, understanding these ideologies will help us understand our own beliefs and those of our friends and associates.

We are surrounded by expressions of ideology. Our parents try to influence our thinking, as do our friends, teachers, religious leaders, and politicians. When we read newspapers or magazines, listen to the radio, watch TV, or go online, we are getting consciously or unconsciously distorted partial views. Because these sources of information often disagree, we are exposed to a range of ideologies. And in the development of our own set of beliefs, we may be influenced by a variety of ideologies, which is one reason that some governments try to limit access to varied sources of information.

As we grow older, we also make conscious choices among beliefs and attitudes, either because we weigh one position against another and conclude that one is preferable according to some standard, or because we simply respect or dislike someone who holds that belief. Through this process of influence and choice, we gradually come to the set of beliefs and attitudes with which we live. This set of beliefs may change, but it changes less as we age; the experiences of a lifetime have led us to these views, and it is extraordinarily difficult to set aside what we have come to believe to be the truth and accept that we have been wrong. Some people do reach such conclusions, usually because they encounter someone whose life experiences have led to different conclusions, thus forcing a reevaluation.

How do we identify an ideology? The most obvious way is through particular words that are associated with the ideology. For example, someone influenced by capitalism will usually speak favorably of the free market; anarchists will usually speak of the state negatively. Most ideologies use such words, and a major clue to changes in an ideology is disagreements over, or changes in, such words. For example, class was once at the absolute center of Marxism, but contemporary Marxists disagree about where it belongs.

IDEOLOGY DEFINED

Scholars disagree on the meaning and importance of ideology. One has even written, "Ideology is the most elusive concept in the whole of social science."[1] As a result, ideology today is what we have come to call an *essentially contested concept,* or a concept about which there is truly fundamental disagreement.[2] Most political debate swirls around such contested concepts, and all the ideologies discussed here contain one or more of these concepts.

This section constructs a definition of ideology, distinguishes political ideologies from other ideologies, and shows how political ideology relates to political theory and political philosophy. Finally, we discuss theorists of ideology and some of the current controversies regarding the nature of ideology and the way it is changing.

An ideology is a system of values and beliefs regarding the various institutions and processes of society that is accepted as fact or truth by a group of people. An ideology provides the believer with a picture of the world both as it is and as it should be, and, in doing so, it organizes the tremendous complexity of the world into something fairly simple and understandable. Ideologies are organized or patterned beliefs. The degree of

---

[1] David McLellan, *Ideology,* 2nd ed. Minneapolis: University of Minnesota Press, 1995: 1.

[2] See W. B. Gallie, "Essentially Contested Concepts," *Proceedings of the Aristotelian Society,* n.s., 56 (1955–56): 167–198; and William E. Connolly, *The Terms of Political Discourse,* 3rd ed. Princeton, NJ: Princeton University Press, 1993. Discussions of the problems connected with this idea can be found in Terence Ball, "Political Theory and Conceptual Change," *Political Theory: Tradition and Diversity.* Andrew Vincent, ed. Cambridge: Cambridge University Press, 1997: 34–36; and Andrew Vincent, *The Nature of Political Theory.* Oxford, England: Oxford University Press, 2004: 98–104.

organization and the simplicity of the resulting picture vary considerably from ideology to ideology, and the ever-increasing complexity of the world tends to blur those pictures. At the same time, however, the core and the fundamental pattern of each ideology remain fairly constant.

Ideologies are stories about the world we live in and our place in that world. When we tell a story, we structure information to communicate our understanding of something to someone else. Stories can, of course, be tall tales or outright lies, but they are still trying to present a pattern that can be accepted as true. An obvious tall tale depends on our recognizing it as such; a lie works only if the hearer believes it to be true.

As in traditional stories, ideologies present a coherent, understandable picture of the world. Believers, telling the story of their beliefs, think they are telling the truth; it is up to the reader, viewer, or listener to sort truth from falsehood. When we read a story, we often suspend our disbelief in it, and while we are still reading the story, watching the film or video, or playing the computer game, the story is real. Some people so want a story to be real that they lose themselves in it and try to change their world to be like the story, rather than accept the story's untruth. Although the best-known cases of this are connected with sophisticated computer games, the political stories we are taught that become ideologies have the same effect on many people. The case for each ideology has positive and negative elements, things that the ideology supports and things that it rejects, and these are mutually reinforcing.

A *political* ideology is, in its simplest formulation, an ideology that focuses on the political. The political system is the way that societies make decisions about their most important values; one scholar defined the political system as "the authoritative allocation of values" for a society;[3] another scholar titled a famous book *Politics: Who Gets What, When, How.*[4] These definitions are much the same. Thus it would be possible simply to insert the word *political* in front of the word *ideology* in the definition given earlier, and the result would be a perfectly acceptable definition of *political ideology.*

This book discusses only *political* ideologies. There are two partial exceptions, two cases where the political aspects of religious belief have become important enough to require treatment: the political ideologies of Islam and Liberation Theology, which started as a political movement within the Roman Catholic Church and has now spread to Protestantism and throughout the Christian world.

Political Philosophy, Political Theory, and Political Ideology

The terms *political ideology, political theory,* and *political philosophy* are frequently used to refer to different ways of thinking about political ideas. The first term, *political ideology,* relates, as we have seen, to the beliefs of a group; that term should never be used in place of either of the other two. The other two terms

---

[3] David Easton, *The Political System: An Inquiry into the State of Political Science,* 2nd ed. New York: Alfred A. Knopf, 1971: 129.

[4] Harold Lasswell, *Politics: Who Gets What, When, How.* New York: McGraw–Hill, 1936. Reprint. *With Postscript (1958).* New York: Meridian Books, 1958.

are often used interchangeably with nothing lost; at other times, it is important to distinguish between them.

Political theory refers to generalizations about politics and society that are based on data, much as any generalization in any science. *Political philosophy,* on the other hand, is explicitly evaluative or normative. It is a set of ideas about how governments and people *should* behave.

All three terms are connected. Every political philosophy is based in part on a political theory. In other words, every statement about how people and governments *should* behave contains a statement about how they *do* behave. In addition, every political ideology contains both political theory and political philosophy, or generalizations about how people and governments do behave and how they should behave. But in a political ideology, these generalizations become beliefs rather than empirical or normative statements about behavior.[5]

Whatever words are used, the important thing to remember is that there are both differences and connections among generalizations about how social and political institutions and the people making them up behave, how they should behave, and the various belief systems that emerge from such generalizations.

SOCIAL MOVEMENTS AND IDEOLOGIES

Most ideologies initially developed in association with the growth and maturation of a social movement. This was obviously the case with the initial development of modern democracy in the seventeenth century, Marxism and anarchism in the nineteenth century, and fascism and National Socialism, feminism, Liberation Theology, and environmentalism in the twentieth century. But in all cases, both scholars and believers have sought and found precedents and precursors. The political ideologies of Islam developed mostly in the nineteenth and twentieth centuries in connection with social movements among Muslims. Nationalism provides a different problem, because there is a fundamental dispute over whether it has been around for many centuries or just a few; and, as we shall see in the next chapter, the answers lead to very different interpretations of nationalism. At present, a new ideology may be emerging that is generally called *globalization* or *globalism*. It has strong supporters and fierce opponents and is already affecting all the other ideologies. The opponents of globalization clearly see themselves as forming a new social movement against the powerful supporters of globalization.

Today, when no social movement is completely unified, one of the most hotly contested areas is the ideology of the movement. Every faction vying for power says that it has the truth. Thus, in addition to conflicts between ideologies, there are deep divisions within ideologies. Only an ideology that has lost its vitality could be free from such differences, and if it were, it would no longer be included in this book.

---

[5] For a recent discussion of the relationship of these three, see Michael Freeden, "Ideology and Political Theory." *Journal of Political Ideologies* Vol. 11:1 (February 2006): 3–22.

IDEOLOGY AND PRACTICE

A central concern of all students of ideology is the extent to which, and the ways in which, ideology affects practice. Political leaders use the language of the dominant ideology of their country to justify their actions, but are these actions actually based on ideology or on expediency? Also, because it is easier to take a strong stand when you are not responsible for the results, politicians are often more ideological when out of power than when in power. Still, ideology has clearly become part of the political landscape in the past quarter century.

The most likely effect of ideology on political action is in limiting options. Except in extraordinary circumstances, political leaders will not perceive as options policies that fall outside their ideology. In this way ideology limits but does not determine practice. However, we have had the opportunity to witness just such an extraordinary break from ideology in Eastern Europe and the former Soviet Union, where both political leaders and ordinary citizens have struggled to free themselves from the preconceptions of communism.

Some people may not even notice the differences between the various sets of beliefs that influence them, but others will be so torn apart by the conflict that they develop serious mental problems. Most of us muddle through, aware that we are not completely consistent in our beliefs and behavior but not terribly bothered by that fact.

Similar situations occur within countries. In most open societies in which many ideologies are recognized and accepted, conflict within the individual is unlikely to become important. But conflicts among ideologies may become obvious, and if the numbers of adherents of conflicting ideologies are large enough and close enough in size, a country's stability can be affected. On the other hand, in a closed system with only one official ideology, an individual who holds beliefs counter to that ideology will probably be intensely aware of the difference and be affected by it. As noted here, such an individual may even be killed for that ideology. The same thing is true for the country as a whole. Ideological differences, including differences *within* the official ideology, become more important and can cause serious conflict.

In any society, different segments of the population will hold different ideologies. For example, within the United States today, the overwhelming majority, if asked, would call themselves believers in democracy. But some would call themselves anarchists, National Socialists, and so forth. Every society exhibits a variety of ideologies. In no case will a society be so completely dominated by a single ideology as to have no ideological alternatives available, even if alternatives are suppressed by the regime.

Many of those willing to label themselves as democrats, or as adherents of some other ideology, do not act as the ideology predicts. But most people build up a pattern of behavior, some aspects of which come directly from the dominant political ideology of the country in which they live. For example, it is a bit surprising that people accept the outcome of elections, rather than fighting for their side when they lose, as recently happened in Kenya. But most people in countries with established democracies are so conditioned to accept losses in elections that they do so without ever thinking about revolt. Just think about the reaction to the 2000 U.S. presidential election. Even though the person who won the most votes lost the election, and many people remain convinced that electoral procedures in a number of states were somewhere between inefficient and corrupt, the result was accepted with little dissent. This acceptance is not always the rule, though, and violent responses to election results occur regularly.

THEORIES OF IDEOLOGY

The word *ideology* was first used by Antoine Louis Claude Destutt, Comte de Tracy (1754–1836) at the end of the eighteenth century to describe an approach to understanding how ideas are formed. But it was the middle of the nineteenth century before the term came to be used regularly with a different meaning, and only in the twentieth century did it become a contested concept.

The Marxist Approach

Marx and Engels Karl Marx (1818–1883) argued that ideologies blind people to facts about their place in society. He described as ideological any set of political illusions produced by the social experiences of a class—that is, a social group defined by its economic role—for example, owners or workers. Marx's colleague Friedrich Engels (1820–1895) called ideology *false consciousness.* For Marx and Engels, a person's membership in a particular class produced a picture of the world shaped by the experiences of that class. Thus it would be almost impossible for an individual class member to form an accurate conception of the world. Marx argued that *socialization*—that is, the process by which an individual comes to learn about and accept the values of the society—is strongly shaped by that person's place in the class system of that society. In other words, he contended that the social setting in which each of us lives determines the broad outlines of the way we think. The members of different classes are both directly and indirectly taught to think and behave in ways appropriate for their own class. This pattern is often called the *social construction of reality.* What we perceive as reality is created by the social world we inhabit; living in a different society, we would perceive a different reality. Other Marxists, like Antonio Gramsci (1891–1937) and Louis Althusser (1918–1990), refined Marx's analysis.

Antonio Gramsci A political activist and social theorist influenced by Marx, Gramsci developed most of his contributions while imprisoned by the Italian Fascists during the last eleven years of his life. Gramsci argued that the ruling classes did not need to dominate the lower classes by force because they used the institutions of socialization—schools, churches, families, and so on—to create a social *hegemony.* This means that people are socialized into viewing the world in the same way that those in the ruling class view it. Being socialized to view the world this way means that the view is accepted subconsciously as common sense or normal, part of everyday life.

Louis Althusser Althusser revised Marx's approach to ideology by arguing that ideology did not simply obscure or hide reality but created a new reality. The belief system becomes part of a person's life; there is no reality outside of it. Workers accept their position as the natural order, which obviously reinforces the position of the ruling class.

Ideology as Necessary Illusion

Ideology can so structure a person's thought and life that it becomes an essential part of them, even if false. Two thinkers, Georges Sorel (1847–1922) and Sigmund Freud (1856–1939) described this phenomenon.

Georges Sorel Sorel argued that mass movements develop visions of the future in which their members do not quite believe but that are an essential part of what motivates them. He called these visions *myths* rather than ideologies. Sorel focused on fairly specific myths, such as the belief in the general strike prevalent among syndicalists, rather than the broader belief systems that this text calls *ideologies*. Also, as the word *myth* implies, the depth of belief is not the same as for an ideology. But myths can galvanize people and are clearly part of all ideologies.

Sigmund Freud Freud made one point that must be noted about beliefs such as ideologies. Freud was specifically concerned with religious belief, but his comments apply equally well to political ideologies. Freud argued that although belief systems are illusions based on the distortion or repression of our psychological needs, they still provide an organized framework for explaining the world and its ills. An accepted explanation, even one that is wrong, can be comforting. Thus Freud, like Marx, saw ideologies as illusions that keep us deluded and content with a difficult, if not intolerable, condition. Freud prescribed psychoanalysis if the illusion becomes sufficiently pathological; Marx prescribed revolution.

Karl Mannheim Although influenced by Marx, Karl Mannheim (1893–1947) was the first thinker to put ideology at the center of social analysis. For Marx, ideologies were illusions that kept members of a class from understanding their true place in society. Mannheim attempted to address the same phenomenon scientifically. He argued that ideology should be treated from two perspectives, which he labeled the "total conception" and the "particular conception" of ideology.[6]

The "total conception" describes the beliefs held in common by a group, such as a social class or an age group. These beliefs are similar to the blinders on a horse, limiting the believer's view of the world to what is acceptable to the ideology. A person whose mind has been sufficiently formed by his or her membership in a group either does not perceive information that conflicts with the belief system or is provided by that belief system with a convenient explanation that allows the contradiction to be set aside without being recognized as a threat.

---

[6] Karl Mannheim, *Ideology and Utopia: An Introduction to the Sociology of Knowledge,* Louis Wirth and Edward Shils, trans. 1936; London: Routledge, 1991: 50.

For Mannheim, an ideology is produced by a failing ruling class to protect itself from the realization of its coming extinction.

The "particular conception" describes the situation in which people recognize the beliefs of opponents as "more or less conscious disguises of the real nature of a situation, a true recognition of which would not be in accord with his interest."[7] This is the belief that the other person's ideas, but not our own, are false representations of the world, illusions or masks that hide the truth from the believer.

Mannheim believed that intellectuals who were not frozen into a class would be capable of recognizing ideologies and of providing a synthesis of perspectives that would help to overcome ideology. For individual believers he recommended education and psychoanalysis.

Ideology and Culture

After Mannheim, other theorists developed approaches to ideology that moved it even further from the negativism of the Marxist approach, from which Mannheim had not rid himself entirely.

Clifford Geertz In 1964 anthropologist and social theorist Clifford Geertz (1926–2006) published the article "Ideology as a Cultural System,"[8] in which he outlined a definition of ideology as a system of symbols. Geertz, like Mannheim, was searching for a relatively neutral definition of the term that would be useful to social scientists. As an anthropologist, Geertz saw ideology deriving from culture, which produces a set of psychologically satisfying symbols that bring order to the world by providing a mechanism through which the world can be understood.

Paul Ricoeur Philosopher Paul Ricoeur (1913–2005) developed a theory of ideology that stressed the importance of foundational myths that pull people together and help create a national identity. But he also pointed out that these myths are false and open to challenge. Thus for Ricoeur, ideology had both positive and negative elements, and he used the word as a neutral term to help in understanding human behavior.

Charles Taylor In *Modern Social Imaginaries* (2004), philosopher Charles Taylor (b. 1931) uses the phrase *social imaginary* in much the way that other writers use *ideology*. Taylor says that "the social imaginary is that common understanding that makes possible common practices and a widely shared sense of legitimacy,"[9] and he says that such understandings are expressed most often in stories and myths.

Michael Freeden The most influential scholar writing on ideology today is Michael Freeden (b. 1944), author of *Ideologies and Political Theory* (1996) and *Ideology: A Very Short Introduction* (2003) and editor of the *Journal of Political Ideologies* (founded 1996). Freeden argues that ideologies are "a distinguishable and

---

[7] Mannheim, *Ideology and Utopia:* 49.

[8] See Clifford Geertz, "Ideology as a Cultural System." In *Ideology and Discontent,* David E. Apter ed. New York: Free Press of Glencoe, 1964: 46–76.

[9] Charles Taylor, *Modern Social Imaginaries.* Durham, NC: Duke University Press, 2004: 23.

unique genre of employing and combining political concepts."[10] They are "distinctive configurations of political concepts."[11]

Each ideology has a set of core concepts, some vary over time and others remain unchanged. Through ideologies we come to know the right meaning of justice, liberty, equality, and so forth, and we "know" that other meanings given to these concepts are wrong.

The "End of Ideology" Debate

In the 1950s and 1960s, a debate started, particularly in the United States, about whether ideological politics had ended in the West.[12] Some writers argued that not only had ideology ended in the West but that its demise was a good thing, because ideology was a bad thing. Ideological politics were seen as divisive—politics that made compromise impossible, drove people apart, and hindered Western progress toward the "good society." Had ideology not gotten in the way, a better society might have been possible in the foreseeable future through the usual practices of compromise politics.

The end of ideology, to the extent it existed at all, is better labeled the *exhaustion with ideology*. By the late 1950s, the twentieth century had seen two world wars; numerous minor wars; the full development of two major new ideologies, communism and fascism; and, in the United States, two major anti-Left campaigns (in the 1920s and 1950s) and a major antifascist campaign during World War II. One response to all this was an attempt to escape from ideology into objectivity. Particularly in the social sciences, attempts were made to eliminate value judgments from research. Although the social sciences are more objective than they were before World War II, scholars rapidly discovered limits to objectivity where human beings are concerned. Also, the development of important political movements—such as the civil rights movement in the United States, which demanded that people take a stand—taught us that understanding a situation as objectively and thoroughly as possible, and taking a position about it, can be complementary actions rather than contradictory ones. And then came the conflict over the war in Vietnam, and the need to take a position shattered whatever remained of the notion that complete objectivity was possible.[13]

A redevelopment of the end of ideology theory greeted the publication in 1989 of "Have We Reached the End of History?" by Francis Fukuyama (b. 1952),

---

[10] Michael Freeden, *Ideologies and Political Theory: A Conceptual Approach*. Oxford, England: Clarendon Press, 1996: 48. See also Freeden's more recent statement, "Editorial: What Is Special about Ideologies?" *Journal of Political Ideologies* Vol. 6, no. 1 (2001): 5–12.

[11] Freeden, *Ideologies and Political Theory*, 4.

[12] For the debate, see Mostafa Rejai, ed., *Decline of Ideology?* Chicago: Aldine-Atherton, 1971; and Chaim I. Waxman, ed., *The End of Ideology Debate*. New York: Funk & Wagnalls, 1968. The book that gave rise to the debate in the United States was Daniel Bell's *The End of Ideology: On the Exhaustion of Political Ideas in the Fifties*. Glencoe, IL: Free Press, 1960.

[13] For an argument regarding the relationship between "facts" and "values," see Hilary Putnam, *The Collapse of the Fact/Value Dichotomy and Other Essays*. Cambridge, MA: Harvard University Press, 2002. Putnam's argument is specifically concerned with economic analysis but reflects broader debates within the social sciences.

republished in his very popular *The End of History and the Last Man* (1992).[14] In this essay, Fukuyama argued that liberalism—his name for democratic capitalism— had obviously won the day and that no other ideology was a serious contender for dominance. For Fukuyama, fundamental contradictions no longer existed in the world, either in ideology or in practice.

In his most recent reflections on his 1960 book *The End of Ideology,* Daniel Bell argues that he was right to say that ideology had ended but says, "I conclude: the 'end of ideology,' as the great historic crossover of beliefs, has run its course, I think. It is now the resumption of history that has begun," by which he appears to mean that the nations or "ethnies" of the world are clamoring for recognition of their unique identities.[15] Even the title of this essay, "The Resumption of History in the New Century," was a direct challenge to Fukuyama's analysis. But Fukuyama now says that he was misunderstood, that the book was about modernization with the "last man" in the title referring to Friedrich Nietzsche's (1844–1901) term for the completely modern citizen.

Ideology and Utopia

The title of Mannheim's book on the subject was *Ideology and Utopia,* and he contrasted utopia and ideology as two very different ways of thinking, saying "the term utopian, as here used, may be applied to any process of thought which receives its impetus not from the direct force of social reality but from concepts, such as symbols, fantasies, dreams, ideas and the like, which in the most comprehensive sense of that term are nonexistent."[16] But the word *utopia*—coined in 1516 to mean "no place," or "nowhere"—has come to mean a vision of the good life.[17] And it is clear that an image of what constitutes the good life lies at the heart of every ideology, and both Mannheim and Ricoeur argued that utopia was an essential element in combating ideology.

The Situation Today

The overwhelming tradition has been that ideology hides truth. Thus it has been considered dangerous by most commentators. Today, influenced by postmodernism, scholars focus on competing ideologies and their "truths" without worrying too much about whether these ideologies are hiding a truth. To each set of believers, the other ideologies are hiding the truth.

---

[14] Francis Fukuyama, *The End of History and the Last Man.* New York: Free Press, 1992. The essay was originally published as "Have We Reached the End of History?" Santa Monica, CA: RAND Corporation, February, 1989.

[15] Daniel Bell, "The Resumption of History in the New Century." In *The End of Ideology: On the Exhaustion of Political Ideas in the Fifties with "The Resumption of History in the New Century."* Cambridge, MA: Harvard University Press, 2000: xxviii.

[16] Karl Mannheim, "Utopia." In *Encyclopedia of the Social Sciences.* Edwin R.A. Seligman, ed. 15 vols. New York: Macmillan, 1935: 15: 201.

[17] See Lyman Tower Sargent, "Utopia." In *New Dictionary of the History of Ideas.* 6 vols. Maryanne Cline Horowitz, ed. New York: Charles Scribner's Sons, 2004, vol 6: 2403–2409; and "Utopianism." In *Routledge Encyclopedia of Philosophy.* 10 volumes. Edward Craig, ed. London: Routledge, 1998, vol. 9: 557–562.

In the recent past, we have witnessed the emergence of numerous new or, more accurately, newly labeled views of the world that are sometimes called ideologies. We have also seen the advocates of certain well-established ideologies, such as democratic capitalism, gain an intellectual self-confidence that was not apparent earlier and adherents of other ideologies, most notably communism, have lost confidence. In addition, as groups have become aware of their ideological ties, they have become more aware of the roots of their beliefs, and forerunners who were not considered important have become more significant.

The competition among ideologies has become more clearly both political and intellectual. The battle is for the hearts and minds of adherents and for political converts; and within ideologies, a quest for coherence and grounding contradicts many of the theories we use to understand ideology, which suggests that any coherence is necessarily false. The ideological map is more complex than ever, so it is even more necessary to understand the theoretical roots of ideologies today than it was in the past.

DO I (YOU) HAVE AN IDEOLOGY?

While I like to think that I select my beliefs, I am also aware of how I am influenced by different ideologies. Of course, as the author of this book, I am likely to be particularly aware of such influences. And I have always thought that one purpose of this book should be to encourage readers to examine their own beliefs, perhaps even to critically evaluate them.

As a teacher I have had relatively few students who saw the world wholly through the viewpoint of an ideology, but I have had students who have taken the position of each of the ideologies in this book: Marxists, Islamists, anarchists, fascists, capitalists, socialists, feminists, quite a few nationalists, and a growing number of environmentalists, all of whom knew the answers to certain questions without needing to think about them. Thus it is clear that some of the people that we meet throughout life will have an ideology in the most complete sense of that term—they will be ideologues. Most of us, though, hold beliefs that are influenced by more than one ideology. One person is influenced by feminism, environmentalism, and Liberation Theology; another is influenced by Marxism and environmentalism; and so on.

In this sense, it is more accurate to say that we have beliefs rather than ideologies, recognizing that those beliefs come, in part, from ideologies. Because these beliefs are often drawn from more than one ideology, there is a potential for conflict among beliefs.

POSTMODERNISM

A new approach to thinking about the world is *postmodernism,* a term coined by Jean-François Lyotard (1924–1998). Some call postmodernism an ideology, but since it is not primarily political, it will not be discussed here as a separate ideology. Still, because it both influences most of the ideologies under discussion and challenges the way we think about ideologies, it needs to be considered briefly.

A crude postmodernism can lead to a position that asserts with absolute certainty that there is no truth; but most postmodernists take a different position, arguing that truth depends on where you stand, also known as *standpoint theory*. Where you stand depends on your identity in terms of gender, nationality, class or social standing, ethnicity, religion, and so on.

In this form, postmodernism has the potential for undermining belief in any ideology, because ideologies have traditionally claimed to have the singular truth, to be universal. Today, influenced by postmodernism, we in the twenty-first century are much more aware of the local and contingent, and if the standpoint is ideological, postmodernism can be seen as actually reinforcing ideologies rather than undermining them. As noted earlier, each ideology is now probably best thought of as composed of subsets of closely related ways of viewing the world, and so each has incorporated the outlook of postmodernism.

A complication for most of us is that we stand in more than one place. We view the world through lenses provided by ideology, gender, race, nationality, ethnicity, religion, and so on. For many people, one of these will dominate, but others look through different glasses at different times, regarding different issues. Most of us manage these shifts in perspective without conflict, often without even being aware that we are doing so. We see ourselves as a whole rather than as multiple selves. In this way what has been known as *identity politics* may be undermined, because it assumes one dominant identity. An approach has developed, called *Queer Theory,* which insists that we all have multiple identities and should not be forced into the box of one identity. Although Queer Theory arose from a concern with sexual identities, it has now been extended into greater multiples.

While postmodernism is not itself political, its political implications are enormous. On the one hand, if truth is multiple, a widely tolerant democracy would seem to be the obvious solution. But as long ago as the seventeenth century, Thomas Hobbes (1588–1679) argued in *Leviathan* (1651) that the lack of what he called a "right reason," or a final authority, produced too much conflict and insecurity. He proposed an authoritarian government to impose an official set of behaviors. If extreme diversity is unacceptable, many people would be willing to impose their answers, and those answers are often based on an ideology.

IDEOLOGIES TO BE CONSIDERED

The ideologies considered in this book have been chosen on two main criteria: their importance in the world today and the desire to present a broad range of political beliefs. Nationalism and globalization; democracy and its two major forms, democratic capitalism and democratic socialism; environmentalism; feminism; and the political ideologies of Islam clearly fall into the first category. Each must be understood before the news of the day can be intelligently grasped. Anarchism clearly belongs in the second category. Although anarchism has never been dominant in any area for long, it still has many adherents and a continuing popularity, and a survey of political ideology would be incomplete without it. The other ideologies included fall somewhere between these two categories. Each is important for an understanding of recent history and current events but not to the same degree as nationalism, democracy, and political Islam. In addition, each represents a point on the spectrum of political beliefs that is not clearly occupied by any of the others.

Nationalism is different from all the other belief systems, because it is part of the other ideologies, and globalization appears to be similar to nationalism in this way. Therefore nationalism and globalization will be discussed first to clarify their effects on the other ideologies. The placement and order of the other ideologies are not arbitrary, but other arrangements are possible. Feminism is placed in its own section, between democracy and Marxism, because it has developed so much internationally that it no longer fits anywhere else.

METHODS OF ANALYSIS

The wide variety of ideologies raises a problem for the analyst. Because each ideology differs significantly from the others, no single approach is appropriate to all of them. Each ideology emphasizes different aspects of society and ignores other aspects stressed by another ideology, so ideologies need to be understood as they exist in the world, rather than on the basis of a formal model. Thus each one will be analyzed as its nature dictates.

Reasons for Comparing Ideologies

It is nevertheless desirable to compare ideologies. Why compare? Political scientists compare political systems and political ideologies for a number of reasons. At the simplest level, we compare to remind ourselves and others of different ways of doing things; in the context of ideologies, differing beliefs exist in the world. It is important to realize that people who hold these beliefs are as sure that they are right as we are that we are right. On a more complicated level, we compare things because it helps us better understand other people and ourselves—to see what both they and we believe. Understanding is important, because we cannot change anything unless we understand it, and because we need to recognize other ways of doing things and believing that might be useful to us.

Through comparison we discover both great differences and great similarities; we discover that differences often hide similarities. We find, for example, that most belief systems rank people in some sort of hierarchy, but we also find that the bases for those rankings differ. Thus we conclude that disagreement exists over what is most important about the differences among people, but that we agree that some basis for making distinctions exists. In other words, we find that a difference is the result of a similarity.

Questions

Any analysis of any part of society is an attempt to answer a series of questions that can be divided into two parts: (1) How should society function? and (2) How does society actually function? Answers to the first question describe the value system. Answers to the second question show us the social system in operation.

The questions that follow provide a fairly complete analysis of the assumptions of an ideology. Using questions like these, it is possible to compare ideologies.

1. Human nature
   a. What are the basic characteristics of human beings as human beings?
   b. What effect does human nature have on the political system?

2. The origin of society and government or the state
   a. What is the origin of society? Why does it develop?
   b. What is the origin of government or the state? Why does it develop?

3. Political obligation (duty, responsibility, law)
   a. Why do people obey the government?
   b. Why should people obey the government, or should they obey it at all?
   c. Is disobedience ever justifiable?
   d. Is revolution ever justifiable?

4. Law
   a. What are the nature and function(s) of law?
   b. Should the regulation of society depend on the immediate decisions of individuals or on sets of rules and regulations that place limitations on all members of society, including political leaders—in other words, the rule of law?
   c. Should there be sets of fundamental laws or constitutions that cannot be changed by the ordinary processes of legislation?

5. Freedom and liberty (rights—substantive and procedural)
   a. Are men and women free in any way vis-à-vis the government?
   b. Should they be free vis-à-vis the government?
   c. Assuming that some type or types of freedom are both possible and desirable, what should these be? Should they be limited or unlimited? Who places the limits?

6. Equality
   a. Are individuals in any way "naturally" equal?
   b. Should they be in any way equal?
   c. Assuming that some type or types of equality are both possible and desirable, what should these be? Should they be absolute or relative? If relative, what criteria should be used to establish them? Who establishes the criteria? Who enforces the criteria?

7. Community (fraternity)
   a. Should ties among individuals composing a group form a bond that takes precedence over the needs and wishes of the individual members of the group?
   b. If this is desirable, how can it be encouraged? If this is undesirable, how can it be discouraged? Who decides?

8. Power (authority)
   a. Should any individual or group of individuals be able to control, determine, or direct the actions of others?
   b. If this is desirable, what form or forms should it take? Should it be limited or unlimited? Who limits it and how?

9. Justice
   a. It is usually assumed that justice is desirable, but what is it? Is it individual or social?
   b. Who decides the characteristics of justice? Who enforces these characteristics?

10. The end of society or government
    a. For what purpose or purposes does society or government exist?
    b. Who decides what these purposes are, or are they consciously chosen?

11. Structural characteristics of government
    a. What is the best or best possible form of government? Why?
    b. Are alternative forms of government equally good?

12. The relationship between religion and government
    a. Should government control religious practice?
    b. Should religion control public policy?
    c. If so, which religion should dominate?
    d. If not, what should the relationship be? Who decides the form this relationship should take?

The Social System

To compare differing ideologies, similar information must be made available for each ideology. In order to achieve some sort of comparability, the complex of interactions among individuals, groups, and institutions that we call *society* has been divided into five segments:

1. Value system
2. Socialization system
3. Social stratification and social mobility systems
4. Economic system
5. Political system

This breakdown is simply a loose set of categories designed to provide some minimal order to the analysis. These categories allow the attitudes found in the various ideologies to be described.

Each chapter of this book attempts to explain the attitudes found in each ideology toward the various institutions and processes of society. As a result, we will see what questions are important within each ideology and establish a basis for comparing them. Before this can be done, it is necessary to understand a bit more about each of these institutions and processes.

Values   The value system is determined by the answers given to the questions listed earlier, which show the hierarchy of values in each society and each ideology. The value system gives us a basis for evaluating each ideology from within itself. To what extent are the expressed values of the ideology compatible with one another? Do the adherents of the ideology live up to the values expressed in the ideology, or do they at least try to? Do followers of the ideology adhere to its values when in power?

Socialization The socialization system is the process by which individuals accept the values of a society as their own. The most important institutions affecting how and the degree to which individuals gain these values are (1) the family system, (2) the educational system, (3) the religious system, and (4) a variety of other influences, such as the mass media and peer group. We are not always sure how the various institutions of socialization operate. It is obvious that a child's outlook on life is strongly influenced by family environment and early school years. It is, perhaps, less clear how the other institutions of socialization influence an individual's outlook on life. We can assume that the same messages repeated in institutions that the individual has been taught to respect, such as the religious and educational systems, have a cumulative effect and thereby become part of the individual's value system. Mass media operates in the same way.

Social Stratification The social stratification system is the way in which a society ranks groups within it. This ranking may be a clearly defined class system, or it may be loose with hazy lines between classes or status groups. Social stratification is usually summed up within a political ideology by the question of equality. Some ideologies contain the idea that everyone within the society should be equal in specified ways. For example, some people talk about equality of opportunity and political equality; others believe in economic and social equality. Only in the absence of economic, social, political, or any other inequalities would there be no social stratification system. Almost no one has ever suggested such complete equality, but each of these more limited types of equality has been suggested or tried at various times.

Social Mobility Every society has a social mobility system that determines the ease or difficulty with which an individual can move among classes or other strata in the society. The system also determines the basis for such movement; for example, in traditional China an individual could move into the upper classes of society by successfully completing a series of examinations. Many contemporary societies have no such formal system but base mobility on standards such as wealth.

The Economic System The economic system is concerned with the production, distribution, and consumption of wealth. The major parts of the economic system that interest us here relate to (1) production, (2) distribution and consumption, and (3) the relationship of the economic system to the political system. We will particularly examine the desired degree of economic equality and the means for achieving this goal. Most ideologies reject extremes of wealth and poverty; therefore, each contains means of correcting the imbalance, such as a graduated income tax or nationalization of industries. But each ideology also differs from others as to what constitutes extremes of wealth and poverty.

These days it is generally accepted that the economic and political systems are closely intertwined. This has not always been the case, and some ideologies still stress the separation of the two systems. Therefore it is particularly important to understand each ideology's position on the appropriate relationship between the economic system and the political system.

The Political System The political system is that segment of society that draws together or integrates all the others. Within the political system, decisions are made that bind the whole society; thus the political system holds the key to understanding the whole ideological and social system. A political ideology does not concern itself only with narrowly defined governmental activity, but rather touches on all aspects of the social system; therefore, a political ideology provides answers, in one form or another, to all of the questions outlined earlier.

Is there, as Mannheim thought, some way of standing completely outside all ideologies, thus making it possible to evaluate them from something at least approaching objectivity? There is a growing consensus that this may not be possible or, at the minimum, is extremely difficult. At the same time, it is essential that we evaluate ideologies and differentiate among them, and that evaluation needs to be based on something reliable. Evaluation cannot be based simply on belief or the lack of belief, although some people find that sufficient. For other people the answer is found in trying, as objectively as possible, to measure the effects of ideologies on human beings or, to include the most radical environmentalists, on the natural order as a whole.

A NOTE ON TERRORISM

On September 11, 2001, the reality of world terrorism was brought home to the United States in the destruction of the World Trade Center and the attack on the Pentagon. Although there had been a prior attack on the World Trade Center in 1993, numerous attacks on American individuals and institutions abroad, and the destruction of the Alfred P. Murrah Federal Office Building in Oklahoma City in 1995, the impact of the September, 11 2001 attacks has been of a much greater magnitude than any of the earlier cases. And the continuing presence of terrorism around the world means that we need to understand it.

Terrorism is not an ideology; it is a form of killing for political ends, and it has been used by many ideologies. It differs from assassination in that it is frequently directed at nonpolitical targets and groups of people rather than individuals. Its purpose, as implied by the word, is to terrorize; but in the terrorists' view, this is justified, because they see their beliefs and their communities as under threat.

Advocates of political murder can be traced far back in history, and in the Middle Ages, a debate ensued over the justification of tyrannicide, the murder of a tyrant. But these actions were aimed at individuals perceived to have earned attack by their personal actions and do not constitute terrorism as we now know it.

Since the nineteenth century, adherents of various ideologies have resorted to terrorism to attack their opponents and publicize their beliefs. Anarchists in the second half of the nineteenth century called these actions "propaganda by the deed." Around the same time, a group of Russian terrorists earned the name *nihilists,* which indicated that their aim was the destruction of current social institutions with no concern for what might replace them. The best-known statement of this position is *Catechism of the Revolutionist* (1869), usually attributed to Sergei Nechaev (1847–1882) and Mikhail Bakunin (1814–1876), although Bakunin's role was limited.[18] In this pamphlet, Nechaev uses the word *revolutionist* where we would use the word *terrorist,* and even most supporters of violent revolution have rejected Nechaev. Typical of the statements in the *Catechism,* and one in which the connection to contemporary terrorism is obvious, is "He [the terrorist] despises public opinion. He despises and hates the present day code of morals with all its motivations and manifestations. To him whatever aids the triumph of the revolution is ethical; all that which hinders it is unethical and criminal."[19]

During the antiwar movement, there were a small number of bombings in the United States. Most of these were directed at institutions like banks and did not target individuals, although some people were killed or badly injured. Later the so-called Unabomber targeted individuals, sending them mail bombs, some of which seriously injured their recipients.

Today terrorism is obviously most closely connected with the events of September 11, Osama bin Laden (b. 1957), and his particular brand of Islam. But terrorism is also related to ethnic nationalism, such as with Basques in Spain and Tamils in Sri Lanka; the American right wing (e.g. Timothy McVeigh [1968–2001] and various militia groups); and religious conflict, such as that between Hindus and Muslims in India.

We tend to identify terrorism with the acts of individuals and small groups, but *state terrorism* describes a state using terrorist acts against its enemies—Iran, Iraq, and Libya have been identified as doing this—or against its own citizens, such as Argentina, Chile, and Peru in the recent past. Thus terrorism is a complex phenomenon driven by many motives and ideologies. It has existed in isolated, irregular acts since the mid-nineteenth century, but has occurred with increasing frequency in the past 25 years.[20]

Terrorism continues as a tool of contemporary politics and warfare, and the responses to it from within the countries affected have raised important issues for many ideologies, particularly democracy and the political ideologies of Islam. Therefore, the effects of terrorism will also be discussed in a number of the following chapters.

---

[18] On the relationship, see Paul Avrich, *Bakunin & Nechaev.* London: Freedom Press, 1974.

[19] The text of the *Catechism* can be found in Max Nomad, *Apostles of Revolution,* revised ed. New York: Collier Books, 1961: 230–235, quoted passage on p. 230.

[20] There has been a flood of books on all aspects of terrorism in the last three years. The Suggested Readings includes a representative sample. William T. Vollmann has produced a remarkable seven-volume reflection on violence in fiction, journalism, and photography that serves as an introduction to terrorism and state terrorism; see his *Rising Up and Rising Down,* 7 vols. San Francisco: McSweeney's Books, 2003.

SUGGESTED READING

Some Classic Works

Althusser, Louis. "Ideology and Ideological State Apparatuses (Notes towards an Investigation)." In Althusser, *Lenin and Philosophy and Other Essays*. Ben Brewster, trans. London: NLB, 1971: 121–173.

Bell, Daniel. *The End of Ideology: On the Exhaustion of Political Ideas in the Fifties*. Glencoe, IL: Free Press, 1960. Republished as *The End of Ideology: On the Exhaustion of Political Ideas in the Fifties with "The Resumption of History in the New Century."* Cambridge, MA: Harvard University Press, 2000.

Geertz, Clifford. "Ideology as a Cultural System." In *Ideology and Discontent*. David E. Apter, ed. New York: Free Press of Glencoe, 1964: 47–76.

Gramsci, Antonio. *Pre-Prison Writings*. Richard Bellamy, ed. Cambridge, England: Cambridge University Press, 1994.

Mannheim, Karl. *Ideology and Utopia: An Introduction to the Sociology of Knowledge*. Louis Wirth and Edward Shils, trans. New York: Harcourt, Brace & Co., 1936; London: Routledge, 1991. The English edition brings together *Ideologie und Utopie* (Bonn, Germany: Cohen, 1929) and other essays by Mannheim.

Marx, Karl, and Friedrich Engels. *The German Ideology*. Vol. 5 of Karl Marx and Frederick Engels, *Collected Works*. 50 vols. New York: International Publishers, 1976.

Shklar, Judith, ed. *Political Theory and Ideology*. New York: Macmillan, London: Collier-Macmillan, 1966.

Books and Articles

Anderson, Perry. *Spectrum*. London: Verso, 2005. A history of contemporary ideas across the political spectrum by a scholar identified with the left.

Bauman, Zygmunt. "Ideology in the Postmodern World." *In Search of Politics*. Cambridge, England: Polity, 1999: 109–131.

Bennett, Tony, Lawrence Grossberg, and Meaghan Morris, eds. *New Keywords: A Revised Vocabulary of Culture and Society*. Malden, MA: Blackwell, 2005.

Revised edition of Raymond Williams, *Keywords: A Vocabulary of Culture and Society* (1985). "Ideology" by Lawrence Grossberg is on pages 175–178 and "Utopia" by Avery F. Gordon is on pages 362–364.

Brennan, Timothy. *Wars of Position: The Cultural Politics of Left and Right*. New York: Columbia University Press, 2006.

Caputo, John D. *On Religion*. New York: Routledge, 2001. Good introduction to the currents of religious change in the twentieth century, including secularism and post-secularism.

Collier, David, Fernando Daniel Hidalgo, and Andra Olivia Maciuceanu. "Essentially Contested Concepts: Debates and Applications." *Journal of Political Ideologies* Vol. 11:3 (October 2006): 211–246.

Eagleton, Terry. *Ideology: An Introduction*. New and updated ed. London: Verso, 2007. Except for the "Introduction to the 2007 Edition" (x–xix), this is a reprint on the 1991 edition.

Freeden, Michael. *Ideologies and Political Theory: A Conceptual Approach*. Oxford: Clarendon Press, 1996.

———. "Ideology." *Routledge Encyclopedia of Philosophy*. 10 vols. Edward Craig, ed. London: Routledge, 1998, 4: 681–685.

———. "Editorial: What Is Special about Ideologies?" *Journal of Political Ideologies* Vol. 6:1 (2001): 5–12.

———. *Ideology: A Very Short Introduction*. Oxford, England: Oxford University Press, 2003.

———. "Ideology and Political Theory." *Journal of Political Ideologies* Vol. 11:1 (February 2006): 3–22.

Freeden, Michael, ed. *Reassessing Political Ideologies: The Durability of Dissent*. London: Routledge, 2001.

Goodwin, Jeff, and James M. Jasper, eds. *The Social Movements Reader: Cases and Concepts*. Malden, MA: Blackwell Publishing, 2003.

Gray, John. *Black Mass: Apocalyptic Religion and the Death of Utopia*. London: Allen Lane, 2007. "Modern politics is a chapter in the history of religion" (page 1).

Griffin, Roger. "Ideology and culture." *Journal of Political Ideologies* Vol. 11:1 (February 2006): 77–99.

Habermas, Jürgen. *The Future of the Human Race*. Cambridge, England: Polity, 2003. Different parts have different translators (William Rehg, Max Pensky, and Hella Beister and Max Pensky). Secularist point of view, which he calls post-metaphysical.

——. "Religion in the Public Sphere." http://www.sandiego.edu/pdf/pdf_library.

Journal of Political Ideologies Vol. 1:1 to present (Founded February 1996).

Lukes, Steven. *Power: A Radical View*. 2nd ed. Houndsmill, England: Palgrave Macmillan, published in association with the British Sociological Association, 2005.

Mazrui, Ali A. "Ideology and African Political Culture." In *Explorations in African Political Thought: Identity, Community, Ethics*. Teodros Kiros, ed. New York: Routledge, 2001: 97–131.

Mészáros, István. *The Power of Ideology*. New York: New York University Press, 1989. Revised and enlarged ed. London: Zed Books, 2005.

Meyer, David S., Nancy Whittier, and Belinda Robnett, eds. *Social Movements: Identity, Culture, and the State*. New York: Oxford University Press, 2002.

Minogue, Kenneth. *Alien Powers: The Pure Theory of Ideology*. 2nd ed. New Brunswick, NJ: Transaction, 2007.

Nash, June, ed. *Social Movements: An Anthropological Reader*. Malden, MA: Blackwell Publishing, 2004.

Rejai, Mostafa. "Ideology." In *Dictionary of the History of Ideas*, Philip P. Wiener, ed. 5 vols. New York: Scribner's, 1973, 2: 552–559.

Talshir, Gayil, Mathew Humphrey, and Michael Freeden, eds. *Taking Ideology Seriously: 21st Century Reconfigurations*. Vol. 8:2 (June 2005) of *CRISPP: Critical Review of International Social and Political Philosophy*.

Taylor, Charles. *Modern Social Imaginaries*. Durham, NC: Duke University Press, 2004.

——. *A Secular Age*. Cambridge, MA: Belknap Press of Harvard University Press, 2007: 874 pages.

Taylor, Victor E., and Charles E. Winquist, eds. *Encyclopedia of Postmodernism*. London: Routledge, 2001.

Thompson, Simon. "Postmodernism." In *New Political Thought: An Introduction*. Adam Lent, ed. London: Lawrence & Wishart, 1998: 143–162.

Žižek, Slavoj. *For They Know Not What They Do: Enjoyment as a Political Factor*. 2nd ed. London: Verso, 2002.

——. *The Sublime Object of Ideology*. London: Verso, 1989.

——, ed. *Mapping Ideology*. London: Verso, 1994.

Terrorism

Ahmed, Akbar, and Brian Forst, eds. *After Terror: Promoting Dialogue among Civilizations*. Cambridge, England: Polity, 2005. Many short essays, including some from major political figures.

Asad, Talal. *On Suicide Bombing*. New York: Columbia University Press, 2007.

Barber, Benjamin R. *Fear's Empire: War, Terrorism, and Democracy*. Rpt. New York: W.W. Norton, 2004 with a new "Preface to the Paperback Edition": 15–29.

Bergen, Peter L. *The Osama bin Laden I Know: An Oral History of al Qaeda's Leader*. New York: Free Press, 2006.

Berkowitz, Peter, ed. *Terrorism, the Laws of War, and the Constitution: Debating the Enemy Combatants Case*. Stanford, CA: Hoover Institution Press, 2005.

Bernstein, Richard J. *The Abuse of Evil: The Corruption of Politics and Religion since 9/11*. Cambridge, England: Polity, 2005. Argues that there is no need to appeal to absolutes.

Björgo, Tore, ed. *Root Causes of Terrorism*. London: Routledge, 2005.

Bloom, Mia. *Dying to Kill: The Allure of Suicide Terror*. New York: Columbia University Press, 2005.

Byman, Daniel. *Deadly Connections: States that Sponsor Terrorism*. Cambridge, England: Cambridge University Press, 2005.

Carr, Matthew. *The Infernal Machine: A History of Terrorism*. New York: New Press, 2006.

Chandler, Michael, and Rohan Gunaratna. *Countering Terrorism: Can We Meet the Threat of Global Violence?* London: Reaktion Books, 2007.

Clarke, Richard A. *Against All Enemies: Inside America's War on Terror.* New York: Free Press, 2004. The author was the National Coordinator for Security, Infrastructure Protection, and Counterterrorism from 1998 to 2003, under both Presidents Clinton and Bush.

Critical Studies on Terrorism Vol. 1:1 to the present (Founded 2008).

Cronin, Audrey Kurth, and James M. Ludes, eds. *Attacking Terrorism: Elements of a Grand Strategy.* Washington, DC: Georgetown University Press, 2004.

Cushman, Thomas, ed. *A Matter of Principle: Humanitarian Arguments for War in Iraq.* Berkeley: University of California Press, 2005.

Defeating the Jihadists: A Blueprint for Action. The Report of a Task Force Assembled and Chaired by Richard A. Clarke. New York: The Century Foundation Press, 2004.

Giraldo, Jeanne K., and Harold A. Trinkunas, eds. *Terrorism Financing and State Responses: A Comparative Perspective.* Stanford, CA: Stanford University Press, 2007.

Goodin, Robert E. *What's Wrong With Terrorism?* Cambridge, England: Polity Press, 2006. Notes that some contend that terrorism is an ideology. The purpose of terrorism is to generate fear, and Goodin argues that some politicians use that fear within democratic societies for their own political ends.

Greenberg, Karen J., ed. *Al Qaeda Now: Understanding Today's Terrorists.* Cambridge, England: Cambridge University Press, 2005.

Habeck, Mary. *Knowing the Enemy: Jihadist Ideology and the War on Terror.* New Haven, CT: Yale University Press, 2006. Argues that extremists put a political spin on the concept of *tawhid* (the belief that there is only one God) and believe that God's laws, as they interpret them, should be implemented, and that competing belief systems can and should be eliminated by force.

Hoffman, Bruce. *Inside Terrorism.* Revised and expanded ed. New York: Columbia University Press, 2006.

Ignatieff, Michael. *The Lesser Evil: Political Ethics in an Age of Terror. The Gifford Lectures.* Princeton, NJ: Princeton University Press, 2004. Concerned with the ethical issues involved when a democracy has to respond to terrorism, also includes a chapter on how democracies can make terrorism less likely.

Kepel, Gilles, and Jean-Pierre Milelli, eds. *Al Qaeda in Its Own Words.* Trans. Pascale Ghazaleh. Cambridge, MA: Belknap Press of Harvard University Press, 2008. Collection including material from Osama Bin Laden, Abdallah Azzam, Ayam al-Zawahiri, and Abu Musab al-Zarqawi.

Krueger, Alan B. *What Makes a Terrorist: Economics and the Roots of Terrorism.* Princeton, NJ: Princeton University Press, 2007. Argues that research has shown that most terrorists do *not* come from poor backgrounds and that terrorists generally come from countries where civil and political liberties are suppressed.

Laqueur, Walter, ed. *Voices of Terror: Manifestoes, Writings, and Manuals of Al-Qaeda, Hamas and Other Terrorists Around the World and Throughout the Ages.* New York: Reed Press, 2004. Part one is based on his *Guerrilla Reader* (1977); part two is from the *Terrorism Reader* (1977); part three is new. The most comprehensive collection of such material.

LeBor, Adam. *"Complicity With Evil": The United Nations in the Age of Modern Genocide.* New Haven, CT: Yale University Press, 2006.

Levitt, Matthew. *Hamas: Politics, Charity, and Terrorism in the Service of Jihad.* New Haven, CT: Yale University Press, 2006.

Lustick, Ian S. *Trapped in the War on Terror.* Philadelphia: University of Pennsylvania Press, 2006.

O'Kane, Rosemary H.T., ed. *Terrorism.* 2 vols. Cheltenham, England: Edward Elgar, 2005. Wide-ranging collection of articles.

Oliver, Anne Marie, and Paul F. Steinberg. *The Road to Martyrs' Square: A Journey into the World of the Suicide Bomber.* Oxford, England: Oxford University Press, 2005.

Posner, Eric A., and Adrian Vermeule. *Terror in the Balance: Security, Liberty, and the Courts.* New York: Oxford University Press, 2007.

Richardson, Louise. *What Terrorists Want: Understanding the Terrorist Threat*. New York: Random House, 2006. U.K. ed. London: John Murray, 2006.

Robin, Corey. *Fear: The History of a Political Idea*. Oxford, England: Oxford University Press, 2004.

Scheffler, Samuel. "Is Terrorism Morally Distinctive?" *Journal of Political Philosophy* Vol. 14:1 (March 2006): 1–17.

Semelin, Jacques. *Purify and Destroy: The Political Uses of Massacre and Genocide*. Cynthia Schoch, trans. New York: Columbia University Press, 2007.

Shaw, Martin. *What Is Genocide?* Cambridge, England: Polity, 2007.

Shultz, Richard H., Jr., and Andrea J. Dew. *Insurgents, Terrorists and Militias: The Warriors of Contemporary Combat*. New York: Columbia University Press, 2006.

Terrorism and Political Violence Vol. 1:1 (Founded January 1989).

TMPR: Totalitarian Movements and Political Religion Vol. 1:1 (Founded Summer 2000).

Waldron, Jeremy. "Terrorism and the Uses of Terror." *Journal of Ethics* Vol. 8:1 (March 2004): 5–35. Particularly useful overview.

Weimann, Gabriel. *Terror on the Internet: The New Arena, the New Challenges*. Washington, DC: The United States Institute of Peace Press, 2006.

Weinberg, Leonard. *Global Terrorism: A Beginner's Guide*. Oxford, England: Oneworld, 2005.

Weiss, Thomas G. *Humanitarian Intervention: Ideas in Action*. Cambridge, England: Polity, 2007. A particularly good introductory overview.

Wilson, Richard Ashby, ed. *Human Rights in the 'War on Terror.'* Cambridge, England: Cambridge University Press, 2005.

Yoo, John. *War by Other Means: An Insider's Account of the War on Terror*. New York: Atlantic Monthly Press, 2006. Continues his argument that the U.S. President has whatever powers he wants during wartime and responds to critics.

Websites

Terrorism

CIA: http://www.cia.gov

Department of Homeland Security: http://www.dhs.gov

FBI: http://www.fbi.gov

UK Home Office: http://www.homeoffice.gov.uk

UN: http://www.un.org/terrorism

2

Nationalism

I s nationalism an ideology? Scholars flatly disagree. On the one hand, Michael Freeden writes that nationalism is not a distinct ideology but what he calls a "thin" ideology, or an ideology that takes on different characteristics depending on which ideology it is connected with.[1] On the other hand, one of the most common topics in the *Journal of Political Ideologies,* which Freeden edits, is nationalism, and many articles there explicitly refer to nationalism as an ideology. Both positions can be defended.

Though views of nationalism differ, it can be found affecting—some would say infecting—other ideologies. Thus many, like Freeden, say that nationalism cannot be called an ideology in the full sense of the word. Nationalism has a set of core attributes that parallel the core attributes of other ideologies; therefore, many, like the authors of the articles in the *Journal of Political Ideologies,* say that nationalism clearly is an ideology. Some even use Freeden's definition of ideology in doing so. My position, which accords with Freeden's notion of nationalism as a "thin ideology," is simply that it is impossible to understand the world of the twenty-first century without understanding nationalism, and its similarities to other ideologies mean that we can plausibly treat nationalism as an ideology.

The importance of nationalism is underscored by Robert Coles (b. 1929), an authority on the political beliefs of children, who wrote, "Nowhere on the

---

[1] Michael Freeden, "Is Nationalism a Distinct Ideology?" *Political Studies* 46.4 (September 1998): 748–765. Another recent argument that nationalism is not an ideology can be found in Mark N. Hagopian, "Ideology," in *Encyclopedia of Nationalism,* Alexander J. Motyl, ed. San Diego: Academic Press, 2001, 1: 385–403.

five continents I've visited in this study has nationalism failed to become an important element in the developing conscience of young people."[2] Another scholar has argued, "No single political doctrine has played a more prominent role in shaping the face of the modern world than nationalism,"[3] and another has written, "Nationalism is the most powerful of political ideologies."[4] Or as the editors of one anthology put it, "It is incontestable that the resurgence of nationalist sentiment in many areas of the world is one of the most important and least anticipated phenomena of contemporary international politics. People are increasingly conscious of their national identities; they are rediscovering their national histories, pressing for recognition of their distinctness, and making various demands under the banner of national self-determination."[5]

Because nationalism has such impact on other ideologies, it must be discussed first. Of course, as will be clear throughout this text, and as Freeden says, ideologies also affect nationalism. This interchange is a clue to one of the greatest difficulties in dealing with nationalism. For many, there are "good" and "bad" forms of nationalism, often meaning "ours" and "theirs" but equally often reflecting a considered analysis of the types of nationalism or the differential impacts of nationalism. The tradition, both popular and scholarly, has been to view nationalism as mostly bad; but a number of recent scholars have pointed out that nationalism has many positive factors. In the United States, we have always had this dual position without recognizing it, because we use *patriotism* for a "good" nationalism and reserve *nationalism* for a "bad" nationalism.

This chapter presents nationalism as a coherent set of beliefs that produces a divergent set of existing nationalisms. It illustrates how important nationalism is today, for good and ill, and addresses a number of countervailing forces that may, in time, diminish the importance of nationalism. These forces include globalization (see Chapter 3); internationalism, or cosmopolitanism; and regionalism.

The root of the word *nationalism* is *nation;* it means a people with a common culture and history that produce an identity. Nations can have the same geographical boundaries as countries; can occur as small, identifiable units within the political boundaries of a country; or can, at times, cross those boundaries. Most countries, often called *nation-states,* are examples of the first sort. The French Canadians in Canada are an example of the second sort. The Romany, or Gypsies, are an example of the third sort; they exist in many countries, have certain traditions in common, and many of them share a common language. A fourth type might be represented by Black Nationalism within the United States; while Black Nationalists perceive themselves as a people with a common culture and history—and call for some form of cultural, economic, or political separation from the United States—they live in many places throughout the

[2] Robert Coles, *The Political Life of Children.* Boston: Atlantic Monthly Press, 1986: 66.

[3] Umut Özkirimli, *Theories of Nationalism: A Critical Introduction.* New York: St. Martin's Press, 2000: 1.

[4] Francisco José Moreno, *Basic Principles of Politics,* 4th ed. Miami, FL: Cefatex International, 2006: 47.

[5] Robert McKim and Jeff McMahon, introduction to *The Morality of Nationalism,* Robert McKim and Jeff McMahon, eds. Oxford, England: Oxford University Press, 1997: 3.

country, rather than as a small, identifiable unit.[6] Immigration is producing a fifth type that has some of the characteristics of a nation, identifiable groups within one country with ties to another country, which may or may not over time become integrated within the new country.

DEFINING NATIONALISM

Most definitions of *nationalism* include the following:

1. National consciousness or awareness of oneself as part of a group
2. National identity or identification with the group
3. Geographical identification or identification with a place with notable exceptions, such as the Romany, or Gypsies
4. Patriotism or love of the group
5. Demands for action to enhance the group

The neutral term *group* is used because commentators disagree about how to define a national group.

There is a difference between consciousness and identity. I can be aware of my membership in a group without identifying myself with it. In fact, there may well be groups that I am aware I belong to, such as by birth or upbringing, that I do not identify with—that I actually reject.

Most of us are born in a nation, but we are not aware of that until later. We have to be taught about all the communities of which we are members. In the language of Benedict Anderson (b. 1936), nations are "imagined communities" because they, like most other communities, are created by the actions of those who, over time, come to believe in or accept certain myths and symbols that powerfully affect those who identify with the community.[7] Philosopher Paul Ricoeur (1913–2005) said that these "foundational symbols" are part of what creates, legitimates, and justifies a nation.[8] Symbols of nationality, such as the flag and the national anthem, evoke such feelings of identification, at times even in those who do not think of themselves as having a strong identification with the country. Sports are particularly good at doing this, especially international competitions such as the Olympics and soccer (soccer in the U.S.; football in the rest of the world) and

---

[6] See, for example, Wilson Jeremiah Moses, ed., *Classical Black Nationalism: From the American Revolution to Marcus Garvey.* New York: New York University Press, 1996; William L. Van Deburg, ed., *Modern Black Nationalism: From Marcus Garvey to Louis Farrakhan.* New York: New York University Press, 1997; Eddie S. Glaude Jr., ed., *Is It Nation Time? Contemporary Essays on Black Power and Black Nationalism.* Chicago: University of Chicago Press, 2002; and Dean E. Robinson, *Black Nationalism in American Politics and Thought.* Cambridge, England: Cambridge University Press, 2001.

[7] Benedict Anderson, *Imagined Communities: Reflections on the Origin and Spread of Nationalism,* revised and extended ed. London: Verso, 1991.

[8] Paul Ricoeur, "Imagination in Discourse and in Action." In *The Human Being in Action: The Irreducible Element in Man, Part II. Investigations at the Intersection of Philosophy and Psychiatry.* Anna-Teresa Tymieniecka, ed. Vol. 7 of *Analecta Husserliana: The Yearbook of Phenomenological Research.* Dordrecht, Holland: D. Reidel, 1978: 135.

rugby world cups. But as already noted, identification is also an active process in which the various symbols are molded into something that affects how we live and interact with others, including those who are members of our nation and those who exist legally or physically outside its boundaries.

One of the most common identifying characteristics of a nation is language. In the United States, Native American children were once punished for speaking their national languages, some of which have been lost altogether or are now endangered, and some states have passed laws mandating the use of English. Language is immensely important as a marker of national identity. Those who watched the closing of the 2004 Olympics in Athens, Greece, will have heard some of the closing ceremony in Greek, which relatively few of the people watching the ceremony around the world would have understood; but to the Greeks, having part of the ceremony in Greek was an important symbol of their nationality.

When people in a country speak different languages, it usually means that different groups of people existed, or still exist, who have separate identities. For example, the country that was known as Czechoslovakia was formed after World War I from two ethnic groups, the Czechs and the Slovaks. After the overthrow of communism, Czechoslovakia became the Czech and Slovak Federative Republic, which, in 1993, became two separate countries: the Czech Republic and Slovakia. Likewise, Yugoslavia was formed after World War I from five ethnic groups and has fragmented into the countries of Bosnia and Herzegovina (a combination that may yet fall apart), Croatia, the Republic of Macedonia, Montenegro, Serbia, and Slovenia, with Kosovo declaring independence from Serbia in 2008. Some countries have recognized Kosovo's independence, while others have either refused to do so or are waiting to see what happens. Serbia, which sees Kosovo as the historic heart of Serbia, strongly rejects its declaration of independence.

I become most conscious of being an American when I am out of the country. Partially this is because others identify me as American, but mostly it is the contrast between what I am used to and what I am surrounded by elsewhere. But before I ever left the country, I was aware of my membership in this group because I grew up surrounded by the symbols of group identity: the flag, the national anthem, July 4th, and Thanksgiving. And my parents and others made the connection between the symbols and the nation explicit. For most of us, this is how national consciousness develops.

National identity is a choice, a conscious act. It means that I identify myself as an American both to myself and to others. For those of us born in this country, there is no universal rite of passage in which we become officially American, such as the naturalization process (note the word meaning "to become natural"), in which someone born in another country becomes a citizen of this one; so identification either takes place gradually or occurs during some rite of passage such as joining the military.

Most of us tend to think of ourselves as having multiple identities based on our "unique" combination of class (a term Americans avoid), ethnicity, gender, and race. When we leave the United States, we are certain to add national identity. Think about how you answer the question asked by yourself or others, who or what are you? This is usually answered in terms of occupation or ethnicity. But outside one's country, national identity is likely to be part of the answer. Sometimes Canadians seem obsessed with what it means to be a Canadian, which is often defined as being different from the United States. Over the past few years, the British have become more concerned with what it means to be British or, alternatively, English, Scottish, or Welsh, with a number of books published on these subjects.

One of the earliest theorists of nationalism, Johann Gottfried von Herder (1744–1803), argued that a basic human need is to belong to a group and that being part of a nation gives us part of our identity. We have a history, ancestors, "roots" that place us in a tradition. We are born in a "stream of tradition" that helps define us as individuals.[9]

In a small country, the geographical dimension of one's nationalism is clear. In the United States, it is not as clear, except perhaps when we leave the country. I have visited 46 of the 50 states, and even though I have a picture of the United States in my head, I cannot say that I have a real sense of the country as a unit, a whole. It is simply too large and diverse for that.

For most Americans, geographic identification is with a region but with the awareness that this region is part of a whole. In smaller countries there may also be a regional identification, but the national boundaries are much clearer, and boundaries and their maintenance are central to the nation and nationalism. Of course, boundaries are clearer the closer you are to them. I was much more aware of the boundary between the United States and Canada when I lived in Minnesota than when I lived in Missouri.

Patriotism, or love of the nation, like most of our loves, depicts the loved one as better than it actually is; because we have created an image of the loved one for ourselves. Remember Benedict Anderson's idea of the nation as an imagined community: We create an image of the nation in a form that fits our needs. This image will have certain core elements like symbols of nationhood (flag, anthem, Statue of Liberty), fundamental documents (the Declaration of Independence, the Constitution), institutions (democracy, electing our leaders), and events (the American Revolution). But other things will be added to this list, such as the Civil War/War between the States, World War II, or the civil rights movement. It is how we create our image of the nation through the mix of images that characterizes the nation we love.[10]

Demands for action are what generally provoke opposition to nationalism. These range from the demand for self-government, to a demand for recognition of a nation within the borders of an existing country (often a request of indigenous populations), to the demand to change borders to enlarge the nation. Such demands may include dismembering an existing country to create one or more new political entities. For example, at the time of independence from Great Britain in 1947, India included what is now Pakistan and Bangladesh, which

---

[9] Isaiah Berlin, "The Bent Twig: A Note on Nationalism," *Foreign Affairs* 51, no. 1 (October 1972): 16.

[10] For a discussion of patriotism in the United States, see John Bodnar, ed., *Bonds of Affection: Americans Define Their Patriotism.* Princeton, NJ: Princeton University Press, 1996.

was part of Pakistan—called East Pakistan—until 1971. Thus, in this case, three countries were created from one, and India and Pakistan have been at war over Kashmir, a region claimed by both, since 1948. These two sides have come close to nuclear war over Kashmir, and both sides have nuclear weapons. In 2004 they began to slowly move toward negotiating the future of Kashmir, but very little progress has been made since then.

As this last example indicates, nationalist demands often lead to conflict, and this has given nationalism a bad name. The current list of examples in which nationalism has produced violence includes the Greeks and the Turks in Cyprus, who are now beginning to talk to each other; the Dutch-speaking Flemish and the French in Belgium; the Basques in Spain; Israel and the Palestinians; the Albanians in the Republic of Macedonia; Northern Ireland; Chechnya in Russia; the Kurds in Iran, Iraq, and Turkey; the Hutu and Tutsi in central Africa; the Sinhalese and the Tamils in Sri Lanka; and Tibet, where the Chinese and the Tibetans are already in a struggle over who should name the next Dalai Lama, and where the Beijing Olympics has provided Tibetans an opportunity to bring their case before the world media—and this list could be much longer.

Nationalism: Ancient or Modern?

One current debate over the nature of nationalism is whether it is an ancient or modern phenomenon. This dispute has connections with the two ways most scholars categorize nationalism today: ethnic or cultural and civic or liberal. Clearly some ethnicities have ancient roots, although the awareness of that ethnicity may be more recent. Thus whether nationalism is ancient or recent has no simple answer.

Until recently, most scholars treated nations and nationalism as a modern phenomenon and argued that a coherent *doctrine* of nationalism came into existence only in the eighteenth century, first in Germany and later in France. The major parts of the mix of ideas that came together to become nationalism were seen as originating in the fourteenth through the sixteenth centuries.[11] As Isaiah Berlin (1909–1997) wrote, "Consciousness of national identity may be as old as consciousness itself. But nationalism, unlike tribal feeling or xenophobia, to which it is related but with which it is not identical, seems scarcely to have existed in ancient or classical times."[12]

Those arguing for ancient roots to nationalism contend that the argument for modernity rests entirely on the experience of western Europe and ignores, for example, China, which existed as a nation centuries before any western European nation. Also, and more important to the current debate over nationalism, those arguing for ancient roots are saying that the source of the nation is the ethnic group and that those arguing for a modern nationalism are confusing nation and state, which is why I have carefully avoided using the word *state*.

---

[11] The best discussion is by Quentin Skinner, *The Foundations of Modern Political Thought.* Cambridge, England: Cambridge University Press, 1978.

[12] Berlin, "Bent Twig," 15.

Nationalism: Ethnic and Civic

The division between ancient and modern versions of nationalism is reflected in the other current conflict between scholars of nationalism: that between cultural or ethnic nationalism and civic or liberal nationalism. Roughly speaking, the former is based on ancient roots and the latter on modern ones, and for most people the distinction is between "bad" (ethnic) and "good" (civic) nationalism.

Civic nationalism reflects positive versions of nationalism or patriotism; shared identity and purpose counteract apathy and isolation, currently considered major problems in the United States. One scholar argues, "Civic nationalism maintains that the nation should be composed of all those—regardless of race, color, creed, gender, language, or ethnicity—who subscribe to the nation's political creed. This nationalism is called civic because it envisages the nation as a community of equal, rights-bearing citizens, united in patriotic attachment to a shared set of political practices and values."[13] And another scholar says, "To make sense, democracy requires a 'people,' and social justice a political community within which redistribution can take place, while the liberal discourse of rights and the rule of law demands a strong and impartial polity."[14] This means that nations and people identifying with nations are necessary for democracy.

One author has noted, "Nations have called forth heroism and sacrifice as well as murder and torture. People have risked their lives to restore democracy and civil rights in their own country, when they could easily have chosen comfortable exile elsewhere. Programmes of health reform, social welfare and environmental repair have gained political support because they appeal to a sense of national identity."[15]

On September 11, 2001, and the days following, Americans could readily see these two faces of nationalism. The terrorists were ethnic nationalists, and much of the response within the United States reflected civic nationalism. But the fact that there were many attacks—from verbal to violent—on Arab Americans, anyone wearing a turban, Muslims, and others thought to be from the Arab world demonstrates that ethnic nationalism is not just a phenomenon found outside U.S. borders.

COUNTERVAILING TENDENCIES

Regionalism

At various times, two or more countries have established ties that have raised questions about the continuing identity of the parts, but turning such agreements into long-term successes has been difficult. For example, in 1964 Tanganyika and Zanzibar established a new country, the United Republic of

---

[13] Michael Ignatieff, *Blood and Belonging: Journeys into the New Nationalism.* New York: Farrar, Straus & Giroux, 1993: 261.

[14] Margaret Canovan, *Nationhood and Political Theory.* Cheltenham, England: Edward Elgar, 1996: 2.

[15] Ross Poole, *Nation and Identity.* London: Routledge, 1999: 1.

Tanzania. And while Tanzania still exists, many Zanzibaris have never been happy with the arrangement; even after 40 years, there is a strong movement for greater autonomy.

The single, most successful effort at regionalism has been among developed nations. The European Union, or EU, originated as the European Coal and Steel Community (ECSC); became the European Economic Community (EEC), popularly known as the Common Market; and then became the European Community (EC). In 1993 the name was changed again to the European Union. The ECSC began with 6 countries; in 2008 the EU had 27 members with Croatia, the Republic of Macedonia, and Turkey as candidates for membership. Turkey is in a somewhat different position from the others due to the widespread opposition to adding a predominantly Islamic country to the EU. Perhaps most striking is the fact that the following countries that were under the influence, sometimes amounting to control, of the former Soviet Union have joined the EU: Bulgaria, Estonia, Hungary, Latvia, Lithuania, Poland, Romania, Slovakia, and Slovenia.

As the EU has grown, it has changed from an almost purely economic union to an economic and political one, although incorporating some of the new countries has been difficult both economically and politically. For many countries in the "old" EU, the biggest problems have been caused by the free movement of labor; tens of thousands of both skilled and unskilled workers have moved from the "new" EU countries to higher paying jobs in the old EU countries, which in some cases has pushed wages down or produced unemployment. In the new EU, the same movement has meant that there are too few skilled workers for the construction projects designed to improve the infrastructure needed for economic development funded by the EU. As a result, the countries joining must recently have done so under some labor movement restrictions.

The European Court of Justice is an appeals court for cases brought under or against national laws. The European Parliament, composed of directly elected members, has begun to act as an independent political body and has even managed to force the EU bureaucracy to become more responsive to it.

The dominant political groups in the EU Parliament are the center/conservative group with 268 seats and the socialists with 200. Three groups that are roughly to the left, but not socialist, have 171 seats in total. The far Right is trying to form a recognized group.[16] Voting for the EU Parliament remains low, but the differences among the member countries is huge, ranging from below 10 percent to above 90 percent.

The EU is a powerful economic bloc, and, for all the problems of transition, its expansion into central Europe has made it even stronger. Officially all interior barriers to trade were dropped in 1992, and on the continent of Europe, this is generally true. In 1998 a European Central Bank was established to set monetary policy for the EU. And in 2001 a single currency, the euro, was instituted and became the only legal currency for most EU countries during the first months

---

[16] On the European Parliament, see Bernard Steunenberg and Jacques Thomassen, eds., *The European Parliament: Moving toward Democracy in the EU.* Lanham, MD: Rowman & Littlefield, 2002.

of 2002.[17] The euro-zone countries aim for convergence of inflation rates, convergence of interest rates, stability of exchange rates, budget deficits of less than 3 percent of GDP (gross domestic product), and national debt levels of less than 60 percent of GDP. The last two are proving to be the most difficult to achieve.

The countries that join the EU must bring their economic, political, and social systems in line with the EU on 31 issues. During the discussions leading to membership, individual countries negotiate transitional periods relating to specific issues, but on the whole, the systems are harmonized with the EU before the countries join. The potential problem after a nation joins is whether the new laws are implemented; if they are not, the EU can take a member state to the European Court of Justice, and individuals and companies can take their own state to court. In a number of areas, candidate countries must harmonize their systems with the EU before they will be considered for membership. For example, Turkey abolished its death penalty to be considered for candidacy.

African countries are trying to form a union similar to the European Union. The Organization of African Unity voted to disband, and an African Union (AU), modeled on the European Union, is being established. The AU is much larger than the EU in that it includes all 53 countries of Africa, some of which are at war with each other. The Constitutive Act of the AU includes all the institutions similar to those that the EU took years to develop, such as a Pan-African Parliament and a Court of Justice. In addition, the AU has developed a detailed program for economic development in Africa called the New Partnership for Africa's Development (NEPAD), which is designed to initiate a program of sustainable development throughout Africa.[18]

It is too early to do more than note this attempt, but the attempt is important in that it is explicitly designed to counteract the nationalism that has divided African countries against each other. The size of the AU suggests that it will not achieve its far-reaching goals, but some members are aware of the problems and hope to move slowly in implementing the proposed institutions. Meanwhile, the AU provides a mechanism through which African leaders can meet and discuss common problems. Also, the AU has managed to assist in conflicts in Africa by providing some peacekeeping troops that operate under the auspices of the AU rather than individual countries.

In addition, a variety of primarily economic regional agreements, such as the North American Free Trade Agreement (NAFTA), the Free Trade Association of the Americas (FTAA), and Asia–Pacific Economic Cooperation (APEC), are slowly encouraging greater regional economic cooperation. And the Central American–Dominican Republic–U.S. Free Trade Agreement, or CAFTA–DR, was signed in 2004. There are also security-based organizations like the North Atlantic Treaty Organization (NATO) and the Southeast Asia Treaty Organization (SEATO), through which governments come together to discuss security issues and, in the case of NATO, sometimes act on them.

---

[17] Three countries in the European Union—Denmark, Sweden, and the United Kingdom—chose not to adopt the euro.

[18] On the African Union, see http://www.africa-union.org and http://www.nepad.org/en.html.

Cosmopolitanism/Internationalism

The emphasis on a whole within which differing peoples and cultures can be accepted is the heart of internationalism or cosmopolitanism. In Western thought this goes back to ancient Greek and Roman philosophers who saw themselves as "citizens of the world." During the same period that gave rise to the nation-state, Dante Alighieri (1265–1321) wrote *Monarchia*, arguing for a worldwide monarchy. But despite significant areas of world cooperation—such as the Universal Postal Union (founded 1874), the International Civil Aviation Organization (founded 1944), and the Food and Agricultural Organization (founded 1945)—a number of international organizations have either failed or been perceived as failures. The League of Nations was founded in 1919 and lasted until 1946, when the United Nations (UN) was formed. The League failed to respond to a number of significant crises, with the Italian takeover of Abyssinia, now Ethiopia and Eritrea, in 1935 and 1936 being the best known of these failures. While the UN has been extremely successful in many of its activities, it is thought of by many, mostly in the United States, as both a failure and a serious threat to national sovereignty. How a failed organization can constitute a threat is rarely discussed.

Space exploration has produced pictures of earth hanging in space surrounded by absolutely nothing (see Chapter 13). The realization that human beings live together with nowhere else to go has led many to believe that some way must be found for all of us to get along peacefully. Cosmopolitanism, or thinking of oneself as a citizen of the world, or at least as a member of the human race that together inhabits a fragile earth, is a growing phenomenon. Many people see themselves as having much in common with others around the world. This usually comes from contact with people from different backgrounds through travel, business or professional contacts, interaction with immigrants, or education with student exchanges and study abroad programs doing a lot to foster greater understanding.

Internationalists believe that the world should be united in some way, but they do not agree on what this way should be. Some, for example, argue for a world government with strong powers. Others argue for some sort of loose confederation. Still others argue for a federal system of government similar to that of the United States, with powers divided between a world government and the government of each country belonging to the federation. Others are unsure what form unity might take but believe strongly that unity is essential.

Many believe that cosmopolitanism is nothing more than a general statement about the need to treat others ethically, because anything more would require a world government, which is simply impossible.[19] On the other hand, many commentators refer to "The Cosmopolitan Manifesto," first published in 1998 and often reprinted, as providing guidelines for a workable cosmopolitanism.[20]

---

[19] See, for example, David Miller, "Cosmopolitanism: A Critique," *CRISPP: Critical Review of International Social and Political Philosophy* 5:3 (Autumn 2002): 80–85. Responses to Miller's article, published in the same issue, include Thomas Pogge, "Cosmopolitanism: A Defence" (pp. 86–91) and Thom Brooks, "Cosmopolitanism and Distributing Responsibilities" (pp. 92–97).

[20] Ulrich Beck, "The Cosmopolitan Manifesto," *New Statesman* 127 (March 20, 1998): 28–30.

In a general sense, cosmopolitanism or internationalism is similar to nationalism. It requires recognition of ties among all individuals in the world, just as nationalism requires recognition of ties among those living in a country. Symbols can help create such ties, and internationalism has few such symbols. Even though people may intellectually recognize ties to others around the world, it is unlikely that they will have a significant emotional identification with the world. Thus internationalism is not likely to be as strong a force as nationalism unless some crisis produces the emotional fervor that would bring about an identification of the individual with a world community. A science fiction cliché has an invasion from outer space acting as the crisis that produces the recognition that we are all human beings living together.

Today, the recognition that actions in one country affect the health and safety of people in another country—through pollution such as acid rain, the destruction of the ozone layer, changes in weather patterns, and other impacts on the global environment—has brought a new urgency and prominence to internationalism. Although few specific policies have changed, there is a growing sense that nations must find ways of cooperating on environmental issues.

In addition, the world now seems to recognize that conflict in one place is dangerous for other places, and the UN is involved in a number of peacekeeping missions. Part of the reason for internationalizing peacekeeping through the UN is that nationalism produces resentment at the involvement of powerful countries like the United States; the use of troops from small countries, particularly countries from the same general area of the world, helps reduce this resentment. Thus nationalism is helping to create at least one instance of internationalism.

But one author notes that "cosmopolitanism is the privilege of those who can take a secure nation-state for granted,"[21] which suggests that cosmopolitanism is not in opposition to nationalism, but instead something that can be built on nationalism.

NATIONALISM IN THE THIRD WORLD

Until the breakup of the former Soviet Union, we were most aware of nationalism in the Third World, now called the Global South by some. In the terminology in use then, the *First World* was the United States and those countries aligned with it; the *Second World* was the Soviet Union and those countries aligned with it; and the *Third World* was everything else, specifically the developing countries that tried to avoid being aligned with either. With the Second World conceptually gone, the Third World is now the most common term in use to describe the underdeveloped or developing countries of the world.[22] Other "worlds" have been added to the list. *Fourth World* is used by some to refer to the poorest of the

---

[21] Ignatieff, *Blood and Belonging,* 13.

[22] "Third World" was first used in 1952 by Albert Sauvy (1898–1990), a French demographer, to refer to those countries trying to find a "third" way between capitalism and communism. For a sympathetic account of the history of the Third World, see Vijay Prashad, *The Darker Nations: A People's History of the Third World.* New York: New Press, 2007.

poor countries and by others to refer to the indigenous or native peoples of the world. Recently others have begun to use *Fifth World* to refer to those who have lost status through immigration.

Stages of Development from Colony to Independence

Most Third World countries have gone through a series of stages in the process of development from the colonial period to independence. The colonial experience was the first stage, followed, not necessarily in order, by the development of a movement for independence; the revitalization of the indigenous culture; political independence; neocolonialism; one-party rule with internal conflict and often a military takeover; and, in a slowly growing number of cases, the establishment of a stable political system. A striking recent case is the 2008 election in Pakistan, in which a dictator managed to lose an election and accepted the result. While it is too early to be sure about long-term stability, the result was truly remarkable.

The Colonial Experience The one experience all Third World countries share is having been colonies. Although Western countries such as the United States, Canada, Australia, and New Zealand were all colonies of Britain at one time, generally the experience is sufficiently in the past that little awareness of it politically, economically, and psychologically remains. For many countries of the Third World, the colonial experience is recent.

Colonies can be characterized as *settlement colonies* and *exploitative colonies*.[23] The first were primarily areas to which people from the home country moved with the intention of staying. The latter were primarily exploited for their natural resources, although settlement colonies were also exploited, and some people settled permanently in colonies that were primarily exploited. In both cases the indigenous population was devastated, and mass murder was common. Joseph Conrad's (1857–1924) novel *The Heart of Darkness* (1902) is a well-known and generally accurate description of the exploitation of the Congo by Belgium. And while Belgium was among the very worst colonial powers, the description fits most other colonies.

Being a colony meant that others made all decisions for their own benefit. Even major decisions were made not in the colony but in Europe; a colonial bureaucracy composed of people sent from Europe made other decisions. In political terms, a colony was just a minor concern in the overall policy of the European power.

Economically, the colony was there to provide raw materials for the "home" country, a place to offload its population, a market for its goods, and cheap labor. Most exploitative colonies were required to limit their economies to one or two cash crops or other raw materials, and they were not allowed to diversify. Little more than minimal processing was done in the colony; that would have required trained workers, and training workers might raise their expectations and pose

---

[23] While *settler* or *settlement colonies* is the standard language used, there is a no agreement on what to call the colonies I have labeled *exploitative*.

problems. Ultimately, this happened; training workers for skilled jobs did raise expectations—and it produced leaders of independence movements.

Even more dangerous was education. Most colonial powers did not educate the indigenous population, although Christian missionaries provided schools and, in fact, educated many leaders of the later independence movements. The fact that most education was provided by Christian missionaries illustrates another fact about the colonial experience—the attack on indigenous culture. This process of deculturation proved traumatic for many people, but it also provided the tools that made independence possible. On the one hand, the imposition of an alien culture stripped many people of their sense of self. Their religions were suppressed, their languages replaced, their customs denigrated, even their clothes and hairstyles were replaced by Western styles. Everything indigenous was treated as inferior, and this attitude was taught in schools.

On the other hand, the acceptance, at least temporarily, of Western culture provided both the intellectual and physical tools needed for independence. The Western traditions of liberty and equality provided the vocabulary needed for movements toward independence. Technical training provided the ability to replace the colonial rulers running the government and the economy. And at least some colonial rulers found it more difficult to treat as inferior someone who dressed and spoke as they did and who had been educated at the same schools and universities.

The process in settlement colonies was somewhat different in that local decision making came easier and earlier than in the exploitative colonies, but the treatment of the indigenous population was much the same. Indigenous rights movements in the settler colonies developed later and have been less successful than the independence movements in exploitative colonies. In fact, it is possible to argue that the damage done to the indigenous populations was much worse in some settler colonies, such as the United States and Australia, than in most exploitative colonies. South Africa is the only former settlement colony in which the indigenous people have regained political power.

Movements for National Liberation

The most common scenario for an independence movement involved years of covert and overt opposition. Most, if not all, independence leaders spent time in prison for their activities; in fact, in many countries prison time became a requirement for gaining acceptance, respect, and credibility.

In most cases independence was actually won through violent revolution or long years of war for independence. India was the major exception: although violent incidents did occur, India's independence leaders, Mohandas K. Gandhi (1869–1948) and Jawaharlal Nehru (1889–1964), used nonviolent techniques to win political autonomy.

The struggle for independence provided a focus for the development or redevelopment of a national identity. It also became the basis for a national culture. In almost all cases, independence movements attempted to ensure that their supporters worked solely for the benefit of the people as a whole rather than for their own benefit. A good example of this approach is found in the

Julius K. Nyerere (1922–1999) was president of the United Republic of Tanzania, formed by uniting Tanganyika and Zanzibar, from 1964 to 1985. He is one of the few leaders of an African independence movement not to be overthrown, though a few attempts were made, and to retire from office. From 1954 on, he was president of the Tanganyika African National Union (TANU), the political party active in bringing independence to Tanganyika. Nyerere was known for his advocacy of African Socialism and what he called *ujamaa*—a Swahili word that he translates as "familyhood"—as the basis for developing Third World economies.

"Rules of Discipline" announced by Kwame Nkrumah (1909–1972), the leader of the independence movement in what was the British colony of Gold Coast, which became Ghana upon gaining independence in 1957. In his "Rules of Discipline," Nkrumah says that those involved in the revolution should "not take a single needle or piece of thread from the masses," "not take liberties with women," "always guide and protect the children," and "always be the servant of the people."[24] Julius K. Nyerere (1922–1999), the leader of the independence movement in Tanganyika, now Tanzania, went even further in the Arusha Declaration. He declared that no member of government or leader in a political party should "hold shares in any company," "hold directorships in any privately owned enterprise," "receive two or more salaries," or "own houses which he rents to others." He stated explicitly that the prohibition extends to spouses.[25] Until independence, and for awhile afterward, such programs worked; but after a time,

---

[24] Kwame Nkrumah, *Handbook of Revolutionary Warfare: A Guide to the Armed Phase of the African Revolution*. New York: International Publishers, 1969: vii.

[25] Julius K. Nyerere, *Ujamaa—Essays on Socialism*. Dar es Salaam, Tanzania: Oxford University Press, 1968: 36.

many leaders of liberation movements used their new power to line their own pockets and those of their families and friends, rather than to help develop the country as a whole. There were exceptions, and Nyerere was one.

The Revitalization of Indigenous Cultures Despite colonization, indigenous cultures were damaged but not destroyed, and national identity required that the culture be revived.[26] Language, literature, and the arts, together with religion and music, were all rediscovered, encouraged, and, with independence, taught in a refashioned educational system. The so-called world music movement has brought the music of indigenous peoples to the attention of people throughout the world.[27] In what may seem a minor move, countries have reestablished traditional names for places that had been given different names by the colonists; for example, what the British had called *Bombay* is now *Mumbai*.

In places where the traditional culture had been nearly destroyed, notably sub-Saharan Africa, the process of revitalization has been slow, but it is still taking place and provides more and more people a recovered sense of self. Still, the continuing Westernization and urbanization that have followed independence have added to the difficulty of establishing a national culture. And the revival of indigenous cultures can also produce problems, because cultures are often tribal rather than national. Nations are artificial creations of the colonial powers, so many countries are experiencing a clash of cultures. Independence is not the solution to all problems that it had seemed to many.

For most Third World countries, political independence, which had been the only goal, suddenly became a step toward the goals of economic independence, political stability, and decent lives for their citizens. The first action needed to achieve these goals was to take effective control of the economy, but this proved difficult.

Neocolonialism After formal independence has been achieved, economic ties with the former colonial power may resemble continued control. This is known as *neocolonialism*. Most new countries have developed some sort of agreement with the former colonists, usually to their mutual advantage. The problem of neocolonialism is a complex one. It is essential for rapid economic development that the new nation trade with older, more established nations. Often the only thing the new nation has to trade is raw materials. In return it gets manufactured

---

[26] See, for example, Sékou Touré, "A Dialectical Approach to Culture," in *Pan-Africanism*, Robert Chrisman and Nathan Hare, eds. Indianapolis: Bobbs-Merrill, 1974: 52–73; Amilcar Cabral, "National Liberation and Culture," Maureen Webster, trans. In Cabral, *Return to the Source: Selected Speeches.* New York: Monthly Review Press, 1973: 39–56; and Cabral, "The Role of Culture in the Battle for Independence," *UNESCO Courier* (November 1973): 12–16, 20.

[27] World Music appears to include all music except that of the developed West, but includes indigenous music from that area. The British Broadcasting Corporation (BBC) Radio 3 awarded the first Awards for World Music in 2002; the current regional categories are Africa, Asia/Pacific, America (including the Caribbean), and Europe/Middle East with additional awards for boundary crossing, newcomers, innovation, and listeners and critics awards. National Public Radio (NPR) has a more limited definition of *World Music* and includes Africa, Latin America, and the Caribbean.

goods or even industries. The problem stems from the fact that raw materials sell on the world market at a much lower price than do manufactured goods. Therefore, the new nation feels it is being exploited by selling a commodity that is relatively inexpensive to purchase one that is relatively expensive.

Such problems make neocolonialism an important and difficult issue for the new nation. It must deal with older, more developed countries, often including its previous colonial ruler, to survive, but it feels it is being exploited in virtually the same way it was while still a colony. Therefore, many new countries have insisted that processing of raw materials take place at home, thus producing an industry, employing people, and giving them some sense that they are not being exploited.

Political Instability   After independence, usually one political party dominated, and it often allowed no significant opposition to develop. One-party rule, it was argued, was necessary to provide the unity and stability needed to forge a new nation. Frequently one-party rule resulted in military coups, because the military was the only alternative center of power. This pattern has left many Third World countries struggling for political and economic survival, searching for an identity that allows them independence from the former colonial powers.

And again because the countries were artificial creations by the colonial powers, conflicts among ethnic groups are common. The genocide in Rwanda in 1994 was centered around an ages-old conflict between the Hutu and the Tutsi. The postelection violence in Kenya in late 2007 and early 2008 was not simply between political parties but also between the dominant tribe, the Kikuyu, and smaller tribes, particularly the Luo.

Another major problem that does not seem to go away is corruption. Vast sums of money are stolen by those in power and moved out of the country, usually to banks in Europe and North America. As a result, the political leaders become more and more afraid of the penalties if they lose an election and will do anything to stay in power. When political change does take place, it proves difficult to ensure that lower level bureaucrats do not conclude that they should act like the previous regime did and enrich themselves as soon as they have the opportunity to do so. Having people at the top who are not corrupt, and who want to establish a new regime free of corruption, does not mean that they will succeed.

NEW NATIONS

Throughout the twentieth century, new nations were created, but national consciousness and identity cannot be created overnight. In most new twentieth-century nations, the experience of being a colony and the movement to overthrow the colonial power helped citizens develop a sense of themselves as a people. But these experiences are not enough to maintain the identity for long.

The ancient/modern, ethnic/civic splits can be seen in the process of creating a nation, or *nation building,* as it used to be called.[28] Identification is easiest if it

---

[28] See Karl Deutsch and William J. Foltz, eds., *Nation-Building.* New York: Atherton Press, 1963.

is based on a single ethnic group that has a consciousness of itself that long precedes the creation of the new nation. It is relatively easy to proclaim a new nation with agreed-on boundaries and a government; it is much harder to imagine that nation into existence in the minds of its inhabitants. Flags, national anthems, and other symbols of nationhood must be accepted by the people and become part of their personal identities before more than an outer shell of a nation can be said to exist.

The first new nation to succeed in developing a national consciousness and identity was the United States.[29] It was a difficult process, even though some states that united had histories as lengthy as 150 years. These states had the initial advantage of a common enemy, Britain, but they also had separate identities in the minds of many of their citizens; and the process of creating an identification with the new nation was long and arduous. The United States went through a civil war before it was clear that a nation had been established, and it reached its current geographic dimensions only in 1959, when Alaska and Hawaii were admitted as the forty-ninth and fiftieth states.

CURRENT TRENDS

Contemporary scholarship indicates that past studies of nationalism neglected three subjects: minorities, women, and postcolonial societies. Postcolonialism has become a major theme of contemporary scholarship, but the other two, though they attract some attention, are still generally neglected.

These neglected subjects are important for different reasons. Minorities are important because they complicate the imagining of the nation. As previously noted, it is fairly easy to imagine a nation composed of one ethnic group but much harder if there are minorities. Assimilation or the belief in assimilation (the "melting pot") has been the traditional strategy to address the problem. This approach suggests that there are no important minorities, just people who are in the process of becoming part of the nation. But today we realize both that the process takes much longer than was previously thought and that assimilation is almost always partial. In other words, minorities remain that identify with both the nation they live in and the one they emigrated from.

Women play particularly important roles in both bearing the future citizens of the nation and in socializing those future citizens. In the latter case, they are likely to give their children their first sense of the nation to which they belong and their future role in it. Thus if women do not identify with the nation, their children are less likely to do so.

In a world of multiple identities, and as feminism becomes more global, with whom should women identify: other women wherever they reside, or just those men and women—or other women—residing in the same country? In other

---

[29] See Seymour Martin Lipset, *First New Nation: The United States in Historical and Comparative Perspective.* New York: Basic Books, 1963.

words, which of their, and our, identities should take precedence? In a world half female, this is obviously an important question for each nation.[30]

Postmodernism/Postcolonialism

Because it is based on "imagined" or "created" communities, nationalism can easily be read from the perspective of postmodernism. Specifically, as postmodernism undermines the idea of universalism—particularly a universalism seen through Western eyes—nationalism becomes extremely important, especially from the postcolonial perspective.[31] Although those of us who are born and stay within the bounds of a country are likely to see the nation as a given, it is not. In the United States, we used to use the metaphor of the melting pot to suggest that in some way those who immigrated to the United States from other places melted together into one whole. (The term originated with a play of that name performed on Broadway in 1908.)[32] What we forgot was that each melting changed the whole, and today many people are more likely to use a metaphor like "tossed salad" to suggest that although a whole is created, the parts of that whole remain recognizable.

This perspective shows how nationalism today reflects postcolonialism, although postcolonialism is itself a contested concept.[33] As Homi K. Bhabha put it, "the founding dictum of the political society of the modern nation—its spatial expression of a unitary people" is "*out of many one*".[34] But it is clear that the multicultural, multiethnic modern state remains multiple.

Secession

Many ethnic groups argue for positions ranging from the recognition of some degree of autonomy for their group within the larger political unit to secession from that unit to establish a new unit. Secession movements exist in most countries today, and most of them are of little significance. But there are important—and often violent—movements: among the Kurds in Iran, Iraq, and Turkey; the Basques in Spain; the Tibetans in China; the Tamils in Sri Lanka; and other less well-known movements elsewhere. And there is an important nonviolent secessionist movement in Great Britain, where the Scottish Nationalist Party won the most seats in the Scottish Parliament in the last election and hopes to hold a referendum on independence.

---

[30] For various perspectives on women and nationalism, see Cynthia Cockburn, *The Space Between Us: Negotiating Gender and National Identities in Conflict.* London: Zed Books, 1998; Caren Kaplan, Norma Alarcón, and Minoo Moallem, eds., *Between Woman and Nation: Nationalism, Transnational Feminisms, and the State.* Durham, NC: Duke University Press, 1999; and Tamar Mayer, ed., *Gender Ironies of Nationalism: Sexing the Nation.* New York: Routledge, 2000.

[31] See Rachel Walker, "Postmodernism," in *Encyclopedia of Nationalism,* 1: 611–630.

[32] Israel Zangwill, *The Melting Pot: Drama in Four Acts.* New York: Macmillan, 1909.

[33] See Leela Gandhi, *Postcolonial Theory: A Critical Introduction.* New York: Columbia University Press, 1998. Offers a discussion of the conflicted nature of postcolonial studies.

[34] Homi K. Bhabha, "DissemiNation: Time, Narrative, and the Margins of the Modern Nation," in *Nation and Narration,* Homi K. Bhabha, ed. London: Routledge, 1990: 294. (Original emphasis).

Although not based on ethnicity, a secessionist movement occurred in the United States during the period of the Civil War, known in the South as the War between the States or the War of Northern Aggression. Abraham Lincoln (1809–1865) is remembered as one of the greatest U.S. presidents because of his dedication to saving the Union, for which he was assassinated. Proponents of secession have argued for it as national self-determination, asking whether a people who want their own state should be able to have it. Opponents, like Lincoln, have argued that the maintenance of the current state should take precedence over the desires of a minority within it.[35] But as suggested by the different language used to describe the Civil War, the world looks different from the point of view of the secessionists; for example, what is known as the 1857 Indian Mutiny in Britain is known as the First War of Independence in India.

In 2008 Kosovo seceded from Serbia, and politicians in the countries that might benefit from the secession are trying to say that this secession is acceptable, but others are not. No country with an important secessionist movement has recognized Kosovo's existence as legitimate. In time Kosovo may succeed in establishing itself as an independent country generally recognized by the international community, but its secession is just as likely to spark another war in the Balkans.

Nationalist Conflicts

Many conflicts in the world today reflect nationalism. Some are of long standing, such as the Basque nationalist movement in northern Spain and southern France, the Zapatistas in Mexico, and the struggle between Israel and the Palestinians. The terrorist attacks on the United States led both the Basques and the Irish Republican Army (IRA) to make conciliatory gestures so as not to be targets of the world campaign against terrorism; and in Northern Ireland, the first stages of reconciliation have been achieved and terrorism has ended. The Basques have returned to terrorism, little has changed in Mexico, and the situation between Israel and the Palestinians has not changed and it seems unlikely to change in the near future.

Nationalism in the United States

Nationalism in the United States mirrors nationalism elsewhere. For the most part, Americans responded to the attacks on the World Trade Center and the Pentagon with the sort of widespread patriotism, the positive support for and identification with country, that represents the best of civic nationalism. "Good" nationalism clearly predominated. On the other hand, a small minority has exhibited the "bad" nationalism, sometimes called *jingoism*, that we condemn as ethnic nationalism when we see it elsewhere. The murder of Muslims and Sikhs—a religion originating in India that is unrelated to Islam but requires its men to wear turbans and beards—illustrates that this sort of nationalism exists in the United States. And the treatment during World War II of Japanese-American

---

[35] On secession movements, see *Theories of Secession,* Percy Lehning, ed. London: Routledge, 1998; and Margaret Moore, *The Ethics of Nationalism.* Oxford, England: Oxford University Press, 2001.

U.S. citizens, who were interned in prison camps, shows that this is not a new phenomenon. The Council on American–Islamic Relations (CAIR) reported 141 Islamic hate crimes in the U.S. in 2004, 153 in 2005, and 167 in 2006.

Indigenous Peoples

In addition to the activities of Native Americans in the United States and the indigenous peoples of Canada,[36] activities that take place largely within the political realm, indigenous peoples' movements exist throughout the Americas. In the Amazon River basin in Brazil, native people are struggling for recognition by the international community and against the oil and other companies that have been given access to the natural resources in the area. Because few South American countries have strict environmental laws, or choose not to enforce those that exist, a number of indigenous people have become involved with environmental activists in an attempt to protect the environment that is central to their way of life. They have generally been ignored, have failed even when their efforts were recognized as just, or have been murdered.

Failed States

There are states where the nation-building process has not worked, called *failed states,* or states that cannot maintain law and order within their boundaries. Liberia is a well-known example: life expectancy is 47 years, 1 of every 16 adults is HIV-positive or has AIDS, and one in seven babies dies in infancy. One positive note is that Liberia recently put into power the first democratically elected female head of state in Africa. Ellen Johnson Sirleaf (b. 1938) was educated in the United States and holds a BA from the University of Colorado and an MA in Economics from Harvard University. If she manages to improve conditions, it will bring hope to other such states; but she faces an extremely difficult task.

The problem with nationalism is that it both unites and divides. Ernest Renan (1828–1892) eloquently described the nation as "a soul, a spiritual principle. Two things, which in truth are but one, constitute this soul or spiritual principle. One lies in the past, one in the present. One is the possession of a rich legacy of memories; the other is present-day consent, the desire to live together, the will to perpetuate the value of the heritage that one has received in an undivided form."[37] At the same time, nationalism defines any nonnational as "other," or "alien," with the implication of fundamental difference, often leading to fear. The alien may be "naturalized" and assimilated, but even these characteristics do not necessarily eliminate the fear of outsiders, which often leads to violence against them.

Thus nationalism is both a positive and a negative force in the world today, pulling people together and pushing them apart. And in one aspect or another, it is a force in all other ideologies.

---

[36] There is no single name for the indigenous peoples of Canada. *Inuit* refers to only Eastern Arctic; *Eskimo* has been partially reinstated because it refers to both Eastern and Western Arctic peoples; *First Nations* excludes Eskimos; and *Indian* is used (and rejected) as is *Native Peoples.*

[37] Ernest Renan, "What Is a Nation?" Martin Thom, trans. In Bhabha *Nation and Narration* (p. 19). Originally given as a lecture entitled "Qu'est-ce qu'une nation?" March 11, 1882.

SUGGESTED READING

Some Classic Works

Anderson, Benedict. *Imagined Communities: Reflections on the Origin and Spread of Nationalism.* Revised ed. London: Verso, 2006. Includes a new chapter "Travel and Traffic: On the Geo-biography of *Imagined Communities*" (207–229), which is largely about its translation into 27 languages and its publication in over 30 countries.

Berlin, Isaiah. "The Bent Twig: A Note on Nationalism." *Foreign Affairs* Vol. 51:1 (October 1972): 11–30. Reprinted in *The Crooked Timber of Humanity: Chapters in the History of Ideas,* Henry Hardy, ed. London: John Murray, 1990: 238–261.

———. "Nationalism: Past Neglect and Present Power." *Partisan Review* Vol. 46:3 (1979): 337–358. Reprinted in *Against the Current: Essays in the History of Ideas,* Henry Hardy, ed. London: Hogarth Press, 1979: 333–355.

Fanon, Frantz. *Black Skin, White Masks.* Charles Lam Markmann, trans. New York: Grove Press, 1967. Reprinted by Grove Weidenfeld, 1991. Originally published as *Peau noire, masques blancs.* Paris: Éditions du Seuil, 1952.

———. *The Wretched of the Earth.* Constance Farrington, trans. New York: Grove Press, 1963. New ed. translated by Richard Philcox with introductions by Jean-Paul Sartre and Homi K. Bhabha. New York: Grove, 2004. Originally published as *Les Damnés de la terre.* Paris: F. Maspero, 1961.

Gandhi, Mohandas Karamchand. *Hind Swaraj and Other Writings.* Anthony J. Parel, ed. Cambridge, England: Cambridge University Press, 1997.

Kohn, Hans. *American Nationalism: An Interpretive Essay.* New York: St. Martin's Press, 1957.

———. *The Idea of Nationalism: A Study in its Origins and Background.* New edition. New Brunswick, NJ: Transaction, 2005. Includes an "Introduction to the Transaction Edition" by Craig Calhoun (ix–l). Originally published New York: Macmillan, 1944.

Mandela, Nelson. *Long Walk to Freedom: The Autobiography of Nelson Mandela.* Boston: Little, Brown, 1994. Reprinted Boston: Little, Brown, 2006.

Nasser, Gamal Abdel. *The Philosophy of the Revolution.* Buffalo, NY: Smith, Keynes & Marshall, 1959.

Nkrumah, Kwame. *The Autobiography of Kwame Nkrumah.* Edinburgh: Thomas Nelson & Sons, 1957.

———. *I Speak of Freedom: A Statement of African Ideology.* New York: Praeger, 1970.

Said, Edward W. *Orientalism.* New York: Pantheon Books, 1978. Reprinted with a new afterword. Harmondsworth, England: Penguin, 1995. Most recent reprint Harmondsworth, England: Penguin, 2003.

Tagore, Sir Rabindranath. *Nationalism.* New York: Macmillan, 1917. Reprinted Westport, CT: Greenwood Press, 1973.

Books and Articles

Abdel-Nour, Farid. "National Responsibility." *Political Theory* Vol. 31:5 (October 2003): 693–719. What responsibility do we have as members of a national community?

Alagha, Joseph Elie. *The Shifts in Hizbullah's Ideology: Religious Ideology, Political Ideology, and Political Program.* Leiden, The Netherlands: Amsterdam University Press, 2006. History 1978 to 2005.

Appiah, Kwame Anthony. *The Ethics of Identity.* Princeton, NJ: Princeton University Press, 2005. Rooted cosmopolitanism.

———. *Cosmopolitanism: Ethics in a World of Strangers.* New York: Norton, 2006. U.K. edition, London: Allen Lane, 2006. Identifies "two strands" to cosmopolitanism: "obligations to others" and taking "seriously the value not just of human life but of particular human lives": (xiv).

Ayittey, George B.N. *Africa Unchained: The Blueprint for Africa's Future.* London: Palgrave Macmillan, 2005. An argument for the freeing of the market in Africa and the development of the entrepreneurial spirit of young Africans with examples of the success of such activities.

Beck, Ulrich. "The Cosmopolitan Manifesto." *New Statesman* Vol. 127: 4377 (March 20, 1998): 28–30.

———. *The Cosmopolitan Vision.* Ciaran Cronin, trans. Cambridge, England: Polity, 2006. Originally published as *Der kosmopolitische Blick oder: Krieg is Frieden.* Frankfurt am Main, Germany: Suhrkamp Verlag, 2004.

Bose, Sumantra. *Contested Lands: Israel–Palestine, Kashmir, Bosnia, Cyprus, and Sri Lanka.* Cambridge, MA: Harvard University Press, 2007.

Brock, Gillian, and Harry Brighouse, eds. *The Political Philosophy of Cosmopolitanism.* Cambridge, England: Cambridge University Press, 2005.

Calderisi, Robert. *The Trouble with Africa: Why Foreign Aid Isn't Working.* New York: Palgrave Macmillan, 2006. Reprint New Haven, CT: Yale University Press, 2006.

Carey, Roane, and Jonathan Shainin, eds. *The Other Israel: Voices of Refusal and Dissent.* New York: New Press, 2002.

Castle, Gregory, ed. *Postcolonial Discourses: An Anthology.* Oxford: Blackwell, 2001.

Chakrabarty, Bidyut. *Social and Political Thought of Mahatma Gandhi.* London: Routledge, 2006.

Cockburn, Cynthia. *The Space between Us: Negotiating Gender and National Identities in Conflict.* London: Zed Books, 1998.

Costa, Josep. "On Theories of Secession: Minorities, Majorities and the Multinational State." *CRISPP: Critical Review of International Social and Political Philosophy* Vol. 6:2 (Summer 2003): 63–90.

Day, Graham, and Andrew Thompson. Consulting Editor Jo Campling. *Theorizing Nationalism: Debates and Issues in Social Theory.* London: Palgrave Macmillan, 2004.

Delanty, Gerard, and Krishan Kumar, eds. *The Sage Handbook of Nations and Nationalism.* London: Sage Publications, 2006. An important collection.

Dieckhoff, Alain, and Christophe Jaffrelot, eds. *Revisiting Nationalism: Theories and Processes.* London: Hurst & Co. in association with the Centre d'Etudes et de Recherches Internationales (Sciences Po), Paris, 2005.

Easterly, William. *The White Man's Burden: Why the west's efforts to aid the rest have done so much ill and so little good.* New York: Penguin, 2006. U.K. ed. Oxford, England: Oxford University Press, 2006.

Ethnicities Vol. 1:1 (Founded 2001).

Feldman, Noah. *What We Owe Iraq: War and the Ethics of Nation Building.* Princeton, NJ: Princeton University Press, 2004. The author was a Senior Constitutional Adviser to the Coalition Provisional Authority in Iraq.

Freeden, Michael. "Is Nationalism a Distinct Ideology?" *Political Studies* Vol. 46:4 (September 1998): 748–765.

Frost, Catherine. *Morality and Nationalism.* London: Routledge, 2006. Compares Ireland and Québec to develop a theory of nationalism.

Fukuyama, Francis. *State-Building: Governance and World Order in the 21st Century.* Ithaca, NY: Cornell University Press, 2004.

Gelvin, James L. *The Israel–Palestine Conflict: One Hundred Years of War.* Cambridge, England: Cambridge University Press, 2005.

Gillingham, John. *European Integration, 1950–2003: Superstate or New Market Economy?* Cambridge: Cambridge University Press, 2003. History of European integration.

———. *Design for a New Europe.* Cambridge, England: Cambridge University Press, 2006.

Goldberg, Michelle. *Kingdom Coming: The Rise of Christian Nationalism.* New York: W.W. Norton, 2006. Popular.

Hardt, Michael, and Antonio Negri. *Empire.* Cambridge: Harvard University Press, 2000.

———. *Multitude: War and Democracy in the Age of Empire.* New York: Penguin Press, 2004.

Harty, Siobhán, and Michael Murphy. *In Defence of Multinational Citizenship.* Cardiff: University of Wales Press, 2005.

Henck, Nick. *Subcommander Marcos: The Man and the Mask.* Durham, NC: Duke University Press, 2007.

Higgins, Nicholas P. *Understanding the Chiapas Rebellion: Modernist Visions and the Invisible Indian.* Austin: University of Texas Press, 2004.

Higonnet, Patrice. *Attendant Cruelties: Nation and Nationalism in American History.* New York: Other Press, 2007.

Hing, Bill Ong. *Deporting Our Souls: Values, Morality and Immigration Policy.* Cambridge, England: Cambridge University Press, 2006.

Hopgood, Stephen. *Keepers of the Flame: Understanding Amnesty International.* Ithaca, NY: Cornell University Press, 2006.

Hutchinson, John, and Anthony D. Smith, eds. *Nationalism: Critical Concepts in Political Science.* 5 vols. New York: Routledge, 2000.

Ichijo, Atsuko, and Gordana Uzelac, eds. *When Is the Nation? Towards an Understanding of the Theories of Nationalism.* London: Routledge, 2005.

Ignatieff, Michael, ed. *American Exceptionalism and Human Rights.* Princeton, NJ: Princeton University Press, 2005.

Immigrants and Minorities Vol. 1:1 (Founded 1982).

The Indigenous World Vol. 1 to the present (Founded 1994).

Isbister, John. *Promises Not Kept: The Betrayal of Social Change in the Third World.* 7th ed. Bloomfield, CT: Kumarian Press, 2006.

Jamal, Amal. *The Palestinian National Movement: Politics of Contention, 1967–2005.* Bloomington: Indiana University Press, 2005.

Joireman, Sandra Fullerton. *Nationalism and Political Identity.* London: Continuum, 2003. Types of nationalism.

Journal of Ethnic and Migration Studies Vol. 1:1 to the present (Founded 1998).

Kaplan, Caren, Norma Alarcón, and Minoo Moallem, eds. *Between Woman and Nation: Nationalism, Transnational Feminisms, and the State.* Durham, NC: Duke University Press, 1999.

Kassir, Samir. *Being Arab.* Will Hobson, trans. London: Verso, 2006. Originally published in 2004. The author was a Lebanese journalist who was assassinated in 2005.

Kateb, George. *Patriotism and Other Mistakes.* New Haven, CT: Yale University Press, 2006. Collection of essays that are relevant to a wide range of topics.

Kennedy, Paul. *The Parliament of Man: The United Nations and the Quest for World Government.* London: Allen Lane, 2006.

Khalidi, Rashid. *The Iron Cage: The Story of the Palestinian Struggle for Statehood.* Boston, MA: Beacon Press, 2006.

Kymlicka, Will. *Politics in the Vernacular: Nationalism, Multiculturalism, and Citizenship.* New York: Oxford University Press, 2001.

Laitin, David D. *Nations, States, and Violence.* Oxford, England: Oxford University Press, 2007.

Legrain, Philippe. *Immigrants: Your Country Needs Them.* London: Little, Brown, 2006.

Levene, Mark. *Genocide in the Age of the Nation State.* 2 vols. I.B. Tauris, 2005. Vol. 1 is *The Meaning of Genocide* and vol. 2 is *The Rise of the West and the Coming of Genocide.*

Lieven, Anatol. *America Right or Wrong: An Anatomy of American Nationalism.* New York: Oxford University Press, 2004.

Loomba, Ania. *Colonialism/Postcolonialism.* 2nd ed. London: Routledge, 2005.

——, Suvir Kaul, Matti Bunzil, Antoinette Burton, and Jed Esty, eds. *Postcolonial Studies and Beyond.* Durham, NC: Duke University Press, 2005.

Lumumba-Kasongo, Tukumbi, ed. *Liberal Democracy and its Critics in Africa: Political Dysfunction and the Struggle for Social Progress.* Dakar, Senegal: Codesria Books in association with London: Zed Books and Pretoria, South Africa: University of South Africa Press, 2005.

Máiz, Ramón. "Framing the Nation: Three Rival Versions of Contemporary Nationalist Ideology." *Journal of Political Ideologies* Vol. 8:3 (October 2003): 251–267.

Mann, Michael. *The Dark Side of Democracy: Explaining Ethnic Cleansing.* Cambridge, England: Cambridge University Press, 2005.

Marcos, Subcomandante. *Our Word Is Our Weapon: Selected Writings.* Juana Ponce de León, ed. New York: Seven Stories, 2001.

Marrow, Helen B. "New Destinations and Immigrant Incorporation." *Perspectives on Politics* Vol. 3:4 (December 2005): 781–799.

Mayer, Tamar, ed. *Gender Ironies of Nationalism: Sexing the Nation.* New York: Routledge, 2000.

Miller, David [Leslie]. *Citizenship and National Identity.* Cambridge, England: Polity Press, 2000.

Mishal, Shaul, and Avraham Sela. *The Palestinian Hamas: Vision, Violence, and Coexistence.* New York: Columbia University Press, 2006. "Preface to the 2006 Edition" (xiii–xxx).

Mkandawire, Thandika, ed. *African Intellectuals: Rethinking Politics, Language, Gender and Development.* Dakar, Senegal: Codresia Books in conjunction with Zed Books, London: 2005.

Morgan, Glyn. *The Idea of a European Superstate: Public Justification and European Integration.* Princeton, NJ: Princeton University Press, 2005.

Morris, Benny. *The Birth of the Palestinian Refugee Problem Revisited.* Cambridge, England: Cambridge University Press, 2004.

Motyl, Alexander J., ed. *Encyclopedia of Nationalism.* 2 vols. San Diego: Academic Press, 2001.

Natali, Denise. *The Kurds and the State: Evolving National Identity in Iraq, Turkey, and Iran.* Syracuse, NY: Syracuse University Press, 2005.

Nationalism and Ethnic Politics Vol. 1:1 to the present (Founded 1995).

Noe, Nicholas, ed. *Voice of Hezbollah: The Statements of Sayyed Hassan Nasrallah.* Ellen Khouri, trans. London: Verso, 2007. Covers material from 1986 to 2006.

Norman, Wayne. *Negotiating Nationalism: Nation-Building, Federalism, and Secession in the Multinational State.* Oxford, England: Oxford University Press, 2006.

Packer, George. *The Assassins' Gate: America in Iraq.* New York: Farrar, Straus and Giroux, 2005. The author is a staff writer for the *New Yorker* who worked in Iraq.

Panitch, Leo, and Colin Leys, eds. *Socialist Register 2003: Fighting Identities: Race, Religion and Ethno-nationalism.* London: Merlin Press, 2002.

Paul, T.V., ed. *The India–Pakistan Conflict: An Enduring Rivalry.* Cambridge, England: Cambridge University Press, 2005.

Pauly, Robert J., and Tom Lansford. *Strategic Preemption: U.S. Foreign Policy and the Second Iraq War.* Aldershot, England: Ashgate, 2005.

Pecora, Vincent P., ed. *Nations and Identities: Classic Readings.* Oxford: Blackwell, 2001.

Prashad, Vijay. *The Darker Nations: A People's History of the Third World.* New York: New Press, 2007.

Qassem, Naim. *Hizbullah: The Story from Within.* Dalia Khalil, trans. London: Saqi, 2005.

Rao, Vijayendra, and Michael Walton, eds. *Culture and Public Action.* Stanford, CA: Stanford Social Sciences, 2004. Discusses the need for economists to understand the concept of culture and the content of different cultures, particularly in the ways they effect development. Website at http://culture and publicaction.org.

Romano, David. *The Kurdish Nationalist Movement: Opportunity, Mobilization, and Identity.* Cambridge, England: Cambridge University Press, 2006.

Roshwald, Aviel. *The Endurance of Nationalism: Ancient Roots and Modern Dilemmas.* Cambridge, England: Cambridge University Press, 2006. Argues that nationalism existed in the classical Greek and ancient Jewish worlds.

Ross, Andrew, and Kristin Ross, eds. *Anti-Americanism.* New York: New York University Press, 2004.

Rotberg, Robert I., ed. *When States Fail: Causes and Consequences.* Princeton, NJ: Princeton University Press, 2004.

Rubin, Barry, and Judith Colp Rubin. *Hating America: A History.* New York: Oxford University Press, 2004. History of anti-Americanism.

Schierup, Carl-Ulrik, Peo Hansen, and Stephen Castles. *Migration, Citizenship, and the European Welfare State: A European Dilemma.* Oxford, England: Oxford University Press, 2006.

Schwarz, Henry, and Sangeeta Ray, eds. *A Companion to Postcolonial Studies.* Malden, MA: Blackwell, 2000.

Sen, Amartya. *Development as Freedom.* New York: Knopf, 1999.

———. *The Argumentative Indian: Writings on Indian History, Culture and Identity.* London: Allen Lane, 2005. New York: Farrar, Straus & Giroux, 2005.

———. *Identity and Violence: The Illusion of Destiny.* New York: W.W. Norton, 2006.

Shulman, David. *Dark Hope: Working for Peace in Israel and Palestine.* Chicago, IL:

University of Chicago Press, 2007. An Israeli working with Palestinians in the peace movement.

Spector, Bertram I., ed. *Fighting Corruption in Developing Countries: Strategies and Analysis*. Bloomfield, CT: Kumarian Press, 2005.

Spencer, Philip, and Howard Wollman. "Good and Bad Nationalisms: A Critique of Dualism." *Journal of Political Ideologies* Vol. 3:3 (October 1998): 255–274.

Spivak, Gayatri Chakravorty. *A Critique of Postcolonial Reason: Toward a History of the Vanishing Present*. Cambridge, MA: Harvard University Press, 1999.

Tamimi, Azzam. *Hamas: Unwritten Chapters*. London: Hurst, 2007.

Tan, Kok-Chor. *Justice without Borders: Cosmopolitanism, Nationalism, and Patriotism*. Cambridge, England: Cambridge University Press, 2004. Argument that the equality that is the goal of cosmopolitanism can accommodate liberal nationalism and patriotism.

Thakur, Ramesh Chandra. *The United Nations, Peace and Security: From Collective Security to the Responsibility to Protect*. Cambridge, England: Cambridge University Press, 2006.

Third World Quarterly Vol. 1:1 to the present (Founded 1979).

United Nations Human Settlements Programme (UN-Habitat). *The Challenge of Slums: Global Report on Human Settlements 2003*. London: Earthscan, 2003.

Uvin, Peter. *Human Rights and Development*. Bloomfield, CT: Kumarian Press, 2004.

Wiredu, Kwasi, ed. *A Companion to African Philosophy*. Malden, MA: Blackwell Publishing, 2004. Includes a number of essays on African thinkers. An important collection.

Wolff, Stefan. *Ethnic Conflict: A Global Perspective*. Oxford, England: Oxford University Press, 2006. Says of nationalism, "At its most basic, it is an ideology that puts the nations first before all other forms of social or political organization" (p. 32).

Young, Robert J.C. *Postcolonialism: An Historical Introduction*. London: Routledge, 2001.

¡Zapatistas! Documents of the New Mexican Revolution (December 31, 1993–June 12, 1994). Brooklyn: Autonomedia, 1994.

Websites

The Nationalism Project: http://www.nationalismproject.org

Free the Slaves: http://www.freetheslaves.net

Third World

Third World Network: http://www.twnside.org.sg

Indigenous Peoples

Center for World Indigenous Studies: http://www.cwis.org

Declaration on the Rights of Indigenous Peoples (Adopted by the United Nations in September 2007): http://www.iwgia.org

Fourth World Journal: http://www.cwis.org/fwj

3

Globalization

An Emerging Ideology?

Both globalization and antiglobalization are being called full-fledged ideologies to the extent that it is necessary to at least consider the possibility that one or more new ideologies are emerging. As has been noted, ideologies generally develop out of social movements, and it is easy to see antiglobalization as a social movement that developed in opposition to globalization. But despite the success of its slogans—"Another World Is Possible" and "Make Poverty History"—at present the antiglobalization movement remains a movement, not an ideology. It simply has not yet come together with a core set of beliefs, and no agreement has been reached on what "Another World" would look like or *how* to "Make Poverty History." Beliefs about what such a world would *not* look like are plentiful, but there is no real agreement even on these; too many different groups are involved, all with different agendas.

Globalization has a set of core beliefs with variants, but it is much harder to see it as a social movement, which is one reason some are not entirely convinced it can be called an ideology. Still, it is clear that something is happening, even though there are disagreements about what it is: perhaps a new ideology; perhaps a new "thin" ideology in Freeden's sense; perhaps, as the antiglobalization forces say, simply a further power-grab by the already powerful forces of either U.S. or world capitalism. This chapter will explore some of the different approaches to the phenomenon called *globalization, globalism,* or, by some of its opponents, *the new (American* for some) *empire/imperialism/colonialism.*

WHAT IS GLOBALIZATION?

If we avoid conspiracy theories, globalization is, at its base, an economic phenomenon brought about, as one economist says, "by the falling cost of distance."[1] The market for goods and labor has become worldwide in addition to being local, national, and regional. Goods can be produced anywhere in the world and shipped anywhere else in the world at much lower cost than in the past. Thus companies search for places to produce their goods that have the cheapest labor and the fewest labor laws—these two generally go together—and the most lenient environmental regulations, the lowest taxes, and so forth. This is the reality of the modern world market, but globalization and antiglobalization as possible ideologies are concerned with the political and social effects of this change in the world market.

Manfred B. Steger (b. 1961) characterizes globalization as "a multidimensional set of social processes that create, multiply, stretch, and intensify worldwide social interdependencies and exchanges while at the same time fostering in people a growing awareness of deepening connections between the local and the distant."[2] His definition makes clear that although economic relationships may be at the basis of globalization, it is the impact of the process that is most important.

Is globalization a positive force, bringing people together, creating jobs, saving the Third World from poverty, and diminishing the likelihood of war? Or is it a negative force, shifting power from individuals and legislatures to unelected corporate leaders and bureaucrats; destroying the environment in the name of profit; shifting jobs from developed countries to Third World countries where wages are low, working conditions poor, and environmental regulations nonexistent; and reinforcing the dominance of the industrialized countries over the rest of the world? These differences are reflected in the different views of the demonstrators at various meetings of world economic leaders, such as the World Trade Organization (WTO) meetings in Seattle, November 30 to December 3, 1999; the G-8 meeting in Genoa, Italy, in July 2001; and with less violence at other such meetings since then.

From the point of view of its advocates, globalization benefits everyone economically and helps spread democracy. It does this by opening up or liberalizing markets and integrating markets worldwide. To the antiglobalization movement, globalization equals Americanization and is about power: it means a new colonization in which Western countries support those who support them. From this point of view, although globalization suggests that it will produce inclusion in the world economy, it in fact produces exclusion from the world economy. In the United States, two antiglobalization movements exist, one from the Left

---

[1] Brian Easton, *Globalisation and the Wealth of Nations*. Auckland, New Zealand: Auckland University Press, 2007: 2.

[2] Manfred B. Steger, *Globalization: A Very Short Introduction* (Oxford, England: Oxford University Press, 2003), 13.

and one from the Right. The Left's argument is based on a worldwide perspective; the Right's argument is based on patriotism. To the antiglobalization forces, globalization amounts to exporting exploitation; to its advocates, globalization exports opportunity. The problem is that both arguments can be supported.

One positive result of globalization, from the point of view of Third World workers, is that corporate codes of behavior developed in the First World have sometimes, usually because of protests within the First World, been applied in the Third World to help oppressed workers there. The best-known example is the international campaign against the wages and working conditions found in Third World suppliers to Nike. Protests and boycotts in North America and Europe helped change conditions in Third World factories. Protests by Third World workers alone, without First World support, generally have little effect.

One clear negative result of globalization is the rapid global spread of diseases such as the so-called bird flu, AIDS, and malaria. But this problem is not entirely new; between 1918 and 1920, the flu killed millions of people worldwide—estimates range from 40 million to 100 million—but it is the rapidity with which disease now spreads due to the ease of international travel that makes the problem much worse. Also, although rats once traveled the world in ships and were introduced into countries where they were not native, other animals, birds, and plants were deliberately introduced to places they were not native for economic and sporting reasons with sometimes devastating effects. Now microbes and insects travel the world on planes and in shipping containers, again sometimes with devastating effects on the countries where they end up.

Offshoring/Outsourcing   One issue in globalization is the movement of jobs from the developed countries to the developing world. An interesting case can be seen by following the U.S. textile industry from its origins in New England to new plants in the American Southeast, Texas, Mexico, and now China. The argument in favor is that everyone benefits from higher wages in poor countries, which still keeps overall costs lower in the developing world than they would be in the developed world. The argument against is that the loss of jobs and lowering of wages in the developed countries has a negative impact that significantly outweighs the cost savings. Not only are jobs lost but the closing of factories can devastate a town or region, which often means that those who have made it into the middle class running the local shops lose their shops and their status. An interesting twist to this story is that companies in India are now outsourcing jobs to countries with lower wages than those paid in India, including some areas of the United States.

A related question currently being investigated is who gains and who loses when jobs are lost: men or women? Many of the jobs lost by women in the developed world are gained by men in the developing world. But some jobs in the developing world go to women, and some writers argue that this will lead to greater freedom and independence for these women. The evidence is mixed. On the one hand, the real beneficiaries are the companies in the developed world; on the other hand, some women in the Third World are getting higher wages than they would have otherwise. It is also often women of color who are losing the low-paying jobs in industrialized countries and women of color in the Third World who are gaining from the new jobs.

The Financial Effects of Globalization One effect of globalization is increased volatility in financial markets and loss of control over national currencies by national governments. As early as 1972, James Tobin (1918–2002) proposed a 0.5 percent tax, later lowered to 0.1 to 0.25 percent, on foreign exchange and bond trading to curb volatility. This idea is now championed by some groups as a mechanism for funding international social programs. The primary organization promoting the idea, with branches in many countries, is the ATTAC (Association for the Taxation of Financial Transactions for the Aid of Citizens).

One of the best-known activists in this, George E. Stiglitz (b. 1943), has focused on the damage that organizations like the World Bank, the International Monetary Fund (IMF), and the World Trade Organization (WTO) have done to the economies of vulnerable nations. Stiglitz is a particularly important campaigner because he was once a Senior Vice President and the Chief Economist of the World Bank, and he shared the Nobel Prize in Economics in 2001. Stiglitz is often labeled as antiglobalization; he actually believes that globalization is both inevitable and desirable but contends that the way it is coming about is damaging both the developing and the developed world. In making his argument, he aligns himself with many on the antiglobalization side of the argument and uses many of their arguments.

Empire and *Empire*

There is much talk today about the creation of a new American empire, but if such an empire is coming into being, it will differ from past empires. Past empires, such as the Greek, Roman, Chinese, Spanish, Arab Muslim, Venetian, Dutch, and British, were all based on acquisition of territory, whereas the new American empire appears to be based primarily on economic dominance backed up by military might and the willingness to use it. Another way of looking at the situation is simply to note that at present, the world is unipolar, with only one very strong economic and military power. But such a situation may not last. The European Union is currently the second strongest economic arena; and China, with its huge population, is rapidly becoming a strong economic force in the world, and it has nuclear weapons.

A recent book that quickly became influential, *Empire* (2000) by Michael Hardt (b. 1961) and Antonio Negri (b. 1933), argues that "over the past several decades, as colonial regimes were overthrown and then precipitously after the Soviet barriers to the capitalist world market finally collapsed, we have witnessed an irresistible and irreversible globalization of economic and cultural exchanges."[3] They contend that a new form of socio-political-economic-cultural organization has emerged, which they label "Empire." "Composed of a series of national and supranational organisms united under a single logic of rule,"[4] it has neither spatial nor temporal boundaries. Thus nations, states, and nationalism are already outmoded and in the process of being supplanted. We are, to Hardt and

---

[3] Michael Hardt and Antonio Negri, *Empire* (Cambridge, MA: Harvard University Press, 2000), xi.

[4] Ibid.

Negri, already living in a postnational era dominated by institutions based in existing states that reach throughout the world.

Hardt and Negri followed *Empire* with *Multitude* (2004), which argues that what they have called *empire* has the potential of creating global democracy, not as a world government but through networks of interconnected communities and individuals. *Empire* clearly tapped into what many believed to be the next great social change. Limited evidence of the potential for the interconnected world suggested in *Multitude* may be seen in movements and organizations such as the World Social Forum, first held in Porto Alegre, Brazil in January 2001; then again in Porto Alegre in 2002, 2003, and 2005; and in Mumbai, India, in 2004. Attendance grew from 20,000 in 2001 to 155,000 in 2005 (80 percent from Brazil). The World Social Forum now meets in various places around the world each year and brings together thousands of individuals and groups under the slogan "Another World Is Possible"—and in opposition to organizations like the World Bank, International Monetary Fund, the World Trade Organization, and the World Economic Forum, which are seen as dominating the world economically and politically. Participants believe that the informal networks being created provide centers of opposition that have the potential for bringing about far-reaching change. For all of its extreme diversity, the World Social Forum brings together people from all over the world who want to bring about significant social reform. This has reinvigorated the Left, and although supporters of globalization suggest that the Left is becoming irrelevant, globalization has created a space in which the Left has become more radical.

IMMIGRANTS AND REFUGEES

The United States is a nation of immigrants, the only difference being when our ancestors arrived, with even the ancestors of the Native Americans appearing to have immigrated here at a much earlier stage in history. Thus the famous poem "The New Colossus" by Emma Lazarus (1849–1887) that appears on the Statue of Liberty:

> Give me your tired, your poor,
> Your huddled masses yearning to breathe free,
> The wretched refuse of your teeming shore.
> Send these, the homeless, tempest-tost to me,
> I lift my lamp beside the golden door.[5]

For various reasons, immigration is today a major issue throughout the developed world. Immigrants are being divided roughly into "political" immigrants, or those fleeing their homelands in fear for their lives, and "economic" immigrants, or those hoping to improve their lives. Of course, the categories overlap, but economic reasons have always propelled the vast majority of immigrants. Today countries are much more welcoming to political than economic immigrants, or to economic immigrants possessing needed skills.

---

[5] http://www.libertystatepark.com/emma.htm

One reason for the concern with immigration is that contemporary economies are less able to absorb large numbers of new, particularly new unskilled or low-skill workers than they once were. Countries are worried that the new immigrants will be unable to find work and will become an economic burden, as well as providing a dissatisfied minority ripe for exploitation by extremist elements. But countries still benefit from immigrant labor, particularly workers who are willing to do the types of jobs that the better-off natives are no longer willing to do, or from skilled migrant workers who bring expertise currently unavailable in the host country. Thus the issue becomes economic need versus cultural rejection, with the rejection often being on both sides.

This concern is related to the problem of ethnic nationalism, because it reflects the worry that ethnic enclaves will develop within countries and resist integration into the national culture. It is related to civic nationalism, because civic nationalism depends on a growing identification with the new nation by immigrant groups. Although we now recognize that it can take years for a new immigrant to become fully identified with the new nation (the melting pot), civic nationalism depends on there being sufficient identification with the new nation to clearly become part of it (the tossed salad).

But how long should it take to become integrated into the new country? In France, fourth and fifth generation French citizens who speak no language other than French but are Muslims are treated as if they are recent immigrants. The riots in France over the past few years resulted from joblessness and poverty among French citizens whose great grandparents immigrated, not among recent immigrants.

Many theorists of civic nationalism are aware of this problem. For example, in *Citizenship and National Identity* (2000), David Miller (b. 1946) argues against multiculturalism and suggests positive steps to incorporate immigrants into their new country. Will Kymlicka, a major theorist of multiculturalism, argues in his *Politics in the Vernacular* (2001) in favor of multiculturalism but also in favor of education for citizenship.

The entire question looks different from the point of view of the immigrant. As mentioned earlier, some people have begun to use the phrase *Fifth World* to refer to immigrants and those who lose status through immigration. For others the whole concept of immigration no longer applies, and they prefer the word *diaspora,* which suggests the scattering of a people. Homi K. Bhabha writes, "I have lived that moment of the scattering of the people that in other times and other places, in the nations of others, becomes a time of gathering."[6]

Globalization involves the mass movement of people around the world, legally and illegally. In most countries, highly skilled people are welcomed. For example, the United States is not currently producing enough engineers and computer scientists to meet its needs and welcomes such immigrants. At the other end of the wage scale, many U.S. crops are picked by illegal migrant workers who are deported if discovered. Farmers say they cannot get the seasonal labor they need to pick their crops, and before September 11, 2001, efforts were being made to provide legal status for many such workers.

---

[6] Homi K. Bhabha, "DissemiNation: Time, Narrative, and the Margins of the Modern Nation." *Nation and Narration.* Homi K. Bhabha, ed. London: Routledge, 1990: 291.

Immigration among the poor is having a striking effect on the position of women. Most women immigrate with their husbands and families rather than on their own, although a growing tendency is for single women to migrate to places where there is already an established community from their country. After immigration, women appear to integrate more quickly into the new country and learn the new language faster than men. This seems to be due to the fact that women, particularly those with children, have to deal with the wider community, whereas men tend to stay within the immigrant community. As a result, some scholars are seeing the empowerment of women through immigration.

A special subcategory of immigrants are refugees, defined as "[Any person who] . . . owing to well-founded fear of being persecuted for reasons of race, religion, nationality, membership of a particular social group or political opinion, is outside the country of his nationality and is unable to, or owing to such fear, is unwilling to avail himself of the protection of that country."[7] Today the definition has been informally extended to cover those forced to flee their homes but who remain within their country of nationality, such as the thousands living in refugee camps in the Darfur region of the Sudan. The UN estimates that in 2000, there were 175 million refugees compared to 33 million in 1910. In those nine decades, world population had grown threefold, but refugee population had grown sixfold, with more than half of that growth taking place between 1965 and 2000.

Such immigrants or potential immigrants are often ill, extremely poor, and without marketable skills. On the other hand, I have recently had students who came to the United States as refugees from the former Yugoslavia—having experienced horrendous violence and the death of one or more of their parents—who have done extremely well in my classes, graduated with honors, been employed locally, or are in or have completed graduate or law school.

HUMANITARIAN INTERVENTION

Another important issue today is what is called *humanitarian intervention,* or intervention in a country by another country or group of countries either to alleviate extreme human suffering or to keep or restore peace. The two best-known recent examples are in the former Yugoslavia, where entire populations were at risk, and in the Darfur region of the Sudan, where its population has faced constant attacks from other regions of the country. The wars in Afghanistan and Iraq are presented by some as examples of humanitarian intervention; others reject that label and say that the war in Iraq at least is simple, old-style colonialism in search of oil. The question involved is what happens to the idea of independent nations if one or more nations can invade another nation, arguing that it is for the good of the country invaded. Who should decide when and where intervention is appropriate? On what grounds, and to whom, can such intervention

---

[7] United Nations High Commission for Refugees, *The State of the World's Refugees: Fifty Years of Humanitarian Action* (Oxford: Oxford University Press, 2000), 23.

be justified? Thus humanitarian intervention raises, in only a slightly new form, the old debate over the nature of a just war.[8]

UNIVERSAL JURISDICTION

A new legal theory that runs directly counter to nationalism is *universal jurisdiction*. This theory—most obviously applied in the case of the former Chilean dictator Augusto Pinochet (1915–2006), who was arrested in the United Kingdom on a Spanish warrant for crimes committed in Chile—says that any court can claim jurisdiction over crimes committed anywhere in the world. Although Pinochet was released on the grounds of ill health, and no other actual case has arisen, the theory has attracted considerable attention.[9]

A related issue is the establishment of the International Criminal Court under a 1998 agreement that has now been signed by over 100 countries; the United States has not signed. The idea behind the International Criminal Court is that individuals accused of crimes could be tried anywhere in the world when no national or local court has, or chooses to take, jurisdiction. The Pinochet case might, for example, have been appropriate for such a court. Many people fear that charges could be brought against people who are unpopular for actions that were perfectly legal under the laws of their own country, or for political acts that would not normally be considered criminal but that political opponents might see as criminal. Historically, the only international criminal trials have been for crimes committed during war, such as the Nuremberg trials after World War II and the trials currently in progress concerning the civil war in Rwanda and the conflicts in the former Yugoslavia. In these examples special tribunals were established just for those cases. A long-established International Court of Justice—its predecessor was established in 1922—only hears cases between states or gives advisory opinions.

IS GLOBALIZATION A NEW IDEOLOGY?

Probably the strongest case for globalization as a new ideology is that made by Manfred B. Steger. He argues that not only are there a number of ideologies of globalism—the word he prefers—including market or imperial globalism, justice

---

[8] For recent discussions, see Jean Bethke Elshtain, *Just War against Terror: The Burden of American Power in a Violent World*. New York: Basic Books, 2003; Charles Reed and David Ryall eds., *The Price of Peace: Just War in the Twenty-First Century*. Cambridge, England: Cambridge University Press, 2007. Considers the issue of just war from contemporary Christian perspectives; Michael Walzer, *Just and Unjust Wars: A Moral Argument with Historical Illustrations*, 4th ed. New York: Basic Books, 2006: "Preface to the Fourth Edition": ix–xviii; and Walzer, *Arguing about War*. New Haven: Yale University Press, 2004.

[9] See Stephen Macedo, ed., *Universal Jurisdiction: National Courts and the Prosecution of Serious Crimes under International Law*. Philadelphia: University of Pennsylvania Press, 2004; and Luc Reydams, *Universal Jurisdiction: International and Municipal Jurisdictions*. Oxford: Oxford University Press, 2004.

globalism, and jihadist globalism, but that the whole basis of ideological thinking is shifting from a national imaginary to a global imaginary.[10]

Steger makes a good case and provides considerable evidence, and it is clear that something is going on that has destabilized ideological thinking. What he calls "market globalism," a term I prefer to "imperial globalism," is certainly in evidence in the arguments of those saying that globalization is a positive force. And what he calls "justice globalism" is certainly in evidence in some of the arguments of the antiglobalization movement. I am not convinced either by the label "jihadist globalism" or that there is a phenomenon parallel with the other two that could be given such a label (see the discussion in Chapter 11).

There seem to be two possible conclusions: First, that Steger is right, and we are witnessing a major shift in the way we think politically. Or, second, we are witnessing the emergence of another "thin ideology," such as nationalism, that becomes attached to and influences all the other ideologies. At present I lean toward the second, but no matter which you choose, significant changes are taking place.

SUGGESTED READING

Classic Works

Meadows, Donella H., Dennis L. Meadows, Jørgen Randers, and William W. Behrens, III. *The Limits to Growth: A Report for the Club of Rome's Project on the Predicament of Mankind.* New York: Universe Books, 1972.

Pestel, Eduard. *Beyond the Limits of Growth: A Report to the Club of Rome.* New York: Universe Books, 1989.

Books and Articles

Abdelal, Rawi. *Capital Rules: The Construction of Global Finance.* Cambridge, MA: Harvard University Press, 2007.

Andreas, Peter, and Ethan Nadelmann. *Policing the Globe: Criminalization and Crime Control in International Relations.* Oxford, England: Oxford University Press, 2006.

Bales, Kevin. *Disposable People: New Slavery in the Global Economy.* Berkeley: University of California Press, 1999. Revised ed., Berkeley: University of California Press, 2004.

———. *New Slavery: A Reference Handbook.* Santa Barbara, CA: ABC–CLIO, 2000. 2nd ed. Santa Barbara, CA: ABC–CLIO, 2004.

———. *Understanding Global Slavery: A Reader.* Berkeley: University of California Press, 2005. Not a reader in the sense of an edited collection. A study of the "new slavery" around the world with recommendations on how people can oppose it. Gives statistics on the estimate of the number of the "new slaves" in each country, including 100,000 to 150,000 in the United States.

Banerjee, Abhijit Vinayak, Roland Bénabou, and Dilip Mookherjee. *Understanding Poverty.* Oxford, England: Oxford University Press, 2006.

Barnett, Michael. "Humanitarianism Transformed." *Perspectives on Politics* 3:4 (December 2005): 723–740. Comment by Janice Stein (pp. 741–744). The articles discuss the changes in humanitarian action due to globalization, primarily its politicization and institutionalization.

Barry, John, and Robyn Eckersley, eds. *The State and the Global Ecological Crisis.* Cambridge, MA: MIT Press, 2005.

Beck, Ulrich. *Power in the Global Age: A New Global Political Economy.* Kathleen Cross, trans. Cambridge, England: Polity, 2005. Originally published in German in 2002.

---

[10] See his *The Rise of the Global Imaginary: Political Ideologies from the French Revolution to the Global War on Terror.* Oxford, England: Oxford University Press, 2008.

———. *What Is Globalization?* Patrick Camiller, trans. Cambridge, England: Polity, 2000. Originally published as *Was ist Globalisierung?* (1997).

Bello, Walden. *Deglobalization: Ideas for a New World Economy.* New updated ed. Dhaka, Bangladesh: University Press/Bangkok, Thailand: White Lotus/Bluepoint, NS, Canada: Fernwood Publishing/Bangalore, India: Books for Change/Kuala Lumpur, Malaysia: SIRD/Cape Town, South Africa/London: Zed Books, 2004. Argument for decentralization. See 122–126 and 133–135 for organizations concerned with globalization that have websites.

Benjamin, Daniel, and Steven Simon. *The Next Attack: The Globalization of Jihad.* London: Hodder & Stoughton, 2005.

Boron, Atilio A. *"Empire" and Imperialism: A Critical Reading of Michael Hardt and Antonio Negri.* Jessica Casiro, trans. London: Zed Books, 2005.

Broad, Robin, ed. *Global Backlash: Citizen Initiatives for a Just World Economy.* Lanham, MD: Rowman & Littlefield, 2002.

Bunker, Stephen G., and Paul S. Ciccantell. *Globalization and the Race for Resources.* Baltimore, MD: The Johns Hopkins University Press, 2005. Concerned with the exploitation of countries for their natural resources, often with the cooperation of the political leaders of the countries involved.

Buckman, Greg. *Globalization: Tame It or Scrap It? Mapping the Alternatives of the Anti-globalization Movement.* Dhaka, Bangladesh: University Press/Bangkok, Thailand: White Lotus/Bluepoint, NS, Canada: Fernwood Publishing/Bangalore, India: Books for Change/Kuala Lumpur, Malaysia: SIRD/Cape Town, South Africa: David Philip/London: Zed Books, 2004. Includes "Useful Globalization Websites" (213–216).

Cabrera, Luis. *Political Theory of Global Justice: A Cosmopolitan Case for the World State.* London: Routledge, 2004.

Caney, Simon. *Justice Beyond Borders: A Global Political Theory.* Oxford, England: Oxford University Press, 2005.

Chomsky, Noam. *Hegemony or Survival: America's Quest for Global Dominance.* New York: Metropolitan Books, 2003.

Christiansen, Flemming, and Ulf Hedetoft, eds. *The Politics of Multiple Belonging: Ethnicity and Nationalism in Europe and East Asia.* Aldershot, England: Ashgate, 2004.

Clarke, Kamari Maxine, and Deborah A. Thomas, eds. *Globalization and Race: Transformations in the Cultural Production of Blackness.* Durham, NC: Duke University Press, 2006.

Coady, Tony, and Michael O'Keefe, eds. *Righteous Violence: The Ethics and Politics of Military Intervention.* Melbourne, Vic, Australia: University of Melbourne Press, 2005. Humanitarian intervention.

Cohen, Daniel. *Globalization and Its Enemies.* Jessica B. Baker, trans. Cambridge, MA: MIT Press, 2006.

Cohen, Steve. *Deportation Is Freedom! The Orwellian World of Immigration.* London: Jessica Kingsley, 2006. An argument for the abolition of all border controls, stressing that the current system is explicitly racist and discriminates on the basis of class, ethnicity, and gender.

Croucher, Sheila L. *Globalization and Belonging: The Politics of Identity in a Changing World.* Lanham, MD: Rowman & Littlefield, 2004.

Davis, Mike. *Planet of Slums.* London: Verso, 2006. Argues that the Structural Adjustment Programs (SAP) mandated by the International Monetary Fund (IMF) before it will lend money has had a devastating impact on the countries involved. With IMF/World Bank help, 46 countries were poorer in 2006 than in 1990; and in 25 countries, more people were hungry (p. 163).

della Porta, Donatella, and Sidney Tarrow, eds. *Transnational Protest and Global Activism.* Lanham, MD: Rowman & Littlefield, 2005.

de Sousa Santos, Boaventura. *The Rise of the Global Left: The World Social Forum and Beyond.* London: Zed Books, 2006.

Dunning, John H., ed. *Making Globalization Good: The Moral Challenges of Global Capitalism.* Oxford: Oxford University Press, 2003. Generally favors global capitalism.

Easton, Brian. *Globalisation and the Wealth of Nations.* Auckland, New Zealand: Auckland University Press, 2007.

Ehrenreich, Barbara, and Arlie Russell Hochchild, eds. *Global Woman: Nannies, Maids, and Sex Workers in the New Economy.* New York: Henry Holt, 2003.

Fabian Globalisation Group. *Just World: A Fabian Manifesto.* London: Zed Books in association with The Fabian Society, 2005. A just world requires "the creation of a new global economic architecture to enable expansionary national economic policies; democratic global governance; equitable trade; and regulation of corporate and governmental action in the global sphere" (p. 3).

Faux, Jeff. *The Global Class War: How America's Bipartisan Elite Lost Our Future—and What It Will Take to Win It Back.* Hoboken, NJ: John Wiley & Sons, 2006.

Feher, Michael, ed. with Gaëlle Krikorian and Yates McKee. *Nongovernmental Politics.* New York: Zone Books, 2007. Nongovernmental Organizations (NGOs).

Friedman, Thomas L. *The World Is Flat: A Brief History of the Globalized World in the Twenty-first Century.* New York: Farrar, Straus and Giroux, 2005. U.K. ed. London: Allen Lane, 2005. Friedman argues that globalization has "flattened" the world, in effect making for a more level playing field and leading to greater potential equality and competitiveness. He instances the flattening by the fall of the Berlin wall, Netscape, workflow software, open-sourcing, outsourcing, supply-chaining, in-sourcing (UPS and Fed Ex), in-forming (search engines), and what he calls "The Steroids" (wireless connections).

Gibney, Matthew J. *The Ethics and Politics of Asylum: Liberal Democracy and the Response to Refugees.* Cambridge, England: Cambridge University Press, 2004.

Glatzer, Miguel, and Dietrich Rueschemeyer, eds. *Globalization and the Future of the Welfare State.* Pittsburgh, PA: University of Pittsburgh Press, 2005. Looks at welfare policies throughout the world and how globalization has changed them.

Goldin, Ian, and Kenneth Reinert. *Globalization for Development: Trade, Finance, Aid, Migration, and Policy.* Washington, DC: The World Bank and Palgrave Macmillan, 2006.

Habermas, Jürgen. *Time of Transitions.* Ciaran Cronin, trans., and Max Pensky, ed. Cambridge, England: Polity, 2006. Originally published as *Zeit der Übergänge.* Frankfurt am Main, Germany: Suhrkampf Verlag, 2001. Essays and interviews on globalization and democracy.

Halper, Stefan, and Jonathan Clarke. *America Alone: The Neo-Conservatives and the Global Order.* Cambridge: Cambridge University Press, 2004.

Harnett, Stephen John, and Laura Ann Stengrim. *Globalization and Empire: The U.S. Invasion of Iraq, Free Markets, and the Twilight of Democracy.* Tuscaloosa: University of Alabama Press, 2006.

Hayden, Patrick, and Chamsy el-Ojeili, eds. *Confronting Globalization: Humanity, Justice, and the Renewal of Politics.* New York: Palgrave Macmillan, 2005.

Held, David, et al. *Debating Globalization.* Anthony Barnett, David Held, and Caspar Henderson, eds. Cambridge, England: Polity Press in association with Open Democracy, 2005.

Hobsbawm, Eric. *Globalisation, Democracy, and Terrorism.* London: Little, Brown, 2007. Collection of essays.

Hopper, Paul. *Living with Globalization.* Oxford, England: Berg, 2006.

The International Journal of Human Rights Vol. 1:1 to the present (Founded 1997).

Jackson, Jeffrey T. *The Globalizers: Development Workers in Action.* Baltimore, MD: Johns Hopkins University Press, 2005.

Jacobsen, Karen. *The Economic Life of Refugees.* Bloomfield, CT: Kumarian Press, 2005. Activist perspective.

Khor, Martin. *Rethinking Globalization: Critical Issues and Policy Choices.* London: Zed Books/Dhaka, Bangladesh: University Press/Bangkok, Thailand: White Lotus/Halifax, NS, Canada: Fernwood Publishing/Cape Town, South Africa: David Philip/Penang, Malaysia: Third World Network/Bangalore, India: Books for Change, 2001.

Levine, Ruth, and the What Works Working Group with Molly Kinder. *Millions Saved: Proven Successes in Global Health.* Washington, DC: Center for Global Development, 2004.

Lynn, Barry C. *End of the Line: The Rise and Coming Fall of the Global Corporation.* New York: Doubleday, 2005. Problems of globalization.

Mishkin, Frederic S. *The Next Great Globalization: How Disadvantaged Nations Can Harness Their Financial Systems and Get Rich.* Princeton, NJ: Princeton University Press, 2006.

Model, David. *Corporate Rule: Understanding and Challenging the New World Order.* Montréal, PQ, Canada: Black Rose Books, 2003.

Moghadam, Valentine M. *Globalizing Women: Transnational Feminist Networks.* Baltimore, MD: The Johns Hopkins University Press, 2005.

Munck, Ronaldo. *Globalization and Social Exclusion: A Transformational Perspective.* Bloomfield, CT: Kumarian Press, 2005. Argues that globalization increases inequality.

Nairn, Tom, and Paul James. *Global Matrix: Nationalism, Globalism, and State Terrorism.* London: Pluto Press, 2005. Argues that globalization and nationalism overlap and that the past is still very much present in the contemporary world.

Naples, Nancy, and Manisha Desai, eds. *Women's Activism and Globalization: Linking Local Struggles and Transnational Politics.* New York: Routledge, 2002.

Nardin, Terry, and Melissa S. Williams, eds. *Humanitarian Intervention: Nomos XLVII.* New York: New York University Press, 2006.

Nee, Victor, and Richard Swedberg, eds. *The Economic Sociology of Capitalism.* Princeton, NJ: Princeton University Press, 2005. Discusses how capitalism is changing under globalization.

Newman, Robert. *The Fountain at the Center of the World.* Brooklyn, NY: Soft Skull Press, 2004. Antiglobalization novel.

Norberg, Johan. *In Defense of Global Capitalism.* Washington, DC: The Cato Institute, 2003. From a libertarian perspective, capitalism is shown as providing freedom and opportunity to even the poorest peasant.

Office of the United Nations High Commissioner for Refugees (UNHCR). *The State of the World's Refugees. 2006: Human Displacement in the New Millennium.* Oxford, England: Oxford University Press, 2006.

Panitch, Leo, and Colin Leys, eds. *Socialist Register 2004: The New Imperial Challenge.* London: Merlin Press, 2003.

———. *Socialist Register 2005: The Empire Reloaded.* London: Merlin Press, 2004.

Patomäki, Heikki. *Democratizing Globalization: The Leverage of the Tobin Tax.* London: Zed Books, 2001.

Porritt, Jonathon. *Capitalism as if the World Matters.* London: Earthscan, 2005. Globalization and its effects on the environment. Discusses the need to retool capitalism.

Roht-Arriaza, Naomi. *The Pinochet Effect: Transnational Justice in the Age of Human Rights.* Philadelphia: University of Pennsylvania Press, 2005. Universal jurisdiction.

Rosecrance, Richard N., and Arthur A. Stein, eds. *No More States? Globalization, National Self-Determination, and Terrorism.* Lanham, MD: Rowman & Littlefield, 2006. Report of a UCLA–Harvard study on the likelihood of new states emerging in current conditions. Generally argues that it is unlikely and that the national liberation movements will fail.

Rupp, George. *Globalization Challenged: Conviction, Conflict, Community.* New York: Columbia University Press, 2006.

Sassen, Saskia, ed. *Deciphering the Global: Its Scales, Spaces, and Subjects.* London: Routledge, 2007. A collection of essays on the effects of globalization on specific communities.

———. *A Sociology of Globalization.* New York: W.W. Norton, 2007.

Shutt, Harry. *A New Democracy: Alternatives to a Bankrupt World Order.* London: Zed Books/Dhaka, Bangladesh: University Press/Bangkok, Thailand: White Lotus/Halifax, NS, Canada: Fernwood Publishing/Cape Town, South Africa: David Philip/Bangalore, India: Books for Change, 2001.

Singer, Peter. *One World: The Ethics of Globalization,* 2nd ed. New Haven, CT: Yale University Press, 2004. Argues that ethically there is only one world; sections/chapters on one atmosphere, one law, one community.

Singh, Kavaljit. *Questioning Globalization.* Delhi, India: Madhyam Books and London Zed Books in association with ASED Asia Europe Dialogue, 2005.

Slaughter, Anne-Marie. *A New World Order.* Princeton, NJ: Princeton University Press, 2004.

Smith, Stephen C. *Ending Global Poverty: A Guide to What Works.* New York: Palgrave Macmillan, 2005.

Smith, Tony. *Globalisation: A Systematic Marxian Account.* Leiden, The Netherlands: Brill, 2006.

Starr, Amory. *Global Revolt: A Guide to the Movement Against Globalization.* London: Zed Books, 2005.

Steger, Manfred B. *Globalism: Market Ideology Meets Terrorism,* 2nd ed. Lanham, MD: Rowman & Littlefield, 2005.

———. *Globalization: A Very Short Introduction.* Oxford, England: Oxford University Press, 2003. 2nd ed. in preparation.

———. "Ideologies of globalization." *Journal of Political Ideologies* Vol. 10:1 (February 2005): 11–30. Argument that globalism, as Steger calls it, already constitutes an ideology.

———, ed. *Rethinking Globalism.* Lanham, MD: Rowman & Littlefield, 2004.

———. *The Rise of the Global Imaginary: Political Ideologies from the French Revolution to the Global War on Terror.* Oxford, England: Oxford University Press, 2008.

Stiglitz, Joseph E. *Globalization and Its Discontents.* New York: W.W. Norton, 2002. Among other arguments, Stiglitz argues that the International Monetary Fund (IMF) pursues the interests of the financial community rather than fulfilling the goals for which it was established (206–213).

———. *Making Globalization Work.* New York: W.W. Norton, 2006.

Tarrow, Sidney. *The New Transnational Activism.* Cambridge, England: Cambridge University Press, 2005.

Taylor, Rupert, ed. *Creating a Better World: Interpreting Global Civil Society.* Bloomfield, CT: Kumarian Press, 2004. Stresses the opponents of globalization as those creating the global civil society.

Todorov, Tzvetan. *The New World Disorder: Reflections of a European.* Andrew Brown, trans. Cambridge, England: Polity, 2005.

Tremayne, Mark, ed. *Blogging, Citizenship, and the Future of Media.* New York: Routledge, 2007.

van den Anker, Christien, ed. *The Political Economy of New Slavery.* Basingstoke: Palgrave Macmillan, 2004. New slavery includes child labor, debt bondage, forced prostitution, and migrant domestic work, among other social ills.

Veseth, Michael. *Globaloney: Unraveling the Myths of Globalization.* Lanham, MD: Rowman & Littlefield, 2005.

Wall, Derek. *Babylon and Beyond: The Economics of Anti-Capitalist, Anti-Globalist, and Radical Green Movements.* London: Pluto Press, 2005.

Wallach, Lori, and Patrick Woodall. *Whose Trade Organization? A Comprehensive Guide to the WTO.* New York: New Press, 2004. Critique.

Walt, Stephen M. *Taming American Power: The Global Response to U.S. Primacy.* New York: W.W. Norton, 2005.

Weinstein, Michael M., ed. *Globalization: What's New.* New York: Columbia University Press, 2005.

Weiss, Thomas G. *Humanitarian Intervention: Ideas in Action.* Cambridge, England: Polity, 2007. A balanced presentation of the issues with examples.

Wolf, Martin. *Why Globalization Works.* New Haven, CT: Yale University Press, 2004.

Woodin, Michael, and Caroline Lucas. *Green Alternatives to Globalisation: A Manifesto.* London: Pluto Press, 2004. Economic localisation, Local Exchange Trading Systems (LETS), local food, and so forth.

Woods, Ngaire. *The Globalizers: The IMF, the World Bank, and Their Borrowers.* Ithaca, NY: Cornell University Press, 2006.

Young, Iris Marion. "Responsibility and Global Labor Justice." *The Journal of Political Philosophy* Vol. 12:4 (2004): 365–388.

Zaniello, Tom. *The Cinema of Globalization: A Guide to Films about the New Economic Order.* Ithaca, NY: ILR Press of Cornell University Press, 2007.

Websites

Amnesty International: http://www.amnesty.org

Asia–Pacific Economic Cooperation (APEC): http://apec.org

Association for the Taxation of Financial Transactions for the Aid of Citizens (ATTAC) in eight languages (Slogan: "The World is Not for Sale"): http://www.attac.org

European Social Forum: http://www.fse-esf.org

Free Trade Area of the Americas (FTAA): http://www.ftaa-alca.org

International Forum on Globalization (IFG): http://www.ifg.org

International Monetary Fund: http://www.imf.org

No One Is Illegal: http://www.noii.org.uk

North American Free Trade Agreement (NAFTA) Secretariat: http://www.nafta-sec-alena.org

Organisation for Economic Cooperation and Development (OECD): http://oecd.org

Our World Is Not for Sale: http://www.ourworldisnotforsale.org

Peoples' Global Action/Acción Global de los Pueblos: http://www.agp.org

World Bank: http://www.worldbank.org

World Economic Forum: http://www.weforum.org

World Social Forum: http://www.wsf.org

World Trade Organization: http://wto.org

4

⚜

The Principles
of Democracy

The word *democracy* comes from two Greek words: *demos* meaning "people" and *kratos* meaning "rule." Therefore, the word means "rule by the people," sometimes called *popular sovereignty,* which can refer to direct, participatory, and representative forms of rule by the people. Today the word has a positive meaning throughout most of the world—so much so that even some political systems with little or no rule by the people are called democratic to connect themselves with this positive image.

The following analysis uses a simple model of the key elements of democracy as it exists today:

1. Citizen involvement in decision making

2. A system of representation

3. The rule of law

4. An electoral system—majority rule

5. Some degree of equality among citizens

6. Some degree of liberty or freedom granted to or retained by citizens

7. Education, particularly but not solely citizenship education

CITIZEN INVOLVEMENT

The most fundamental characteristic of any democratic system, truly its defining characteristic, is the idea that citizens should be involved in making political decisions, either directly or through representatives of their choosing. These two approaches can be characterized in one of two ways:

1. *Direct democracy*—Citizens take part personally in deliberations and vote on issues. Citizens debate and vote on all laws.

2. *Representative democracy*—Citizens choose (elect) other citizens to debate and pass laws.

Voting on issues personally is the defining activity of a citizen in a direct democracy. Although direct democracy has only rarely been practiced as a means of governing a country, most people have experienced such involvement at a lower level. Almost everyone in the West has, at some time, had a chance to discuss and vote on an issue. This may have taken place at a school or university; in a church, mosque, or synagogue; in a union or club meeting; or in one of the hundreds of other groups that allow voting members to decide at least some questions that concern the membership.

In addition, most people have voted in an election in some such organization, thereby taking part in one of the basic steps of choosing a representative; fewer people, but still a substantial number, have cast their votes to elect a public official. These are the defining activities of a citizen in a representative democracy.

Other forms of citizen involvement include actively participating in a political party or interest group, attending and participating in political meetings or public hearings, discussing politics with friends or colleagues, or contacting a public official about an issue. A growing area of involvement is for citizens to work for or against issues that will be voted on during an election. This area is growing because interest groups and groups of citizens are bringing more issues directly to the electorate through initiative petitions or referenda (see the definitions in the glossary and the discussion later in this chapter).

In a representative system, citizen involvement helps to ensure that public officials are accountable and responsive to the people. Candidates for public office must convince voters of good reasons to vote for them rather than their opponents. In particular, elected officials are expected to show that they respond to the changing needs and demands of their constituents. Of course, no system can guarantee responsive public officials, but having to run for reelection helps.

In addition, involvement is thought to be good for citizens. Defenders of democracy believe that being involved in decision making, even if this means simply voting in an election, expands the horizons of voters and makes them more aware of issues. Involvement encourages a feeling of responsibility, a sense of belonging to a community, and knowledge. Involved citizens become better, more complete people. This is particularly true for those whose involvement goes beyond the vote to more active participation. Of course, this positive effect depends on citizens being informed about the issues involved and demonstrates why education is important.

Defenders of democracy ask a simple question: Who else should make political decisions? A monarch? A political boss? Bureaucrats? The rich? The poor? An ethnic or racial majority? Who knows the interests of the average citizen better than the average citizen?

In some countries, including the United States, many people—sometimes even the majority—do not bother to vote. In the 2000 U.S. presidential election, just 51 percent of eligible voters participated. The 2004 turnout of 59.6 percent was the highest since 1968, when 60.84 percent voted; in 1964, turnout was 61.92 percent. The lowest turnouts in late-twentieth century presidential elections included 1986, with 36.40 percent, and 1990, with 36.52 percent. Turnouts are counted in two ways: the percentage of people eligible to vote (VEP) and percentage of people of voting age (VAP). The former is much more accurate in that it excludes noncitizens and others who are for some reason not eligible to vote, such as, in the United States, convicted felons.

Not voting does not mean that decisions will not be made; someone will still make them. Do high levels of nonvoting undermine democracy? Does it matter? These questions have produced a number of approaches to either justify the system that exists or propose changes in it. These approaches include elitism, pluralism, corporatism or neocorporatism, and participatory democracy. The first three all assume that democracy is working fairly well with low levels of participation. In addition, these three approaches recognize and support differences in power within the political system; in other words, they contend that inequalities of power are acceptable, possibly even a good thing. Participatory theories take the position that democracy is not working as it should and that ways must be found to increase participation. In addition, participatory theories claim that the differences in power supported by the other three approaches are part of the problem and definitely not a good thing. In the 2004 presidential election, the official results showed that more than 19 people got votes—18 plus an unknown number of write-ins. But only the top two candidates got more than a half percent of the vote.

Elitism

The elitist approach asserts that democracy is "a method of making decisions which ensures efficiency in administration and policy making and yet requires some measure of responsiveness to popular opinion on the part of the ruling elites."[1] In this view, citizen involvement functions primarily as a check on political leaders while maintaining competition among rival elites. The arguments for elitist theories center on efficiency and the perceived inability of voters to make informed decisions. The citizen casting his or her vote is, in this view, simply a mechanism for deciding among competing elites. Given the complexity of the modern world and the issues involved, so the argument goes, it is impossible for the average citizen to know enough to participate intelligently in decision making. But competition is still thought desirable, so the vote is used to choose the group that will be given temporary power.

---

[1] Jack L. Walker, "A Critique of the Elitist Theory of Democracy," *American Political Science Review* Vol. 60 (June 1966): 286.

Opponents of elitism argue that (1) efficiency is not as important as the positive influence of participation on the citizen, and (2) the average citizen is capable of understanding most issues. The elitist theorists contend, in effect, that classical representative democracy does not—even cannot—work in the modern world; their opponents argue that a truly informed citizenry is even more important than in the past, even if new problems make effective participation difficult to achieve. But they also argue that people need to be actively encouraged to participate and given the means of informing themselves regarding the issues.

Pluralism

Closely related to the elitist view is pluralism, in which the political system is seen as composed of interest groups competing for power with none strong enough to dominate. As long as competition exists and is fair, no single interest can gain too much power; each interest will always be held in check by the other interests. Advocates contend that pluralism is the best system for a representative democracy, because it protects citizens from too much centralization of power and allows diverse interests to be expressed. In the United States today, pluralism connects neatly to the growth of interest in multiculturalism, the structuring society around competing and cooperating cultures. But it is important to note that pluralism is about distribution of power, and multiculturalism is about toleration of difference.

Most modern societies are pluralistic in that they are composed of a variety of groups based on characteristics such as wealth, race, gender, ethnic or national origin, profession, and religion. Defenders of pluralism argue that this diversity should be recognized and protected. Thus pluralism includes both a positive awareness of the group basis of most contemporary societies and the belief that democracy needs to incorporate that awareness. Pluralists in the United States assert that pluralism supplements the system of checks and balances enshrined in the U.S. Constitution with additional checks on power. Outside the United States, pluralists stress that competition among groups is often the primary means of limiting centralized power.

Critics of pluralism make two major points: First, according to the antipluralists, the only thing of interest to the competing elites is staying in office; all values are secondary to this overriding goal. Thus the suggestion that pluralism protects freedom is false. Pluralism is a protection for freedom, or any other value, only as long as it works to the political benefit of the competing groups. Second, antipluralists note that the supposedly competing groups cooperate to maintain the present system and their positions of power within it. As a result, pluralism—and the groups that compete within it—are obstacles to change, particularly as they try to avoid the emergence of new groups that might successfully compete for power.

Corporatism

Corporatism—or *neocorporatism,* as some of its proponents prefer to call it to distinguish it from a similar idea found in fascism—contends that interest groups both compete and cooperate with each other and share power with government bureaucracies. Interest groups do not merely consult with government but are fully integrated into the process of policy making and implementation. Today that cooperation is almost the norm in that the legislative process usually directly involves representatives of interest groups (lobbyists) providing information to legislators and more and more often in the actually writing of legislation. Critics of corporatism argue that it simply justifies greater power on the part of unelected people, that the similar concept in fascism is no accident, and that corporatism explicitly denies the power of citizens to control their own lives.

Participatory Democracy

Critics of elitism, pluralism, and corporatism often suggest that more, not less, direct participation on the part of the citizens is the best approach to democracy; and the most direct challenge to these approaches is found among those who say that the low level of citizen involvement is a problem that must be solved. Advocates of participatory democracy see elitism, pluralism, and corporatism as disregarding the most fundamental principle of democracy: citizen involvement. Thus, they propose moving the system away from representative democracy in the direction of direct democracy.[2]

The participatory democrat argues that individuals should not be bound by laws they did not participate in making. In other words, people must be consulted in the making of laws that will affect them. If they are not consulted, the laws should be considered invalid.

In addition to asserting that a more participatory democracy can work, advocates of this position contend that only with greater participation can the other principles of democracy be fulfilled. According to this argument, people will never be politically equal or free unless they become active and involved citizens. Most contemporary defenders of participatory democracy do not oppose representation but contend that voters must be more directly consulted and involved in decision making and that representatives should be kept on a shorter leash.

Opponents of participatory democracy argue that it simply goes too far and is impractical. It would be fine if it were possible, but it cannot be achieved in our complex world. Also, they say, the fact that many choose not to vote raises questions about any participatory theory, although advocates of increased participation say people choose not to vote because they think their vote makes no real difference. Critics assert that contemporary political decisions require both expertise and time, things unavailable to the average citizen. Therefore representative democracy is necessary, and the differences reflect differences in what we mean by *representation*.

REPRESENTATION

If direct participation is difficult to achieve or is not a good idea, then it is necessary to develop a way for people to participate indirectly. The primary means of doing this has been through representatives, people chosen by citizens to act for them. In other words, citizens delegate to one of their number the responsibility

---

[2] See, for example, Carole Pateman, *Participation and Democratic Theory.* Cambridge: Cambridge University Press, 1970; and Benjamin R. Barber, *Strong Democracy: Participatory Politics for a New Age.* Berkeley: University of California Press, 1984.

for making certain decisions. The person chosen may be a delegate from a geo-graphical area, of a certain number of people (representation by area or popula-tion), or some other identifiable group, as in systems that set aside seats to be elected by a specific group. The citizens represented are called the *constituents,* or the representative's *constituency.*

The word *represent* is used in a number of different ways that help provide an understanding of the situation:

1. Something *represents* something else when it is a faithful reproduction or exact copy of the original.
2. Something that symbolizes something else is said to *represent* it.
3. A lawyer *represents* a client when he or she acts in place of or for the client.

Clearly, the third meaning is closest to the way we think of a representative in democracy; but it is not that simple, because no constituency is composed of citizens whose interests are identical. As a result, there are two main approaches to the relationship between the representative and her or his constituency, with most representatives fitting somewhere between the two.

Some representatives try to reflect the varied interests of their constituents as precisely as possible, but others take the position that they were elected to make the best decisions they can for the nation as a whole. The latter position was first put forth by Edmund Burke (1729–1797), who said,

> To deliver an opinion is the right of all men; that of constituents is a weighty and respectable opinion, which a representative ought always rejoice to hear, and which he ought always most seriously to consider. But *authoritative* instructions, *mandates* issued, which the member is bound blindly and implicitly to obey, to vote for, and to argue for, though contrary to the dearest conviction of his judgment and conscience—these are things utterly unknown to the laws of this land, and which arise from a fundamen-tal mistake of the whole order and tenor of our Constitution.
>
> Parliament is not a *congress* of ambassadors from different and hostile interests, which each must maintain, as an agent and advocate, against other agents and advocates; but Parliament is a *deliberative* assembly of *one* nation, with one interest, that of the whole; where, not local purposes, not local prejudices, ought to guide, but the general good, resulting from the general reason of the whole. You choose a member, indeed; but when you have chosen him, he is not a member of Bristol [England, where Burke was campaigning], he is a member of *Parliament.* If the local constituent should form a hasty opinion evidently opposite to the real good of the rest of the community, the member for that place ought to be as far as any other from an endeavor to give it effect.[3]

Here Burke presents a case for the representative as an independent agent, a representative solely in the sense of being elected by the people in a particular area.

---

[3] Speech to the Electors of Bristol (1774), in *The Works of the Right Honorable Edmund Burke,* 7th ed. Boston: Little, Brown, 1881; Vol. 11:96 (emphasis in the original).

In doing this, Burke specifically rejects representation in the third sense, the representative as agent for some individual or group.

Seldom if ever will an elected official fit exactly one and only one of the roles assigned by the theories of representation. Even the most Burkean representative will act as a constituency agent at times or on certain issues. The typical representative is likely to act as a constituency agent whenever constituents are actively concerned with a particular issue or to assist individuals or groups of constituents when they need help in dealing with a bureaucracy. At the same time, the typical representative is likely to act as a Burkean representative on issues that do not directly concern the constituency, and thus about which little or no pressure is received from the constituency. But today no representative can ever take their constituents for granted; they must be a constituent representative some of the time.

As we have already seen in the discussion of participatory theories, an issue that concerns some theorists is how to give representative democracy some attributes of direct democracy. In the United States such practices as the *initiative, referendum,* and *recall* were developed to allow people to play a direct role in political decision making, and these devices are being used extensively at present.

The problem is seen most clearly in the thinking of Jean-Jacques Rousseau (1712–1778), who said, "Thus deputies of the people are not, and cannot be, its representatives; they are merely its agents, and can make no final decisions. Any law which the people have not ratified in person is null, it is not a law."[4] Here Rousseau has used two of our definitions of *represent.* For him a representative is not an independent agent but one who acts only with constituent approval.

Rousseau realized that in a large country, direct democracy is impractical, even impossible; and although he maintained the ideal of direct democracy, he did discuss representation in a more favorable light. He said,

> I have just shown that government weakens as the number of magistrates [elected officials] increases; and I have already shown that the more numerous the people [are], the more repressive force is needed. From which it follows that the ratio of magistrates to government should be in inverse proportions to the ratio of subjects to sovereign; which means that the more the state expands, the more the government ought to contract; and thus that the number of rulers should diminish in proportion to the increases of the population.[5]

Rousseau would have liked to have seen a country small enough for every person to be his[6] own representative; but as population increases, this becomes more and more difficult. Thus the number of rulers must of necessity diminish through the establishment of some type of representative system; and the larger

---

[4] Jean-Jacques Rousseau, *Du contrat social*. Paris: Le Renaissance de Livre, 1762: 86.

[5] Rousseau, *Du contrat social:* 59.

[6] In Rousseau's case it is fairly clear that he would not extend direct political involvement to women. On Rousseau's treatment of women, see Susan Moller Okin, "Rousseau," in Okin, *Women in Western Political Thought*. Princeton, NJ: Princeton University Press, 1979: 99–194.

Jean-Jacques Rousseau (1712–78) is best known as a political philosopher. His works *Discours sur les sciences et les arts* (*Discourse on the Arts and Sciences,* 1750), *Discours sur l'origine et les fondements de l'inégalité* (*Discourse on the Origin and Foundations of Inequality,* 1755), *Émile* (1762), a treatise on education, *Du contrat social* (*The Social Contract,* 1762), and others placed him in the forefront among critics of contemporary society. He argued that civilization was corrupting and that a return to a simpler society in which each individual could fully participate was the remedy for the current social ills. His arguments were used as justifications for the French Revolution. The meaning, intent, and effect of Rousseau's ideas are still widely debated; interpretations of his thought range from the belief that he was one of the founders of modern totalitarianism to the belief that he was an important defender of democracy.

the country, the more powerful those representatives must be. Rousseau believed that the closer a system can come to a direct democracy through an increase in the number of magistrates, the better the system will be; but this is only possible in a very small country.

THE RULE OF LAW

In a democracy, elected representatives participate in making laws but are still bound by them. Once passed, the law is supreme, not those who made it. Representatives can participate in changing a law, but until it is changed, they, along with everyone else, must obey it.

This apparently simple notion came about only after a long struggle. It was one of the basic principles demanded in the early conflicts that led to the establishment of democratic institutions. Before that, monarchs claimed that they had been appointed by God to rule—called *the divine right of kings*—and were, therefore, above the law. The principle involved is that a society should be able to bind itself by the rules it has chosen, and no individual or institution should be outside those rules. It must be noted that although the rule of law is a long-established democratic principle, it is still the case that from time to time, powerful political figures conclude that the law does not really apply to them.

Of course, the rule of law can be complex. For example, not all laws—perhaps even few—are so clear that everyone agrees on their meaning. Therefore, every country has procedures for interpreting the meanings of laws, and those interpretations can change over time. In the United States, for example, the Supreme Court ruled in *Plessy* v. *Ferguson* (163 US 537 [1896]) that racially segregated facilities were legal under the U.S. Constitution. In *Brown* v. *Board of Education of Topeka* (347 US 483 [1954]), it ruled that they were not.

Another way in which the rule of law is not so simple is that some laws conflict, or at least appear to conflict, with other laws. Countries have to rely on some mechanism for deciding which law takes precedence and must be obeyed. In the United States, the Supreme Court has the role of deciding which laws conflict with the U.S. Constitution, and the Court is the ultimate arbiter of all disputes over conflicting laws. Other countries have a wide variety of institutions to make this determination, but some means is always available to do so.

Of course, the ability to make this determination gives power to whomever makes it, and a major controversy has arisen in the United States over what different groups have interpreted as political decision making by the Supreme Court. But what is deemed "political" seems to depend on whether the group agrees or disagrees: if they agree, it is an appropriate use of judicial authority; but if they disagree, it is a political decision.

THE ELECTORAL SYSTEM

The means of choosing representatives is central to making democracy work, and considerable conflict has arisen over procedures to do this. As we learned during the presidential vote counts in Florida in 2000 and in Ohio in 2004, the details of electoral procedure can be a significant factor in determining the outcome of an election. What might appear to be simple questions raise serious issues, but these only arise in very close elections. Consider the following questions:

1. For what period of time should someone be elected?
2. Should elected representatives be allowed to be reelected to the same office? If so, how many times? If not, can they be elected again later, after not holding the office for a set time? How long?
3. What percentage of the vote does a person need to get elected? Fifty percent plus one—called a *simple majority*—works nicely if there are only two candidates, but it poses problems otherwise.
4. If there are more than two candidates, should there be a second election, called a *runoff*, to choose between the two highest vote-getters in the first election?
5. Are there any circumstances in which more than a simple majority should be required?
6. How large should a representative assembly be?
7. How many representatives should be chosen from each area or for what population size? For example, in the United States, the Senate is composed of two representatives from each state, and the House of Representatives is composed of one representative from each Congressional district. Historical reasons exist for these arrangements, but they could be changed by amending the Constitution.

All of these questions have been disputed at times, and most still are. Also, many countries are currently going through what is being called *democratization,* in which these questions *must* be answered in the process of establishing representative institutions where none had existed. Many of these countries are having trouble finding the right answers and have yet to achieve stable democratic political systems. The long-term violence in late 2007 and 2008 that followed the elections in Kenya reflects the importance of honest elections.

The electoral process begins with the selection of candidates. The means by which this takes place varies from country to country and even within countries. In some cases, the system is entirely under the control of political parties, and a citizen must become active in a party to influence the choice of candidates. In other cases, although the political party is still important, an election—in the United States this is called a *primary*—is held to reduce the number of candidates. In this situation, citizens can influence the final list of candidates by voting, donating money to a candidate, or working actively for a candidate.

For a citizen who simply wants to vote intelligently, deciding whom to vote for will depend largely on the available information. For many offices a high percentage of voters vote on the basis of party identification alone; others depend on information provided by the candidate's campaign and the media. Reliable information is not always easy to come by, and voters often feel they are forced to choose without the information necessary to make a fully informed decision. This may be one reason for the low voter turnout in some countries: Getting adequate information can take more effort than some voters are willing to expend. And sometimes simply making a decision that reflects your own beliefs is hard. For example, at a recent local election in my area, both candidates took positions I liked, and both took positions I disliked, and it was a fairly dirty campaign. In these circumstances, the temptation to not vote is strong, and it is hardly surprising that many people choose not to. But not voting is giving the decision on who holds power to others; some countries, therefore, *require* their citizens to vote.

The normal rule of elections is that the side with the most votes wins, but it is always important to remember that this does not mean that those with the most votes are right; it just means that because more people voted for A rather than B, A must be accepted until the next election gives people the chance to change to B or C if they wish. Majority rule tends to be based on the assumption that any issue has only two sides. If, for example, there are three candidates in an election, majority rule becomes more complicated, because it is harder to determine what the majority wants. But having more than two candidates provides the opportunity for a greater possibility that a variety of positions will be represented in the election. But we have already seen the disadvantage of such an arrangement—if no one receives a clear majority, does this constitute majority rule?

To avoid these problems, various governments have made it difficult or impossible for more than two sides to be represented on the ballot, and other governments have used a system called *proportional representation* (PR), which allocates seats in the legislature on the basis of the percentage of votes cast for an individual or party. In a simple example of PR, using a 100-seat legislature like the U.S. Senate, if a minor party got 10 percent of the vote, it would get 10 seats. In the usual system, in which only the party that gets the majority of votes in a district is seated, the minor party would almost certainly get no seats.

Another way to make a representative system more representative is to change from single-member to multiple-member districts. In the usual system, one person is elected from each district, but some places elect two or more people from a district. In most but not all cases, this results in more women and minorities being elected.[7]

A final institutional arrangement designed to protect minorities is the common practice in the United States of requiring more than a simple majority on certain issues, such as money issues and amending basic sets of rules, such as in constitutions. The purpose is to protect the rights of the minority, the idea being that at least on some issues, a minority with strongly held opinions should not be dictated to by the majority.

The electoral system, although seemingly only a mechanism for determining the composition of the government for the next few years, actually provides the major, and sometimes the sole, means of political participation for individuals living in a large, complex, modern society. The electoral system, therefore, takes on peculiar importance for democratic theory. Because it often provides a significant, perhaps the only, means of political participation, the electoral system is the key to whether the system is democratic. When entering the voting booth, individuals must be sure their votes will be counted, that the election provides some choice, and that the choice is meaningful in that voters are actually free to vote for any of the options. It is also important to remember the most obvious point; that is, that an individual is allowed to vote in the first place. Finally, each vote should be equal to any other vote, although in the nineteenth century, proposals for plural votes based on some criterion such as education were fairly common.[8]

These questions of electoral procedure bring into focus other important problems. The electoral system, in addition to providing a means of political participation, is designed to guarantee the peaceful change of political power from one individual or group to another. This in turn raises the issue of leadership, a question confronting democratic theorists since ancient Athens. The importance of leadership in democratic theory is particularly significant in representative democracy. Whatever theory of representation is accepted, the elected official is given some political power not directly held by constituents. This power can be removed through the electoral process, but in the meantime, it is held by an individual who can directly participate in political decision making to the extent of the power vested in the office. In addition, the official may exercise political leadership by helping form or inform the opinions of constituents and others by

---

[7] On the different systems and their relationship to democracy, see Douglas J. Amy, *Behind the Ballot Box: A Citizen's Guide to Voting Systems*. Westport, CT: Praeger, 2000; Richard S. Katz, *Democracy and Elections*. New York: Oxford University Press, 1997; and G. Bingham Powell, *Elections as Instruments of Democracy: Majoritarian and Proportional Visions*. New Haven, CT: Yale University Press, 2000.

[8] See, for example, John Stuart Mill, *Considerations on Representative Government*, Currin V. Shields, ed. New York: Liberal Arts Press, 1958: 136–143.

James Madison (1751–1836) was secretary of state (1801–1809) during the presidency of Thomas Jefferson and served as the fourth president of the United States (1809–1817). Madison is now remembered mostly as one of the authors of *The Federalist Papers* (1787–1788) and as a major contributor to the drafting of the U.S. Constitution. Madison was concerned with the problem of minority rights and argued that the Constitution as written would provide adequate protection for minorities.

Library of Congress

defining the political issues he or she believes significant and by propagandizing for particular positions while ignoring others.[9]

Historically, most democratic theorists have been concerned with limiting the political power held by any individual or group within a society while at the same time providing intelligent and capable leadership. For example, James Madison (1751–1836), an important figure in the framing of the U.S. Constitution and the fourth president of the United States, was greatly worried about the possibility of some faction, including a "majority faction," gaining political power and exercising it in its own interest.

In the tenth number of *The Federalist Papers* (1787–1788), Madison suggested that the best protectors of freedom are the division of powers between the states and the national government; the separation of powers among the executive, legislative, and judicial branches of government found in the U.S. Constitution;[10] and the diversity of a large country. Others involved in the writing and defense of the Constitution advocated an enlightened aristocracy exercising political power but periodically checked through election, rather than rule by the people. In other words, they accepted Burke's theory of representation and made it the essence of their theory of government.

A central problem with majority rule, and the purpose of all these proposals to limit it, is the tendency of majorities to suppress minorities. Systems such as proportional representation, requirements for more than 50 percent of the vote, and Madison's proposals regarding the U.S. Constitution are attempts to ensure that minorities are protected from the majority.

---

[9] On leadership, see Arnold M. Ludwig, *King of the Mountain: The Nature of Political Leadership.* Lexington: University Press of Kentucky, 2002.

[10] The idea of the separation of powers came mostly through the writings of the French political theorist Montesquieu (1689–1755), particularly his *De l'esprit des lois* (*The Spirit of the Laws;* 1748).

EQUALITY

Although equality has been discussed for centuries, it became centrally important only in the twentieth century. Today equality is one of those concepts, called *essentially contested concepts,* that produce fundamental disagreement (see Chapter 1). For some people the achievement of some form of equality is absolutely essential; for others the achievement of any form of equality is impossible; for still others, even if some form of equality were possible, it would not be desirable. Part of this disagreement comes from lumping together very different types of equality into one concept. *Equality* as a general concept includes five separate types of equality: political equality, equality before the law, equality of opportunity, economic equality, and equality of respect or social equality.

If there is a strict sense of equality applicable to human beings, it is sameness in relevant aspects.[11] But the phrase "in relevant aspects" modifying "sameness" shows that we have to define carefully what is relevant in talking about equality; failure to do this is another source of disagreement over the meaning and importance of equality.

Political Equality

The importance of defining *relevant aspects* can be seen even in what would appear to be the simplest form of equality, political equality. If we assume the existence of some form of representative democracy, *political equality* refers to equality at the ballot box, equality in the ability to be elected to public office, and equality of political influence.

Voting   Equality at the ballot box entails the following:

1. Each individual must have reasonably easy access to the place of voting.

2. Each person must be free to cast his or her own vote as he or she wishes.

3. Each vote must be given exactly the same weight when counted.

These conditions constitute an ideal and are much harder to fulfill than they at first appear. There are a number of reasons for this difficulty.

First, there is the question of *citizenship.* To vote you must be a citizen. Each country has regulations defining who is a citizen and how citizenship is acquired. For example, in most countries, if you are born in that country, you are a citizen. But if your parents are citizens of another country, you may have the right to be a citizen of their country, but there may be restrictions on your ability to be a citizen of the country in which you were born. Some countries allow their citizens to simultaneously be citizens of another country; others do not. Citizenship also can be gained by being *naturalized,* or granted citizenship, by a country. Naturalization usually requires a formal process culminating in a ceremony in which allegiance is sworn to the new country.

---

[11] See the discussion in *Nomos IX: Equality,* J. Roland Pennock and John W. Chapman, eds. New York: Atherton Press, 1967. Of particular interest is the article "Egalitarianism and the Idea of Equality" by Hugo Adam Bedau (pp. 3–27).

Citizenship can also be lost. In many, though not all, countries, swearing allegiance to another country will result in the loss of citizenship. In the United States, serving in the military of another country is supposed to result in the loss of U.S. citizenship, although it has not always been enforced. Each country has its own rules on the loss of citizenship: in some countries it is virtually impossible to lose citizenship, whereas in others many different actions can result in such loss.

Second, there is an age requirement for voting. Each country establishes an age at which citizens are first allowed to vote. At present the most common voting age is 18, although there are exceptions; for example, the voting age in Indonesia is 17 and in India, 21.

Third, various people have had the right to vote taken away from them. In the United States, for example, about five million people convicted of certain crimes have lost the right to vote in some states; and in some states, the loss continues after the sentence has been served.[12] At times various countries have formally limited the right to vote. Examples of such limitations are requirements that a voter own a specified amount of property or belong to a particular religion; race and gender have also served as limitations and in some places still do.

In addition, there are many informal avenues of inequality. First, and perhaps most obvious, are racial and sexual discrimination. Even with legal limitations on voting removed, women and minorities in many countries still vote at a much lower rate than males of the racial majority. Second, some older and many disabled voters may have difficulty getting to the polling place. For example, the polling place in my area requires voters to negotiate two sets of stairs, and although arrangements can be made to vote without having to use the stairs, some voters do not know this or feel that the effort required is too great and choose not to vote. This example illustrates that the right to vote can be taken away simply by not thinking through what is required to actually vote.

People who cannot influence what names are printed on the ballot—that is, people who cannot choose the candidates—are not equal to those who can. There are two ways to influence the choice of who becomes a candidate: money and active participation in the political system. For many people the lack of money makes it difficult to participate actively, but most people who do not participate simply choose not to, and that choice has an effect.

Finally, each voter votes in a district, which should be roughly equal in population to other districts. If one district has a much larger population than another, each vote is diluted in that it does not have the same strength in determining the outcome as a vote in a smaller district. The closer the districts are in population size, the closer the votes will be in strength. For example, to take an extreme case, if voter A lives in a district of 50,000 voters, and voter B lives in one with only 10,000, B's vote will be worth five of A's. Some countries, such as the United States, require that district boundaries be changed regularly—usually

---

[12] In many democracies, people imprisoned can still vote; and in all but a few, those who have been released from prison can vote. On the issue, see Elizabeth A. Hull, *The Disenfranchisement of Ex-Felons*. Philadelphia, PA: Temple University Press, 2006; and Jeff Manza and Christopher Uggen, *Locked Out: Felon Disenfranchisement and American Democracy*. New York: Oxford University Press, 2006.

after each census—to achieve this form of equality. The process is called *reapportionment*. But the shape of the district can be manipulated to produce a desired result for or against a political party or ethnic or racial group. This process is called *gerrymandering* after Elbridge Gerry (1744–1814), a Massachusetts politician and signer of the Declaration of Independence who drew districts lines to ensure the victory of his party.

Running for Office Equality in the ability to be elected to public office means that everyone who has the vote can be elected to public office, although particular offices usually have age qualifications and other specific requirements, such as residence in a specified area. In many countries it has become very expensive to run for public office; hence equality in the ability to be elected to public office has been seriously eroded. Most countries have seen attempts to limit the effect of wealth by legally controlling campaign spending. Some countries, such as Great Britain, strictly limit the amount that candidates can spend. It has been estimated that an average, recent U.S. Senate campaign cost $10 million. In the United Kingdom, by contrast, candidates spent well under $200,000 in a campaign for the British Parliament and under $90,000 in campaigns for the European Parliament.

In addition, social constraints may restrict running for office. Traditionally in the United States, it has been difficult or even impossible for women, African Americans, Hispanics, and other ethnic minorities, to name just a few groups, to become serious candidates for office. Religious preferences have also played a role; John F. Kennedy (1917–1963) was the first Catholic President of the United States, and national office is effectively closed for Jews and Muslims at present. Similar situations, although with different groups, exist in most countries. Although members of such groups may have the legal right to run for office, that right has been meaningless, because there was no chance they could be elected. To avoid this, many countries set aside seats based on ethnicity or gender. In the United States, districts used to be drawn to guarantee white representation; some are now drawn to guarantee black representation. Also, Hispanics are now better represented because their numbers have grown substantially in recent years. The fact that Barack Obama (b. 1961) won the nomination of the Democratic Party to run for the presidency in 2008 suggests that a significant change may be taking place in the United States regarding race. Since this book had to be printed before the election, it is impossible to say more.

Political Influence Political equality also refers to an equality of political influence among citizens. Such equality means that all who choose to participate can do so without any formal limitations based on their membership in any religious, racial, ethnic, gender, or economic category. The point is the lack of legal limitations prohibiting participation. Of course, all these categories have at times both formally affected political influence and informally affected people's ability to participate and the likelihood that they will choose to participate. In much of the world, most of these limitations still exist.

Equality before the Law

Equality before the law resembles the definition of equality as sameness in relevant aspects, because it means that all people will be treated in the same way by the legal system; and it is not hedged about by so many formal definitions of relevant aspects. Depictions of justice usually show a blindfolded woman holding a scale. The scale is an indication that the issues will be weighed; the blindfold indicates that they will be weighed fairly, taking into account nothing beyond the issues of the case.

Because a major function of law and legal procedures is to establish general rules that all people are expected to accept, law, by its nature, is an equalizing force in society if it is enforced fairly. Clearly, equality before the law in practice is undermined by the socioeconomic inequalities that exist in all societies. But equality before the law is one of democracy's clearest goals.

pol. eq

Equality of Opportunity

The third type of equality is related to social stratification and mobility systems. *Equality of opportunity* means, first, that every individual in society can move up or down within the class or status system depending on that individual's ability and application of that ability. Second, it means that no artificial barrier keeps anyone from achieving what they can through ability and hard work. The key problem in the definition of equality of opportunity is the word *artificial,* which refers to characteristics that do not affect inherent abilities. Race, gender, religion, ethnic or national origin, and sexual orientation are most often cited as such artificial barriers.

Social stratification and mobility systems vary greatly from society to society. We tend to think of social status and mobility as easy to measure, because we link them to an easily quantifiable object: money. In most Western societies today, that measure is a fairly accurate guide to status (except at the level of the traditional aristocracy) and the major means of gaining or losing status. But even in the West, it is not quite that simple, because status depends on the respect a position in society is given, as well as the income that goes with the position. For example, clergy are not generally well paid but are accorded a status higher than their income. In a society that accords status on the basis of some other value, such as education, money would not automatically bring status. Equality of opportunity depends on the value accorded status.

Economic Equality

The fourth aspect of equality, economic equality, is rarely used to refer to economic sameness, but a complete discussion of the subject cannot ignore this definition. In this sense *economic equality* could mean that every individual within a society should have the same income, and Edward Bellamy (1850–1898), in his popular novel *Looking Backward* (1888), proposed such a definition. This definition is normally avoided because most advocates of economic equality are more concerned with the political and legal aspects of equality and with equality of opportunity than with strict financial equality. In addition, complete equality of income could be unfair to everyone, because it would not take into account the differing needs of different individuals. Of course, if income levels were sufficiently high, differences in need would be irrelevant, because all individuals would have enough no matter what their needs were; and this was Bellamy's assumption. But few exponents of economic equality expect such high income levels; therefore, what constitutes basic or fundamental human needs is a matter of considerable concern.

The usual argument for economic equality is that every individual within a society must be guaranteed a minimum level of economic *security*. The stress is on security, not equality. Such security would allow the individual to become a fully active citizen. The major contention, the key to the argument, is that without some degree of security, citizens will not be in a position to participate effectively, even in the limited role of voter.

Extreme levels of poverty effectively bar an individual from participation in the life of the community and can create continuing inequalities. This effect is particularly significant in education. A child in a typical middle-class or lower middle-class home has had toys and other objects that help teach many skills essential to learning. A simple thing such as having a book read aloud a number of times shows the child the turning of the pages and indicates that the English language is read from left to right, thus setting up a pattern the eyes will follow. The child who has not had this preparation will start out behind the child who has. Certain skills are essential even for relatively unskilled jobs that a child learns by playing with toys. A child who has simple toys to play with is learning these skills; a child who does not have such toys will not gain these skills and will have to learn them later or be barred from even those unskilled jobs. The effect of such deprivation on a child's life can be profound, and we are unsure whether some of these effects can be reversed for children who are already in our school systems. Thus children at age 5 or 6 may already have handicaps they will never be able to overcome. There are exceptions: Some children brought up in families that have suffered generations of extreme poverty do make it. However, the overwhelming majority do not.

Does great inequality in income eliminate equality of opportunity? How great an inequality is permissible? How can the extremes be brought closer together? We will look at these problems in greater detail as we discuss the differences between democratic capitalism and democratic socialism in the next chapter.

Equality of Respect or Social Equality

The fifth type of equality, equality of respect or social equality, is in some ways the most difficult to define, but it has become central to discussions of equality. At its base is the belief that all human beings are due equal respect simply because they are human; we are all equal in our fundamental humanity. Social equality is derived from this belief. *Equality of respect* refers to a level of individual interpersonal relations not covered by any of the other aspects of equality. The civil rights movement in the United States once developed a slogan,

Thomas Jefferson (1743–1826), the third president of the United States, was involved in almost all the issues that dominated American political life during his lifetime. Of all the things he accomplished, Jefferson thought his three most important actions were writing the Declaration of Independence, writing the Virginia Act for Establishing Religious Freedom, and founding the University of Virginia.

"Black Is Beautiful," which illustrates the point. In Western society, the color black has long connoted evil, as in the black clothes of the villain in early movies about the Old West. Advertising on television and in magazines used to reinforce this stereotype by never using black models. The slogan "Black Is Beautiful" was directed particularly at African-American children to teach them that it was good, not bad, to be black, and that they could be black and still respect themselves and be respected by others.

In a narrow sense, social equality means that no public or private association may erect artificial barriers to activity within the association. Again, there is the problem of defining *artificial,* but generally we use it in the same sense described earlier; that is, to denote characteristics—such as gender, sexual orientation, race, ethnic or national origin, or religion—that do not affect an individual's inherent abilities. Examples of this type of equality might be the lack of such barriers to membership in a country club or the use of a public park. Thus *social equality* refers to the absence of the class and status distinctions that raise such barriers. In this sense, it includes aspects of equality of opportunity.

Education is believed to be one of the main mechanisms for overcoming inequality, but in many countries, education is also a means of preserving inequalities. For example, in Britain large numbers of students are educated privately in what are called *public schools.* These students then proceed to the best universities and generally into the best jobs; and this same process takes place in most countries but on a smaller scale. Thus these students are cut off from the broader society, and privilege, antagonism, and ignorance establish the basis for significant social inequality. Some countries, including Britain, have tried to overcome such patterns by establishing schools that bring together people from a wide variety of backgrounds in an attempt to eliminate class or racial ignorance and animosity.

FREEDOM, LIBERTY, AND RIGHTS

Historically, the desire for equality has often been expressed as an aspect of liberty. When Thomas Jefferson (1743–1826), drafting the Declaration of Independence, spoke of equality he meant that people were equal in the rights they had. Equality of opportunity is often thought of as a right. On the other hand, many people believe that attempts to achieve a degree of economic equality conflict directly with attempts to maintain economic liberty.

The words *liberty, freedom,* and *right* are most often used interchangeably. Although some distinguish carefully among the meanings, it is not necessary to do so. All three refer to the ability to act without restrictions or with restrictions that are themselves limited in specified or specifiable ways. *Freedom* is the most general term. *Liberty* usually refers to social and political freedom. *Right* usually refers to specific, legally guaranteed freedoms. Also, *right* has been broadened to include basic human or natural rights. Finally, rights have become the focus of those in the United States who wish to expand constitutional guarantees and protections. As a result such questions as "Does the U.S. Constitution provide for a right of privacy?" or, more recently, "Is there a right to die?" have become the center of legal, political, and philosophic debate.

There is no such thing as complete freedom. In the first place, one must maintain life and perform a number of essential bodily functions. It is possible to choose when one eats, drinks, sleeps, and so on, but one cannot choose not to eat, drink, or sleep for long. In the second place, there are other people. Although they are essential for a complete life, they are restricting. An old adage states, "Your freedom to swing your arm stops at my nose." Although superficial, it does point out that the existence of others must be taken into account and that other people can limit free action.

A democratic society should be fairly free and open rather than controlled. It is the general assumption of democratic theory that whatever does no damage to the society as a whole, or to the individuals within it, should be the concern of no one but the individual or individuals involved.

Natural Rights and Civil Rights

The most influential approach to liberty is found in the distinction between the rights a person has or should have as a human being and the rights derived from government. The former are often called *natural rights,* although *natural* is now more and more often replaced with *human;* the latter are called *civil rights.* Although the trend today is either to reject the concept of natural rights altogether and call all rights civil rights, the traditional distinction is still useful.

Many democratic theorists, such as John Locke (1632–1704), have argued that human beings, separate from all government or society, have certain rights that should never be given up or taken away. People do not give up these rights on joining a society or government, and the society or government should not attempt to take these rights away. If a government does try to take them away, the people are justified in revolting to change the government. Not all theorists make this last argument, but the point is that natural rights establish limits. The

John Locke (1632–1704) was an important British philosopher and political thinker of the seventeenth century. His most important works were his *Essay Concerning Human Understanding* (1689) and, in political thought, *Two Treatises of Government* (published in 1690 but written earlier). The first of the two treatises attacked the divine right of kings as put forth by Robert Filmer (1588–1653). The second treatise is an argument for rule by consent of the governed, a defense of private property and majority rule, and a justification for revolution. The U.S. Declaration of Independence was based on the second treatise, and Locke was a major influence on a number of thinkers in the United States at the time of the revolution and the drafting of the U.S. Constitution.

Bill of Rights in the U.S. Constitution is a good example. Many of the amendments in the Bill of Rights begin, "Congress shall make no law regarding. . . ." The wording clearly indicates a limit on governmental activity. Isaiah Berlin (1909–1997) calls this approach *negative liberty*. By this term he describes the area of life within which one "is or should be left to do or be what he is able to do or be, without interference by other persons."[13]

In the United States, tradition emphasizes the danger of possible interference from government. Certain areas of life—such as speech, religion, press, and assembly—have been defined as areas of negative liberty, in which each person is left to do, on the whole, what she or he wants. Negative liberty as practiced illustrates the complexity of democracy. Government is seen as the most likely agent to attempt to restrict liberty. Government is also the major protector of liberty, and it must protect people even against itself. This is one reason many Western democracies have established systems of checks and balances within the government. No segment of government should be able to rule unchecked by any other segment; as a result, the rights of citizens are protected.

Berlin also developed a concept that he called *positive liberty*. He used it to refer to the possibility of individuals controlling their own destiny or their ability to choose among options. For Berlin, positive liberty is the area of rational self-control or "self-mastery." For others, positive liberty means that the government should ensure conditions in which the full development of each individual is possible.[14] On the whole, as will be seen in the next chapter, democratic

---

[13] Isaiah Berlin, "Two Concepts of Liberty." In Berlin, *Four Essays on Liberty*. London: Oxford University Press, 1969: 121–122.

[14] See, for example, the argument in Christian Bay, *The Structure of Freedom*. Stanford, CA: Stanford University Press, 1958; and Bay, *Strategies of Political Emancipation*. Notre Dame, IN: University of Notre Dame Press, 1981.

capitalists stress negative liberty, and democratic socialists stress positive liberty, while trying to maintain most of the negative liberties.

The most important natural right—the right of self-preservation—is basic to this understanding of positive liberty. This right can be interpreted to mean that every person has a right to the necessary minimum of food, clothing, and shelter needed to live in a given society. Because standards vary considerably from society to society, the necessary minimum might vary a great deal.

From this perspective, positive liberty might include the right to an education equal to one's ability and the right to a job. This approach to positive liberty logically extends to establishing as a right anything that can be shown to be essential to the development, and perhaps even the expression, of each person's potential as a human being.

Thus positive liberty can include as rights a wide variety of economic and social practices in addition to the political rights that usually come to mind when speaking of rights. The Universal Declaration of Human Rights adopted by the United Nations in 1948 includes such rights in its definition of human rights. For example, Article 22 states that "everyone, as a member of society, has the right to social security and is entitled to realization, through national effort and in accordance with the organization and resources of each State, of the economic, social and cultural rights indispensable for his dignity and the free development of his personality." Another checklist is produced by Freedom House and asks a set of questions regarding civil and political rights, and all countries are evaluated on this basis.[15] Positive liberty is not usually extended this far; the Universal Declaration has been accused of having a Western bias, and a revised Islamic version exists (see Chapter 11), but these examples illustrate the complexity of the questions involved.

Other so-called natural rights have also been widely debated. One of the most controversial is the right to property. Some contend that there must be a nearly absolute right to acquire and accumulate private property, because ownership of property is an avenue to the full development and expression of the human personality. Others argue that private property must be limited, because the control of such property gives additional power to those who own it. (Additional arguments for and against the institution of private property will be considered in Chapter 5.)

Although there is widespread disagreement on specific natural rights, it is generally agreed that after the formation of government, these rights must become civil rights, or rights specifically guaranteed and protected by the government—even or particularly against itself. This formulation of liberty raises many difficulties, the most basic of which is the assumption that a government will be willing to guarantee rights against itself. Many thinkers have assumed that representative democracy with frequent elections will solve this problem. Any such government should recognize that an infringement of people's civil rights would ensure its defeat in the next election. Experience has shown this is not necessarily true, and the result has been apathy, civil disobedience, and revolution, with

---

[15] The text of the Universal Declaration can be found at http://www.un.org/Overview/
rights.html. For the Freedom House list and evaluations, see http://www.freedomhouse.org.

apathy currently the greatest concern in most developed democracies. At the same time, protecting liberties is still considered a primary duty of a democratic political system and a central part of democratic theory.

Types of Liberty

It is more difficult to define types of liberty than types of equality; but, loosely, civil rights include the following specific liberties or freedoms:

1. The right to vote

2. Freedom of speech

3. Freedom of the press

4. Freedom of assembly

5. Freedom of religion

6. Freedom of movement

7. Freedom from arbitrary treatment by the political and legal system

The first six of these are areas of life that the democratic argument says should be left, within broad limits, to the discretion of the individual. Of these six, freedom of movement is the least commonly discussed among theorists of democracy. The seventh item, freedom from arbitrary treatment, is simply a way of stating positively the belief that government must protect the citizen from government. The various freedoms—particularly those of speech, press, assembly, and religion—are closely related. Among the other means by which freedom has been expressed are toleration, silence of the law, and unenforceability.

The Right to Vote   The right to vote without interference is, of course, the key to the ability to change the system. It is the ultimate check on government and the true guarantor of any freedom.

Freedom of Speech   With some minimal disagreement, most thinkers consider freedom of speech the most important freedom. Within democracy freedom of speech has a special place. The right to vote does not mean much if it is impossible to hear opposing points of view and to express an opinion. The same reasoning is behind the freedoms of press and assembly. The rights to publish opinion and to meet to discuss political issues are fundamental if people are to vote intelligently. The right to vote implies, even requires, a right to information and the free expression of opinion both orally and in writing. Freedom of speech requires freedom of assembly; freedom to speak is meaningless without the possibility of an audience.

John Stuart Mill (1806–1873) explained the importance of freedom of speech and press in a slightly different way in his classic *On Liberty* (1859):

> This, then, is the appropriate region of human liberty. It comprises, first, the inward domain of consciousness; demanding liberty of conscience in the most comprehensive sense; liberty of thought and feeling; absolute freedom of opinion and sentiment on all subjects, practical or speculative, scientific, moral, or theological. The liberty of expressing and publishing opinions may

seem to fall under a different principle, since it belongs to that part of the conduct of an individual which concerns other people; but, being almost of as much importance as the liberty of thought itself and resting in great part on the same reasons, is practically inseparable from it.[16]

For Mill, thought requires the freedom to express oneself orally and in writing. The search for truth requires that challenge, debate, and disagreement be possible. Mill argued this from four different perspectives:

> First, if any opinion is compelled to silence, that opinion may, for aught we can certainly know, be true. To deny this is to assume our own infallibility.
>
> Secondly, though the silenced opinion be an error, it may, and very commonly does, contain a portion of truth; and since the general or prevailing opinion on any subject is rarely or never the whole truth, it is only by the collision of adverse opinions that the remainder of the truth has any chance of being supplied.
>
> Thirdly, even if the received opinion be not only true, but the whole truth; unless it is suffered to be, and actually is, vigorously and earnestly contested, it will, by most of those who receive it, be held in the manner of a prejudice, with little comprehension or feeling of its rational grounds. And not only this, but, fourthly, the meaning of the doctrine itself will be in danger of being lost or enfeebled, and deprived of its vital effect on the character and conduct; the dogma becoming a mere formal profession, inefficacious for good, but cumbering the ground and preventing the growth of any real and heartfelt conviction, from reason or personal experience.[17]

Without freedom of expression truth is lost, is never found, becomes mere prejudice, or is enfeebled. Assuming that there is truth to be found, freedom of expression is essential; if there is no truth to be found, freedom of expression is even more important as the only device available to sort out the better opinion from the worse.

Speakers' Corner on the northeast corner of Hyde Park in London, across from where people used to be executed for their religious beliefs, is open every Sunday morning to anyone with the urge to speak. It was designed as a "safety valve" and appears to have functioned as such for some time. Today it is mostly viewed as entertainment.

Freedom of the Press Mill joined speech and press closely together and, for political concerns, the argument that a generally free press is essential in a democracy is almost noncontroversial. But there are areas of concern outside the strictly political realm, most obviously related to the publication of pornography, and there are even concerns about some more narrowly political issues.

If freedom of the press is absolute, there should be no restrictions on the publication of pornography. With some exceptions, much pornography depicts

---

[16] John Stuart Mill, *On Liberty,* 4th ed. London: Longman, Reader & Dyer, 1869: 26.

[17] Mill, *On Liberty,* 95.

individuals of one of two groups—women or children—as objects to be used, often violently, by another group: men. Viewed this way, pornography is an issue with strong political overtones and illustrates a central concern of contemporary students of democracy, the conflict of rights. Whose rights should be protected, the publishers and consumers of pornography or the women and children who are turned into consumer goods?

A more narrowly political issue involves the publication of material designed to incite the overthrow of government by violence. Absolute freedom of the press would require the government to ensure that those trying to overthrow it have the right to publish calls for its overthrow and even manuals on how to produce bombs and directions on where and how to place them. Many people find such a position ludicrous; many find it perfectly reasonable.

A third issue is governmental secrecy. Some, particularly those working for the press, contend that the press should have free access to the whole government decision-making process. Others, especially those working in government, argue that government should be free to choose what the press is allowed to know and publish. Most people fall somewhere in between, believing that some governmental actions must be secret and that other actions, ranging from a few to most, should not be secret. The problem is that governments decide what must be secret, and this leads to distrust. There is no way around this problem, and the press and government will inevitably be at odds about the extent of permissible secrecy.

A related issue is self-censorship by the press. Privately owned media, mostly in the developed world, must attract and keep readers, viewers, or listeners to make a profit. Some sensationalize material to attract a larger audience; others limit what they report, or structure the language they use, to avoid upsetting their owners, corporate sponsors, or the audience they have already attracted. Both tendencies distort the information available and undermine the ability of the public to use the information provided by the press to make decisions about important political questions.

In the United States, conservatives consistently argue that most journalists are liberals who bias their reporting to support the liberal position. Liberals argue that most media outlets are owned by wealthy conservatives and that they require reporting slanted to support the conservative position. Although it is impossible to be certain, on the whole journalists are more liberal than their bosses; but most media outlets and journalists strive for accuracy and balance. Some on both sides do not, and they deliberately distort the news; so both conservatives and liberals are, at times, correct in their judgments.

Historically, newspapers and news magazines separated reporting and opinion, with pages devoted to opinion clearly marked. Today both print and electronic media are less careful in making such a separation, and getting accurate and balanced news is more difficult than it used to be. At the same time, electronic media provide a range of news sources never before available, and the Internet in particular is a source of serious investigative reporting, the expression of minority viewpoints, and bias presented as objectivity.

The growth of blogs—originally *Web log* or *Weblog,* then *We blog,* and now just *blogs* or *to blog*—that cover every imaginable activity or subject, including politics, is transforming political reporting. Most news outlets have their own blogs, and the speed with which information, true or false, can become available and spread makes secrecy much harder to maintain. And many bloggers are in effect amateur investigative reporters, competing to post information before others; a blog was even designed for those wanting to leak information, Wikileaks. In early 2008, Wikileaks was closed down by order of a U.S. court but is still readily accessible through other countries (my route went through Belgium). This provides an excellent example of how difficult it is to control the Internet, but, as will be seen later in this chapter, China has been quite successful in doing just that.

Tension between the press and government is unavoidable and probably healthy. Western democracies criticize countries with a controlled press while trying to keep their own press from publishing things they want kept secret. The degree of press freedom varies among democracies. There is no such thing as a completely free press, but a fairly high degree of such freedom is essential in a democracy; because in the modern world, the communication of political ideas requires the right to publish those ideas.

Freedom of Assembly The freedom to speak requires the freedom to have an audience. Although in broadcasting the audience need not be gathered in one place, the ability to meet together to discuss political issues, make decisions on those issues, and choose candidates is clearly still fundamental to a functioning democracy.

The political issues related to freedom of assembly are issues of public order. Should parades and demonstrations that may produce violence be allowed? What limitations on assembly are permissible to keep traffic moving or to prevent violence? All governments, from the local to the national, in all democracies constantly face the problem of how to regulate assembly without making it politically ineffective. Some governments clearly use the excuse of necessary regulation through the need for permits, for example, to limit the freedom of assembly, but on the whole such attempts have proved ineffective.

Freedom of Religion Freedom of religion is usually supported on precisely the same grounds Mill used to defend freedom of speech and press, and worshipping together requires the freedom of assembly. Even if we are certain that we have the whole truth—perhaps particularly if we are certain—we should always distrust our own presumed infallibility and welcome the continuation of the search. Freedom of religion has, particularly in North America, come to be identified with the separation of church and state. The search for religious truth, in this view, requires that government be a neutral bystander, neither favoring nor suppressing any aspect of that search.

In many countries this issue takes a more complex form. Some countries have an established church or a church that is officially recognized by the government and that may receive financial and other public support. In addition, many countries have political parties that are tied, directly or indirectly, to religious bodies. In Europe most of these parties are labeled *Christian Democrats* or some variant thereof. These parties are often conservative.

In such circumstances the quest for freedom of religion becomes more problematic. But every religion has at some time faced the question of its relationship to political power. This issue is particularly important today in the Third World, and until recently deeply divided the Roman Catholic Church (See the discussion of Liberation Theologies in Chapter 12 for some current issues within Christian churches). And in many Islamic countries, the notion of separation of church and state is simply rejected.

Two somewhat contradictory bases for the separation of church and state exist: one argues that it is important to protect the state from domination by the church, or one church in particular; the other argues that it is important to protect the church from the state. In other words, putting the arguments together, the state should neither control nor be controlled by religion, and religion should neither control nor be controlled by government. Both arguments are grounded in historical experience. For example, the Puritans who settled Plymouth Colony in 1620 did so because they could not practice their beliefs the way they wanted to in Great Britain. They did not establish separation of church and state or religious freedom; they legislated their religious beliefs. But Maryland was founded by Roman Catholics, and Pennsylvania by Quakers (members of the Society of Friends). Therefore, for perfectly practical reasons, as the colonies came together it was found necessary to separate church and state. In addition, between 1620 and 1789, when the Bill of Rights was added to the U.S. Constitution, religious toleration had become generally accepted. This was reflected in one of the most important U.S. statements of religious freedom, Thomas Jefferson's "Act for Establishing Religious Freedom," adopted by Virginia in 1779. With the growth of toleration, the state was prohibited from requiring membership and support of any particular denomination, and no church was able to insist that the state support it and it alone. This left citizens the right to practice their religious beliefs as they choose.

The reality is not quite so clear-cut. The U.S. Congress has a Christian chaplain; U.S. currency has "In God We Trust" on it; in most Christian countries most testimony in court begins with swearing to tell the truth with one's hand on the Bible, and there are many more such examples. Some people advocate closer ties between church and state; other people advocate greater, even complete, separation; and the Supreme Court regularly tries to draw acceptable lines between the two, none of which last very long.

Freedom of Movement Freedom of movement is less commonly included among the basic freedoms, but it is as important as the others because the ability to move freely is a major protection for other freedoms. Some restrictions are already in effect. Many democratic countries, particularly in Europe, require their citizens to carry identity papers and, for example, require hotels to record the number on these papers when someone registers. All countries require passports for foreign travel. And the growth of government programs means that most countries have records of the location of and changes of permanent address for a growing number of citizens. But in no democracy is it necessary to get prior approval from a government to travel within its borders; and most important, within a democracy people can freely move from place to place for political activity.

Freedom from Arbitrary Treatment Freedom from arbitrary treatment by the political and legal system also protects the other freedoms. All democratic societies have clearly established procedural rights designed to guarantee that every individual will be treated fairly by the system. Without these procedural rights, the substantive rights of freedom of speech, press, and so on would not be as secure. Basic guarantees include those found in the U.S. Bill of Rights, such as freedom from cruel and unusual punishment (designed to prohibit torture, now an issue in the debate over capital punishment—and even the issue of torture has returned); the right to a writ of *habeas corpus,* a Latin term meaning to "have the body," which is the right to demand that a prisoner be brought before an officer of the court so that the lawfulness of the imprisonment can be determined; and the right to a trial by a jury of your peers.[18]

In addition to these issues, the process of jury selection has become so sophisticated that lawyers hire experts to advise them on how to choose a jury that will either acquit a person or find them guilty.[19]

Toleration Toleration means that you accept another person believing or doing something that you believe to be wrong. Religious toleration is the most obvious case, and in some ways it is the most difficult. If I am certain that my way is the only one that leads to salvation, I am unlikely to tolerate an opposing belief that I am convinced endangers that salvation. Religious toleration is, in fact, a relatively recent phenomenon; as late as the seventeenth century, the word *tolerance* had a negative meaning and *intolerance* a positive one. Within a relatively short time, though, the connotation of the words shifted: tolerance became a virtue and intolerance a vice, although even now many do not tolerate beliefs or behaviors they are convinced are wrong. Today most people accept toleration and extend it beyond religion to other beliefs and ways of life. In this way, freedom includes a large area in which we accept other people even though we disagree with them.

Politically, toleration is basic to modern democracy because one key to democracy is the recognition and acceptance of basic disagreements among citizens. The diversity of the population and the protection of that diversity are extremely important. Toleration must exist or democracy cannot work, but it can be difficult. It requires us either to feel sufficient empathy for a position we reject, so that we may accept its believers, or to be able to simply accept that fundamental disagreements will be part of the life of a citizen in a democracy; neither attitude is easy to achieve.

Currently, religious disputes and disagreements have made toleration both more of a concern and more difficult, because the question arises of whether to tolerate someone who would not tolerate you. This issue has always been there

---

[18] What constitutes a peer is at times an issue. Must there be African-American members of a jury when an African-American is on trial? And should this selectivity be extended to women, ethnic and religious groups, and so forth?

[19] On this issue, see Joel D. Lieberman and Bruce D. Sales, *Scientific Jury Selection.* Washington, DC: American Psychological Association, 2007; and Bruce D. Sales and Daniel W. Shuman, *Experts in Court: Reconciling Law, Science, and Professional Knowledge.* Washington, DC: American Psychological Association, 2005.

regarding extremists who insist on the right of free speech but who would abolish it once in power. Today, the debate centers on whether to tolerate the small minority of Islamists (see Chapter 11) who use the traditional freedoms in order to oppose them.

The Silence of the Law and Unenforceability   Two other areas of freedom should be noted briefly: the silence of the law and unenforceability. It is part of the Anglo-American tradition that if no law prohibits an action, that action is within the area of individual discretion until such a law is written. In the United States, when the law is written, it cannot affect actions that preceded it. In many other countries, newly passed laws can be used to find past acts illegal. Also, the experience of Prohibition in the United States indicated that there are unenforceable laws, laws that people simply will not accept. Thus unenforceability can also be seen as an aspect of freedom.

Liberty is limited to some extent by all political systems. The democratic system has built-in safeguards that protect individuals from having their freedoms too severely restricted. Of course, these safeguards do not always work. The most fundamental of these safeguards is the basic characteristic of a democracy—that people have some control over their government. Democratic theorists have never adequately addressed the problem of severe restrictions of rights that are desired or acquiesced to by the majority. Thus a problem for democracy is how to achieve sufficient tolerance of differences so that the majority is willing to protect the rights of the minority. For many the answer is education.

EDUCATION

Education as a fundamental principle of democracy may be mildly controversial, but it should not be. Democratic theorists such as John Locke, Jean-Jacques Rousseau, and John Stuart Mill wrote treatises on education that tied their political theories loosely or tightly to the need for an educated populace. In the United States, the founders believed education essential to an effective democracy. In fact, the statement that an educated citizenry is necessary in a democracy is commonplace. The argument regarding the need for education is fairly simple: Citizens are required to choose among candidates and issues. To do so they must have the basic skills of reading, writing, and arithmetic—rather illiterately known as the *three Rs*—because information provided is often communicated in print, because it may be necessary for citizens to communicate in writing, and because numbers are used extensively. Equally important, citizens must be able to evaluate the information, weigh pros and cons, and decide what positions best correspond to their interests. Of course, citizens must also be able to correctly identify those interests.

A democracy can operate without an educated populace. India is a functioning democracy with a high level of illiteracy. But a democracy of illiterates is limited unless the culture actively encourages oral dissemination of information and discussion of issues. The elitist model of democracy would have no trouble with a high level of illiteracy, but every other approach to democracy would find it an issue requiring solution. Thus it is fair to say that an educated populace is a prerequisite of a fully functioning democracy.

The principles of democracy all relate to one another, and all stem from the most fundamental democratic principle: citizen involvement. Politically, equality and freedom both characterize and protect citizen involvement. They characterize citizen involvement in that democracy demands the freedom to vote and equality of the vote; they protect citizen involvement because a free and equal electorate can insist on the maintenance of that freedom and equality. A free and equal electorate needs education to ensure that freedom and equality are meaningful and to make informed choices as citizens. Today the electoral system is the major avenue for the expression of citizen involvement, and of course the system of representation is the purpose and result of the electoral system and the way in which citizens are involved.

CURRENT TRENDS

The principles of democracy do not change, but their interpretation does. The most obvious current trend is the ongoing process of democratization, in which countries without a democratic tradition are trying to establish the institutions of democracy. But there are also other significant trends, some of which will remain unsettled for the foreseeable future.

Democratization

If any ideology is dominant today, it is democracy. Most countries at least pretend to be democratic in the most minimal sense of holding elections. And many countries are going through a process called *democratization*. Thus it is particularly important today to understand what range of meanings can be applied to *democracy*. Does it mean merely holding elections, even though the electoral process is corrupt? If the elections are honestly run, is that enough? If more is required, what is necessary? What constitutes a full democracy, and do any exist?[20]

Since 1989 and the fall of the Berlin Wall, democratization—the process by which countries establish democratic institutions and procedures and, even more important, a culture of democracy—has been a major topic of discussion. Putting such institutions and procedures in place is fairly easy; making them work is often difficult, but it is possible. Democratization continues in the Third World, where elections are common, but the development of a democratic culture lags far behind; and some of the countries of Central Europe and the former Soviet Union face similar problems. Some countries in Central Europe had democratic institutions before World War II, but few current citizens have any experience with democracy. Few of the countries that emerged from the former Soviet Union

---

[20] For one statement about what constitutes a full democracy, see Juan J. Linz and Alfred Stepan, *Problems of Democratic Transition and Consolidation*. Baltimore, MD: Johns Hopkins University Press, 1996: 3–7.

Louise Gubb/Corbis Saba

Nelson Rolihlahla Mandela (b. 1918) helped transform the African National Congress (ANC) into a mass movement opposed to apartheid or racial separation in South Africa. He helped lead a movement of mass civil disobedience, for which he was arrested, tried, found guilty, and given a suspended jail sentence, even though the court found that he had always advocated peaceful action. A lawyer, Mandela was active both in the courts and on the streets to fight against the growing number of apartheid laws. He was charged with treason and arrested. When the trial collapsed, he called for a new constitution for South Africa based on democratic principles. After a new constitution was adopted that strengthened apartheid, Mandela accepted that violence was necessary and led the military wing of the ANC that attacked governmental and economic activities. He was arrested for leaving the country illegally and for incitement to strike; he was found guilty and sentenced to five years in prison. While in prison, he was charged with sabotage and sentenced to life in prison. Having refused a number of offers of release if he renounced his principles, he served his sentence from 1964 to 1990. After his release, he was elected President of the now-legal ANC, and in 1994 he was the first State President of South Africa elected under a system of racial equality. He served until 1999.

have ever experienced democracy. And in the Third World, democratic institutions borrowed from the previous colonial rulers were put in place; but again, those citizens have little or no previous experience with these institutions. In a few cases, the Czech Republic and India for example, democracy has taken root; but in some of the new democracies it is fragile. As a result, dictators of various sorts exist throughout the Third World, in many countries of the former Soviet Union, and in a few Central European countries. Russia, for example, has established institutions that look democratic, but there is no democratic culture (see Chapter 8 for the current situation).

Given the extreme poverty of many Third World countries, many argue that development must come first, and then democracy will follow. But Amartya Sen (b. 1933), who won the Nobel Prize in economics in 1998, contends that development and at least some features of democracy are inseparable:

> Development requires the removal of major sources of unfreedom: poverty as well as tyranny, poor economic opportunities as well as systematic social deprivation, neglect of public facilities as well as intolerance or overactivity of repressive states. Despite unprecedented increases in overall opulence, the contemporary world denies elementary freedoms to vast numbers—perhaps even a majority—of people.[21]

Sen says that the establishment of such freedoms will spur economic development.

Civil Society

The culture that supports democracy includes a concept that has a long history but had largely been forgotten until the process of democratization reminded us of its importance. *Civil society* refers to the largely voluntary associations and interactions found in the family, clubs, neighborhood associations, religious organizations, and so forth that operate outside the formal political system. In these social interactions, people learn tolerance, the process of winning and losing elections (learning how to lose being particularly important), living with rules determined by the group, and other key democratic values.

Civil society also includes economic relationships and institutions that are outside direct political control, such as private banking and the free market. Just as democratic values must be learned, so must the attitudes and behaviors appropriate to private economic life, such as profit and loss, the ability of enterprises to both succeed and fail, and the need to be responsible for one's own future economic health. Many argue that a healthy civil society is essential to the existence of both democracy and private economic institutions.

In Central Europe and the former Soviet Union, the problem is how to create a civil society in a country where most such associations were controlled by the state. In the Third World, the problem is how to create a specifically democratic civil society in places where private institutions have been based on hierarchical relationships of clans, ethnic groups, religions, tribes, and so forth.

The United States used to be described as a country based on voluntary associations. But recently, as popularly explained in *Bowling Alone: The Collapse and Revival of American Community* (2000) by Robert D. Putnam (b. 1941), Americans are much less likely to be members of such associations than they used to be. For many, this suggests that even in the United States, civil society is less vital than it must be to support a vibrant democratic culture.

Consociational Democracy One approach to democratization tries to balance groups that are opposed to each other in fundamental ways by redefining some of the usual organizational structures. *Consociational democracy* is in essence a system of formal power sharing in which each significant group in a country is guaranteed a

[21] Amartya Sen, *Development as Freedom*. New York: Knopf, 1999: 3–4.

place in the governing bodies and has a veto on some issues. In addition, representation is based on proportionality, and each group controls its own affairs.[22] The central problem in such a system is getting the groups to agree in the first place. Disagreements on who is to be included and what issues will be covered by the veto are other problems, but the system is designed to avoid the division of countries into separate nations. For a time it seemed to be working in Lebanon, but pressures from outside that country have undermined the initial successes.

Group Rights

A focus of attention that relates to many other contemporary points of contention is the issue of group rights. When we think of legally enforceable rights, we tend to think solely in terms of individuals, although the fact that in the United States corporations are legally classified as individuals complicates the issue. Today many believe they are deprived of rights solely based on their membership in a group and that the rights of groups should be protected. The argument goes, if I lose my rights or I am discriminated against because of my membership in a group, shouldn't my rights be protected as a member of a group?

The assumption has been that individuals make up groups and, as a result, there is no need to have rights for groups. But the issue today is the belief that in practice only some individuals are in fact protected, and those whose rights are not protected are in that situation because they are members of a group.

Some of these claims are based on the American myth of the "melting pot," in which ethnic, religious, and other differences are supposed to disappear. But of course racial and gender differences have never disappeared. Many contend that without group rights, the pressure to conform to the majority violates people's ability to practice their religion—particularly if that religion is not Christian—and to maintain their ethnic identity, speak their native language, have a sexual orientation other than heterosexual, and so forth, putting them at risk of prosecution and persecution, or at least threatening their cultural identity.

Of course, the obvious problem is deciding what groups need their rights protected. Most of us are members of multiple groups. Some are more important to us than others, and most of us might easily say that we most identify with our ethnic group, our religious group, or some other identifiable group; but others might not find this as easy. Are all groups worthy of legal protection? And what if the culture of one group includes discrimination against members of another group? This issue is now of growing importance. As a result of these problems, a number of approaches to groups have developed.

Multiculturalism To what extent should a society with a dominant culture or cultures teach children about the dominant culture rather than the minority cultures? Put another way, what right do children have to learn about their heritage, rather than being forced to learn about the dominant culture? These two ways of putting what is essentially the same question illustrate the problem. Those in the dominant culture have as much right to value their culture as those in the minority cultures,

---

[22] On consociational democracy, see Arend Lijphart, *Democracy in Plural Societies: A Comparative Exploration.* New Haven, CT: Yale University Press, 1977: 25–52.

but do they have a right to impose it? In the past this practice was never questioned. Today people in minority cultures are demanding that their cultures also be taught; this is called *multiculturalism,* and it raises questions of majority versus minority rights and how to make a diverse society genuinely pluralistic.

As noted in the previous chapter, the issues raised by multiculturalism are also part of the current debate around immigration. Immigration enriches societies both culturally and economically while raising issues of autonomy, citizenship, and rights. In Chapter 7 we will discuss to what extent a democratic culture, in the name of multiculturalism, should allow practices such as child marriage and restrictions on women's rights that are part of certain immigrant cultures but illegal in the new country.

Difference   How can individual and group differences be recognized and valued in a society that believes in equality, and should they be? In a development that has changed the focus of debate, a shift has occurred; stemming primarily from debates within feminism (see Chapter 7), and from a concern with the sameness component of equality, a recognition has emerged that difference is important and valuable and should be protected, even fostered. The argument does not depend on whether the differences are based on biology or are socially constructed.

Although the definition of equality as "sameness in relevant aspects" does not prohibit a focus on difference, the emphasis since the beginning of the civil rights movement has been on sameness. The change is to move the focus to what is a *relevant* difference. Thirty years ago such an emphasis was used as an excuse to take rights from minorities; the assumption today is that such rights are so well established that it is safe to recognize relevant differences.

The issue comes back to one of the fundamental questions of democracy: How do we balance the interests of the majority and the minority? Or as may more accurately reflect the current situation in the United States, how do we balance the interests of various minorities given that there is no overall or general minority—only temporary majorities and minorities on specific issues?

For example, what does *equality* mean to someone who is disabled? Immediately after World War II, various European countries tried to compensate for war injuries by giving those disabled in the war easier access to certain jobs and transportation, and they established other programs to integrate the physically disabled as much as possible into postwar society. The United States had similar but much more limited programs. With time these programs gradually disappeared; but recently, and now beginning in the United States, people with disabilities have been gaining recognition by stressing that they must be compensated for their disabilities so they can fully participate in society; and the return of disabled serviceman links the issue back to the earlier programs. The establishment of legally protected rights moves in this direction. Again, note the connection between rights and equality.

Groups advocating for people with disabilities have also attempted to change the language used to describe them. The earlier usage was "handicapped." Later usage has included "disabled," "people with disabilities," and "differently abled." I taught at a public university that happened to be located on hilly terrain. Some years ago, before there were advocacy groups for the disabled, some faculty and students decided to demonstrate the difficulties faced by students in wheelchairs by spending a few days trying to get around the campus in wheelchairs. In many places it was virtually impossible to get between buildings, into buildings, or from parking lots to buildings. On the whole, the university responded positively by removing certain barriers, replacing steps with ramps, and providing a parking area that was close to and on the same level as the center of the campus. But not until laws requiring access were passed did other barriers disappear, and problems still remain.

Most efforts to bring about equality of opportunity for the disabled have focused on those with observable physical disabilities; those with less obvious problems have had difficulty getting the help they need. For example, because she had no outward signs of disability, a student with heart problems that restricted the distance she could walk was regularly chastised by other disabled students for using parking set aside for the disabled.[23]

Deliberative Democracy

A new approach to democratic participation is called *deliberative democracy*, a theory that has developed along somewhat different lines in Europe and the United States with variants in each. One generally accepted definition calls it "a form of government in which free and equal citizens (and their representatives), justify decisions in a process in which they give one another reasons that are mutually acceptable and generally accessible, with the aim of reaching conclusions that are binding in the present on all citizens but open to challenge in the future."[24] The purpose is to encourage participation, provide communication between citizens and leaders, and recognize fundamental disagreements that need to be discussed. A basic problem in democracy is whether it can function where differences are deep. How does democracy handle issues when those on one side are absolutely convinced that they are right and the other side is wrong? How does democracy address a situation in which a temporary majority is willing to impose its version of the truth on a sizable minority? How does democracy deal with a situation in which "informing" voters becomes manipulating them with half-truths and outright lies? Deliberation has the potential of avoiding the second and third problems and reducing the first by encouraging people to listen to each other.

A specific proposal is for a national Deliberation Day, a holiday to be held two weeks before a national election. On Deliberation Day, actually two days to encourage wider participation, registered voters would meet in neighborhood groups to discuss the issues raised by the election. Participants would be paid $150 both to encourage them to attend and so they could afford to do so.[25]

---

[23] For the Americans with Disabilities Act of 1990, see http://www.usdoj.gov/crt/ada/pubs/ada.txt. On disability issues, see Ruth O'Brien, ed., *Voices from the Edge: Narratives about the Americans with Disabilities Act.* New York: Oxford University Press, 2004; and Susan Stefan, *Unequal Rights: Discrimination against People with Mental Disabilities and the Americans with Disabilities Act.* Washington, DC: American Psychological Association, 2001.

[24] Amy Gutmann and Dennis F. Thompson, *Why Deliberative Democracy?* Princeton, NJ: Princeton University Press, 2004: 7.

[25] Bruce Ackerman and James S. Fishkin, *Deliberation Day.* New Haven, CT: Yale University Press, 2004.

Deliberative democracy assumes a degree of trust in the system, something that many believe is lacking today. Deliberative democracy also assumes that citizens will have the ability to participate and evaluate; but many are concerned that citizens in some democracies, including the United States, lack the information needed to do so. As a result, education is again a significant issue.

Education Today

Education has become a major debate in a number of democracies. The issues vary, but central to all of them are questions about what education is necessary for a democratic citizen in the twenty-first century, and who should decide the content of that education.

One concern is how to educate citizens. This applies both to children as they grow up and immigrants hoping to become citizens of their new country. Given the apparent level of apathy in the United States, many people feel that it has become essential to educate for citizenship, to help people realize the advantages of active, involved participation.

A number of studies have shown that people in many democracies, including the United States, know little about how their political systems work. For example, in a 1998 study of fourth-, eighth-, and twelfth-grade students in the United States, at least 30 percent of students scored below what was considered the basic level of information.[26] This lack of knowledge about how the system works, combined with a lack of knowledge regarding the issues, is considered dangerous to democracy, which has always been based on the assumption of an educated and informed populace. As a result of similar concerns in England, an Advisory Group on Citizenship was established; it issued a report in 1998— popularly known as the Crick Report after its Chair Sir Bernard Crick (b. 1929)— titled "Education for Citizenship and the Teaching of Democracy in Schools." This report suggested adding material on citizenship to the curriculum.[27] But Britain, like many Western democracies, has a national curriculum; whereas in the United States, such decisions are left up to either the states or local school boards, which makes the issue much more complicated.[28]

In the modern world, the knowledge and evaluative skills necessary to judge the issues might appear to require considerable formal education—and that is part of the current controversy. What constitutes an educated populace? On this

---

[26] U.S. Department of Education, Office of Educational Research and Improvement, National Center for Education Statistics, *The NAEP 1998 Civics Report Card for the Nation* (NCES 2000–457) by A. D. Lutkus, A. R. Weiss, J. R. Campbell, J. Mazzeo, and S. Lazer. Washington, DC: 1999. For specific information, see http://nces.ed.gov/nationalreportcard/civics/findings.asp/ or page x of the report. For a study, see Henry Milner, *Civic Literacy: How Informed Citizens Make Democracy Work.* Hanover, NH: Tufts University; published by the University Press of New England, 2002.

[27] The report can be seen at the website of the Qualifications and Curriculum Authority: http://www.qca.org.uk. In an e-mail message to me in October 2004, Professor Crick reported that Scotland is in the process of adopting similar provisions.

[28] For some comparisons among countries, see Derek Heater, "The History of Citizenship Education: A Comparative Outline," *Parliamentary Affairs* Vol. 55:3 (July 2002): 457–474; and Heather Marquette and Dale Mineshima, "Civic Education in the United States: Lessons for the UK," *Parliamentary Affairs* Vol. 55:3 (July 2002): 539–555.

question basic divisions exist. Some people believe that knowledge of how the government functions is sufficient. Others believe that formal education in the principles of democracy and how to evaluate arguments is necessary. Many positions between these are taken, with the only agreement in most democracies being that the educational system is not doing what it should. Although much has been said and written about the need to do something to ensure that citizens can cast an informed vote, little has actually been achieved.

In the United States, many people stress the right of parents to choose the sort of education they want their children to receive, including whether certain subjects are taught as part of the curriculum. The most famous U.S. legal case on this issue is *Wisconsin* v. *Yoder* (406 US 205 ([1972]), in which an Amish community in Wisconsin was exempted from sending their children to school beyond the elementary grades on the grounds that as members of their community, they did not need further education.

Today the issues center more around alternatives to public education, such as homeschooling (see the discussion in Chapter 9) and charter schools, in which parents choose significantly different educational patterns for their children. Charter schools originated in the 1980s and 1990s as a movement designed to improve elementary and secondary education by providing alternatives to public education as it currently existed; and charter schools have had support from both major political parties. Since Minnesota established the first one in 1991, some 3,000 such schools have been established with mixed results. A number failed quickly, some have shown potential to produce educational innovation, and many are producing the same results as the schools they were meant to replace. The political issue, and the issue for democracy, that charter schools and homeschooling raise is that of who will determine what education is appropriate to produce the next generations of informed citizens.

The Revival of the Initiative, Recall, and Referendum

The initiative, recall, and referendum were developed in the late nineteenth and early twentieth centuries to bring direct citizen participation into state and local politics. Initially they were used sparingly and then generally fell out of use almost completely. But in the late twentieth century, the initiative and referendum were revived, particularly on the West Coast, and were used by both citizen groups and corporations to put issues on the ballot to force the legislature to act. Some states see dozens of such measures on a ballot with a great deal of money spent supporting and, less often, opposing the proposals. The recall is used less often and rarely succeeds, but it has the power to change officeholders between regularly scheduled elections; this was shown in California in 2003, when a recall election removed one governor and replaced him with another.

It is difficult to judge the results of this revival. Citizens have been able to force legislatures to act when they had chosen not to; however, proposals are often presented in a deliberately misleading way, and the actual effects are difficult to determine. Also, the ability to fund a campaign may determine the result.[29]

---

[29] On the initiative today, see Richard J. Ellis, *Democratic Delusions: The Initiative Process in America*. Lawrence: University Press of Kansas, 2002.

National Security and Civil Liberties

A recurrent issue for democracy is the relationship between civil liberties and national security. Since the attacks on the United States in 2001, this issue has resurfaced, and Americans are deeply divided over how to balance the two, or even whether a balance is desirable. Some people believe that national security should take priority, but others believe that civil liberties should prevail.[30]

It is essential to understand both sides of this issue. Security is essential for democracy to function, so the case for national security is also a case for the full functioning of the democratic system. Civil liberties are, of course, an absolutely fundamental aspect of democracy. The problem is one of balance. National security must not be an excuse for destroying democratic institutions, and civil liberties must not be an excuse for allowing them to be destroyed.

The basic question is to what extent fundamental freedoms should be limited in the name of national security, and this is not the first time the United States has faced the issue. In fact, such concerns go back to 1798 and the "Alien and Seditions Acts," which Congress passed at the request of President John Adams (1735–1826) to give him the power to limit free speech, deport or imprison aliens, and make it harder to become a U.S. citizen. The real purpose of the acts was to limit the power of Adams's then political rival, Thomas Jefferson (1743–1826), who had the support of most new citizens—which illustrates the potential misuse of such laws.

The issue of limits on basic freedoms arises most often in connection with war, and examples of the limitations on freedom in the name of security can be found in the Civil War, World Wars I and II, the Korean War, the Vietnam War, and the first and second Gulf Wars. Two periods in which civil liberties were severely restricted in the name of national security, the Red Scare of the 1920s and the McCarthy era of the 1950s and 1960s, were not directly connected to wars.

In addition to legal restrictions, there is a fear factor; people limit their activities out of fear of reprisals, real or imaginary. I recall being told as an undergraduate during the end of the McCarthy era to never sign a petition if I ever wanted a government job, because my name would go on a list. It may or may not have been true, but it shows the way that fear can make people choose to limit the exercise of their freedoms even when such exercise is perfectly legal. Such statements are being made again today, and again it is difficult to know if there is any truth to them.

A specific issue is how free a press can be in a crisis. The British press was critical of the British government over Iraq and other issues; the U.S. press generally chose not to be critical and was even criticized worldwide for its unquestioning presentation of the official position. The choice to limit what is generally considered a major protector of freedom—a press willing and able to criticize and question government—is now being debated within the media and among citizens.

---

[30] See Helen Cothran, *National Security: Opposing Viewpoints.* Farmington Hills, MI: Greenhaven Press, 2004. A collection of brief essays on both sides of the issue. In addition, the Suggested Reading includes texts arguing for each side.

Democracy and Politics

In ancient Athens, citizens took lessons in rhetoric to learn how to persuade their fellow citizens in the legislative assembly. Thus, from the very beginning of democracy, the necessity to persuade, bargain, compromise, build coalitions, and so forth—in other words, to engage in politics—was understood. Today some people suggest that these processes are somehow not worthy of democracy, but others see them as the essence of the democratic process.

This division is not new. Aristophanes (c. 448/445–386/80 BCE) satirized the teachers of rhetoric, called *Sophists,* from which we get the word *sophistry,* meaning subtly deceptive reasoning or argumentation, as a people without a sense of right and wrong. American political vocabulary used to be full of descriptive terms and phrases: *log rolling* meant vote trading among legislators; *backstabbing* meant attacking an opponent, usually falsely; and the term *jumping on the bandwagon* meant attaching yourself to an obvious winner. Politics also governed the process by which the U.S. Constitution was developed, signed, and ratified—along with all the good and bad laws passed in all democratic countries.

Politics in a representative system provides the main vehicle for political participation, in that the choice of candidates and elections are decided through politics by the people who choose to participate; those who choose not to participate are in fact making a choice to leave the decision to others. We now use the more neutral phrase, "the political process," but it is the same thing; and those who shun "politics" are rejecting the way democracy works.

Certainly, politics can too often be "dirty". Well-timed lies and manufactured events have won elections. Money can be immensely influential, so much so that a significant part of a politician's job in the United States these days is raising money, day in and day out without end, and many people believe that this undermines democracy. Elections have been rigged, voting machines have been set to produce a predetermined outcome, the dead have voted, and the advent of computer voting has provided a field day for hackers.

Electronic Voting The continuing problem of ensuring that election results reflect the votes cast has moved on with the development of a number of systems of electronic voting. So far, such systems have frequently had counting errors, and we know that every system of voting tried so far—oral, paper ballot, voting machine, punch card, and electronic—has been vulnerable to manipulation; and so far no security system has proven invulnerable to hackers. Whether electronic systems will prove to be more or less subject to manipulation than earlier systems has yet to be determined, but since anyone with a computer and the knowledge might be able to get access to the system, the potential for greater vulnerability exists and must be guarded against.

Democracy and the Internet Quite a few people see the Internet as an essentially democratic space that has real potential for reviving democracy in the face of spreading apathy. Others see the Internet as an essentially anarchic space deeply antagonistic to democracy. As with so many opinions about the Internet, both are right. An excellent example of how both can be right at the same time is Wikipedia, which from moment to moment can, in one article, range from an excellent source of information—created by the collective efforts of many, even hundreds, of individuals—to a political or personal rant and back again. Those who run Wikipedia are being forced to be more directly involved and authoritarian to maintain the integrity of the information. Such participant systems are immensely popular, and sites such as YouTube and FaceBook have become places that millions of people visit, sometimes many times a day, to keep in touch with friends and make new ones. Such sites are also the haunt of pedophiles and other sexual predators and criminals seeking to steal identities. It has become clear that these sites, together with the mobile, have revived the sort of social networking that Putnam's *Bowling Alone* saw as having disappeared; but at the same time, anonymous peer-produced sites continue to foster social isolation.

The fact that governments keep trying to figure out ways to control the Internet suggests that they see it as a danger. At some time or other, most democratic governments have proposed regulating or controlling the Internet. Authoritarian governments have, with considerable success, worked the hardest to do so, often with the cooperation of companies. For example, Google and Yahoo both released names and other personal data to Chinese authorities, who used the information to punish dissidents; other companies, both in the U.S. and elsewhere, have assisted the Chinese government in censoring the writings of dissidents by removing the writings from websites. In addition, the "Great Firewall of China" blocks access to Internet sites not approved by the Chinese government; it operates on the basis of equipment knowingly provided by U.S. companies for that purpose.

On the other hand, the Internet has become almost uncontrollable and is effectively used by dissidents in many countries to post materials governments do not want seen, and the Internet has become one of the main locations for free speech and press. In addition to social networking spaces, blogs have done the most to enhance such freedoms. There are something like 100 million blog posts a day, with about a third each in English and Japanese; and the cultural differences between English and Japanese come through clearly. Although relatively few blogs are political, that still means thousands exist. English blogs are much more likely to be political than Japanese blogs, but political blogs can be found in most languages. Egypt and Syria, assisted by Internet companies, have jailed bloggers; China, Iran, Morocco, and South Korea—a democracy—have worked with companies to limit access to blogs and bloggers; and the U.S. military has tried, largely unsuccessfully, to limit the blogs of those serving in Iraq.

An interesting case is the use of the Internet by the Tamils in their conflict with the government of Sri Lanka. The Tamil Tigers, often called a terrorist group, are a secessionist movement that wants to establish a Tamil state they call "Eelam," which they believe to be the Tamil homeland. Eelam would be a long crescent on the east coast of Sri Lanka. A number of Tamil websites, including chat rooms, have been established to improve communications, and the Internet has become the main mechanism of public life for Tamils. One of the direct effects has been democratization of decision making, which has directly changed policy over time. Thus technology can both enhance democracy and limit it.

SUGGESTED READING

Classic Works

Bentham, Jeremy. *An Introduction to the Principles of Morals and Legislation* (printed 1780 but not published until 1789). J.H. Burns and H.L.A. Hart, eds. Oxford, England: Oxford University Press, 1996.

Berlin, Isaiah. *Liberty: Incorporating "Four Essays on Liberty."* Henry Hardy, ed. Oxford: Oxford University Press, 2002.

Burke, Edmund. *Reflections on the Revolution in France* (1790). Frank M. Turner, ed. New Haven, CT: Yale University Press, 2003. Includes essays on the text.

Dahl, Robert A. *A Preface to Democratic Theory.* Expanded ed. Chicago, IL: University of Chicago Press, 2006.

The Constitution of the United States of America (1787).

Declaration of Independence of the United States (1776).

Hamilton, Alexander, John Jay, and James Madison. *The Federalist Papers* (1787–1788). Isaac Kramnick, ed. New York: Penguin, 1987.

Locke, John. *Two Treatises of Government* (first edition dated 1690; probably written sometime between 1679 and 1682). Ian Shapiro, ed. New Haven, CT: Yale University Press, 2003. Includes essays on the text.

Macpherson, C. B. *The Real World of Democracy.* Oxford, England: Clarendon Press, 1966. Reprinted Oxford: Oxford University Press, 1997.

Mill, John Stuart. *On Liberty* (1859). David Bromwich and George Kateb, eds. New Haven, CT: Yale University Press, 2003. Includes essays on the text.

Montesquieu, Charles-Louis de Secondat. *De l'esprit des lois* (*The Spirit of the Laws;* 1748). Anne E. Cohler, Basia Carolyn Miller, and Harold Samuel Stone, trans. and eds. Cambridge, England: Cambridge University Press, 1989.

Rousseau, Jean-Jacques. *Du contrat social* (*The Social Contract;* 1762). Maurice Cranston, trans. New York: Penguin, 2004.

Wollstonecraft, Mary. *A Vindication of the Rights of Woman* (1792). Miriam Brody, ed. New York: Penguin, 2004.

Books and Articles

Abrams, Floyd. *Speaking Freely: Trials of the First Amendment.* New York: Viking, 2005. An argument for a robust freedom of the press illustrated through court cases in which the author participated.

Ackerly, Brooke A. "Deliberative Democratic Theory for Building Global Civil Society: Designing a Virtual Community of Activists." *Contemporary Political Theory* Vol. 5:2 (May 2006): 113–141.

Ackerman, Bruce A. *Before the Next Attack: Preserving Civil Liberties in an Age of Terrorism.* New Haven, CT: Yale University Press, 2006.

Alexander, Jeffrey C. *The Civil Sphere.* Oxford, England: Oxford University Press, 2006.

Alford, C. Fred. *Rethinking Freedom: Why Freedom Has Lost Its Meaning and What Can Be Done To Save It.* New York: Palgrave Macmillan, 2005.

American Democracy in an Age of Rising Inequality: Task Force on Inequality and American Democracy. Washington, DC: American Political Science Association, 2004. http://www.apsanet.org/ imgtest/taskforcereport.pdf. Accessed July 12, 2007. The January 2006 Vol. (40:1) issue of *Political Science & Politics* includes a number of essays discussing this report.

An-Na'im, Abdullahi Ahmed, ed. *Human Rights under African Constitutions: Realizing the Promise for Ourselves.* Philadelphia: University of Pennsylvania Press, 2003.

Barber, Benjamin R. *Strong Democracy: Participatory Politics for a New Age.* 20th anniversary ed. Berkeley: University of California Press, 2003.

Barry, Brian. *Culture and Equality: An Egalitarian Critique of Multiculturalism.* Cambridge, MA: Harvard University Press, 2001.

Baum, Bruce. *The Rise and Fall of the Caucasian Race: A Political History of Racial Identity.* New York: New York University Press, 2006. Minority rights.

Bay, Christian. *The Structure of Freedom.* Stanford, CA: Stanford University Press, 1958. Reprinted Stanford, CA: Stanford University Press, 1970. Stresses the importance of economic and psychological security for freedom.

Behrouzi, Majid. *Democracy as the Political Empowerment of the People: Direct-Deliberative e-Democracy.* Lanham, MD: Lexington Books, 2005.

Benhabib, Selya. *The Rights of Others: Aliens, Residents and Citizens.* Cambridge, England: Cambridge University Press, 2004. A symposium on this book with a response by Benhabib is in the *European Journal of Political Theory* Vol. 6:4 (October 2007): 397–462.

Benkler, Yochai, and Helen Nissenbaum. "Commons-based Peer Production and Virtue." *The Journal of Political Philosophy* Vol. 14:4 (December 2006): 394–419. Democracy and Web 2.0. Open-source software like Linux, Wikipedia, and other participant systems.

Bennett, W. Lance, Regina G. Lawrence, and Steven Livingston. *When the Press Fails: Political Power and the News Media from Iraq to Katrina.* Chicago, IL: University of Chicago Press, 2007.

Berg-Schlosser, Dirk, and Norbert Kersting. *Poverty and Democracy: Self-Help and Political Participation in Third World Cities.* London: Zed Books, 2003.

Bork, Robert H. *Coercing Virtue: The Worldwide Rule of Judges.* Washington, DC: AEI Press, 2003. Compares the Unites States with Canada and Israel.

Bork, Robert H., ed. *"A Country I Do Not Recognize": The Legal Assault on American Values.* Stanford, CA: Hoover Institution Press, 2005.

Boyte, Harry C. *Everyday Politics: Reconnecting Citizens and Public Life.* Philadelphia: University of Pennsylvania Press, 2004.

Breyer, Stephen. *Active Liberty: Interpreting Our Democratic Constitution.* New York: Vintage, 2005. The author is a current member of the U.S. Supreme Court.

Brown, Mark B. "Citizen Panels and the Concept of Representation." *Journal of Political Philosophy* Vol. 14:2 (June 2006): 203–225. Citizen juries, consensus conferences, and planning cells should be added to other forms of representation in deliberative democracy.

Burley, Justine, ed. *Dworkin and His Critics with replies by Dworkin.* Malden, MA: Blackwell, 2004.

Burnell, Peter J, ed. *Democratization Through the Looking-Glass.* Manchester, England: Manchester University Press, 2003. Reprinted, New Brunswick, NJ: Transaction Publishers, 2006. Democratization examined from a number of disciplinary perspectives and in a number of geographic areas.

Burns, James MacGregor. *Running Alone: Presidential Leadership—JFK to Bush II. Why It Has Failed and How We Can Fix It.* New York: Basic Books, 2006. The dangers of personal leadership.

Campbell, Tom. *Rights: A Critical Introduction.* London: Routledge, 2006.

Carter, Jimmy. *Our Endangered Values: America's Moral Crisis.* New York: Simon & Schuster, 2005. Argument for the separation of church and state specifically against his fellow Baptist co-religionists, who, he argues, have abandoned a fundamental tenet of their traditional beliefs.

Cheema, G. Shabbir. *Building Democratic Institutions: Governance Reform in Developing Countries.* Bloomfield, CT: Kumarian Press, 2005.

Chomsky, Noam. *Failed States: The Abuse of Power and the Assault on Democracy.* New York: Metropolitan Books/Henry Holt & Co., 2006. U.K. ed. London: Hamish Hamilton, 2006. Presents the United States as a failed state with a particular concern for the "democratic deficit" in the United States.

Connolly, William E. *Pluralism.* Durham, NC: Duke University Press, 2005.

Crick, Bernard. *Democracy: A Very Short Introduction.* Oxford, England: Oxford University Press, 2002.

Dahl, Robert A. *Democracy and Its Critics.* New Haven, CT: Yale University Press, 1989.

———. *How Democratic Is the American Constitution?* 2nd ed. New Haven, CT: Yale University Press, 2003.

———. *On Democracy.* New Haven, CT: Yale University Press, 1998.

———. *On Political Equality.* New Haven, CT: Yale University Press, 2006.

Dalton, Russell J. *Democratic Challenges, Democratic Choices: The Erosion of Political Support in Advanced Industrial Democracies.* Oxford, England: Oxford University Press, 2004.

Davis, Darren W. *Negative Liberty: Public Opinion and the Terrorist Attacks on America.* New York: Russell Sage Foundation, 2006.

De Feyter, Koen. *Human Rights: Social Justice in the Age of the Market.* Dhaka, Bangladesh: University Press/Bangkok, Thailand: White Lotus/Black Point, NS, Canada: Fernwood Publishing/Bangalore, India: Books for Change/Kuala Lumpur, Malaysia: SIRD/Cape Town, South Africa: David Philip/London: Zed Books, 2005.

DeParle, Jason. *American Dream: Three Women, Ten Kids, and a Nation's Drive to End Welfare.* New York: Viking, 2004. Argues that on the whole welfare reform has made little difference, with little real improvement but little demonstrable worsening either.

Dershowitz, Alan. *Rights from Wrongs: A Secular Theory of the Origin of Rights.* New York: Basic Books, 2004. Rights come from our experience with injustice and are discovered by trial and error. He applies this understanding to a number of current issues.

Diamond, Larry [Jay], and Leonardo Morlino, eds. *Assessing the Quality of Democracy.* Baltimore, MD: Johns Hopkins University Press, 2005. How to measure quality; includes case studies.

Diamond, Larry, Marc F. Plattner, and Philip J. Costopoulos, eds. *World Religions and Democracy.* Baltimore, MD: Johns Hopkins University Press, 2005.

Dierenfield, Bruce J. *The Battle over School Prayer: How* Engel v. Vitale *Changed America.* Lawrence: University Press of Kansas, 2007. For the case, see 320 US 421 (1962).

Donnelly, Jack. *Universal Human Rights in Theory and Practice.* 2nd ed. Ithaca, NY: Cornell University Press, 2003.

Dworkin, Ronald. *Justice in Robes.* Cambridge, MA: Belknap Press of Harvard University Press, 2006.

———. *Sovereign Virtue: The Theory and Practice of Equality.* Cambridge, MA: Harvard University Press, 2000. Argues there is no conflict between liberty and equality.

Feldman, Leonard C. *Citizens Without Shelter: Homelessness, Democracy, and Political Exclusion.* Ithaca, NY: Cornell University Press, 2004.

Fisher, Dana R. *Activism, Inc. How the Outsourcing of Grassroots Campaigns Is Strangling Progressive Politics in America.* Stanford, CA: Stanford University Press, 2006. An argument against the commercialization of grassroots campaigning, in which companies hire individuals to campaign rather than having campaigning by volunteers.

Fishkin, James S., and Peter Laslett, eds. *Debating Deliberative Democracy.* Malden, MA: Blackwell, 2003.

Fung, Archon. "Deliberation Before the Revolution: Toward an Ethics of Deliberative Democracy in an Unjust World." *Political Theory* Vol. 33:3 (June 2005): 397–419.

Fung, Archon, Mary Graham, and David Weil. *Full Disclosure: The Perils and Promise of Transparency.* Cambridge, England: Cambridge University Press, 2007.

Garry, Patrick M. *Rediscovering a Lost Freedom: The First Amendment Right to Censor Unwanted Speech.* New Brunswick, NJ: Transaction, 2006.

Gastil, John, and Peter Levine, eds. *The Deliberative Democracy Handbook: Strategies for Effective Civic Engagement in the 21st Century.* San Francisco, CA: Jossey-Bass, 2005.

Gheissari, Ali, and Vali Nasr. *Democracy in Iran: History and the Quest for Liberty.* Oxford, England: Oxford University Press, 2006.

Giacomello, Giampiero. *National Governments and Control of the Internet: A Digital Challenge.* London: Routledge, 2005.

Goldfarb, Jeffrey C. *The Politics of Small Things: The Power of the Powerless in Dark Times.* Chicago, IL: University of Chicago Press, 2006.

Goldman, Merle. *From Comrade to Citizen: The Struggle for Political Rights in China.* Cambridge, MA: Harvard University Press, 2005. Examines the beginnings of the process of opening up the political system.

Goldsmith, Jack, and Tim Wu. *Who Controls the Internet: Illusions of a Borderless World.* Oxford, England: Oxford University Press, 2006.

Greenwalt, Kent. *Religion and the Constitution. Volume 1: Free Exercise and Fairness.* Princeton, NJ: Princeton University Press, 2006.

Habermas, Jürgen. "Religious Tolerance— The Pacemaker for Cultural Rights." *Philosophy* Vol. 79:1 (January 2004): 5–18.

Halperin, Morton H., Joseph T. Siegle, and Michael M. Weinstein. *The Democracy Advantage: How Democracies Promote Prosperity and Peace.* New York: Routledge, 2005.

Hamilton, Marci A. *God vs. the Gavel: Religion and the Rule of Law.* Cambridge, England: Cambridge University Press, 2005. An argument that religion should not be used to protect individuals and institutions that have harmed others and that freedom of religion should not be treated as an absolute.

Hannay, Alastair. *On the Public.* London: Routledge, 2005. Discusses the nature of the "public" and the "public sphere."

Harris-Lacewell, Melissa Victoria. *Barbershops, Bibles and BET: Everyday Talk and Black Political Thought.* Princeton, NJ: Princeton University Press, 2004. BET (Black Entertainment Television) is a cable station

Harrison, Lawrence E. *The Central Liberal Truth: How Politics Can Change a Culture and Save It From Itself.* Oxford, England: Oxford University Press, 2006.

Hay, Colin. *Why We Hate Politics.* Cambridge, England: Polity, 2007. Argues that though people may have withdrawn from the formal political process, many are still involved in politics more broadly defined.

Held, David. *Models of Democracy.* 3rd ed. Cambridge, England: Polity, 2006.

Hewitt, Hugh. *Blog: Understanding the Information Reformation That's Changing Your World.* Nashville, TN: Nelson Books, 2005.

Holohan, Anne. *Networks of Democracy: Lessons from Kosovo for Afghanistan, Iraq, and Beyond.* Stanford, CA: Stanford University Press, 2005.

Honig, Bonnie. *Democracy and the Foreigner.* Princeton, NJ: Princeton University Press, 2001.

Hunt, Lynn. *Inventing Human Rights: A History.* New York: W. W. Norton, 2007.

Ivie, Robert L. *Democracy and America's War on Terror.* Tuscaloosa: University of Alabama Press, 2005. Argues that the war on terror is undermining democracy and that democracy is one of the most effective weapons against terrorism.

Jordan, Barbara. *Speaking the Truth with Eloquent Thunder.* Max Sherman, ed. Austin: University of Texas Press, 2007.

Kendall, Frances E. *Understanding White Privilege: Creating Pathways to Authentic Relationships Across Race.* New York: Routledge, 2006.

Keren, Michael. *Blogosphere: The New Political Arena.* Lanham, MD: Lexington Books, 2006.

Kornbluh, Felicia. *The Battle for Welfare Rights: Politics and Poverty in Modern America.* Philadelphia: University of Pennsylvania Press, 2007. History.

Kymlicka, Will. *Multicultural Odysseys: Navigating the New International Politics of Diversity.* Oxford, England: Oxford University Press, 2007. Discusses the problems that have arisen with the spread of what Kymlicka calls *liberal multiculturalism.*

Leib, Ethan. *Deliberative Democracy in America: A Proposal for a Popular Branch of Government.* University Park: Pennsylvania State University Press, 2004. Proposes a fourth branch of government to replace the initiative and referendum that would make laws using civic juries.

Lever, Annabelle. "Privacy Rights and Democracy: Contradiction in Terms?" *Contemporary Political Theory* Vol. 5:2 (May 2006): 142–162.

Lipset, Seymour Martin, ed. *The Encyclopedia of Democracy.* 4 vols. Washington, DC: Congressional Quarterly, 1995.

Lukacs, John. *Democracy and Populism: Fear & Hatred.* New Haven, CT: Yale University Press, 2006.

Lumumba-Kasongo, Tukumbi, ed. *Liberal Democracy and its Critics in Africa: Political Dysfunction and the Struggle for Social Progress.* Dakar, Senegal: Codesria Books in association with London: Zed Books and Pretoria, South Africa: University of South Africa Press, 2005.

Macedo, Stephen, et al. *Democracy at Risk: How Political Choices Undermine Citizen Participation and What We Can Do About It.* New York: Brookings Institution Press, 2005. Nineteen authors argue for more citizen involvement.

Magnette, Paul. *Citizenship: The History of an Idea.* Katya Lang, trans. Colchester, England: ECPR Press, 2005. Originally published in French in 2001.

McKinnon, Catriona. *Toleration: A Critical Introduction.* London: Routledge, 2006.

Meijer, Martha, ed. *Dealing with Human Rights: Asian and Western Views on the Value of Human Rights.* Oxford, England: WorldView Publishing/Bloomfield, CT: Kumarian Press, in association with The Netherlands Humanist Committee on Human Rights (HOM), 2001.

Modood, Tariq. *Multiculturalism: A Civic Idea.* Cambridge, England: Polity, 2007. An introduction to the subject.

Moreno-Riaño, Gerson, ed. *Tolerance in the Twenty-First Century: Prospects and Challenges.* Lanham, MD: Lexington Books, 2006.

Mouffe, Chantal. *On the Political.* London: Routledge, 2005. Argues that politics as a way of dealing with fundamental disagreements is still essential.

Mutua, Makau. *Human Rights: A Political and Cultural Critique.* Philadelphia: University of Pennsylvania Press, 2002. From an African perspective; sees human rights as a Western phenomenon.

Mutz, Diana C. *Hearing the Other Side: Deliberative versus Participatory Democracy.* Cambridge, England: Cambridge University Press, 2006.

Nelson, Samuel P[eter]. *Beyond the First Amendment: The Politics of Free Speech and*

Pluralism. Baltimore, MD: Johns Hopkins University Press, 2005.

Perlmutter, David D. *Blogwars: The New Political Battleground.* Oxford, England: Oxford University Press, 2008.

Phelan, Shane. *Sexual Strangers: Gays, Lesbians, and Dilemmas of Citizenship.* Philadelphia, PA: Temple University Press, 2001.

Pinello, Daniel R. *America's Struggle for Same-Sex Marriage.* Cambridge, England: Cambridge University Press, 2006.

Pinkney, Robert. *Democracy in the Third World.* 2nd ed. Boulder, CO: Lynne Rienner, 2003.

Pogge, Thomas. *World Poverty and Human Rights.* 2nd ed. Cambridge, England: Polity, 2008.

Polletta, Francesca. *Freedom is an Endless Meeting: Democracy in American Social Movements.* Chicago: University of Chicago Press, 2002.

Posner, Richard A. *Law, Pragmatism, and Democracy.* Cambridge, MA: Harvard University Press, 2003.

———. *Not a Suicide Pact: The Constitution in a Time of National Emergency.* New York: Oxford University Press, 2006. Based on his contention that constitutional rights are created by the justices of the Supreme Court, he argues that the courts must find a pragmatic balance between individual liberties and security.

Prothero, Stephen, ed. *A Nation of Religions: The Politics of Pluralism in Multireligious America.* Chapel Hill: University of North Carolina Press, 2006. Discusses, from a variety of perspectives, how the separation of church and state operates in a multicultural, multireligious U.S.

Putnam, Robert D. *Bowling Alone: The Collapse and Revival of American Community.* New York: Simon & Schuster, 2000.

Raaflaub, Kurt A., Josiah Ober, and Robert W. Wallace, with chapters by Paul Cartledge and Cynthia Farrar. *Origins of Democracy in Ancient Greece.* Berkeley: University of California Press, 2007.

Ringen, Stein. *What Democracy Is For: On Freedom and Moral Government.* Princeton, NJ: Princeton University Press, 2007. Seeks greater decentralization.

Roberts, Alasdair [Scott]. *Blacked Out: Government Secrecy in the Information Age.* Cambridge, England: Cambridge University Press, 2006.

Robin, Corey. *Fear: The History of an Idea.* New York: Oxford University Press, 2004.

Robinson, Mary. *A Voice for Human Rights.* Kevin Boyle, ed. Philadelphia: University of Pennsylvania Press, 2006.

Rodzvilla, John, comp. and ed. *We've Got Blog: How Weblogs Are Changing Our Culture. From the Editors of Perseus Publishing.* Cambridge, MA: Perseus Books, 2002.

Roosevelt, Kermit, III. *The Myth of Judicial Activism: Making Sense of Supreme Court Decisions.* New Haven, CT: Yale University Press, 2006.

Rosanvallon, Pierre. *Democracy Past and Future.* Samuel Moyn, ed. New York: Columbia University Press, 2006. Discusses the problem democracy is having with the "dissociation of legitimacy and trust" (p. 238).

Ross, Daniel. *Violent Democracy.* Cambridge, England: Cambridge University Press, 2004. Argues that democracy has historically been violent.

Roussopoulos, Dimitrios, and C. George Benello, eds. *Participatory Democracy: Prospects for Democracy.* Montréal: Black Rose Books, 2005. New edition of their *The Case for Participatory Democracy* (1970).

Santos, Bonaventura de Sousa, ed. *Democratizing Democracy: Beyond the Liberal Democratic Canon.* London: Verso, 2005. Participatory democracy throughout the world.

Schell, Jonathan. *The Unconquerable World: Power, Nonviolence, and the Will of the People.* New York: Henry Holt, 2003. An argument that peaceful responses to the world's problems are more effective than military ones.

Shelby, Tommie. *We Who Are Dark: The Philosophical Foundations of Black Solidarity.* Cambridge, MA: Belknap Press of Harvard University Press, 2005. Argues in favor of the continuing importance of black solidarity.

Snyder, R. Claire. *Gay Marriage and Democracy: Equality for All.* Lanham, MD: Rowman & Littlefield, 2006.

Soros, George. *The Age of Fallibility: The Consequences of the War on Terror.* New York: Public Affairs, 2006. U.K. ed. London: Weidenfeld & Nicolson, 2006. Argument for an open society and that the war on terror is creating a closed one.

Stout, Jeffrey. *Democracy and Tradition.* Princeton, NJ: Princeton University Press, 2004. Argument that liberal democracy needs space for religious arguments.

Sullivan, Shannon. *Revealing Whiteness: The Unconscious Habits of Racial Privilege.* Bloomington: Indiana University Press, 2006.

Sunstein, Cass R. *Laws of Fear: Beyond the Precautionary Principle.* Cambridge, England: Cambridge University Press, 2005. Argues against the too general application of the Precautionary Principle, which asserts that government should protect citizens against potential harms. Argues for the need to balance freedom and security.

———. *Republic.com 2.0.* Rev. ed. Princeton, NJ: Princeton University Press, 2007.

———. *Why Societies Need Dissent.* Cambridge, MA: Harvard University Press, 2003.

Tamanaha, Brian Z. *On the Rule of Law: History, Politics, Theory.* Cambridge, England: Cambridge University Press, 2004.

Thompson, Dennis F. *Restoring Responsibility: Ethics in Government, Business and Healthcare.* Cambridge, England: Cambridge University Press, 2005.

Tilly, Charles. *Democracy.* Cambridge, England: Cambridge University Press, 2007.

Trigg, Roger. *Religion in Public Life: Must Faith Be Privatized?* Oxford, England: Oxford University Press, 2007. An argument for religion in public life.

Urbinati, Nadia. *Representative Democracy: Principles and Genealogy.* Chicago, IL: University of Chicago Press, 2006. Principles of representation and some theorists of representation.

Vermeule, Adrian. "Submajority Rules: Forcing Accountability upon Majorities." *The Journal of Political Philosophy* Vol. 13:1 (March 2005): 74–98. Includes rules that allow a minority to force a recall or put an initiative on a ballot and a number of legislative rules that force broader consideration. Argues that for all their potential problems, such rules lead to greater accountability.

Villalón, Leonardo A., and Peter VonDoepp, eds. *The Fate of Africa's Democratic Experiments.* Bloomington: Indiana University Press, 2005. Describes the successes and failures of a number of countries.

Wacquant, Loïc. *Urban Outcasts: A Comparative Sociology of Advanced Marginality.* Malden, MA: Polity, 2008.

Wark, McKenzie. *A Hacker Manifesto.* Cambridge, MA: Harvard University Press, 2004.

White, Stuart. *Equality.* Cambridge, England: Polity, 2007. Key Concepts in the Social Sciences.

Williams, Melissa S., and Jeremy Waldron, eds. *Nomos XLVIII: Toleration and Its Limits.* New York: New York University Press, 2008.

Wuthnow, Robert. *America and the Challenges of Religious Diversity.* Princeton, NJ: Princeton University Press, 2005. Argues, based on detailed research, that Americans generally support religious diversity but know very, very little about any religion other than own.

Zukin, Cliff, Scott Keeter, Molly Andolina, Krista Jenkins, and Michael X. Delli Carpini. *A New Engagement? Political Participation, Civic Life and the Changing American Citizen.* New York: Oxford University Press, 2006.

Websites

Core documents of U.S. democracy: http://www.gpoaccess.gov/coredocs.html

Deliberative Democracy Consortium: http://www.deliberative-democracy.net

The Democracy Online Project: http://democracyonline.org

National Association of Evangelicals. For the Health of the Nation: An Evangelical Call to Civic Responsibility http://www.nae.net/images/civic_responsibility2.pdf

Public Interest Research Groups: http://www.uspirg.org

UN Office of the High Commissioner for Human Rights. International Human Rights Instruments: http://www.unhchr.ch/html/intlinst.htm

U.S. charter schools: http://www.uscharterschools.org

5

⚜

Capitalism, Socialism, and Democracy

To most citizens of North America, democracy and capitalism are so closely tied that the idea of an alternative seems foolish; to many citizens of other countries in other parts of the world, it is self-evident that democracy and socialism are the only possible partners. In the United States, the word *socialist* is so negative that using this word produces rejection of an idea without further discussion; in many countries the word *capitalist* has the same effect. To put it mildly, there has been much disagreement and misunderstanding exists concerning these two economic systems.

But these two systems also have much in common. Both democratic capitalists and democratic socialists believe that they can provide a good life for all if allowed to fully implement their beliefs. Both argue about power, who should have it, and what limits there should be on its exercise. And in the twenty-first century, both camps face many of the same issues, such as the problem of corporate and governmental bureaucracy and corporate and governmental corruption and the poverty that neither has been able to eliminate.

The discussion that follows is intended to clarify the meaning of *capitalism* and *socialism* and show why adherents of each claim to be the only true democrats. Thus the emphasis is on the arguments for and against capitalism and socialism as supportive of democracy. Both positive and negative arguments are presented, because in each case, much of the argument for one alternative is based on the argument against the other. Both capitalism and socialism can be found combined with democratic and authoritarian political systems; therefore it is particularly important to understand how both advocates and critics see their relationship to democracy.

DEMOCRATIC CAPITALISM

Only a few years ago, many thought that the argument between capitalism and socialism was over, with capitalism the victor. With the collapse of the authoritarian socialism called *communism,* capitalists had renewed confidence and proclaimed the free market as the savior of humankind. This left many of capitalism's defenders contending that the problems capitalism encountered had been the result of a loss of faith in the free market, rather than any inherent problem with the system. The resurrected belief in the free market made the whole argument much simpler than when most capitalists supported what they called the *mixed economy;* but it also simplifies and focuses the attack on capitalism, because the operations of the free market are the traditional point of attack.

The crisis brought about by subprime mortgage loans being offered to people with poor credit, a practice that depended on constant economic growth for its success, found bankers demanding that government provide greater regulation and pay for their losses, which suggests that the banks' faith in the free market has waned. On the whole, governments have complied with the demands of the bankers, because not doing so would make the crisis even worse and damage the world economy even more than it has already. But perhaps more important from the political viewpoint, people holding mortgages vote. No one yet (mid 2008) knows how much money is involved, what banks are at risk, and how many more people could lose their homes.

The Principles of Democratic Capitalism

Traditional capitalism, *free market capitalism,* or *laissez-faire capitalism,* is characterized by:

- Private ownership of property
- No legal limit on the accumulation of property
- A free market with no government intervention in the economy
- The profit motive as the driving force
- Profit as the measure of efficiency

The fundamental position as stated by Adam Smith (1723–1790), the Scottish economist and moral philosopher who is generally thought of as the intellectual father of capitalism, is that human beings are most effectively motivated by self-interest.[1] In economic terms, this means that individuals should be free (the free market) to pursue their interests (profit). The result should be the most efficient economic system, and, as a result, everyone will benefit. Goods will be produced that sell as cheaply as possible because, if they do not, someone else will step in and replace that manufacturer. Jobs will be created by entrepreneurs searching for a way to make a profit. The entire economy will be stimulated and grow, thus producing a higher standard of living for everyone, as long as the entrepreneur

---

[1] For an extensive history of the development of capitalism, see Fernand Braudel, *Civilization and Capitalism, 15th–18th Century,* 3 vols. New York: Harper & Row, 1982–1984.

is free to operate and can make a sufficient profit. Workers can choose to spend their money on consumer goods or, by saving, enter the competition by going into business for themselves. Some will fail, some will succeed, and some will succeed beyond all expectations. All commentators agree that capitalism tends to increase production; even Karl Marx (1818–1883), the founder of communism, said this. But critics of capitalism, like Marx, argue that the human costs are too high. Adam Smith argued that the human costs might at times be high but that these costs are clearly outweighed by the advantages. His description of the working conditions in a pin factory could easily have been written by an anticapitalist, but he contended that eventually even these workers would benefit.

The Mixed Economy A different model of capitalism, generally called the *mixed economy,* dominated in the middle years of the twentieth century. First, in the culmination of a trend that began in the late nineteenth century, government regulation of the economy was accepted. Regulation came about because, as the English economist John Maynard Keynes (1883–1946) argued and generally convinced other economists, depressions can be avoided by regulating the economy, specifically by using public expenditure to pump money into the economy and soak up excess unemployment. By doing this, prosperity for all without serious fluctuations—the so-called boom-and-bust cycle—could be virtually guaranteed.

Second, banks closed during the Great Depression, causing the loss of people's life savings, and pensions disappeared along with the companies that had provided them. These events left many people without the financial support they had counted on for their old age. As a direct result, government-administered retirement systems were established in most Western countries. In the United States this was the beginning of the Social Security system, which was initially

Library of Congress

Adam Smith (1723–1790) is best known as the author of *An Inquiry into the Nature and Causes of the Wealth of Nations* (1776), better known under the short title *The Wealth of Nations*. In *The Wealth of Nations*, Smith presented a history of economics in Europe, a description of manufacturing in his day, and, most important, a set of recommendations. The key argument is that individuals, each pursuing his or her own self-interest, will produce the greatest benefits for everyone. He applied this idea to the operations of the economic system and thereby became famous for providing the moral justification for, and part of, the intellectual foundation of capitalism.

designed to be self-supporting; monies paid in by employees and employers would accumulate and be paid out on retirement. The expansion of the program to most of the population, the expansion of benefits, and the rapid increase in the number of people who not only lived long enough to retire but then lived a long time after retirement combined to undermine the financial base of the system.

On the same principle that people should be protected from radical shifts in economic fortune, other programs were added. Countries varied in the speed and extent of expansion of such governmental intervention in the economy; the United States was probably the slowest economically developed democracy to add programs, and it added far fewer than most. In the United States most programs were established in the so-called War on Poverty during the presidency of Lyndon Johnson (1908–1973), from 1963 to 1969. These programs were then greatly expanded during the presidency of Richard Nixon (1913–1994), who succeeded Johnson in 1969 and served until 1974.

The argument for regulation makes the following points:

- The amount of property and money held by individuals directly affects the amount of money they spend.
- The amount individuals spend directly affects the amount any industry can produce.
- The amount industry can produce affects the number of people it can hire.
- The number of people industry can hire again affects the amount of money available to be spent by individuals for the products of industry.
- The number of products industry can produce affects its profit.

Therefore the argument is that some limitation on the amount of property or money that can be held by any individual helps, rather than hurts, the capitalist system, because it forces the money to circulate more widely. Thus even some strong supporters of capitalism argue that limited regulation is needed.

Some believe that even with regulation, capitalism tends to lead to too much conflict between owners or managers and workers; in Japan, corporations used to provide what were, in essence, lifetime contracts for workers. In return they expected the workers to have a real identification with the corporation. Some such contracts still exist, but the practice is no longer standard. In other Asian countries, such as Singapore, a free market is combined with an authoritarian political system that, although democratic in the sense that elections are held, regulates many details of daily life. For a time it was argued that the rapid growth of the economies of many Asian countries was the result of such modifications. Today, due to the strength of the Chinese economy, the argument is again being made.

A number of countries have tried to replace the conflict or adversary model of industrial relations that has dominated democratic capitalism with a model that sees management and labor as dependent on each other for success. Continuing attempts to modify that relationship have so far had only limited success, and avoiding conflict is also one goal of the corporatist or neocorporatist theory of democracy described in the previous chapter. Corporatists want workers and employers to join with government in ensuring the smooth running of the economy.

During the 1980s and 1990s, most Western countries reduced government regulation, cut back assistance and pension programs, and privatized parts of the economy that had been publicly owned or operated. The extent of economic regulation has clearly dropped, but many programs have proved immensely popular with citizens and are politically difficult or impossible to eliminate. And, as noted earlier, the first years of the twenty-first century have seen requests for a return to increased regulation from both capitalists and opponents of capitalism.

Capitalism and Democracy

For capitalists, democracy requires capitalism; they believe it supports the central democratic value of freedom. Capitalists also believe that freedom is based on private property, and capitalism, by stressing private property, makes economic freedom central. Capitalists also believe that economic freedom is a primary support for political liberty. Economic freedom means that everyone is free to enter the marketplace, accumulate property without limit, and use that property as they choose. Capitalists see two potential sources of control that must be blocked: monopolies and government. Monopolies, they believe, will always be temporary if the free market is allowed to operate; therefore, the real problem is government.

Free-market capitalists argue that any government regulation destroys the basis for the capitalist system and, hence, individualism and liberty. They contend that the free market helps create pluralism and diversity. The defenders of some government regulation—but not control—of the economy say that the absence of government regulation itself destroys the democratic capitalistic system, because a few people can control the economy, and even the government, through monopolies. Other negative effects of a lack of government regulation are sometimes mentioned, but the development of monopolies is the most important politically.

Monopolies The problem of monopolies was illustrated in the United States during the first growth of industrialism and particularly the great expansion of the railroads. Men like J. P. Morgan (1837–1913) virtually controlled the American economy and thereby the American government. This monopolistic tendency, some capitalists argue, destroys the capitalist system by radically limiting competition. The system is not competitive when only a few companies can set prices. Under such circumstances, few people with new ideas or approaches are able to try them out; it is not talent that succeeds in such a system but the monopolist's will. This situation does not fit the traditional myth of the capitalist system in which the clerk becomes corporation president by hard work. The clerk of a monopolist might become a corporate leader someday, but not necessarily by hard work: the key to success would be the whim of the monopolist.

The most important effect of monopoly, viewed from the perspective of democracy, is that the monopolist can control the government. Such control severely restricts the degree to which democracy can exist, because it might even negate the effect of popular participation in political decision making. President Dwight D. Eisenhower (1890–1969; president 1953–1961), in his farewell address, warned the American people about a military–industrial complex that he contended was close to ruling the United States through informal channels. Eisenhower was concerned about the close relationship between the military and the large industries that produced military goods under contract to the Pentagon. He was also concerned with the fact that many high-ranking officers "retired" after 20 years in the military to take jobs in the industries with which they had negotiated contracts and with which their former colleagues would be negotiating future contracts. He believed that these relationships and the growth of the sector of the economy providing goods to the military were leading to a dangerous concentration of economic and political power. This could happen even more readily under a monopolistic system.[2] Some limits have been put on both civil service and military retirees using the business connections they had developed in their previous situation during the first years after retirement, but the situation described by Eisenhower still exists.

Many capitalists believe that the competitive pressures of a truly free market will prevent the development of monopolies. They also believe that any monopoly that develops will not last long because of the same pressures. One reason monopolies are expected to collapse is that their dominance of the market will reduce their incentive to innovate or take risks. In these circumstances, people with new ideas and the risk-taking capitalist mentality will bring new goods to the market and undermine the power of the monopoly.

What might be called the problem of the near monopoly—such as with Microsoft and Google, who so dominate their areas of information technology that serious competition is difficult—has competitors asking for governmental regulation. Both the U.S. government and the European Union have regularly taken Microsoft to court over practices they consider monopolistic; but, win or lose, little change has resulted.

Economic theorists now argue that the free market does not in fact work the way that Adam Smith indicated, that human beings do not enter the market as rational actors intending to maximize profit but as human beings who allow a number of other factors to effect their behavior in the market. One of the founders of the field of behavioral economics, Daniel Kahneman (b. 1934), was awarded the Nobel Prize in Economics in 2002 for "having integrated psychological research into economic science."

Economic Freedom   Thus even within capitalism, the desired extent of economic freedom is the subject of debate. The basic premise is that capitalism allows more freedom for the individual than any other economic system. Any individual with sufficient interest and funds can buy stock in any number of companies. Stockholders become part owners of a company and can, if time and money permit, participate in some decisions of the company at annual meetings, although this opportunity is limited for the small shareholder.

And, as noted earlier, capitalists believe that capitalism provides greater political freedom than any other system. As Milton Friedman (1912–2006) put it, "The

---

[2] Some critics argue that this happened some time ago. See, for example, Paul A. Baran and Paul M. Sweezy, *Monopoly Capital: An Essay on the American Economic and Social Order.* New York: Monthly Review Press, 1966.

kind of economic organization that provides economic freedom directly, namely, competitive capitalism, also promotes political freedom because it separates economic power from political power and in this way enables the one to offset the other."[3] This separation can be compared to a checks-and-balances system such as that in the U.S. Constitution. Government power is limited by centers of economic power that also limit one another. These centers of economic power are in turn limited by government, which is also subject to regular elections. If both economic and political power are centralized in government, there is no check on the activities of government except through the vote.

The individual is free to enter the economic system subject to some government regulation and some limitation due to the existence of many large corporations. The individual succeeds or fails depending on his or her willingness to work hard and the desire of the consumer, manipulated to some extent by advertising, to buy the product. This is economic freedom and shows the relationship of capitalism to equality of opportunity. Every person should be able to become a capitalist and have the potential to get rich. Most small businesses actually fail, many are successful in that they continue as small businesses, and a few succeed exceptionally, like Microsoft and Google.

Equality of Opportunity To the extent that capitalists support equality, they mean equality of opportunity, because unless there is a real opportunity to work and to use one's talents to advance, the capitalist argument for economic and political freedom is less convincing.

Equality of opportunity was one motivation behind the development of welfare systems designed to ensure that no one is too severely hurt by economic competition. And the political purpose of welfare programs is to ensure that no one is excluded from full and equal citizenship, that all are in a position to participate politically. At their simplest level, welfare programs have been concerned with the aged, who have contributed to society but who may need help to provide for retirement when many costs, such as medical bills, tend to rise while incomes decline. Welfare systems also recognize that people who cannot provide for themselves can be a burden on society and human resources that could benefit society are wasted without some support being given to these people. Welfare programs have been quite successful in some places and on some dimensions, but as we will see, they have also had unintended and unexpected consequences.

Capitalism and Welfare In the mid-1990s, politicians in most developed democracies came to the conclusion that the systems designed to provide assistance to the poor had developed fundamental problems and were keeping people out of jobs, rather than helping them until they were in a position to enter or reenter the job market. Bolstered by a strong economy and a low unemployment rate, so-called welfare-to-work programs were implemented to force people into the job market by setting dates upon which their welfare payments would stop. In the United States, the states came up with a wide variety of such programs with

---

[3] Milton Friedman, *Capitalism and Freedom*. Chicago: University of Chicago Press, 1962: 9.

different dates for the cutoff, different job training programs, various incentives to get a job, and disincentives to stay on welfare. Initially these programs were huge successes, with large numbers of welfare recipients entering or reentering the workforce and welfare rolls dropping dramatically. But two problems have emerged, one expected, the other not planned for. The first is that some people on welfare have serious health problems, both mental and physical, or other issues that make it difficult to get or keep a job. The second problem is that the economy is no longer as strong, and many people recently hired off the welfare rolls are being fired, not through any fault in their job performance, but because companies are cutting back.

Criticism of Democratic Capitalism

Critics of capitalism focus on the extremes of wealth and poverty, the power over the political process that such wealth gives its owners, and the extreme inequality between employer and employee that exists under capitalism. Some of these points have also bothered defenders of capitalism. Other criticisms attack the institution of private property, the free market, and the profit motive. Recently there has been growing criticism of the inefficiencies found in most corporations, which would be called bureaucratic inefficiencies if referring to governments, and corruption, both petty and large enough to seriously damage big companies.

Results   There are two related issues in the criticism of capitalism's results: power and poverty. The power issue can be framed generally by asking how much power one person should have in a democratic society. Great wealth gives potential power in a political system, and critics assert that such wealth makes rule by the people impossible. Defenders of capitalism argue either that the rich are a minority, and therefore the majority can defeat them in an election, or that limited regulation can solve the problem. But the essence of the argument is that the benefits of capitalism outweigh any danger.

Great wealth appears to accompany extreme poverty. On a worldwide basis, the "extremely poor" are defined as those earning less that $1.08 per day, and the "poor" defined as those earning less than $2.16 per day.[4] Over one billion people live on less than a dollar a day. While the extreme poverty seen in these figures can be quite shocking, poverty is also relative; it depends in part on the cost of living in a particular place at a particular time and the perception of what is thought of as a normal standard of living. The "normal" life as shown on TV in the developed world makes the poverty of those who cannot afford "normal" feel more intense. And the growing disparity between the top, middle, and bottom can make even those who can afford the normal feel poorer. For example, in 2005, the real after-tax income of the top 1 percent in the U.S. rose almost $180,000, roughly three times the total income of those in the middle 20 percent, whose income rose about $400; the income of the bottom fifth rose about $200.

---

[4] See Abhijit V. Banerjee and Esther Duflo, "The Economic Lives of the Poor." *The Journal of Economic Perspectives* Vol. 21.1 (Winter 2007). http://econ-www.mit.edu/faculty/download_pdf.php?id=1346. Accessed February 10, 2008.

Critics of capitalism say that such extremes are inevitable in a capitalist system and are wrong; no one should be condemned to a life of poverty so that a few individuals can be rich. Defenders of capitalism reply either that poverty is the fault of the poor, who have not worked hard enough, or that poverty will be overcome through the economic growth that capitalism makes possible.

Most defenders of capitalism, and in the United States most people, believe the power of an employer over an employee to be simply in the nature of things. But critics of capitalism see this exercise of power as undemocratic and demeaning to the worker. In addition, many people believe that the power relationship between employer and worker fosters undemocratic attitudes, leading to authoritarianism in the employer and servility in the worker. This was clearly the case in Britain in the nineteenth and early twentieth centuries.

Private Property Critics of capitalism state that the private control of property used to manufacture and distribute goods is wrong, because it gives too much to a few people. Today the power of private property is obvious as many companies relocate their operations for various reasons. Critics contend that such factors as the effect on a community, the well being of employees, and the economic strength of a country should be taken into account in economic decision making. They usually argue that the creation of the value of property is social, not private; that is, it is created by groups of people working together, including those who invest, those who manage, and those who labor, all working within a structure of legal rules. Therefore social effects should outweigh the bottom line in decision making. Capitalists respond that if wealth is to be produced, they must consider their competitive situation first in any decision. Giving social factors precedence would make capitalists uncompetitive and ultimately force them out of business to the detriment of all concerned.

The Profit Motive Capitalists believe that the profit motive drives people to succeed and create wealth; their critics argue that, even if true, it is wrong. They assert that the competition fostered is personally and socially unhealthy. Capitalists reply that competition is natural and healthy, both personally and socially, and that it is the major source of effort and excellence.

The Free Market Critics of capitalism argue that there is no such thing as a free market and that the whole point of business activity is to control or dominate the market, not compete freely in it. They also say that the free market, to the extent there is one, is inefficient. Capitalists, of course, state that a free market either exists or could in most circumstances, and that such a market is the only truly efficient mechanism for producing and distributing goods.

Inefficiency Capitalism prides itself on being more efficient than public ownership, and today privatization is defended as obviously more efficient than leaving activities in public hands. But this is not necessarily the case. The cartoon strip *Dilbert*, which is extremely popular among people working in private enterprises, is almost always about the inefficiencies brought about by poor management. It is, of course, a cartoon strip and thus exaggerated, but it reflects the reality of most large organizations, both private and public. Efficiency in capitalism is in fact defined very narrowly in terms of how much money is made, not now much money could have been made if the company was internally efficient. The ideology says that an inefficient enterprise will be replaced by a more efficient one; that may be true in the long run, but if all enterprises are internally inefficient, huge resources are wasted.

Corruption Part of the inefficiency of corporations is due to what might be called *petty corruption*. All enterprises spend a lot of money trying to ensure that expense accounts are reasonably honest, which they clearly would not do if they could expect employees to file honest ones. While fiddling of expense accounts is a standard joke, it is in fact theft from the company and ultimately from the shareholders.

The corruption that makes the news is the corruption that threatens the existence of companies, like that which destroyed Enron and recently threatened the existence of the large French bank *Société Générale*. Both inefficiency and corruption are part of the critique of socialism made by capitalism, so it is important to recognize that the problems are not entirely on one side.

As can be seen, the disagreements are fundamental. They will come up frequently in succeeding pages, particularly because the same issues are often involved in the discussion of socialism.

DEMOCRATIC SOCIALISM

The word *socialism* refers to *social* theories rather than to theories oriented to the individual. Because many communists now call themselves *democratic socialists,* it is sometimes difficult to know what a political label really means. As a result, *social democratic* has become a common new label for democratic socialist political parties.

The Principles of Democratic Socialism

Democratic socialism can be characterized as follows:

- Much property held by the public through a democratically elected government, including most major industries, utilities, and transportation systems
- A limit on the accumulation of private property
- Governmental regulation of the economy
- Extensive publicly financed assistance and pension programs
- Social costs and the provision of services added to purely financial considerations as the measure of efficiency

Publicly held property is limited to productive property and significant infrastructure; it does not extend to personal property, homes, and small businesses. And in practice in many democratic socialist countries, it has not extended to many large corporations.

Socialism has a long history, which some advocates like to trace back to biblical sources. It is more accurate to see socialism as originating in response to the excesses of early industrial capitalism; but many socialists, particularly those calling themselves Christian socialists, found their inspiration in the New Testament.

Still, the origins of contemporary democratic socialism are best located in the early to mid-nineteenth century writings of the so-called utopian socialists, Robert Owen (1771–1858), Charles Fourier (1772–1837), Claude-Henri Saint-Simon (1760–1825), and Étienne Cabet (1788–1856). All these writers proposed village communities combining industrial and agricultural production, owned, in varying ways, by the inhabitants themselves. Thus the essence of early socialism was public ownership of the means of production. These theorists also included varying forms of democratic political decision making, but they all distrusted the ability of people raised under capitalism to understand what was in their own best interest.

Karl Marx, discussed in detail in Chapter 8, rejected these early socialists and developed his own version of socialism, which he called *communism*. There is considerable controversy among scholars regarding Marx's own attitude toward democracy, but two lines of thought developed from Marx: one emphasizing democracy and one, the dominant line, rejecting it. However, other socialists rejected Marx, and later in the century two American writers, Edward Bellamy (1850–1898) and Henry George (1839–1897), produced versions of public ownership with what they saw as democratic control, although again both placed some limitations on democracy. In his last work, *Equality* (1897), Bellamy dropped most of those limitations.

In Britain a form of socialism developed, called *Fabian Socialism*—now embodied in the Fabian Society—that emphasizes the democratic elements of democratic socialism: electoral success, the rational presentation of their position (in innumerable publications), careful study of the current social situation, and gradualism.

Since that time many democratic socialist political parties, such as the Labour Party in the United Kingdom and the Social Democratic Party in Sweden, have been elected to office, been defeated and left office, and later returned to office or remained in opposition. The best-known adherents of this position have been Willy Brandt (1913–1992) of Germany, Olof Palme (1927–1986) of Sweden, and Michael Harrington (1928–1989) of the United States. Recently, five socialists have been elected to the presidency of countries in South America. Three of them—Luíz Inácio Lula da Silva (b. 1945) of Brazil, elected in 2002; Tabare Vazquez (b. 1940) of Uruguay, elected in 2004; and Álvaro Colom Canalleros (b. 1951) of Guatemala, elected in 2007—are clearly democratic socialists. The fourth, Evo Morales (b. 1959) of Bolivia, is an Aymara Indian, elected in 2006. His party is called the Movement Toward Socialism, and his credentials as a democrat have been questioned by some. The fifth, Hugo Chavez (b. 1954) of Venezuela, elected in 1998, is a controversial figure; and although he has been forced to back down on some of his proposals, he has become more authoritarian. In all five cases, their campaigns succeeded in part due to the electorates' unhappiness with the extent of poverty in their countries, poverty that was successfully portrayed as the result of the operations of the free market.

If one assumes citizens should control their political lives and contribute to political decision making, it is only a short step to the democratic socialist argument that citizens should have some say in economic decision making. There is no question that economic decisions in connection with, for example, an automobile manufacturing industry—or, as has recently been seen, banking—have a tremendous impact on an entire country. Therefore, say democratic socialists, there must be some means for the people to oversee such economic decisions through their elected representatives. But what economic decisions are significant? What are key industries for a national economy? Democratic socialists argue that elected representatives of the people should answer these questions and that the answers are likely to vary from country to country. In addition, the forms of governmental control and regulation and the extent of public ownership of industry will vary depending on the decisions made by the elected representatives of the people, checked at the polls by the people themselves.

Another rationale for democratic socialism, perhaps the most appealing one, is what might be called the *humanitarian argument*. Democratic socialists believe that only when the people control the economic system will solutions to basic social problems, such as hunger and disease, be possible. Only under democratic socialism can the people insist on solutions; therefore, they argue, democratic socialism is essential to overcome the most basic problems of society.

When we say the public holds much property, this refers to property crucial to the functioning of the economic system. It does not mean there is no private property. For example, in Sweden, which most Americans think of as a socialist country, few major industries are governmentally owned. Some democratic socialists, theorists, and systems do not limit the amount of private property that can be held by an individual, but most do. There is no necessity within democratic socialist theory for such limitations. On the other hand, most approaches suggest some degree of income redistribution and thereby justify limited private property.

Paulo Fridman /Corbis

Luíz Inácio Lula da Silva (b. 1945) is the President of the Federative Republic of Brazil. Known in Brazil as "Lula," originally a nickname that he added to his legal name, he was a union organizer and strike leader. In 1980 the *Partido dos Trabalhadores* (PT) or Workers' Party was formed, and in 1986 da Silva was elected to congress. He has run for president in every election since 1989 and was elected in 2002 after campaigning from a somewhat more centrist position than he had previously taken.

Socialism and Democracy

The fundamental assumption underlying democratic socialism is that participation in political decision making should be extended to include economic decision making. Democratic socialists say that because the economy and politics are so closely intertwined, voters should be able to control their economic futures through the government they elect. Such voter control presupposes government's ability to control much of the economy through ownership or regulation of its most important parts.

The government of a democratic socialist system regulates the part of the economy it does not own directly. This regulation is designed to ensure that privately owned businesses operate in the best interest of society as a whole rather than simply for private profit. This point illuminates the ethos of democratic socialism.

In addition to the democratic proposition proclaimed in the basic assumption outlined earlier, democratic socialism suggests that liberty cannot be maintained without economic security. This argument resembles the democratic capitalist argument for welfare as a means of attaining equality of opportunity, but it is broader in that it demands more than equality of opportunity. The democratic socialist says neither the right to vote nor any other form of liberty is possible unless every person within the society is economically secure. If insecure, citizens will be incapable of exercising personal liberty. Such economic security is possible, it is argued, only with an extensive welfare system.

Welfare The typical democratic socialist welfare system includes an extensive medical care system, which is provided either free or at minimal cost and usually includes prenatal care, dental care, and eye examinations, in addition to more typical health services. Access to alternative medical practitioners and procedures like acupuncture or homeopathic treatment was not originally included in most countries but is now being added in some places. An obvious practical rationale for a wide-ranging health care system is that a healthy individual can contribute more to society than a sick one. Therefore, it is to the advantage of society to ensure the health of all. This is the fundamental rationale of any welfare system—an individual who is maintained at the minimum level of life can contribute to society. The welfare system also takes care of those who have already contributed to society and cannot care for themselves. Thus the welfare system provides money for food, housing, and other minimum necessities.

The Problem of Bureaucracy Bureaucracy presents one of the greatest problems for democratic socialism. Whether in business or government, it is difficult for a bureaucracy to be as well informed or as responsive to the needs of the people or industry it serves as would be ideal. Because bureaucracies are not directly responsible to the people, many argue that a large bureaucracy threatens the public control that the democratic socialist is trying to preserve. In democratic capitalism the economy is controlled privately, therefore powerful people are not directly accountable to the electorate. In democratic socialism bureaucrats who are not directly accountable to the electorate replace these people. In addition, because bureaucrats remain while politicians and governments change, it is not unusual for the bureaucrats to follow their own policies rather than those of the elected representatives.

This problem is fundamental to the nature of a bureaucracy. Bureaucracies administer laws (rules) established by the normal processes of legislation. These rules are applied equally, or in the same way, to all people, even though people differ. Attempts to allow flexibility generally produce charges of favoritism, corruption, discrimination, and other forms of illegality. Quite simply, flexibility seems to undermine the equal application of rules, even though that equal application may seem unfair. Thus bureaucracy raises a problem: How can rules be applied unequally but fairly? Laws are rules, and rules by their nature are supposed to apply to everyone in the same way. People are different, and they have different needs. How can a bureaucracy do its job in these circumstances?

We have seen how democratic socialism often faces the same problems for which it criticizes democratic capitalism. Still, the democratic socialist argues that people control the bureaucracy through their elected representatives and that the government can immediately change the operations of the bureaucracy when it becomes cumbersome or ineffective. Democratic capitalists counter that under capitalism, people control the economic system through the market.

Most university students will be familiar with how inefficient bureaucracies can be. While their purpose is to provide a service to both the institution and the students, such bureaucracies appear to inevitably develop rules and regulations that benefit the bureaucracy rather than those they are intended to serve. In this they are just like governmental and corporate bureaucracies. The novel *The Castle* (1926, English translation 1930) by Franz Kafka (1883–1924) effectively describes someone caught in the meshes of a bureaucracy.

Many countries, both democratic socialist and democratic capitalist, have instituted an *ombudsman*—the word derives from a Swedish term for *deputy*, or *representative*—who hears and investigates complaints about a bureaucracy. Sometimes the ombudsman is empowered to make sure the causes of the complaints are corrected. Of course, elected representatives, particularly in the United States, also play this role.

Democratic countries recognize the problem of bureaucracy and have attempted to correct it. At the same time, the relatively independent nature of a bureaucracy may provide some protection for liberty. One agency may force another to respond better than it would on its own. Thus conflicts among parts of the bureaucracy may have a positive result.

Criticism of Democratic Socialism

Critics of democratic socialism have two basic arguments focusing on the destruction of the free market and the centralization of power. Although many socialists now accept "market socialism," a phrase that democratic capitalists see as a contradiction in terms, critics contend that the free market of competitive capitalism is essential for the efficient production and distribution of goods. Socialists have found that a limited market is more efficient and better able to respond to consumer demands than completely centralized regulation and, they argue, it is more fair than a completely unregulated market.

In a related criticism, opponents of socialism say that interference with the free market through government ownership and regulation puts too much power in the hands of government. This, they contend, leads inevitably to even greater centralization of power and the destruction of democracy. A more limited version of the same argument suggests that even if democracy is not destroyed, freedom will necessarily be limited in a democratic socialist regime. Democratic socialists respond that the electoral process is capable of checking any such tendency if it does occur, but they see no reason that it should.

Related to both criticisms is the question of what motivates the socialist bureaucrat. As we saw, the capitalist believes that human beings are motivated by self-interest, or the profit motive. Self-interest, capitalists argue, will always make socialism unworkable. The socialist argues that the bureaucrat is motivated by the desire to serve. The capitalist laughs. The socialist responds that while the profit motive—the socialist might call it "greed"—may be necessary under capitalism, socialism makes it possible to be motivated by a desire to serve the public.

As much distance exists between socialism and its critics as between capitalism and its critics. But both socialists and capitalists are making the same claim: each group contends that it is best for democracy.

Market Socialism

Market socialism is the most significant addition to the vocabulary of democratic socialism in many years. Supporters of market socialism accept the democratic capitalist argument that centralized economic power is inefficient, and they agree with democratic capitalists that markets promote greater freedom. But market socialists contend that democratic capitalism places power in the hands of the rich and that large corporations are as inefficient as large government. They contend that such large corporations can function only by controlling the market and, therefore, that regulated markets protect the weak, prevent monopolies, and produce markets at least as free as those under unregulated democratic capitalism.

In addition, market socialists insist that a functioning welfare system must protect people from the inevitable shifts of a market economy. Thus market socialists have not abandoned the principles of democratic socialism but have moved in the direction of a mixed economy with variously owned enterprises—private, public, worker, and cooperative—competing within a regulated market.[5]

Developmental Socialism

Economic systems have been developed that are neither capitalist nor communist. The most original such creation has been called *African socialism* and *communitarian socialism* but is best known as *developmental socialism*. It originated in the work of Julius Nyerere (1922–1999) of Tanzania; Léopold Sédar Senghor (1906–2001) of Senegal; U Nu (1907–1995) of Myanmar, formerly Burma; and India's Vinoba

---

[5] The classic studies of market socialism, predating the current interest in it, are Oscar Lange and Fred M. Taylor, *On the Economic Theory of Socialism,* Benjamin E. Lippincott, ed. Minneapolis: University of Minnesota Press, 1938; New York: McGraw-Hill, 1964; and Alec Nove, *Efficiency Criteria for Nationalised Industries.* London: George Allen & Unwin, 1974.

Bhave (1895–1982); and it stresses social solidarity and cooperation as the means of developing the economy. Developmental socialism also emphasizes the establishment of a network of close social and economic ties to help form national identity.

A good illustration of the basic idea of developmental socialism is found in the Swahili word Nyerere uses for socialism, *ujamaa*—familyhood. As he put it, "The foundation, and the objective, of African socialism is the extended family."[6] The extended family—consisting of a wide range of relatives who work cooperatively and share all family resources—is the model for village and tribal socialism. All members of the village are fed, clothed, and housed as well as the group can afford. The aged and the ill are supported. Developmental socialism explicitly rejects the class divisions of communism. All are workers, and there is little or no tradition of an indigenous exploiting class.

In Nyerere's socialism all people must recognize that they are part of a single group working together to achieve a common end. This end is designed to achieve economic security and human dignity by changing the distribution system. "There must be something wrong in a society where one man, however hardworking or clever he may be, can acquire as great a 'reward' as a thousand of his fellows can acquire between them."[7] A cardinal principle in Nyerere's socialism reflects the fact that in traditional African society, as in Native American societies, land could not be owned, only used. But developmental socialism failed due to corruption, particularly the misuse of power by bureaucrats and politicians for personal benefit, internal conflicts, and changing world economic conditions.

The Third Way

Just as the phrase *Third World* was coined to refer to countries trying to find a position between capitalist and communist countries, *Third Way* refers to the attempt to find a place between capitalism and socialism.[8]

Generally, socialists condemn the Third Way as capitalism, and capitalists condemn it as socialism; but what it tries to suggest is that the economy cannot operate effectively under either the free market or state control, however democratically those state controllers have been elected. Thus it has affinities with market socialism, but it is often not socialist enough for supporters of market socialism. It also has affinities with the mixed economy of capitalism, but it is often not capitalist enough for supporters of the mixed economy. The essence of the Third Way is clearly to be *both* capitalist and socialist, to have both a strong state with a strong public sphere and a strong market economy. As this suggests, the Third Way is rather undefined, and perhaps it is best thought of as taking the position that policy should be based on what works to achieve the desired goal; and Third Way politicians pride themselves in being pragmatists.

---

[6] Julius K. Nyerere, *Ujamaa: Essays on Socialism*. Dar Es Salaam, Tanzania: Oxford University Press, 1968: 11.

[7] Nyerere, *Ujamaa*, 3.

[8] The phrase is most associated with Anthony Giddens (b. 1938). See his *The Third Way: The Renewal of Social Democracy*. London: Polity Press, 1998; *The Third Way and Its Critics*. London: Polity Press, 2000; and the collection he edited, *The Progressive Manifesto: New Ideas for the Centre-Left*. Cambridge, England: Polity, 2003.

Third Way theorists also take seriously the welfare function of the state. They generally argue that the state should focus on working women, preschool children, and children in single-parent households. They also argue for universal day care, improved health care, and greater work flexibility. All these policies, it is felt, require state implementation.

ECONOMIC DEMOCRACY

Many people from different ideological perspectives have consistently raised the question of the degree to which democratic approaches can be applied to various aspects of the economy. For example, in many experiments—some successful, some not—companies have been owned and democratically operated by their workers. This means that the workers set policy and hire and fire management. Such businesses are operating successfully in many Western countries, including, most notably, Spain and the United States.

A growing trend is for workers in a company to own a substantial share of the stock with the company run by a board of directors and managers, much like any other company. This is not an example of economic democracy unless the workers actively make decisions that give them significant authority.

The argument for economic democracy is the same as that for political democracy outlined in the previous chapter. Robert A. Dahl (b. 1915) has weighed the theoretical arguments for and against economic democracy in *A Preface to Economic Democracy* (1985). He concludes, "A system of self-governing enterprises would be one part of a system of equalities and liberties in which both would, I believe, be stronger, on balance, than they can be in a system of corporate capitalism."[9]

COOPERATION

Cooperation, a significant economic movement of long standing that some adherents relate to democratic capitalism and others to democratic socialism, is having a recent revival after a temporary decline in interest. Cooperation takes two forms: producer cooperatives and consumer cooperatives, and some include both. Both are well known and exist throughout the world, although today they are probably most common in the Third World. A third form, the housing cooperative, is currently most visible in the cohousing movement and is discussed in the next section. In all forms of cooperation, decision making within the cooperative is democratic, usually as direct involvement based on majority rule, although some cooperatives use consensual systems. Larger operations have representative systems with representatives checked by regular meetings of the entire membership.

A *consumer cooperative* is a group of people who form a nonprofit organization to purchase goods in large quantities. Thus they can pass on the savings from the bulk purchase, eliminate some levels of distribution, and not add profit

---

[9] Robert A. Dahl, *A Preface to Economic Democracy.* Berkeley: University of California Press, 1985.

to the price. If goods are sold to nonmembers, any profit made by the coopera-tive is distributed to the members.

A *producer cooperative* is a group of people who form an organization to pro-duce and distribute goods, usually under the management of the workers. Profits are distributed among the workers. Agricultural cooperatives usually involve the processing and distribution of goods together with the joint purchase of expensive equipment but do not normally involve the joint ownership of land. Producer cooperatives frequently establish cooperative financial institutions such as banks, credit unions, and insurance agencies.

Consumer cooperation originated in 1844 with the Rochdale Society of Equitable Pioneers in England. The Rochdale Pioneers, as they are known, estab-lished a series of basic principles that cooperatives, with some updating, still fol-low. These principles include open membership; one member, one vote; limited rate of return on equity capital; surplus returned to the members or reinvested in the business; continuous education; and cooperation among cooperatives.

COMMUNAL LIVING

Communes, now known as *intentional communities,* are generally thought of as a phenomenon of the sixties, but they have experienced a revival. Many communi-ties founded in the sixties are at least 40 years old, and others are being founded regularly. Many are religious communities in which people join to practice a particular religious way of life; but in many secular communities, the appeal is communal life itself. A subset of these communities that bridges the gap between democratic capitalism and democratic socialism is *cohousing.* The rapidly grow-ing cohousing movement establishes communities in which the dwellings are individually owned but in which there are community-owned land and build-ings, where communal interaction is encouraged architecturally and culturally, and where decision making is democratic. Cohousing is both urban and subur-ban and is a recent development of cooperative housing, which was primarily an urban phenomenon.[10]

CURRENT TRENDS

Most current issues affect both democratic capitalism and democratic socialism.

Corruption   Corruption undermines both capitalism and socialism and is not hard to find in most countries. Capitalists argue that the free market will root out corruption or that limited regulation will uncover it. Socialists argue that

---

[10] For directories to such communities, see Sarah Bunker, Chris Coates, and Jonathan How, eds. *Diggers & Dreamers: The Guide to Communal Living 2008/2009.* London: Diggers and Dreamers Publications, 2007; and *Communities Directory: A Comprehensive Guide to Intentional Communities and Cooperative Living. 2007 Edition.* 5th ed. Rutledge, MO: The Fellowship for Intentional Community, 2007.

regulation and political oversight will root out corruption. Both are right. Because corruption is continually being uncovered, there is a good chance that it is more common than we know. Both capitalists and socialists argue that corruption is inevitable in the other system due to the power given to either the wealthy or the bureaucrats. Given the degree of corruption, both may be right, so the question becomes how to ensure that it does not do much damage.

Poverty According to the International Monetary Find (IMF), the richest 20 percent of the world's population controls over 80 percent of the world's gross domestic product (GDP), and the poorest 20 percent has less than 1.5 percent; the poorest 60 percent of people have only about 7 percent of world GDP. An even more striking statistic is that the richest four people (men) in the world have greater wealth than the poorest seventy-two countries combined. The GDP of those countries is almost $96 billion; the net worth of the four richest men is almost $97 billion.

Poverty is a significant issue throughout the world, and extreme differences between the rich and poor, in both income and power, can undermine support for any economic system. The poorest of the poor tend to be located in the Third World, and a number of proposals have been made to help these countries. One common suggestion is to forgive the debt of the poorest countries; but although canceling the debt would give the countries a second chance, it would not address the underlying causes, which range from corruption to a poorly educated workforce to a lack of resources. Solving the problem will require active investment in education and infrastructure, not simply canceling debt.

One of the difficult issues for capitalism is how to approach such intractable issues as poverty at home and abroad. The establishment of welfare systems in capitalist countries is one of the answers. But one of the other answers, reinforced by all religions, is charity, which ranges from a personal donation to a local activity to the large-scale activity usually called *philanthropy*. Such giving is not only directed at difficult social problems, such as poverty, but includes donations to art galleries, symphony orchestras, university buildings and programs, and a wide range of other institutions. But the politically important aspect of charity/philanthropy is that directed at social issues. Examples of such philanthropists include Andrew Carnegie (1835–1919), who used the money he made in the steel industry to build public libraries throughout the world and established the Carnegie Endowment for International Peace—which still exists—in 1910 to promote world peace. The Ford Foundation, which also still exists, was founded by the Ford family in 1936 to promote world peace and reduce poverty.

Today the best-known philanthropic foundation is the Bill and Melinda Gates Foundation, which targets health and extreme poverty, particularly in Africa, and in the United States focuses on education and access to information technology. The Gates Foundation was radically increased in size in 2006 when Warren Buffett (b. 1930) donated stock worth, at the time, over $30 billion spread over a number of years to the Foundation. Therefore at present the Foundation spends, for example, roughly the same amount each year on world health as the World Health Organization.

Such foundations benefit from significant tax benefits (they may be tax exempt, and donations are to a large extent tax deductible in some countries, such as the United States). Therefore foundations' activities are to a degree subsidized by and regulated by governments. For example, in the United States, such organizations are required to spend at least 5 percent of their assets each year. Unlike the foundations established by Carnegie and the Fords, the Gates have announced that all assets are to be spent within 50 years of their deaths, and the Buffett donation required that the money donated be given away within a year of receiving each year's donation.

Because such foundations involve themselves in areas in which governments are also involved, they are inevitably controversial, particularly when, like the Gates Foundation, they spend more money than the governments. Support or opposition tends to depend on whether or not a person approves or disapproves of what the foundations are trying to do and how they go about it. For example, no one opposes better health, but do you try to achieve such a desirable goal by supporting the spread of private medicine or public health services? How much money actually ends up directly improving lives, rather than in administrative costs, corruption, and waste, is always an issue; but the same issue exists with government programs. Some foundations are better than governments at controlling such issues, but some are worse.

Given the size of philanthropic organizations today,[11] they are being criticized from both the Left and Right, with capitalists arguing that they distort the free market and socialists arguing that they undermine successful public programs and that the charity is simply a mask for the pursuit of profit. Particularly when, as in some African countries, foundations have more money to spend than the national government has, they can either undermine or support the democratic process.

Fordism and Post-Fordism

All economic systems are undergoing a transition from Fordism, named after Henry Ford (1863–1947), which features assembly-line mass production and consumption, to post-Fordism, which relies on flexible production, automation and information technology, niche marketing, just-in-time-delivery, and globalization (discussed in Chapter 3). Some critics of post-Fordism stress the degree to which this approach entails a reorganization of the labor market that requires more part-time work, subcontracting or outsourcing, offshoring, and the need to break labor unions.

Fordist systems still exist throughout the world, but much production has been shifted from the First to the Third World, where labor is cheaper; and such offshoring is an aspect of post-Fordist systems. But post-Fordist production is clearly becoming the norm, and this worries both capitalists and socialists, though it worries socialists much more. Both are concerned that such systems will undermine national economies and produce large-scale unemployment;

---

[11] The Gates Foundation is not the largest. The largest, the Stichting INGKA Foundation, operates under laws that make it difficult to know what it actually does.

underemployment, or work below the skill level of the worker; and part-time employment—all of which drive down wages so people cannot consume as much. Socialists and some capitalists believe that regulation can solve these problems, but most capitalists argue that the changes are improving the overall productive capacity of the world. This, they say, raises the standard of living in the Third World, thus raising the level of consumption there, which will offset any drop of consumption elsewhere.

Offshoring jobs from one country to another has the potential of developing serious political opposition to the free market in those countries losing jobs. People disagree over whether such job relocation benefits the economy losing jobs. Those in favor point to the lower cost of goods; those against say that the lost wages exceed the savings in consumption costs.

MICROFINANCE[12]

The United Nations designated 2005 as the International Year of Microfinance. Muhammad Yunus (b. 1940), founder of the Grameen Bank, the best-known microfinance institution, was awarded the Nobel Peace Prize in 2006 together with the bank itself: nine female borrowers represented the bank when the prize was awarded. Microfinance provides credit and savings services to farmers, operators of small enterprises or microenterprises, and, in particular, to women who are starting small businesses, primarily in developing countries. The loans are very small—hence the terms *microfinance* and *microenterprise*—but for the people involved, they mean the difference between abject poverty and the first step on the very bottom rung of the ladder to independence.

The Grameen Bank was founded in Bangladesh—*grameen* means *village* in Bengali—and because they discovered that loans given to women were both more productive and more likely to be repaid than those given to men, 97 percent of their almost seven million borrowers are women. More than $5 billion has been lent, and the default rate is 1.5 percent, which is lower than most mainstream banks. Initial loans are around $45 and the interest rate is 20 percent. If the initial loan is repaid, further loans are made at lower interest rates, around 5 percent to 8 percent. The bank is financially independent and has needed no donor money since 1995.

The Grameen bank works closely with loan recipients to assist them in learning the skills necessary to run their small businesses. One example of such a business that has become common throughout Bangladesh is the "telephone lady." Since landlines are almost nonexistent, and most people cannot afford a mobile, the loan is used to buy a mobile, which is then rented to others to

---

[12] On microfinance, see Sam Daley-Harris, ed. *Pathways Out of Poverty: Innovations in Microfinance for the Poorest Families.* Bloomfield, CT: Kumarian Press, 2002; Malcolm Harper, ed., *Microfinance: Evolution, Achievements and Challenges.* London: ITDG Publishing/New Delhi, India: Samskriti, 2003; Marguerite S. Robinson, *The Microfinance Revolution: Sustainable Finance for the Poor. Lessons from Indonesia. The Emerging Industry.* Washington, DC: The World Bank/New York: Open Society Institute, 2001; and Stuart Rutherford, *The Poor and Their Money.* New Delhi, India: Oxford University Press, 2000.

make calls. After the initial loan has been repaid, later loans are often made to build houses—640,000 houses have been built—and to send children to school; 30,000 scholarships per year are given out, and many of these children are now doctors, teachers, or in other professions.

The Grameen model has grown from simply giving loans to advising on significant lifestyle changes that include creating improved water and sanitation facilities, eating better, getting more physical exercise, eliminating child marriage and the giving of dowries, and reducing family size. All these activities are seen as essential to reducing poverty, but none of them are possible without the initial small loans.[13]

The Grameen Bank model has spread throughout the world, and Grameen Banks have even been established in inner city areas in the United States. For example, Yunus opened eleven microfinance banks in New York City in the Spring of 2008. Alternative models of microfinance have been developed, including those intended to make a profit for the lenders, which remains controversial in the growing microfinance community. And in his Nobel Peace Prize acceptance speech, Yunus criticized the emphasis on the bottom line, arguing that entrepreneurs should add doing good to profit maximization.

SHOULD ALL MARKETS BE FREE?

One question that has arisen is whether or not there should be free markets in whatever can be traded. For example, it has been proposed that there should be a free, legal market in body parts—an illegal one exists already.[14] Should whomever wants to buy a kidney be able to do so from whomever is willing to sell one? The argument in favor is that because an illegal market exists already, it would be better to legalize and regulate the trade. Since prohibition does not work, make it legal and control it, which will also reduce the power of organized crime that benefits from the illegal trade.[15] The argument against is essentially moral; that it is simply wrong to buy and sell body parts. Such a market would, of course, introduce a radical inequality in health care. Currently, although the system is quite complicated, the idea is that those needing a new kidney the most will get one before someone with a lesser need. Under a market system, whomever could pay the most would get one first.

Free Markets and National Interest International free markets can destabilize national economies. Those arguing for completely free markets do not always argue for completely free trade and choose to protect their own industries to avoid losing the industries and the jobs they create. Under most administrations, the

---

[13] See Muhammad Yunus with Alan Jolis, *Banker to the Poor: The Autobiography of Muhammad Yunus, the Founder of the Grameen Bank*. London: Aurum Press, 1998: 115–116 and 222–223 for lists of what loan recipients are encouraged to do.

[14] See, for example, James Stacey Taylor, *Stakes and Kidneys: Why Markets in Human Body Parts are Morally Imperative*. Aldershot, England: Ashgate, 2005.

[15] The same argument has been applied to certain illegal drugs.

United States calls for free trade even as it protects U.S. farmers and industries from what is deemed "unfair" competition, often based on lower labor costs in other countries. One example of a free market that has seriously damaged national economies, and has great potential for doing so again, is the currency market. At present the world currency market handles about $4 trillion, in U.S. dollars, every day—more than the annual GNP (Gross National Product) of the United States. Experts can make immense fortunes by trading on tiny changes in the value of currency, and the activities of George Soros (b. 1930) did serious damage to the British economy in 1992; he was blamed by Asian leaders for making the 1997 Asian financial crisis much worse by buying and selling different Asian currencies.

At present both China and Japan hold over $700 billion in U.S. securities each, which, if sold, could badly damage the U.S. economy. Of course, both countries benefit from a strong U.S. economy and would themselves be hurt by a damaged U.S. economy. But their holdings also give them political power, and China in particular has threatened to use its economic power unless the United States changes some of the policies of which China disapproves.

Privatization *Privatization* is taking something provided by government and contracting to have it provided by private enterprise, which expects to be able to provide some benefit at a lower cost while making a profit. The public gains an infusion of money when the contract is let, payments are made, or the enterprise sold; and it is expected to save administrative costs. However, the public can lose future income and, depending on the contract, it may also lose a degree of control over the quality of the service.

When privatization first became popular, it tended to be applied to local services—such as garbage collection, street cleaning, and building maintenance— with contracts specifying the level of service required (e.g. hospitals have to be cleaner than schools). Even though all of the contracts were not as carefully written as they should have been, and not all of the companies managed to live up to the contract requirements, it worked reasonably well. Later, under so-called Public–Private Partnerships, privatization was extended to the building and operation of such things as prisons, transportation services, and schools. Here again some of the agreements were not carefully thought through, and some serious problems arose, but many such agreements worked as intended.

In Iraq we have seen many of the services to the U.S. military, and services normally carried out by the military, contracted out to private companies and to what are called "Private Military Contractors"; *mercenary* is no longer an acceptable label. But these contractors, who have regularly outnumbered American troops, were made exempt from local law; and they did not, in many cases, fall under U.S. jurisdiction. This situation has produced substantial problems, which raises the question about what limits should be placed on privatization, particularly since many of the services have proven to be less efficient (i.e., they cost more) than when undertaken by the military.

Delivery of Services An issue that troubles both capitalists and socialists is how to bring the advantages of the information revolution to isolated areas. In the early twentieth century, governments generally required that electrical and telephone companies run lines to isolated farms; but that was an era when farmers were a significant percentage of the electorate, and not doing so might have cost votes. Today, building such lines simply is not going to happen, and alternative means need to be found. In many places, construction has begun on small power generators based on gasoline, the sun, wind, or water to provide electricity. The popularity of mobile phones means that telephone lines are no longer necessary, but towers still have to be built; and while this is going on, huge areas of the world exist where mobiles will not work, and this is true even in developed countries. An invention that has brought greater information to isolated areas, the wind-up radio, is being distributed by some foundations, particularly in Africa.

An example that shows what can be done through both government involvement and a capitalist seeing a niche is the small, affordable car. In Germany under National Socialism, the government required the development of such a car; the result was the Volkswagen (*peoples' car*), which of course became one of the largest automobile manufacturers in the world. In 2008 an Indian entrepreneur saw a market for such a car and will begin producing one—initially for the Indian market but with plans to expand throughout the world—that will sell for about $1000 U.S. dollars. He estimates he could sell millions in India alone.

SUGGESTED READING

Democratic Capitalism

Some Classic Works

Bell, Daniel. *The Cultural Contradictions of Capitalism.* New York: Basic Books. 1976. 20th anniversary ed. New York: Basic Books, 1996.

Friedman, Milton, with the assistance of Rose D. Friedman. *Capitalism and Freedom.* 40th anniversary ed. Chicago: University of Chicago Press, 2002.

Keynes, John Maynard. *The Economic Consequences of the Peace.* New York: Harcourt, Brace & Howe, 1920. Recent reprint New Brunswick, NJ: Transaction Books, 2003.

———. *The General Theory of Employment, Interest, and Money.* New York: Harcourt Brace, 1936. Recent reprint London: Palgrave Macmillan, 2006.

Smith, Adam. *An Inquiry into the Nature and Causes of the Wealth of Nations.* (1776) 2 vols. Oxford, England: Clarendon Press, 1976.

Von Mises, Ludwig. *Bureaucracy.* New Haven, CT: Yale University Press, 1944. Reprinted New Rochelle, NY: Arlington House, 1969.

Books and Articles

Abdelal, Rawi. *Capital Rules: The Construction of Global Finance.* Cambridge, MA: Harvard University Press, 2007.

Alperovitz, Gar. *America Beyond Capitalism: Reclaiming Our Wealth, Our Liberty, and Our Democracy.* New York: John Wiley & Sons, 2005.

Avant, Deborah. *The Market for Force: The Consequences of Privatizing Security.* Cambridge, England: Cambridge University Press, 2005.

Baker, Raymond W. *Capitalism's Achilles Heel: Dirty Money and How to Renew the Free-Market System.* Hoboken, NJ: John Wiley & Sons, 2005.

Banerjee, Abhijit V., and Esther Duflo. "The Economic Lives of the Poor." *The Journal of Economic Perspectives* Vol. 21:1 (Winter 2007). http://econ-www.mit.edu/faculty/download_pdf.php?id=1346. Accessed February 10, 2008.

Barber, Benjamin R. *Con$umed: How Markets Corrupt Children, Infantilize Adults, and Swallow Citizens Whole.* New York: W.W. Norton, 2007.

Baumol, William J., Robert E. Litan, and Carl J. Schramm. *Good Capitalism, Bad Capitalism, and the Economics of Growth and Prosperity*. New Haven, CT: Yale University Press, 2007.

Berger, Suzanne, and the MIT Industrial Performance Center. *How We Compete: What Companies Around the World Are Doing to Make It in Today's Economy*. New York: Currency/Doubleday, 2006. Additional material at http://www.howwecompete.com.

Bevir, Mark, and Frank Trentmann, eds. *Markets in Historical Contexts: Ideas and Politics in the Modern World*. Cambridge, England: Cambridge University Press, 2004.

Bogle, John C. *The Battle for the Soul of Capitalism*. New Haven, CT: Yale University Press, 2005. An attack on the way the financial system has been used that undermined trust in capitalism by a successful mutual fund CEO.

Boltanski, Luc, and Ève Chiapello. *The New Spirit of Capitalism*. Gregory Elliott, trans. London: Verso, 2005. Originally published as *Le nouvel esprit du capitalisme*. Paris: Éditions Gallimard, 1999. The ideology of managerial capitalism.

Booth, Philip, ed. *Towards a Liberal Utopia?* 2nd ed. London: Institute of Economic Affairs, 2006. Liberal here means free market, and the book includes a number of essays proposing the changes needed to bring British society closer to a fully functioning free market. Also includes other essays presenting the position of the Institute of Economic Affairs.

Bornstein, David. *The Price of a Dream: The Story of the Grameen Bank*. New York: Simon & Schuster, 1996. U.K. ed. Oxford, England: Oxford University Press, 1996.

Braudel, Fernand. *Civilization and Capitalism, 15th–18th Century*. 3 vols. New York: Harper & Row, 1982–1984.

Counts, Alex. *Give Us Credit*. New York: Times Books, 1996. The Grameen Bank principles applied to Chicago.

Duménil, Gérard, and Dominique Lévy. *Capital Resurgent: Roots of the Neoliberal Revolution*. Derek Jeffers, trans. Cambridge, MA: Harvard University Press, 2004. A study showing the negative effects of the neoliberal economic agenda.

Epstein, Richard with a commentary by Geoffrey E. Wood. *Free Markets Under Siege: Cartels, Politics, and Social Welfare*. Thirty-third Wincott Lecture, 13 October 2003. London: The Institute of Economic Affairs, 2004.

Foley, Duncan K. *Adam's Fallacy: A Guide to Economic Theology*. Cambridge, MA: Harvard University Press, 2006. "Adam" is Adam Smith.

Gantman, Ernesto R. *Capitalism, Social Privilege and Managerial Ideologies*. Burlington, VT: Ashgate, 2004.

Goodwin, Michele. *Black Markets: The Supply and Demand of Body Parts*. New York: Cambridge University Press, 2006.

Kelso, Louis O., and Mortimer J. Adler. *The Capitalist Manifesto*. New York: Random House, 1958. Reprinted Westport, CT: Greenwood Press, 1975.

Klein, Naomi. *The Shock Doctrine: The Rise of Disaster Capitalism*. New York: Metropolitan Books, 2007. A detailed and heavily documented study of the way capitalism exploits natural disasters together with the cooperation of advocates of the free market with dictators.

Lichtenstein, Nelson, ed. *American Capitalism: Social Thought and Political Economy in the Late Twentieth Century*. Philadelphia: University of Pennsylvania Press, 2006. A collection of essays on contemporary American capitalism from a wide range of perspectives.

Muller, Jerry Z. *The Mind and the Market: Capitalism in Western Thought*. New York: Alfred A. Knopf, 2002. Excellent introductory history of capitalist thought by a sympathetic scholar.

Nee, Victor, and Richard Swedberg, eds. *The Economic Sociology of Capitalism*. Princeton, NJ: Princeton University Press, 2005. Discusses how capitalism is changing under globalization.

Nelson, Julie A. *Economics for Humans*. Chicago, IL: University of Chicago Press, 2006.

Norberg, Johan. *In Defense of Global Capitalism.* Washington, DC: The Cato Institute, 2003. From a libertarian perspective, capitalism as providing freedom and opportunity to even the poorest peasant.

Novak, Michael. *The American Vision: An Essay on the Future of Democratic Capitalism.* Washington, DC: American Enterprise Institute for Public Policy Research, 1978.

———. *The Spirit of Democratic Capitalism.* New York: American Enterprise Institute for Public Policy Research/Simon & Schuster, 1982.

Prasad, Monica. *The Politics of Free Markets: The Rise of Neoliberal Economic Policies in Britain, France, Germany, and the United States.* Chicago, IL: University of Chicago Press, 2006.

Rand, Ayn [pseud.]. *Capitalism: The Unknown Ideal.* New York: New American Library, 1966. Includes three essays by Alan Greenspan (b. 1926), the long-serving chairman of the U.S. Federal Reserve Bank (1988–2006).

Rasor, Dina, and Robert Bauman. *Betraying Our Troops: The Destructive Results of Privatizing War.* New York: Palgrave Macmillan, 2007.

Rockwell, Llewellyn H., Jr. *Speaking of Liberty.* Auburn, AL: Ludwig von Mises Institute, 2003.

———, ed. *The Free Market Reader: Essays in the Economics of Liberty.* Burlingame, CA: The Ludwig von Mises Institute, 1988.

Sachs, Jeffrey D. *The End of Poverty: Economic Possibilities for Our Time.* New York: Penguin, 2005. U.K. ed., *The End of Poverty: How We Can Make It Happen in Our Lifetime.* London: Penguin, 2005. Detailed proposals to end "extreme" poverty and an argument for why it makes sense economically to do so.

Schwarz, John E. *Freedom Reclaimed: Rediscovering the American Vision.* Baltimore, MD: Johns Hopkins University Press, 2005. Argues that the free market version of freedom undermines traditional personal and political freedoms.

Seldon, Arthur. *Introducing Market Forces into "Public" Services.* Vol. 4 of *The Collected Works of Arthur Seldon.* Colin Robinson, ed. Indianapolis, IN: Liberty Fund, 2005.

Sennett, Richard. *The Culture of the New Capitalism.* New Haven, CT: Yale University Press, 2006.

Sowell, Thomas. *On Classical Economics.* New Haven, CT: Yale University Press, 2006.

Stiglitz, Joseph E., and Andrew Charlton. *Fair Trade for All: How Trade Can Promote Development.* Oxford, England: Oxford University Press, 2005.

———, José Antonio Ocampo, Shari Spiegel, Ricardo French-Davis, and Deepak Nayyar. *Stability with Growth: Macroeconomics, Liberalization, and Development.* Oxford, England: Oxford University Press 2006.

Taylor, James Stacey. *Stakes and Kidneys: Why Markets in Human Body Parts are Morally Imperative.* Aldershot, England: Ashgate, 2005. Argues for a minimally regulated market in organs, specifically kidneys, as a moral imperative.

Tsai, Kellee S. *Capitalism Without Democracy: The Private Sector in Contemporary China.* Ithaca, NY: Cornell University Press, 2007. Explores the development of a private sector within a China still controlled by the Communist Party.

Véron, Nicolas, Matthieu Autret, and Alfred Galichon. *Smoke & Mirrors, Inc.: Accounting for Capitalism.* George Holoch, trans. Ithaca, NY: Cornell University Press, 2006.

Williams, Colin C. *A Commodified World? Mapping the Limits of Capitalism.* London: Zed Books, 2005. Argument that it is not necessary for everything to become a commodity, an analysis of uncommodified areas of today's economies, and a suggestion of a way to enhance those areas.

Yankelovich, Daniel. *Profit With Honor: The New Stage of Market Capitalism.* New Haven, CT: Yale University Press, 2006. Argues that U.S. capitalists need to develop a new set of norms to regulate themselves and avoid greater government regulation.

Democratic Socialism

Some Classic Works

Crossman, R. H. S., ed. *New Fabian Essays.* London: Turnstile Press, 1952.

Dahl, Robert A. *A Preface to Economic Democracy.* Berkeley: University of California Press, 1985.

Lange, Oskar, and Fred M. Taylor. *On the Economic Theory of Socialism.* Edited by Benjamin E. Lippincott. Minneapolis: University of Minnesota Press, 1938. Reprinted New York: McGraw-Hill, 1964.

Lipset, Seymour Martin, and Gary Marks. *It Didn't Happen Here: Why Socialism Failed in the United States.* New York: Norton, 2000.

Nove, Alec. *The Economics of Feasible Socialism Revisited.* 2nd ed. London: HarperCollinsAcademic, 1991.

———. *Efficiency Criteria for Nationalised Industries.* London: George Allen & Unwin, 1973.

Nyerere, Julius K. *Ujamaa: Essays on Socialism.* Dar es Salaam, Tanzania: Oxford University Press, 1968.

Senghor, Léopold Sédar. *On African Socialism.* Mercer Cook, trans. New York: Praeger, 1964.

Shaw, George Bernard, ed. *Fabian Essays in Socialism.* London: Fabian Society, 1889.

Books and Articles

Albert, Michael. *Realizing Hope: Life Beyond Capitalism.* London: Zed Books/Black Point, NS, Canada: Fernwood Publishing, 2006. Parecon is short for participatory economics.

Aronowitz, Stanley. *Left Turn: Forging a New Political Future.* Boulder, CO: Paradigm Publishers, 2006. Argues that the United States needs a new radical political party and discusses alternatives to market capitalism.

Barsky, Robert F. *The Chomsky Effect: A Radical Works Beyond the Ivory Tower.* Cambridge, MA: MIT Press, 2007.

Bourdieu, Pierre. *Firing Back: Against the Tyranny of the Market 2.* Loïc Wacquant, trans. London: Verso, 2003.

Chang, Ha-Joon, and Ilene Grabel. *Reclaiming Development: An Alternative Economic Policy Manuel.* Dhaka, Bangladesh: University Press/Bangkok, Thailand: White Lotus/Bluepoint, NS, Canada: Fernwood Publishing/Bangalore, India: Books for Change/Beirut, Lebanon: World Book Publishing/Kuala Lumpur, Malaysia: SIRD/Penang, Malaysia: TWN/Cape Town, South Africa: David Philip/London: Zed Books, 2004.

Ezorsky, Gertrude. *Freedom in the Workplace?* Ithaca, NY: Cornell University Press, 2007.

Friedman, Benjamin M. *The Moral Consequences of Economic Growth.* New York: Alfred A. Knopf, 2005. Argues that progressive politics has been associated with periods of economic growth and that periods of weak growth are associated with retrenchment. Argues that economic growth produces "greater opportunity, tolerance of diversity, social mobility, commitment to fairness, and dedication to democracy" (p. 4).

Holloway, John. *Change the World Without Taking Power: The Meaning of Revolution Today.* London: Pluto Press, 2002. New ed. London: Pluto Press, 2005 with an "Epilogue" (pp. 216–245, 258–264). Anticapitalist.

Isbister, John. *Capitalism and Justice: Envisioning Social and Economic Fairness.* Bloomfield, CT: Kumarian Press, 2001.

Lofy, Bill. *Paul Wellstone: The Life of a Passionate Progressive.* Ann Arbor: University of Michigan Press, 2005.

Lowes, David E. *The Anti-Capitalist Dictionary: Movements, Histories, & Motivations.* Black Point, NS, Canada: Fernwood Publishing/Kuala Lumpur, Malaysia: SIRD/London: Zed Books, 2006.

McGilvray, James, ed. *The Cambridge Companion to Chomsky.* Cambridge, England: Cambridge University Press, 2005. Includes "Chomsky on Values and Politics."

Panitch, Leo. *Renewing Socialism: Democracy, Strategy, and Imagination.* Boulder, CO: Westview Press, 2001. Economic and political democracy plus environmentalism.

Pei, Minxin. *China's Trapped Transition: The Limits of Developmental Autocracy.* Cambridge, MA: Harvard University Press, 2006.

Pimlott, Ben, ed. *Fabian Essays in Socialist Thought.* London: Heinemann, 1984.

Qaddafi, Muammar al-. *The Green Book.* 10th ed. Tripoli, Libya: The World Centre for Studies and Research of The Green Book, 1987. This edition includes all three parts. The revised translation was prepared by a committee chosen by the World Centre for Studies and Research of The Green Book.

Tormey, Simon. *Anti-Capitalism. A Beginner's Guide.* Oxford, England: Oneworld Publications, 2004.

Unger, Roberto Mangabeira. *The Self Awakened: Pragmatism Unbound.* Cambridge, MA: Harvard University Press, 2007. A statement of his general philosophy to be read with his more explicitly political works.

———. *What Should the Left Propose?* London: Verso, 2005. Detailed proposals for democratic socialist policies fostering "high-energy democracy."

Websites

Democratic Capitalism

Mont Pelerin Society: http://www.montpelerin.org

Ludwig von Mises Institute: http://www.mises.org

Democratic Socialism

Journal of the Research Group on Socialism and Democracy: http://www.sdonline.org

Socialist Party UK: http://www.socialism.org.uk

6

ψ

Conservatism, Liberalism, and Democracy

onservatism and liberalism within democracy must be treated in three different ways, because they are three different things. First, they are general sets of attitudes toward change, human nature, and tradition. Second, they are specific positions taken at different times and places by identifiable groups of people. Third, they have different histories in different countries, although these histories are so complex that the same individuals are sometimes included in the histories of both. Today, we generally trace the histories of Western conservative and liberal traditions back to the seventeenth and eighteenth centuries. For North Americans, the histories are primarily connected with British political thought with limited French and German influence.

The language in use regarding both conservatism and liberalism can be confusing, and this chapter discusses traditional conservatism, neoconservatism, traditional or classical liberalism, neoliberalism, and social liberalism, sometimes called *welfare liberalism*. The words can be particularly confusing for exchange students, because, for example, in the United Kingdom, liberalism tends to mean classical liberalism; and in the United States, it tends to mean social liberalism—and sometimes the two "neos" are used to refer to the same thing or very nearly the same thing. As a result, conversations can get confusing when you think you are using words that the other will understand in the same way you do.

Two related subjects are also discussed in this chapter, communitarianism and the extreme Right. Although even communitarianism's most ardent defender—its founder and primary theorist, Amitai Etzioni (b. 1929)—believes that it has declined in recent years, it remains a clear variant of conservatism that has been explicitly rejected by most liberals. Parts of the extreme Right are closely related to conservatism, and parts are not; the parts that are not are discussed in Chapter 10. What conservatives might want to call the extreme Left is discussed in the previous chapter and in Chapter 9. Libertarianism, which has been both accepted and rejected by American conservatives, is also discussed in Chapter 9.

Some writers choose to treat conservatism and liberalism as separate ideologies rather than as tendencies within democracy, as they are presented here. Neither approach is perfect, but the approach used here captures the complexity of attitudes toward democracy by showing that, in addition to democrats who are capitalist and democrats who are socialist, there are democrats who are liberal and democrats who are conservative. In the United States almost all democrats are capitalists and are either liberal or conservative. In some countries there are liberal and conservative democratic socialists as well as liberal and conservative democratic capitalists.

Conservatism and liberalism also differ from place to place and time to time. For example, a Canadian conservative will emphasize one thing, and a Japanese or Swedish conservative will emphasize another. And a conservative in the United States at the beginning of the twenty-first century does not believe the same things a U.S. conservative did in 1890. In fact many conservatives believe that they are the true liberals.

Even though conservatives often think of liberals as extremists and vice versa, both liberals and conservatives are found in the middle of the political spectrum; they both want to maintain the basic institutions and processes of the society in which they live. Other terms used include *reactionary,* one who wants to move dramatically in the direction of an idealized past society, and *radical,* one who wants dramatic change in the direction of a vision of a better society that has not yet existed. The term *reactionary* has generally disappeared, because it is actually radical to desire some idealized society that never existed.

CONSERVATISM

A core principle of conservatism is the desire to conserve something, although conservatives disagree over just what should be conserved. Conservatism within democracy today has the following characteristics:

1. Resistance to change
2. Reverence for tradition and a distrust of human reason
3. Rejection of the use of government to improve the human condition; ambivalence regarding governmental activity for other purposes
4. Preference for individual freedom but willingness to limit freedom to maintain traditional values
5. Antiegalitarianism—distrust of human nature

These defining principles of conservatism do not change much over time, and later in the chapter, we will see how they are applied today in the United States.

Modern Anglo-American conservatism is traceable to Edmund Burke (1729–1797), although he had precursors, and a variety of alternative traditions exist in various countries. Burke is most noted for his emphasis on tradition. As he wrote in his most famous book, *Reflections on the Revolution in France* (1790),

> In states there are often more obscure and almost latent causes, things which appear at first view of little moment, on which a very great part of its prosperity or adversity may most essentially depend. The science of government being therefore so practical in itself, and intended for such practical purposes, a matter which requires experience, and even more experience than any person can gain in his whole life, however sagacious and observing he may be, it is with infinite caution that any man ought to venture upon pulling down an edifice which has answered in any tolerable degree for ages the common purposes of society, or on building it up again, without models and patterns of approved utility before his eyes.[1]

Here we see both Burke's concern with the wisdom of the past and with the complexity of social and political life. This latter concern leads to the conservative rejection of the liberal emphasis on rational planning.[2] Life is too complicated for human beings to comprehend and control, and some factors in society do not lend themselves to rational planning.

Burke also stressed another point that is part of contemporary conservatism: private property. "Nothing is a due and adequate representation of a state that does not represent its ability, as well as its property."[3] And, Burke notes, both ability and property are inherited unequally.

Friedrich August von Hayek (1899–1992), whose *The Road to Serfdom* (1944) provided an ethical defense of free markets, wrote, "Conservatism proper is a legitimate, probably necessary, and certainly widespread attitude of opposition to drastic change."[4] Although his point is correct, it is too specific. Conservatives not only oppose "drastic change," as he says, but are hesitant about any change. As one writer put it, "The conservative does not oppose change, but he does resist it."[5] Conservatives do not unthinkingly oppose change; they resist and question it because they are wary of social experimentation. They believe that something that has worked, even if not very well, is better than something untried and unknown.

---

[1] Edmund Burke, *The Works of the Right Honorable Edmund Burke,* revised ed. (Boston: Little, Brown, 1865), Vol. 3: 312.

[2] See, for example, Michael Oakeshott, "Rationalism in Politics," in Oakeshott, *Rationalism in Politics and Other Essays.* New York: Basic Books, 1962: 1–36.

[3] Burke, *Works,* 3: 297–298.

[4] F. A. von Hayek, "Why I Am Not a Conservative," in *The Constitution of Liberty.* London: Routledge & Kegan Paul, 1960: 397.

[5] Jay A. Sigler, introduction to *The Conservative Tradition in American Thought,* Jay A. Sigler ed. New York: Capricorn Books, 1969: 13.

Edmund Burke (1729–1797) is best known as the founder of modern conservatism. His most famous work is *Reflections on the French Revolution* (1790), in which he argued that society is a complex web of relationships among the past, present, and future. He contended that social institutions slowly evolve over time to fit needs and conditions and that, therefore, tampering with tradition is likely to bring grief rather than improvement. He was an advocate of slow, gradual change; he did not reject change altogether, nor did he argue for the return to some idealized past.

The second characteristic of conservatism, a reverence for tradition, is composed of a number of subsidiary points, including traditional moral standards, religion (with few exceptions), and the assumption that the longer an institution has existed, the more likely it is to be worth preserving. Reverence for tradition springs from the conservative's basic distrust of reason as a means of improving humanity's lot. Conservatives do not reject reason completely, but they would rather trust tradition, because they believe that tradition contains the accumulated wisdom of past generations. Note also how closely connected the first and second characteristics are—honoring tradition entails resistance to change.

This point is quite simple and clear-cut. The only really complicating factor is that conservatives (and liberals) change over time regarding the specifics they wish to preserve. The world changes, and conservatives change with it. They do not want to conserve all the past; they want to conserve what they believe is the best of the past.

The third characteristic presents the major dilemma in conservative thought. Overall, conservatives believe governmental power should be reduced, and individuals should make their own way in the world. (Note the similarity to traditional capitalism.) But there is ambivalence here. Governmental power to support traditional moral standards and limit an individual's freedom regarding them is perfectly acceptable to many conservatives and utterly unacceptable to other conservatives. As Russell Kirk (1918–1994) put it, conservatives believe "genuinely ordered freedom is the only sort of liberty worth having: freedom made possible by order within the soul and order within the state."[6]

The case must not be overstated, however. On the whole, conservatives reject the use of government to improve the human condition because (1) they are

---

[6] Russell Kirk, "Prescription, Authority, and Ordered Freedom," in *What Is Conservatism?* Frank S. Meyer, ed. New York: Holt, Rinehart & Winston, 1964: 24.

convinced the use of government does not necessarily improve the human condition, and (2) they believe people left alone can do a better job. The first point is the key. It asserts that the use of government for social betterment will actually produce the opposite. People, according to most conservatives, will come to rely on government and lose the ability to help themselves.

Conservatives have held this position very consistently. Edmund Burke, writing in the eighteenth century, held it; Bernard Bosanquet (1848–1923), writing at the beginning of the twentieth century, held it; and modern conservatives, such as Russell Kirk and William F. Buckley, Jr. (1925–2008) continued to hold it. Kirk's *The Conservative Mind* (1953) provided one of the bases for the redevelopment of modern conservatism; and two of the journals he founded, *Modern Age* in 1957 and *University Bookman* in 1960, provided outlets for conservative writers, and both are still being published. Buckley's *National Review* (founded in 1955) was the most important political magazine for conservatives throughout the second half of the last century.

Most conservatives believe that some people are better than other people and, therefore, should be honored more by society. As Kirk put it, "Aye, men are created different; and a government which ignores this law becomes an unjust government, for it sacrifices nobility to mediocrity; it pulls down the aspiring natures to gratify the inferior natures."[7] This is precisely the reason that conservatives are ambivalent about both government and individual freedom: Governmental help will hurt persons of the better sort, and the poorer sort will not be helped.

Conservatives recognize that people differ on the basis of factors such as class, gender, intelligence, and race; and they believe that sometimes this recognition implies superiority or inferiority, but it does not necessarily do so. Conservatives believe that inferiority and superiority exist but does not necessarily tie such superiority and inferiority to factors like class, gender, intelligence, and race.

Some argue that as American conservatism became more successful it clearly became a separate ideology that includes the neoconservatives, who are most concerned with foreign policy; the religious Right, who are most concerned with social questions such as abortion and the family; and anti-tax conservatives, who are primarily concerned with reducing the size and power of government. But at the same time, many supporters of each of these positions reject the other two, and there are significant divisions over specific policy positions within each.

LIBERALISM

Just as the root word in *conservatism* is *conserve,* the root word in *liberalism* is *liberty.* Some scholars find liberalism in ancient Greece and Rome, but liberalism is most commonly traced to the English revolutions of the seventeenth century. Politically, liberalism originated in the revolution of the 1640s and the Levellers, particularly the Putney debates, in which Colonel Thomas Rainsborough (1610–1648) argued for widening the electoral franchise, saying, "I think that the poorest he

---

[7] Kirk, "Prescription," 34.

that is in England hath a life to live, as the greatest he; and therefore truly, sir, I think it's clear, that every man that is to live under government ought first by his own consent to put himself under that government; and I do think that the poorest man in England is not at all bound in a strict sense to that government that he hath not had a voice to put himself under."[8] Intellectually, liberalism stems from the writings of John Locke (1632–1704), who developed the arguments for consent, majority rule, and rights, particularly property rights.

Today most liberals argue that liberalism is primarily concerned with liberty, and they trace their roots to John Stuart Mill (1806–1873) and his little book *On Liberty* (1859), which stressed freedom of thought and speech. But the liberal emphasis on liberty has taken two differing routes from Mill to the present: One approach is really a continuation of Locke's concern with rights, including property rights. The other approach developed in the late nineteenth and early twentieth centuries in the writings of T. H. Green (1836–1882) and others, who argued that some people need help to be able to exercise their liberty. This argument was the beginning of what became known as *welfare liberalism*.

These varied strands bring us to a liberalism that today can be described as having the following characteristics:

1. A tendency to favor change
2. Faith in human reason
3. Willingness to use government to improve the human condition
4. Preference for individual freedom but ambivalence about economic freedom
5. Greater optimism about human nature than conservatives

These defining principles of liberalism do not change much over time, and later in this chapter, we will see how they are applied today in the United States.

In his speech in 1960 accepting the nomination of the New York Liberal Party, John F. Kennedy (1917–1963) defined what was then seen as liberalism by saying, "If by a 'liberal' they mean someone who looks ahead and not behind, someone who welcomes new ideas without rigid reactions, someone who cares about the welfare of the people—their health, their housing, their schools, their jobs, their civil rights, and their civil liberties—someone who believes that we can break through the stalemate and suspicions that grip us in our policies abroad, if that is what they mean by a 'liberal,' then I'm proud to say that I'm a 'liberal'."[9]

Hubert H. Humphrey (1911–1978), who was the standard-bearer of liberalism in mid-twentieth century America, once wrote, "Liberals fully recognize that change is inevitable in the patterns of society and in the challenges which confront man."[10] Marcus G. Raskin (1934–2002) made the same point in stronger language, saying, "If there is a fundamental liberal principle it is the recognition

---

[8] From A. S. P. Woodhouse, ed., *Puritanism and Liberty: Being the Army Debates (1647–9) from the Clarke Manuscripts with Supplementary Documents,* 2nd ed. London: Dent, 1974: 59.

[9] http://www.presidency.ucsb.edu/ws/index.php?pid=74012. Accessed February 12, 2008.

[10] Hubert H. Humphrey, introduction to Milton Viorst, *Liberalism: A Guide to Its Past, Present, and Future in American Politics.* New York: Avon Books, 1963: vii.

John Stuart Mill (1806–1873) was the most influential philosopher in the English-speaking world in the nineteenth century. His major political works were *On Liberty* (1859), *Considerations on Representative Government* (1861), *Utilitarianism* (1861), and *The Subjection of Women* (1869). Mill developed and modified the philosophy of utilitarianism of Jeremy Bentham (1748–1832), but is best known today for his defense of freedom in *On Liberty*. With his wife, Harriet Taylor (1807–1858), Mill began to explore the subordinate role of women in contemporary society, and he became an advocate of women's rights.

of change in all things as an inevitable condition of living." [11] Liberals generally believe people should keep trying to improve society. Somewhat less optimistic about progress than they once were, liberals still believe beneficial change is possible. Such change can come about through the conscious action of men and women, as unforeseen side effects of decisions, or through the operation of various social forces. But there will be change, and the liberal is convinced it can be directed and controlled for human benefit.

Liberals do not desire radical change that would do away with the basic structure of the current system. On this point, the difference between liberalism and conservatism is a matter of degree rather than kind. Liberals want more change and tend to favor social experimentation, but they want this only within the framework of the current political, legal, and economic system. Liberals are not radicals.

Change is welcomed because liberals trust human reason to devise solutions to human problems. This faith in the potential of reason is the key to the liberal credo—only with such faith can they accept the use of governmental power to improve the human condition. This faith assumes that social experimentation is valid and that it is better to use such power as we have to control change than to allow change to control us.

Liberals contend that some people must be helped to live better lives and fulfill their individual potential, and they believe such assistance can work. Conservatives believe just the opposite—helping people may make it impossible for them to fulfill their potential as individuals. Liberals argue that people, though capable of reason and reasoned action, are often caught in situations in which self-help, even if possible, is difficult and that government should help. Instead of injuring people, such assistance has the potential to give them the impetus to do more for themselves. The liberal assumption is that even though not everyone will respond, it is better to attempt to help than to do nothing, and liberals believe government is in the best position to provide help.

Liberals believe that help through governmental activity will enhance, rather than limit, individual freedom. They argue that a person, once relieved of some basic problems, can enlarge his or her sphere of activity and improve both life and mind. Still, liberals are somewhat ambivalent about human nature. They contend that most problems derive from impersonal social and economic forces acting on humanity. Human reason can solve the problems, but an unaided human being cannot. This is why liberals are ambivalent about economic freedom; they are afraid that one result of an unregulated economy would be great differences in individual power, which would be used to the detriment of the weaker members of society. ✳

Liberalism strongly stresses individual freedom. The role of the government must be limited—it cannot invade the rights and freedoms of the individual. Human beings will err, but liberals have always thought that error is far better than the suppression of error. This belief follows from the belief in the value and inevitability of change. If change is good and will always occur, today's error may be tomorrow's truth. ✳

Of course, liberals disagree among themselves as much as conservatives do. The disagreements among liberals today are primarily focused on how to balance governmental activity and personal freedom and what role the government should have in the economy. Present disagreements are not about fundamentals but are very much matters of degree; but as we will see later in this chapter, these translate into significantly different policy choices, as do the disagreements among conservatives. As general tendencies, liberalism and conservatism are primarily attitudes toward change within the democratic tradition, resting uneasily between reaction and radicalism. ✳

John Rawls

The most important contribution to liberalism in the second half of the twentieth century was the publication of *A Theory of Justice* (1971) by John Rawls (1921–2002). In this work, Rawls set out to establish the fundamental principles of social justice. To do this he undertook a thought experiment in which he imagined people in what he called "the original position," in which people are assumed not to know what talents and abilities they have or what position they hold in society. They do not know what race they are, or whether they are rich or poor, powerful or weak.[12] They are then asked to choose the principles on

---

[12] Rawls and other theorists of justice were criticized by Susan Moller Okin for not recognizing the importance of gender in their theories. Rawls in particular was criticized for not seeing how important a lack of knowledge of gender would be in the original position. See Okin's *Justice, Gender, and the Family*. New York: Basic Books, 1989.

which to build a society. Rawls argued that the following principles would be chosen in such a situation:

1. Each person must have an equal right to the most extensive basic liberty compatible with a similar liberty for others.

2. Social and economic inequalities must be arranged so they are both (a) reasonably expected to be to everyone's advantage and (b) attached to positions that are open to all.[13]

The second principle is intended to ensure equality of opportunity, and these principles are meant to be applied in order. Thus equality of rights has a higher priority than equality of opportunity. Rawls argued that justice requires that everyone have a wide range of basic liberties, including the freedoms discussed in Chapter 4, and those rights that are essential to personal integrity, such as the right to personal property.

Rawls contended that these are the fundamental principles of liberalism. The publication of *A Theory of Justice* set off a long debate among political theorists over all aspects of the book, but particularly about the thought experiment and the priorities that Rawls had assigned to the values he believed would result from it. In *Political Liberalism* (1993) Rawls made explicit that he saw his arguments as contributions to contemporary political debate, as well as contributions to a general theory of justice. He stated that we must recognize that our societies are composed of people with irreconcilable fundamental beliefs. As he put it, "The problem of political liberalism is: How is it possible that there may exist over time a stable and just society of free and equal citizens profoundly divided by reasonable though incompatible religious, philosophical, and moral doctrines?"[14] To answer the question, Rawls subtly modified the two principles just stated to read as follows:

1. Each person has an equal claim to a fully adequate scheme of basic rights and liberties, which scheme is compatible with the same scheme for all; and in this scheme, the equal political liberties, and only those liberties, are to be guaranteed their fair values.

2. Social and economic inequalities are to satisfy two conditions: first, they are to be attached to positions and offices open to all under conditions of fair equality of opportunity; and second, they are to be of the greatest benefit to the least advantaged members of society.[15]

He expanded on this argument in *The Law of Peoples* (1999), in which he considered the extent of and limits to toleration of nonliberal peoples, an issue that has become a major issue in liberal circles.

One critique of Rawlsian liberalism developed into a debate between liberals and what came to be called *communitarians*.

---

[13] John Rawls, *A Theory of Justice*. Cambridge, MA: Harvard University Press, 1971: 60.

[14] John Rawls, *Political Liberalism*. New York: Columbia University Press, 1993: xviii.

[15] Rawls, *Political Liberalism*, 5–6.

COMMUNITARIANISM

The core principle of communitarianism is community. According to the communitarian critique of liberalism, liberalism overemphasizes the individual to the detriment of the community. Liberals say that the communitarian alternative destroys liberty. In this debate, liberals focus on the desirability of developing autonomous individuals who are protected from government by universally applicable rights. Communitarians focus on the community, rather than the individual, as the basis for personal and political identity and moral decision making. Communitarians argue that, to some extent, all individuals are created by and embedded in specific communities. Our beliefs, moral systems, and senses of self come from the community or communities of which we have been and are a part.

The political conclusions drawn by communitarians vary across the political spectrum from Left to Right, although the Right has been most clearly identified with communitarianism. Some left-wing communitarians see it as simply an extension of participatory democracy with a greater concern for the community in which the participation takes place. Thus communitarianism could be seen as a development of the emphasis on community that was found in the New Left,[16] but this is not how most communitarians see it.

Most communitarians are conservatives who believe that the growth of legally enforceable individual rights has gone too far, to the detriment of society as a whole. They believe that there must be a renewed focus on personal, family, and community responsibility. Are individuals responsible to and for themselves? Or, as products of the communities of which they are a part, are they responsible to the community, and the community to them? Most important from the liberal point of view: Should we accept the dominance of community values if those values include the elimination of minority rights? In a sense, this is asking who constitutes the community. Is it the current majority in some geographic area? Are they allowed to simply impose their values on everyone else in that area?[17]

These questions are at the heart of the confused state of liberalism and conservatism in the United States today. People want to live the lives they choose without interference, and they worry about interference from both government and their neighbors, whose vision of the good life may be different from theirs and who might want to impose those values on them. This concern is not without justification: There are people who want us all to live their way. We usually call them *extremists*.

THE EXTREME RIGHT

There are a number of groups and individuals on the extreme Right, and because extremism is often in the eye of the beholder, some commentators lump together people who have relatively little in common. The most visible act of the extreme

---

[16] See Lyman Tower Sargent, *New Left Thought: An Introduction.* Homewood, IL: Dorsey Press, 1972.

[17] See The Communitarian Network at http://www.gwu.edu/~ccps and Amitai Etzioni, ed., *The Essential Communitarian Reader.* Lanham, MD: Rowman & Littlefield, 1998.

Right in the United States was the bombing of the Alfred P. Murrah Federal Office Building in Oklahoma City in 1995 by Timothy McVeigh. Whatever combination of reasons there may have been for the bombing, one motive was to attack a symbol of the federal government. Many on the extreme Right contend that the bombing was in fact a government plot with the bomb set off by government agents to incriminate those on the Right, which indicates the attitude toward the national government of the extreme Right and the depth of its belief in conspiracies.[18] Generally speaking, those in this part of the extreme Right hold that the county is the highest legitimate government. This part of the extreme Right tends to take an anti-international position and is strongly opposed to the United Nations.

Although the extreme Right is in favor of property rights, it has no use for large corporations or financial capitalism, symbolized by Wall Street. They believe a conspiracy among wealthy capitalists exists to control the economy for their own benefit and that the federal government is part of this conspiracy.

A common theme on the extreme Right is racism. Anti-Semitism is common, with both Jews and Arabs grouped together. African Americans are defined as America's major problem, and the goal is a purely Caucasian country. One example of a racist and anti-Semitic program can be found in *The Turner Diaries* (2nd ed., 1980), a novel that Timothy McVeigh had with him when captured and one that a number of far-right groups in the United States treat as a blueprint for a future race war. All the groups are small, but most of them are bigger than Hitler's initial political party.[19] The extreme-racist Right is particularly popular with the group of disaffected people generally called *skinheads*. All white music festivals, which are overwhelmingly male, feature bands with names like "The Bully Boys"; and groups such as the National Alliance, which has been for many years the most important of the organizations of the racist right, receive much of their funding through record sales.

Many issues that bother the extreme Right are the same as those that bother others: globalism, the difficulty of surviving on small farms and in small businesses, crime, drugs, big government, the power of large corporations, changing patterns of marriage and family life, education, and so forth. The central difference is that they see these problems through the lens of race, very broadly defined; thus globalization, corporate power, big government, and related issues are often viewed through the lens of anti-Semitism as a Jewish conspiracy. Many other problems are blamed on African Americans, Hispanics, and immigrants, and conspiracies are almost always central to the extreme Right's worldview.

As a result, solutions proposed by the extreme Right tend to be fairly simplistic. If all our problems are due to conspiracies, and we get rid of the conspiracy, the problems will go away. Of course, if the conspiracy is worldwide and

---

[18] See Michael Barkun, "Religion, Militias and Oklahoma City: The Mind of Conspiratorialists," *Terrorism and Political Violence* Vol. 8:1 (Spring 1996): 50–64.

[19] For more on these groups, see Lyman Tower Sargent, ed., *Extremism in America: A Reader.* New York: New York University Press, 1995. For a history, see Michael Barkun, *Religion and the Racist Right: The Origins of the Christian Identity Movement.* Chapel Hill: University of North Carolina Press, 1994. On conspiracy theories, see Barkun, *Culture of Conspiracy: Apocalyptic Visions in Contemporary America.* Berkeley: University of California Press, 2003.

centuries old, as they think some are, it is hard to see how to make it go away. Some have taken to violence, but for all the headlines, that is fairly rare. Most just want to be left alone. Some achieve this by retreating to an isolated part of the country—Idaho and eastern Washington are favorite spots—and homeschooling their children, living as much as possible in a cash-only or barter economy to avoid the attention of government, and generally cutting as many ties with the outside world as possible.

But some find staying out of sight inadequate and want to change the world they reject. Many journals, pamphlets, books, videos, and records are published by the extreme Right, but today the Internet is a major means of communication.

CURRENT TRENDS

The divisions between conservatism and liberalism are mostly long-standing, but in some cases, they are focusing on new issues. One division discussed throughout this book is multiculturalism. On the whole conservatives oppose it and liberals support it, but some liberals raise doubts about the rights of individual members of groups versus the rights of groups as a whole, fearing that these could conflict with each other.[20]

One issue continues to show a clear conservative–liberal division: how to stimulate the economy. On the whole conservatives want to give money to large corporations and the wealthy on the assumption that that is the most effective way to get the money into the economy productively and create jobs. Liberals, on the other hand, tend to want to give money to the poorest people, both to help them directly, and because the poor are most likely to spend the money immediately, thus putting it into the economy. Both conservatives and liberals want the same result but favor different approaches.

The Rule of Law From time to time, the differences in what the law—or a constitution—says or means moves from the pages of law reviews and treatises on jurisprudence to the pages of popular journals and daily newspapers. Today there are diametrically opposed views within the legal community on a wide range of issues and these differences are clearly influenced by different ideologies, particularly conservatism and liberalism. The most basic questions regarding the scope of the law, whether there is a legal right to privacy and the extent of police powers, for example, are currently being debated and the result of these debates will affect the lives of every person.

One of the debates has largely disappeared: Conservatives used to be incensed by what they called "judicial activism," or political decision making by the U.S. Supreme Court, but what they really disliked was the content of the

---

[20] See Brian Barry, *Culture and Equality: An Egalitarian Critique of Multiculturalism*. Cambridge, MA: Harvard University Press, 2001; and Susan Moller Okin, with respondents, *Is Multiculturalism Bad for Women?* Joshua Cohen, Matthew Howard, and Martha C. Nussbaum, eds. Princeton, NJ: Princeton University Press, 1999.

decisions. Now that the Court is more attuned to conservative positions, that argument is not heard so much.

But significant disagreement persists on what standard judges should use in making decisions. Legal pragmatists, such as Richard Allen Posner (b. 1939), who generally takes a conservative stance, argue that judges should simply use their own value preferences. Others, such as Ronald Dworkin (b. 1931), who generally takes a liberal stance, argue that the values of judges cannot be avoided but must be defended using precedent, legal reasoning, and so on. Legal positivists, such as H. L. A. Hart (1907–1992), have argued that judges' values are irrelevant.

CONTEMPORARY CONSERVATISM
IN THE UNITED STATES

Two groups of people share the label *conservative* in the United States today: traditional conservatives and neoconservatives who differ on specific issues and therefore can usually be clearly identified. Three sets of issues can be used to define contemporary conservatives (and liberals): social, fiscal, and foreign policy issues. The mixture of positions on each of these and the emphasis placed on them define the differences. Briefly, these positions can be characterized as follows:

- Social—a belief in traditional values centering on the home, family, and religion. At present this includes the belief that the appropriate place for women is in the home; a strong opposition to abortion; support for required prayer in schools; and opposition to the teaching of sex education and evolution, among other subjects.

- Fiscal—a belief in capitalism, opposition to most government regulation of the economy, and support for a balanced budget.

- Foreign policy—a belief in a strong military, support for our allies whatever their political position, and opposition to giving authority to international organizations like the United Nations.

The differences in these forms of conservatism are primarily ones of emphasis.

The Role of Religion With few exceptions, religion is central to conservatism, and it has become even more important in the last few decades. Evangelical Christians had traditionally not been involved in politics, but this changed when the Rev. Jerry Falwell (1933–2007) founded the Moral Majority as an explicitly political movement within evangelical Christianity to support conservative social causes, particularly regarding abortion, the family, national defense, and Israel. Although Falwell disbanded the Moral Majority in 1989 to dedicate his time to Liberty University, which he established in 1971, by that time a wide range of other groups had been established with similar agendas. The deep involvement of religion and religious leaders in American politics is now clear, although it does not entirely support a conservative agenda in that a growing number of evangelical leaders are arguing that government must become an active rather than an uninvolved part of the solution to social problems. I have only mentioned the activities of Protestants here, because they are currently the most important politically; but similar movements exist within the Roman Catholic Church and among Jews and Muslims.

Traditional Conservatism

What I call *traditional conservatism* is closest to the general characterization of conservatism outlined previously, but it has faded from view recently under pressure from neoconservatism. This does not mean that such conservatives do not exist; they have always been the mainstream of conservative thought, both in numbers and influence, and remain so. They are simply not getting the publicity that the other brands of conservatism are getting.

Traditional conservatives are more likely to support some government regulation of the economy than are neoconservatives, but they are still fiscal conservatives. They are much less likely to be social conservatives than are neoconservatives. Although they support traditional moral values, they do not generally favor using government power to enforce them. Traditional conservatives are also foreign policy conservatives, but in all three areas, they emphasize gradual change and continuity rather than immediate, radical change.

Neoconservatism

The name *neoconservative* actually originated with former liberals who felt that liberalism had lost its way in the 1960s and 1970s, with Irving Kristol (b. 1920) usually identified as its founder. But what is now called *neoconservatism* developed through a number of stages under different names and through amalgamation with conservatives of somewhat different outlooks. One stream of neoconservatism was originally called the *Radical Right,* and it developed in the 1950s in opposition to communism. As such, most Radical Right programs were negative and oppositional. Later it expanded its outlook, became the *New Right,* and was concerned with social issues, such as abortion, busing to integrate schools, pornography (a concern shared with some feminists), prayer in schools, and local control of education, which are all seen as fundamentally moral questions.

This is now the dominant outlook of neoconservatism. It is primarily concerned with issues centering on the family, religion, and education. All these issues are, they argue, basically about morals. They generally believe that the proper place for women is in the home caring for and educating their children, and they strongly oppose any position that can be seen as supporting nontraditional sexual relations, such as the movement for gay rights. They believe the role of schools is to teach parentally approved values and "the basics"—reading, writing, and arithmetic—and that schools should require Christian prayer and teach intelligent design, rather than evolution, in biology classes (neoconservatives do not believe in the separation of church and state).

These positions might seem to pose a dilemma for neoconservatives. They oppose government activity that imposes moral positions with which they disagree, but they are willing to use government to impose their own moral positions.

But there is no dilemma, because they see a simple division of right and wrong on moral questions and believe government has an appropriate role to support the "right" morality and oppose the "wrong" morality. To them, tolerance of what they know to be the wrong positions is unacceptable.

Neoconservatives are strongly conservative on foreign policy, with the conservatism formerly driven by anticommunism now driven by support for a strong military. Patriotism seems to be the motivation behind most foreign policy positions. In the contemporary environment of world politics, they see the United States as the rightly dominant power, and they believe humanitarian military intervention can advance U.S. policy.

On fiscal policy, neoconservatives argue for a free market and against government regulation, because they see these positions as essential to political freedom. For many neoconservatives, capitalism and the free market are absolutely central, and reducing nonmilitary government expenses and lowering taxes are among their primary goals. A problem for many neoconservatives is that although they had consistently opposed deficit spending, in office they have presided over one of the greatest increases in the budget deficit since World War II. Traditional conservatives, and some who identify themselves as neoconservatives, have expressed deep concern over this issue. The argument that the growing deficit is not a serious problem, because the U.S. economy is strong and will grow in a way that will take care of the deficit, is contradicted both by the desire to cut taxes to stimulate growth—tax revenue is needed to pay the debt—and the slowing of the economy in early 2008.

CONTEMPORARY LIBERALISM
IN THE UNITED STATES

Liberalism has been in considerable disarray for the past few decades, and liberals have been less sure about their policies than they used to be; but the extreme unpopularity of the administration of George W. Bush (b. 1946) has led to a reinvigorated liberalism that is likely to remain no matter who wins the 2008 presidential election. The movement has been away from government regulation of the economy to acceptance of the position that less regulation, but not *no* regulation, might be a good idea. Liberals have also concluded that the welfare system needs to be redesigned but not entirely scrapped. The old liberal faith that the government could help people help themselves, and the belief that recession and depression could be avoided by stimulating the economy, have been challenged but not entirely discarded. Liberals still stand for expanded personal freedom and therefore find themselves constantly at odds with the neoconservatives. Liberals still believe that greater human equality is a desirable and achievable goal and thus usually oppose conservatives, who reject the belief in equality as not reflecting the reality of the human race.

Liberals can be characterized on the same three measures as conservatives, but with less agreement on the mix of the three than what is found among conservatives. On social, fiscal, and foreign policy, liberals can be characterized roughly as follows:

- Social—a belief in freedom of choice. Today this tends to mean support for the pro-choice position on abortion and advocacy of the rights of women and minorities, including gay rights and rights for the disabled.

- Fiscal—a belief in the use of government intervention in the economy to regulate it.

- Foreign policy—a belief in the need to work within the international community for the peaceful resolution of conflicts. The stress is on cooperation and aid with a related reduction in emphasis on defense and the military.

There are two groups of liberals in the United States today: traditional liberals and what are called *neoliberals*.

The Role of Religion Liberals are often depicted as being antireligion and secular, supporting a belief system called *secular humanism*. While some liberals fit this image, it is a false depiction of liberalism in the United States. Clearly much of the civil rights movement was religiously based, as exemplified by the leadership of Rev. Dr. Martin Luther King (1929–1968). Much of the opposition to the war in Vietnam was based in churches and led by ministers. Jimmy Carter (b. 1924) is a Southern Baptist whose most recent publications argue that his coreligionists are abandoning their traditional concern for the poor. Canadian philosopher Charles Taylor (b. 1931) won the Templeton Prize for Progress Toward Research or Discoveries about Spiritual Realities in 2007. Taylor, a practicing Catholic, has long argued that societies must balance the secular and the spiritual, and he has chastised his fellow liberals for forgetting the necessity of the spiritual.

The connection between religion and liberalism can probably be traced to the Social Gospel of the late nineteenth and early twentieth centuries, led by writers like Baptist minister Walter Rauschenbusch (1861–1918). Illustrative of the Social Gospel movement was one of the best-selling novels of the time, *In His Steps* (1897), by Charles M. Sheldon (1857–1946), a Kansas minister. In the novel, people begin to ask themselves what Jesus would do before taking any action, with society transformed as a result.

But contemporary liberals are more likely to be secularists than are contemporary conservatives, and although the term is meant as an attack, secular humanism can be seen as a belief system parallel to religion. Unfortunately, those who could be called secular humanists often simply do not see what their opponents are talking about. But their opponents generally fail to understand the secular humanist belief system. It is essential that both the words *secular* and *humanism* be understood, because the focus of liberal secularists is on the improvement of the human condition, and they argue that religious belief gets in the way of the knowledge necessary to do that. Religious liberals like Taylor argue that religion provides the very values that the secularists pursue.

Because they are currently the most important politically, here I have only mentioned the activities of Christians, but similar movements exist among Jews and Muslims.

Traditional Liberalism

Traditional liberalism, in this sense a tradition dating back to the 1930s, is described by its opponents as advocating big government, deficit spending, and expensive welfare programs. Traditional liberals see themselves as advocates of working people, the poor, and minorities against big business and as supporters of civil rights for African Americans, women, and ethnic and other minorities against the repression of government and business. Thus they see themselves as defenders of freedom and equality. They believe that only government is powerful enough to achieve these goals; therefore, they favor strong government. Liberals are unified on goals but divided on means. All liberals believe in an egalitarian society with protection for civil rights, but they are divided on how to achieve it. And in recent years, liberals have tried to expand civil rights to the disabled, indigenous groups, and gays and lesbians.

Neoliberalism

Neoliberals have identified themselves as fiscal conservatives while remaining social and foreign policy liberals, albeit with a slight shift to the conservative side in both cases. Neoliberals stress that they are concerned with getting the system to work rather than with ideology, and in this they are like the Third Way discussed in the previous chapter. They want to change the pattern of government spending because it is, they say, too high and inefficiently handled. They want a strong defense but more government oversight of military spending. They want efficient and effective welfare programs. Generally they want what they consider to be a realistic liberalism that faces rapid social and economic change. Today neoliberals dominate the Democratic Party in the United States.

SUGGESTED READING

Conservatism

Some Classic Works

Buckley, William F., Jr. *Up from Liberalism.* 25th anniversary ed. New York: Stein & Day, 1984.

Burke, Edmund. *Reflections on the Revolution in France.* 1790. Indianapolis, IN: Hackett, 1987. There are a number of good editions; I recommend the one edited by J. G. A. Pocock.

Falwell, Jerry. *Listen America!* Garden City, NY: Doubleday, 1980.

Hayek, Friedrich A. von. *The Constitution of Liberty.* London: Routledge & Kegan Paul, 1960.

————. *The Road to Serfdom.* 50th anniversary ed. Chicago: University of Chicago Press, 1994.

Huntington, Samuel P. "Conservatism as an Ideology." *American Political Science Review* Vol. 51:1 (June 1957): 454–473.

Kendall, Willmoore. *The Conservative Affirmation.* Chicago: Henry Regnery, 1963.

Kirk, Russell. *The Conservative Mind, from Burke to Santayana.* Chicago: Henry Regnery, 1953. 7th revised ed. with the subtitle *from Burke to Eliot.* Washington, DC: Regnery Publishing, 1995.

————. *A Program for Conservatives.* Revised ed. Chicago: Henry Regnery, 1962. Originally published 1954.

Viereck, Peter [Robert Edwin]. *Conservatism Revisited: The Revolt Against Ideology.* New Brunswick, NJ: Transaction, 2005.

————. *The Unadjusted Man: A New Hero for Americans. Reflections on the Distinction Between Conforming and Conserving.* Boston, MA: Beacon Press, 1956. Critique of conservatism by a well-known conservative theorist.

Books and Articles

Berkowitz, Peter, ed. *Varieties of Conservatism in America.* Stanford, CA: Hoover Institution Press, 2004. Distinguishes among classical conservatism, libertarianism, and neoconservatism.

Bloom, Allan. *The Closing of the American Mind: How Higher Education Has Failed Democracy and Impoverished the Souls of Today's Students.* New York: Simon & Schuster, 1987.

Bork, Robert H. *Coercing Virtue: The Worldwide Rule of Judges.* Washington, DC: AEI Press, 2003. Compares the United States with Canada and Israel.

Brown, Wendy. "Neoliberalism, Neoconservatism, and De-Democratization." *Political Theory* Vol. 34:6 (December 2006): 690–714.

Buchanan, James M. *Why I, Too, Am Not a Conservative: The Normative Vision of Classical Liberalism.* Cheltenham, England: Edward Elgar, 2005. Title refers to an article by Hayek and makes strong distinctions between what he calls "classical liberalism" and contemporary conservatism. In particular he distinguishes the conservative emphasis on hierarchy among humans with the classical liberal rejection of hierarchy and accepts "the [Adam] Smithean assumption of natural equality" (p. 5). Says that this means that the conservative cannot be a democrat.

Buchanan, Patrick. *Right from the Start.* Boston: Little, Brown, 1988.

Comfort, Nathaniel C., ed. *The Panda's Black Box: Opening up the Intelligent Design Controversy.* Baltimore, MD: Johns Hopkins University Press, 2007.

Critchlow, Donald T. *Phyllis Schlafly and Grassroots Conservatism: A Woman's Crusade.* Princeton, NJ: Princeton University Press, 2005.

Dreher, Rod. *Crunchy Cons: How Birkenstocked Burkeans, Gun-Loving Organic Gardeners, Evangelical Free-Range Farmers, Hip Home-schooling Mamas, Right-Wing Nature Lovers, and Their Diverse Tribe of Countercultural Conservatives Plan to Save America (or at least the Republican Party).* New York: Crown Forum, 2006. Conservatives who do not fit the usual model.

Dunn, Charles W., and J. David Woodard. *The Conservative Tradition in America.* Revised ed. Lanham, MD: Rowman & Littlefield, 2003.

Flippen, J. Brooks. *Conservative Conservationist: Russell E. Train and the Emergence of American Environmentalism.* Baton Rouge: Louisiana State University Press, 2006.

Frank, Thomas. *What's the Matter With Kansas? How Conservatives Won the Heart of America.* New York: Metropolitan Books, 2004.

Fukuyama, Francis. *America at the Crossroads: Democracy, Power, and the Neoconservative Legacy.* New Haven, CT: Yale University Press, 2006. Disassociates himself from what neoconservatism has become, particularly in foreign policy.

Hacker, Jacob S., and Paul Pierson. *Off Center: The Republican Revolution and the Erosion of American Democracy. With a New Afterword.* New Haven, CT: Yale University Press, 2006.

Harvey, David. *A Short History of Neoliberalism.* Oxford, England: Oxford University Press, 2005.

Hasian, Marouf [Arif] Jr. *In the Name of Necessity: Military Tribunals and the Loss of American Civil Liberties.* Tuscaloosa: University of Alabama Press, 2005.

Honderich, Ted. *Conservatism: Burke, Nozick, Bush, Blair?* London: Pluto Press, 2005.

Intercollegiate Review: A Journal of Scholarship and Opinion (Founded 1965).

Kirk, Russell. *The American Cause.* Gleaves Whitney, ed. Wilmington, DE: ISI Books, 2002. Originally published in 1957.

————. *The Politics of Prudence.* Bryn Mawr, PA: Intercollegiate Studies Institute, 1993. Denies that conservatism is an ideology, but his definition of ideology applies only to ways of thinking he dislikes. See Chapter II "Ten Conservative Principles" (pp. 15–29).

————. *Redeeming the Time.* Jeffrey O. Nelson, ed. Wilmington, DE: ISI Books, 1996.

Kristol, Irving. *Reflections of a Neoconservative: Looking Back, Looking Ahead.* New York: Basic Books, 1983.

McDonald, W. Wesley. *Russell Kirk and the Age of Ideology.* Columbia: University of Missouri Press, 2004.

Modern Age (Founded 1957).

Norton, Anne. *Leo Strauss and the Politics of American Empire.* New Haven, CT: Yale University Press, 2004. Characteristics of neoconservatism.

Ong, Aihwa. *Neoliberalism as Exception: Mutations in Citizenship and Sovereignty.* Durham, NC: Duke University Press, 2006. Argues that many countries, particularly in Asia, are combining a supposedly noninterventionist neoliberalism with interventionist policies both economically and socially.

Posner, Richard. *The Problematics of Moral and Legal Theory.* Cambridge, MA: Belknap Press of Harvard University Press, 1999: 241. "Pragmatist judges always try to do the best they can do for the present and the future, unchecked by any felt *duty* to secure consistency in principle with what other officials have done in the past." [Original emphasis].

Rosen, Gary, ed. *The Right War? The Conservative Debate on Iraq.* Cambridge, England: Cambridge University Press, 2005.

Ruse, Michael. *The Evolution–Creation Struggle.* Cambridge, MA: Harvard University Press, 2005.

Ryn, Claes G. "Peter Viereck and Conservatism." In Peter Viereck, *Conservatism Revisited: The Revolt Against Ideology.* New Brunswick, NJ: Transaction, 2005: 1–49.

Scully, Matthew. *Dominion: The Power of Man, the Suffering of Animals, and the Call to Mercy.* New York: St. Martin's Press, 2002. Animal rights from the point of view of the Christian Right.

Stelzer, Irwin, ed. *The Neocon Reader.* New York: Grove Press, 2004. UK ed. as *Neoconservatism.* London: Atlantic Books, 2004.

Sullivan, Andrew. *The Conservative Soul: How We Lost It, How To Get It Back.* New York: HarperCollins, 2006. Defines *conservatism* as "a political philosophy based on doubt, skepticism, disdain for attempts to remake the world, and suspicion of most ambitious bids to make it better" (p. 6).

Thompson, Michael J., ed. *Confronting the New Conservatism: The Rise of the Right in America.* New York: New York University Press, 2007.

Toplin, Robert Brent. *Radical Conservatism: The Right's Political Religion.* Lawrence: University Press of Kansas, 2006.

University Bookman (Founded 1960).

Yoo, John. *The Powers of War and Peace: The Constitution and Foreign Affairs After 9/11.* Chicago: University of Chicago Press, 2005. Argues that in foreign affairs, and particularly regarding war, the Constitution does not limit the President in any way. Author was an adviser to President George W. Bush.

Young, Matt, and Taner Edis, eds. *Why Intelligent Design Fails: A Scientific Critique of the New Creationism.* New Brunswick, NJ: Rutgers University Press, 2004.

Liberalism

Some Classic Works

Cumming, Robert Denoon. *Human Nature and History: A Study of the Development of Liberal Thought.* 2 vols. Chicago: University of Chicago Press, 1969.

De Ruggiero, Guido. *The History of European Liberalism.* R. G. Collingwood, trans. London: Oxford University Press, 1927. Reprinted Boston: Beacon Press, 1959.

Dworkin, Ronald. *Taking Rights Seriously.* London: Duckworth, 1977. New Impression with a Reply to Critics. London: Duckworth, 1978.

Flathman, Richard E. *Toward a Liberalism.* . . . Ithaca, NY: Cornell University Press, 1989.

Hartz, Louis. *The Liberal Tradition in America.* New York: Harcourt Brace, 1955.

Pateman, Carole. *The Problem of Political Obligation: A Critical Analysis of Liberal Theory.* New York: John S. Wiley & Sons, 1979. Reprinted Cambridge, England: Polity in association with Blackwell, 1985.

Rawls, John. *Justice as Fairness: A Restatement.* Erin Kelly, ed. Cambridge, MA: Belknap Press of Harvard University Press, 2001.

———. *The Law of Peoples,* with "The Idea of Public Reason Revisited." Cambridge, MA: Harvard University Press, 1999.

———. *Political Liberalism.* New York: Columbia University Press, 1993.

———. *A Theory of Justice.* Cambridge, MA: Belknap Press of Harvard University Press, 1971. Revised ed.: Oxford, England: Oxford University Press, 1999.

Books and Articles

Barry, Brian. *Why Social Justice Matters.* Cambridge, England: Polity, 2005.

Berkowitz, Peter, ed. *Varieties of Progressivism in America.* Stanford, CA: Hoover Institution Press, 2004.

Birt, Robert E., ed. *The Quest for Community and Identity: Critical Essays in Africana Social Philosophy.* Lanham, MD: Rowman and Littlefield, 2002.

Brown, Wendy. *Regulating Aversion: Tolerance in the Age of Identity and Empire.* Princeton, NJ: Princeton University Press, 2006.

Chauncey, George. *Why Marriage: The History Shaping Today's Debate Over Gay Equality.* New York: Basic Books, 2004.

Cheah, Pheng. *Inhuman Conditions: On Cosmopolitanism and Human Rights.* Cambridge, MA: Harvard University Press, 2006.

Dawson, Michael C. *Black Visions: The Roots of Contemporary African-American Political Ideologies.* Chicago: University of Chicago Press, 2001.

Dworkin, Ronald. *Law's Empire.* Cambridge, MA: Belknap Press of Harvard University Press, 1986.

———. *A Matter of Principle.* Cambridge, MA: Harvard University Press, 1985.

———. *Freedom's Law: The Moral Reading of the American Constitution.* Oxford, England: Oxford University Press, 1996.

———. *Is Democracy Possible Here? Principles for a New Political Debate.* Princeton, NJ: Princeton University Press, 2006.

Echols, James, ed. *I Have a Dream: Martin Luther King and the Future of Multicultural America.* Minneapolis, MN: Fortress Press, 2004.

Evans, Mark, ed. *The Edinburgh Companion to Contemporary Liberalism.* Edinburgh, Scotland: Edinburgh University Press, 2001.

Flathman, Richard E. *Freedom and Its Conditions: Discipline, Autonomy, and Resistance.* New York: Routledge, 2003.

———. *Pluralism and Liberal Democracy.* Baltimore, MD: Johns Hopkins University Press, 2005. Stress on pluralism.

Freeden, Michael. "European Liberalisms: An Essay in Comparative Political Thought." *European Journal of Political Theory.* Vol. 7:1 (January 2008): 7–30.

———. *Liberal Languages: Ideological Imaginations and Twentieth-Century Progressive Thought.* Princeton, NJ: Princeton University Press, 2005. A collection of previously published essays.

Freeman, Samuel, ed. *Cambridge Companion to Rawls.* Cambridge, England: Cambridge University Press, 2002.

Gitlin, Todd. *The Intellectuals and the Flag.* New York: Columbia University Press, 2006.

Gruskin, Sofia, Michael A. Grodin, George J. Annas, and Stephen P. Marks, eds. *Perspectives on Health and Human Rights.* New York: Routledge, 2005.

Harrison, Lawrence E. *The Central Liberal Truth: How Politics Can Change a Culture and Save It From Itself.* Oxford, England: Oxford University Press, 2006.

Insole, Christopher J. *The Politics of Human Frailty: A Theological Defence of Political Liberalism.* London: SCM Press/Notre Dame, IN: University of Notre Dame Press, 2004. Sees liberalism as based on the recognition of the fallen nature of humanity and argues that theologies that attack liberalism are misrepresenting liberalism.

Ishay, Micheline R. *The History of Human Rights: From Ancient Times to the Globalization Era*. Berkeley: University of California Press, 2004.

Jumonville, Neil, and Kevin Mattson, eds. *Liberalism for a New Century*. Berkeley: University of California Press, 2007. Argues that liberalism has to revive the best of its past and make a case for its positions. Much on the history of American liberalism and its agreements and disagreements with conservatism in the twentieth century.

Lofy, Bill, ed. *Politics the Wellstone Way: How to Elect Progressive Candidates and Win on Issues*. Minneapolis: University of Minnesota Press, 2005.

Madsen, Richard, and Tracy B. Strong, eds. *The Many and the One: Religious and Secular Perspectives on Ethical Pluralism in the Modern World*. Princeton, NJ: Princeton University Press, 2003.

Massey, Douglas S. *Return of the "L" Word: A Liberal Vision for the New Century*. Princeton, NJ: Princeton University Press, 2005.

Mattson, Kevin. *When America Was Great: The Fighting Faith of Postwar Liberalism*. New York: Routledge, 2004.

Mead, Lawrence M., and Christopher Beem, eds. *Welfare Reform and Political Theory*. New York: Russell Sage Foundation, 2005.

Michaels, Walter Benn. *The Trouble With Diversity: How We Learned to Love Identity and Ignore Inequality*. New York: Metropolitan Books, 2006.

Nussbaum, Martha C[raven]. *Frontiers of Justice: Disability, Nationality, Species Membership*. Cambridge, MA: The Belknap Press of Harvard University, 2005. Justice must incorporate those who cannot be part of the Rawlsian contract.

O'Leary, Kevin. *Saving Democracy: A Plan for Real Representation in America*. Stanford, CA: Stanford University Press, 2006. Proposes a system for greater citizen involvement that would begin with a 100-person assembly in each Congressional district that would discuss the issues their local representative had to vote on.

Pearce, Nick, and Julia Margo, eds. *Politics for a New Generation: The Progressive Moment*. Houndsmill, England: Palgrave Macmillan, 2007.

Peters, John Durham. *Courting the Abyss: Free Speech and the Liberal Tradition*. Chicago: University of Chicago Press, 2005. Free speech throughout history.

Phillips, Anne. "Defending Equality of Outcome." *The Journal of Political Philosophy* Vol. 12:1 (March 2004): 1–19.

Raskin, Marcus G. *Liberalism: The Genius of American Ideals*. Lanham, MD: Rowman & Littlefield, 2004.

Ringen, Stein. *The Possibility of Politics: A Study in the Political Economy of the Welfare State*. New ed. New Brunswick, NJ: Transaction Publishers, 2006. Originally published in 1987.

Sandel, Michael J. *Public Philosophy: Essays on Morality in Politics*. Cambridge, MA: Harvard University Press, 2005. Essays arguing for liberal positions regarding the great moral issues of the day.

Schierup, Carl-Ulrik, Peo Hansen, and Stephen Castles. *Migration, Citizenship, and the European Welfare State: A European Dilemma*. Oxford, England: Oxford University Press, 2006.

Schwartzman, Lisa H. *Challenging Liberalism: Feminism as Political Critique*. University Park: Pennsylvania State University Press, 2006.

Shanley, Mary Lyndon. *Just Marriage: A New Democracy Forum*. Joshua Cohen and Deborah Chasman for *Boston Review*, eds. New York: Oxford University Press, 2004. Argument and responses regarding the status of marriage in the United States.

Starr, Paul. *Freedom's Power: The True Force of Liberalism*. New York: Basic Books, 2007. See also http://www.freedomspower.com.

Swaine, Lucas. *The Liberal Conscience: Politics and Principle in a World of Religious Pluralism*. New York: Columbia University Press, 2006.

Turner, Rachel S. "The 'rebirth of liberalism': The origins of neo-liberal ideology." *Journal of Political Ideologies* Vol. 12:1 (February 2007): 67–83.

Walzer, Michael. *Politics and Passion: Toward a More Egalitarian Liberalism*. New Haven,

CT: Yale University Press, 2004. Argument against deliberative democracy.

Wellstone, Paul. *The Conscience of a Liberal: Reclaiming the Compassionate Agenda.* Minneapolis: University of Minnesota Press, 2001.

Western, Bruce. *Punishment and Inequality in America.* New York: Russell Sage Foundation, 2006.

Wilkinson, Richard G. *The Impact of Inequality: How to Make Sick Societies Healthier.* New York: New Press, 2005. Shows the impact of inequality on human health. Notes that Greece has a higher life expectancy than the United States and that the people of Harlem have shorter lives than those in Bangladesh.

Communitarianism

Some Classic Works

Bell, Daniel. *Communitarianism and Its Critics.* Oxford, England: Clarendon Press, 1993.

Etzioni, Amitai. *The Common Good.* Cambridge, England: Polity Press, 2004.

———. *The Spirit of Community: Rights, Responsibilities, and the Communitarian Agenda.* New York: Crown, 1993.

Books

Bauman, Zygmunt. *Community: Seeking Safety in an Insecure World.* Cambridge, England: Polity Press, 2001.

Etzioni, Amitai. *The Monochrome Society.* Princeton, NJ: Princeton University Press, 2001.

———. *The New Golden Rule: Community and Morality in a Democratic Society.* New York: Basic Books, 1996.

———, ed. *The Essential Communitarian Reader.* Lanham, MD: Rowman & Littlefield, 1998.

Tam, Henry [Benedict]. *Communitarianism: A New Agenda for Politics and Citizenship.* New York: New York University Press, 1998.

The Extreme Right

Classic Work

Macdonald, Andrew [pseud.] [William Luther Pierce]. *The Turner Diaries.* 2nd ed. Washington, DC: National Alliance, 1980.

Books and Articles

Balmer, Randall. *Thy Kingdom Come: How the Religious Right Distorts the Faith and Threatens America. An Evangelical's Lament.* New York: Basic Books, 2006.

Blee, Kathleen M. *Inside Organized Racism: Women in the Hate Movement.* Berkeley: University of California Press, 2002.

Clark, Victoria. *Allies for Armageddon: The Rise of Christian Zionism.* New Haven, CT: Yale University Press, 2007.

Dobratz, Betty E., and Stephanie L. Shanks-Meile. *The White Separatist Movement in the United States: "White Power, White Pride!"* Baltimore, MD: Johns Hopkins University Press, 2000.

Ehrenberg, John. *Servants of Wealth: The Right's Assault on Economic Justice.* Lanham, MD: Rowman & Littlefield, 2006.

Hedges, Chris. *American Fascists: The Christian Right and the War on America.* London: Jonathan Cape, 2007.

Holsinger, Bruce. *Neomedievalism, Neoconservatism, and the War on Terror.* Chicago: Prickly Paradigm Press, 2006.

Kaplan, Jeffrey, ed. *Encyclopedia of White Power: A Sourcebook on the Radical Racist Right.* Walnut Creek, CA: AltaMira Press, 2000.

Morgan, Robin. *Fighting Words: A Tool Kit for Combating the Religious Right.* New York: Nation Books, 2006.

Norris, Pippa. *Radical Right: Voters and Parties in the Electoral Market.* Cambridge, England: Cambridge University Press, 2005.

Phillips, Kevin. *American Theocracy: The Peril and Politics of Radical Religion, Oil, and Borrowed Money in the 21st Century.* New York: Viking, 2006. Strongly against radical religion.

Quarles, Chester L. *Christian Identity: The Aryan American Bloodline Religion.* Jefferson, NC: McFarland & Co., 2004.

Sargent, Lyman Tower, ed. *Extremism in America: A Reader.* New York: New York University Press, 1995.

Suprynowicz, Vin. *The Ballad of Carl Drega: Essays on the Freedom Movement, 1994 to 2001.* Reno, NV: Mountain Media, 2002.

Tebble, Adam James. "Exclusion for Democracy." *Political Theory* Vol. 34:4 (August 2006): 463–487. Points out that identity politics, usually thought of as a liberal or Left phenomenon, is central to some right-wing political movements.

Thompson, Michael J., ed. *Confronting the New Conservatism: The Rise of the Right in America.* New York: New York University Press, 2007.

Toplin, Robert Brent. *Radical Conservatism: The Right's Political Religion.* Lawrence: University Press of Kansas, 2006.

Wallis, Jim. *God's Politics: Why the Right Gets It Wrong and the Left Doesn't Get It.* San Francisco: HarperSanFranciso, 2005. U.K. ed. with the subtitle *A New Vision for Faith in America.* London: Harper-Collins, 2006. From the point of view of a liberal evangelical.

Weinberg, Leonard, and Ami Pedahzur, eds. *Religious Fundamentalism and Political Extremism.* London: Frank Cass, 2004. Originally published as the Winter 2003 issue of *Totalitarian Movements and Political Religions.*

Websites

Conservatism

The American Enterprise Institute for Public Policy Research: http://www.aei.org

The Cato Institute: http://www.cato.org

The Heritage Foundation: http://www.heritage.org

Liberalism

Act Up (AIDS Coalition to Unleash Power): http://www.actup.org

Alternative Radio. Audio Energy for Democracy: http://www.alternativeradio.org

The Brookings Institution: http://www.brook.edu

Human Rights Watch: http://www.hrw.org

Liberal International: http://www.liberal-international.org

National Association for the Advancement of Colored People (NAACP): http://www.naacp.org

Public Citizen: http://www.citizen.org

Communitarianism

The Communitarian Network: http://www.gwu.edu/~ccps

Institute for Communitarian Policy Studies: http://www.gwu.edu

The Extreme Right

National Alliance: http://www.natall.com

Resistance Records: http://www.resistance.com

7

Feminism

Feminism is a well-established ideology with certain core positions and a range of variants that move in somewhat different directions. Feminism is also an international movement that cuts across class, national, racial, ethnic, and religious barriers even though those same barriers reveal significant differences.

One subject on which feminists agree is the need to replace what they see as the system of male dominance, or *patriarchy,* that affects all social institutions. Clearly, feminism focuses on the position of women in society and the roles they play, but feminists argue that improving the status of women will also benefit all human beings whatever their gender.

An obvious example of the problems women can face were the laws the Taliban imposed in Afghanistan, laws that are being reimposed in areas under Taliban control once again. Such laws require most women to stay at home unless accompanied by a male relative; they also prohibit the employment and education of women and require them to wear the *burqa,* a traditional head-to-toe covering. The Taliban also restricts men's freedom in many ways but much less severely; for example, men are required to wear beards. Extreme measures such as those imposed on women in Afghanistan are rare, but women face a wide variety of major and minor restrictions, both customary and legal, throughout the world.

One of the slogans of the women's movement in the sixties was "The Personal Is The Political"; our understandings of ourselves and our relations with others, even those closest to us, are all at least partly political, at least partly power relations. Given the ability of the socialization process to form the understanding people have of their social roles, often women themselves do not recognize the restrictions that limit them; and the modern women's movement has often focused on *consciousness raising,* or helping first women and then men to become aware of the limits imposed on women by both law and custom. The 1960s saw the rapid growth of feminism and thousands of consciousness-raising groups in North America and Europe.

THE DEVELOPMENT OF FEMINISM

Debates over the social roles of men and women go back to classical and biblical times. Both the Old and New Testaments contain passages that have been used to argue either that women are inferior or that women are equal. Plato's (c. 427 to 347 B.C.) *Republic* has been interpreted as contending both that women should be treated as equals to men and that women are naturally inferior.

Such debates are a constant of Western history. For example, in March 1776, Abigail Adams (1744–1818) wrote to her husband John Adams (1735–1826), then involved in the movement for American independence and, later, second president of the United States, entreating him to "Remember the Ladies" in the laws drawn up for the newly independent country. John Adams responded, "I cannot but laugh," and continued, "We know better than to repeal our Masculine systems."[1]

At about the same time in England, Mary Wollstonecraft (1759–1797) was writing the first major work arguing for rights for women. Her *Vindication of the Rights of Woman* (1792) was part of a European and American movement to develop a theory of individual human rights. Thomas Paine's (1737–1809) *The Rights of Man* (1791–1792) and the French *Declaration of the Rights of Man and Citizen* (1789) are other expressions of the movement, but in most cases, these rights were only for men. Thus Wollstonecraft's book was an early plea, generally neglected at the time, that the radical thinkers of the day should argue for human rights rather than man's rights.

Earlier, writers such as Mary Astell (1668–1731), in *A Serious Proposal to the Ladies* (1694), and Sarah Scott (1723–1795), in *A Description of Millenium Hall* (1762), had concluded that women would never be treated as independent beings so they argued that women should separate themselves from men. And, as we shall see, some women still believe today that real freedom for women can come only through separation from men.

In the nineteenth century, the women's movement began as a general movement for sexual equality and ended dominated by a single issue: the campaign for the vote. In the United States, this pattern was repeated with the attempt to pass the Equal Rights Amendment (ERA), which was for a time the sole political focus of the U.S. women's movement. In both cases the general feminist arguments tended to get lost in the political campaign.

---

[1] L. H. Butterfield, ed., *Adams Family Correspondence,* vol. 1. Cambridge, MA: Belknap Press of Harvard University Press, 1963: 370, 382.

In the first half of the nineteenth century in the United States, women like Angelina Grimké (1805–1879), Sarah Grimké (1792–1873), Margaret Fuller (1810–1850), and Frances Wright (1795–1852) became involved in the movement to abolish slavery and, from there, moved into other areas of reform including the rights of women. As Angelina Grimké put it, "I recognize no rights but human rights—I know nothing of man's rights and women's rights."[2] Later, Elizabeth Cady Stanton (1815–1902), Susan B. Anthony (1820–1906), and others argued for a wide-ranging emancipation of women. As Anthony put it in a famous statement to the court upon being found guilty of voting (a sympathetic clerk had allowed her to cast a ballot), "You have trampled underfoot every vital principle of our government. My natural rights, my civil rights, my political rights, are all alike ignored. Robbed of the fundamental privilege of citizenship, I am degraded from the status of a citizen to that of a subject."[3]

Similar movements existed in most western European countries plus Australia and New Zealand, and they generally followed the same pattern of radical demands for equality, giving way to the sole demand for the vote. In Britain three works in the nineteenth century were particularly important in establishing the early stages of the women's movement. *Appeal of One-Half of the Human Race, Women, Against the Pretensions of Other Half, Men* (1825) by William Thompson (1775–1833) and Anna Doyle Wheeler (1785–1848), whom he credited with many of the ideas in the book but whose name does not appear on the title page; *The Enfranchisement of Women* (1851) by Harriet Taylor (1807–1858); and *The Subjection of Women* (1869) by John Stuart Mill (1806–1873) all pointed to the mistreatment of women. Although these works stressed documenting the status of women legally and socially, they also argued for the vote and for equality before the law.

In 1848, a convention in Seneca Falls, New York, was called "to discuss the social, civil, and religious conditions and rights of woman."[4] This convention passed the famous Declaration of Sentiments, modeled on the U.S. Declaration of Independence. It stated that "it is the duty of the women of this country to secure to themselves their sacred right to the elective franchise."[5] It also stated, much more radically, in words similar to those of Henry David Thoreau's (1817–1862) "On the Duty of Civil Disobedience" (1849), that "all laws which prevent women from occupying such a station in society as her conscience shall dictate, or which place her in a position inferior to that of man, are contrary to the great precept of nature, and therefore of no force or authority."[6]

In Britain, Emmeline Pankhurst (1858–1928) was one of the leaders in the movement for the vote. Her group, the Women's Social and Political Union, used civil disobedience in their campaign. As a result, Pankhurst and many of her

---

[2] Angelina E. Grimké, *Letters to Catherine E. Beecher in Reply to an Essay on Slavery and Abolitionism Addressed to A. E. Grimké, Revised by the Author.* Boston: Printed by Isaac Knapp, 1838; Reprinted, New York: Arno Press and the *New York Times,* 1965: 118.

[3] Elizabeth Cady Stanton, Susan B. Anthony, and Martha Joslyn Gage, eds., *History of Woman Suffrage,* vol. 2. New York: Fowler & Wells, 1881; Reprinted, New York: Arno Press and the *New York Times,* 1969: 687.

[4] *History of Woman Suffrage,* vol. 1: 67.

[5] *History of Woman Suffrage,* vol. 1: 72.

[6] *History of Woman Suffrage,* vol. 1: 72.

Culver Pictures, Inc.

The campaign to extend the vote to women was one of the longest-running reform movements in Western democracies. In most countries, women did not gain the right to vote until well into the twentieth century. The campaign for the vote included activities such as this parade, along with marches, petitions, fasts, violent protests, and demonstrations in which women chained themselves to the doors of public buildings. Their efforts involved virtually all the tactics used in later protest movements. The suffrage movement was a single-issue campaign; as such, many feminists today believe that it detracted from attempts to bring about more radical changes in the condition of women. At the time, many women felt that with the vote, women would be able to bring about greater changes. So far this has not been true, and in some countries change has begun but well after they had hoped it would.

followers were repeatedly jailed, thus bringing more attention to the movement. Her daughters Christobel (1880–1958) and Sylvia (1882–1960) were also active feminists; Sylvia attacked the institution of marriage and bore a child out of wedlock.

Before World War I, the single most important issue for the women's movement besides the vote was birth control. The most prominent figure in the birth control movement was Margaret Sanger (1883–1966), but others, notably the U.S. anarchist Emma Goldman (1869–1940), whose broad radical agenda included many issues of particular interest to women, supported her. Others in the United States who were concerned with more than the vote included Charlotte Perkins Gilman (1860–1935), whose journal *The Forerunner* was a forceful advocate for women. Her *Women and Economics* (1898) was a widely acclaimed study that argued for the need to restructure social institutions to permit women to work. Her utopian novel *Moving the Mountain* (1911) fictionally shows such a changed society. Jane Addams (1860–1935) exemplified and argued for an active role for women in improving life in the cities and is best known as the founder of the famous Hull House in Chicago, which was an early project to help the poor, and particularly poor women. She was also deeply involved in the peace movement at the time of World War I.

When the vote was won, it had little noticeable effect on social policy. But during World War II, women were encouraged to join the workforce for the war effort and learned to do things they had been taught were impossible for women. After the war these same women were told to go back home and give up the money and independence they had come to expect. The publication in France in 1949 of Simone de Beauvoir's (1908–1986) *Le Deuxième Sexe* (published in English in 1952 as *The Second Sex*), a study of the treatment of women by various academic disciplines, helped fan the anger at this loss.

Still, it was not until the 1960s and the publication of *The Feminine Mystique* (1963) by Betty Friedan (1921–2006), combined with the rejection of women's issues by the New Left, that a renewed feminist movement began. Although this burgeoning movement was predominantly white, a number of African-American women also became active in the cause. Today the women's movement is acutely aware of the importance of speaking to the needs of minority women and of women in the developing nations. And these women are finding their voices and speaking for themselves, and in doing so, they often reject the approach taken by women in the developed world.

THE PERSONAL IS THE POLITICAL

In opposing all forms of discrimination, feminists have argued that the term *political* needs to be redefined. If, as some would have it, politics are about power, then politics exists between men and women both individually and in groups. Power relations exist between friends and lovers and within families. For example, in the family, who makes decisions and how they are made are political questions, as are questions about who spends how much and on what, who allocates tasks around the house, and the division of labor reflected in such allocation.

An interesting case is housework. This is an important issue, because it includes the traditional sexual division of labor in which men work outside the home for a wage and, if a man's wage is high enough, the woman does not work. But if the man's income is not high enough to pay for servants, the woman works at home without a wage. And, of course, if a woman works outside the home, in the traditional division of labor, she still does the housework. Housework is the largest sector of unwaged labor in the economy, and anyone attempting to replace that unpaid labor with paid labor finds that certain aspects of it command substantial wages because, although the work is not well paid, long hours are required. Cooking and child care can be very expensive; regular cleaning is not cheap, and high-quality work is hard to find. Housework is also repetitive and not particularly exciting work. Many people—men and women alike—if given a choice do not do it.

For these reasons, housework illustrates just how political work allocation is in a modern household. Generally, although increased awareness has produced a change toward men helping more around the house (the word *help* implies assistance freely donated, not required), the traditional pattern remains common, with the added factor that the woman works outside the home for a wage, as well as doing the same work in the home as before. In other words, the pattern of sexual division of labor that once applied only to the poor has spread to the middle class. Thus both the economics and the internal dynamics of housework illustrate the maxim that the personal is the political. Similar questions affect all relations between women and men.

Another way of describing the situation in which women find themselves can be seen in an expansion of the notion of the personal as the political. If all human relationships are power relationships, whatever else they may also be, women as individuals and as a group have been among the powerless and, with some exceptions, are less powerful than men even in the developed world and still mostly powerless elsewhere. An example can illustrate the point: When men were telephone operators and secretaries, these positions were adequately paid and had some prestige; when these positions became "women's work," they changed into low-paid positions with little prestige. And women were excluded from many positions. For example, in *Bradwell* v. *Illinois* (83 U.S. [16 Wall] 130 [1872]), the U.S. Supreme Court upheld an Illinois law that prohibited women from practicing law, and in most areas of the United States, only single women were allowed to teach in elementary and secondary schools.

The fact that we are aware of power relations where we previously failed to notice them does not mean that such relations are necessarily subject to public policy, but our changed awareness does raise the complicated question of the relationship between the public and the private and what activities should belong to each sphere. Many things we consider private have entered the public arena. For example, until recently spousal and, to a slightly lesser extent, child abuse were not considered appropriate subjects for public action. In most states in the United States, it was, until the last few decades, legally impossible for a man to rape his wife; he literally owned access to her body, and she had no right to deny him that access. Thus a central debate raised by feminism is what, if anything, remains private and not subject to public or political scrutiny. At present, the answer is not clear, but the boundaries set by both public opinion and the law have clearly moved toward including more life experiences within the public realm. At the same time, significant opposition to such changes remains.[7]

SEXISM

Sexism is the belief that women are inferior to men, just as *racism* is the belief that one group of people is inferior or superior based on factors such as skin color. But sexism and racism are just examples of the much broader point that people are oppressed both individually and as groups by socially constructed

---

[7] For an analysis of the position, see Jyl Josephson and Cynthia Burack, "The Political Ideology of the Neotraditional Family," *Journal of Political Ideologies* Vol. 3:2 (June 1998): 213–231. For advocacy, see Phyllis Schlafly, *Feminist Fantasies*. Dallas: Spence, 2003.

patterns of beliefs, attitudes, and practices. Like racism, sexism is pervasive in language, art, literature, and religion. More obviously, sexism pervades politics and the economy, and it is part of what feminists oppose and hope to eliminate. Eliminating sexism will be extremely difficult because it is, as feminists contend, part of all Western languages and part of many dearly held beliefs, including religious beliefs.

Socialization

Feminists argue that the process of socialization should not eliminate options for women and that women should be allowed to see all the possibilities open to them, not just a few. For example, as mentioned earlier, at one time women could not be secretaries or telephone operators; these jobs were reserved for men, both because women were not thought capable of doing them and because women were not expected to have paid employment. But, of course, poor women have always worked in paid employment, and women on farms have always worked along with other family members. And feminist historians have discovered multitudes of women who have refused to be limited by stereotypes of acceptable female behavior. This illustrates how the work of recovering the history of women—African Americans, ethnic minorities, and other groups— provides psychological support for individuals living today and a basis for political arguments against discrimination.

In addition, feminists contend that women are socialized to accept both physical and mental mistreatment. Rape has been considered the most underreported crime in the United States, but the "discovery" of the extent of incest and child abuse indicates a number of rarely reported crimes, almost all of which are crimes against women and children. Feminists argue that these crimes are underreported for several reasons. First, women who report rape must still generally deal with male police officers; even if—too rarely—they are sensitive to the woman's trauma, they are still men. Second, the legal system has traditionally treated the woman as the responsible party; victims have often been blamed for "allowing" themselves to be victimized. Third, women have been taught to accept such abuse from men and to consider it almost normal. This socialization process, along with women's common fear of leaving their abusive homes because of the financial consequences, also encourages women to accept abuse from husbands or companions.

Feminists note that in addition to physical abuse, women are subject to pervasive mental abuse. It consists, in large part, of attacks on women's self-esteem and treating women as objects or things rather than as individuals or persons. Clearly rape is the most extreme form of treating a person as an object, but many other ways of abusing women do not involve physical abuse.

Physical and mental abuse are part of the oppression of women, as is the fact that in many jobs, women are not paid the same as men for doing the same work and are often sexually harassed at work. In addition, although overt political discrimination has been reduced, more subtle forms are still common.

Language

Feminists have often been both criticized and laughed at for proposing changes in language use to remove the male bias. But taking the argument seriously and looking at the history (some feminists note that the word *history* itself can be read as "his story" and prefer to use "herstory") of language use, we can see the force of their point. For example, a female first-year university student is called a fresh*man*. Why? Not long ago women could not attend university, and the term implies that. Of course, language use changes, and most people now use fresh*man* to refer to both male and female first-year students; but the word is a relic of past sexual discrimination.[8]

As another example, when Thomas Jefferson drafted the Declaration of Independence and wrote, "All men are created equal," did he mean all human beings or just male human beings? We do not really know what Jefferson meant, but we do know that for many people at the time, the words referred only to white, male human beings. And when we read the writings of major thinkers of the past, we often do not know what the word *man* means; we can read it to mean all human beings, but we may miss what the author intended us to understand.

A particularly interesting example can be seen in the novel *The Left Hand of Darkness* (1969) by Ursula K. Le Guin (b. 1929). When *The Left Hand of Darkness* was originally published, relatively little awareness existed regarding the gendered character of language, and Le Guin called her characters, who changed gender at different points in their lives, "he." The twenty-fifth anniversary edition (1994) of *The Left Hand of Darkness* addressed the criticism Le Guin received for her lack of awareness by providing sample chapters with four different sets of pronouns: one using invented pronouns and genderless personal nouns and titles; one using feminine pronouns and personal nouns, rather than the masculine of the original; one using pronouns that reflected the changes her characters go through, neuter and gendered at different life stages; and one using masculine and feminine pronouns for the same character, as that person goes through a transition. Understanding of the text varies remarkably depending on the set of pronouns and personal nouns used, which makes this exercise by Le Guin a striking contribution to the debate on language.

Religion

Orthodox Judaism makes a rigid division between men and women, with men and women separated during worship and with women defined as inferior. Liberal Judaism advocates, but does not always practice, equality. Women have been rabbis in reform congregations for some years but have only recently been allowed to become rabbis in conservative ones, and the acceptance of women as rabbis is spreading slowly, even where the policy is to allow it.[9]

---

[8] See Dale Spender, *Man Made Language,* 2nd ed. London: Routledge & Kegan Paul, 1985.

[9] See *On Being a Jewish Feminist: A Reader.* Susannah Heschel, ed. New York: Schocken Books, 1983.

Even though in the New Testament Christ is portrayed as treating men and women equally, the same pattern of gender discrimination holds true in Christianity. Almost as soon as the first Christian churches were organized, women were placed in subordinate roles. In fact, some of the earliest heresies centered on the advocacy of equality for women, and such heresies continued to appear from time to time, particularly around the Reformation and again in seventeenth-century England.[10]

Christian churches today are still divided over the role of women. The Episcopalian Church in the United States decided, after a long, intense debate, to admit women to the priesthood. As a result, many women have joined the priesthood, amounting to over a quarter of the Episcopalian clergy, and an African-American woman has been consecrated as a bishop in the United States. Some Episcopalian churches and priests left the denomination as a result. The Roman Catholic Church excludes women from the priesthood. Most Protestant denominations encourage the ordination of women as ministers, but still relatively few women are ministers in most churches.

These divisions reflect a deep ambivalence about women in Christianity, particularly in the Roman Catholic Church. Two women, Eve the rebel and temptress and Mary the mother of Christ, can symbolize the conflict. Roughly the position has been that to the extent that women emulate Mary and remain subordinate to men, they are correctly fulfilling their natures; to the extent that they emulate Eve they are dangerous. As a result, many feminists see Eve, the rebel, as a symbol of the real strength of women. And recently there has developed a critique of the patriarchy of the established churches around the figure of Mary Magdalene, who, in some places in the Bible, is described as one of the Apostles and was the first person to see Christ after his Resurrection. But the message that most churches present to women is one of subordination to men.

A feminist theology emerged from Liberation Theology (see the discussion of Feminist Liberation Theology in Chapter 12) and has developed in a number of different directions both in parallel with Liberation Theology and separate from it (one of those directions relates to ecofeminism, discussed in Chapter 13). For most feminist theologians in the West, the initial concern was critical and had to do with identifying the ways that patriarchy dominated and permeated religious belief and practice; and the most significant changes have come in practice, with substantially more women becoming ministers and holding positions of authority in their denominations.

In Islam men and women worship separately, just as in Orthodox Judaism, and there are no women imams (religious leaders) that have ever been officially recognized. But just as in Christianity and Buddhism, a feminist movement exists in Islam; and in some Western countries, women have unofficially held important religious roles during the early stages of the establishment of a new mosque.

---

[10] See Elaine Pagels, *The Gnostic Gospels.* New York: Random House, 1979; Norman Cohn, *The Pursuit of the Millennium: Revolutionary Millenarians and Mystical Anarchists of the Middle Ages.* London: Granada, 1970; and Christopher Hill, *The World Turned Upside Down: Radical Ideas during the English Revolution.* London: Temple Smith, 1972.

THE FEMINIST RESPONSES

Feminists agree on some responses to sexism, but they also disagree. Almost all feminists agree that fundamental answers to the problem of women's position in modern society include freedom and equality, but disagreements persist over both the meaning of these terms and how to achieve the desired result. All feminists agree that any changes should not benefit women alone. They oppose racism, sexism, and discrimination based on sexual orientation, and they argue that discrimination against any human being is an attack on all human beings; and they agree that men will also benefit from a free and egalitarian society.

Feminist responses can be classified in a number of ways, but none is entirely satisfactory because all of them tend to group people who have important disagreements and to separate people who agree on significant questions. No set of categories is currently acceptable, and many of the suggested categories are nonpolitical. The categories I use are reform or liberal, Marxist, socialist, integrative or transformative, and separatist or radical. Some commentators add a term to describe conservative antifeminists, but because they are antifeminists, I do not include them here (in addition, ecofeminism is discussed in Chapter 13). Following Angela Miles (b. 1946),[11] I have chosen to call the middle group *transformative* feminism, because this generally tries to recognize and incorporate the concerns of all feminists while taking a strong political stand.

Reform or Liberal Feminism

Reform feminists argue that the basic pattern of society is generally acceptable but that changes are needed so women are not put at a disadvantage because of their gender. Reform feminists want an equal opportunity to compete with men, and they propose that the means be found, such as improved and expanded day care facilities and improved parental leave policies, to more readily allow women to combine paid employment and motherhood. Obviously, these proposals also suggest that men must change their attitude toward sharing responsibility for child rearing, housework, and all other aspects of traditionally unpaid labor, which used to be called "women's work."

Reform feminists in the United States were particularly supportive of the Equal Rights Amendment, which reads in its entirety as follows:

Section 1. Equality of rights under the law shall not be denied by the United States or by any State on account of sex.

Section 2. The Congress shall have the power to enforce, by appropriate legislation, the provisions of this article.

Section 3. This amendment shall take effect two years after the ratification.[12]

---

[11] She used "integrative feminism" in her *Integrative Feminisms: Building Global Visions 1960s–1990s*. New York: Routledge, 1996, but changed to transformative in her "Local Activisms, Global Feminisms, and the Struggle Against Globalization." *Canadian Woman Studies/Les Cahiers de la femme* 20.3 (Fall 2000): 6–10.

[12] http://www.equalrightsamendment.org

Forces that considered the amendment dangerously radical or unnecessary defeated its passage. The most effective opponent—a conservative woman, Phyllis Schlafly (b. 1942)—has continued her opposition to feminism in her most recent book, *Feminist Fantasies* (2003).

Marxist Feminism

In its earliest manifestations, Marxism had a split personality regarding women. Marxists often said that women's issues must wait until after the class revolution. On the other hand, in 1884 Friedrich Engels (1820–1895) published *Origins of the Family, Private Property, and the State,* in which he noted the central role of women and the family in the development and maintenance of the social system. Engels thereby put what was called "the woman question" at the forefront of issues Marxists needed to solve, and many women were attracted to Marxism because of this.

In the last quarter of the twentieth century, feminists noted both of these tendencies within Marxism; and although many believed that Marx's analysis of capitalism was correct and pointed in useful directions, most concluded that Marxists in the twentieth century had generally ignored the insights of Engels and others and had adopted the "wait until after the revolution" approach. And because the so-called Marxist revolutions in China, Russia, and other countries did not produce the significant changes in women's roles that had been promised, considerable disillusionment resulted. As a result, today many Marxists argue that the insights of feminism need to be added to Marxism.

Socialist Feminism

Contemporary socialist feminists are perhaps best seen as democratic socialists with a focus. They reject the Marxist tendency to put class before gender, race, sexual identification, ethnicity, and the other ways in which human beings identify and classify themselves. And in doing so, they stress democratic decision making and the acceptance of difference within community.

Transformative Feminism

Transformative feminists have shown how men have created a male-centered way of understanding the world that severely limits our ability to conceptualize human relations that are not hierarchical and patriarchal. The goal of these feminists is to break through those mental barriers as well as the political, economic, and cultural barriers that keep all human beings from becoming fully human. For example, Nancy Hartsock (b. 1943) has noted that feminists have reconceptualized the notion of power. Power as dominance gives way to power as "energy and competence."[13] All our ways of thinking need to undergo a similar revolution.

---

[13] Nancy C. M. Hartsock, *Money, Sex, and Power: Toward a Feminist Historical Materialism.* New York: Longman, 1983: 224–225.

Hence transformative feminists are arguing for a fundamental transformation of not only our political and economic lives but our social, cultural, and personal lives as well. As Angela Miles says, "The alternative value core of transformative feminisms in all their variety is the holistic, egalitarian, life-centered rejection of dominant androcentric, dualistic, hierarchical, profit-centered ideology and social structures."[14] The goal is to achieve equality while recognizing difference or specificity.

Separatist or Radical Feminism

Separatist feminism, with some exceptions, argues for lesbianism and a woman-centered culture. Shulamith Firestone (b. 1945) argues for the abandonment of the biological family in *The Dialectic of Sex* (1970), and the development of a woman's culture can be seen in the works of Judy Chicago (b. 1939) and others.

There are significant separatist subcultures, both female and male, with everything from bars to music festivals to publishing houses, and lesbian communes exist in all Western countries. The lesbian subculture includes publishing houses that publish lesbian crime fiction, science fiction, romance, and other so-called genre fiction as well as nonfiction aimed at a lesbian readership. Much of this has to do with wanting a culture that speaks to the interests and needs of a variety of people, but it also provides space in which it is possible for a person to be who they are.

While gay men and lesbians cooperate on political issues that affect both groups, the divisions are deep. This is hardly surprising; at an important level, both groups are defined by the rejection of the other group, and both groups want to associate with the same sex as much as possible. Of course, it is never quite that simple, and the overwhelming majority of gays and lesbians have close friendships with members of the opposite sex.

Still, gay men often feel that lesbians have it easy in that the public expression of affection between women has always been more acceptable than the public expression of affection between men; and, of course, AIDS (Acquired Immune Deficiency Syndrome) has killed relatively few lesbians but tens of thousands of gay men. But lesbians feel that gay men are still men, socialized as men, and no more capable of treating women as equals than any other man.

One striking phenomenon is that, with the revival of utopian literature in the 1970s, a large number of books describing lesbian utopias have been published but almost none about gay male utopias. The lesbian utopias mostly depicted a positive, singe-sex future, but the gay male works are mostly depictions of negative futures or dystopias in which gay men were even more oppressed than at present.

CURRENT TRENDS

Feminism is developing a critical apparatus for analyzing contemporary society that is challenging all contemporary ideologies. Feminist philosophers and political philosophers are proposing new ways of understanding the world. Feminist economists are analyzing the economic roles of women and suggesting a transformation

---

[14] Miles, *Integrative Feminisms*: xi.

of economic life. Specifically, feminists have discovered the central role that women play in the agricultural economies of Third World countries and are arguing that the bias-rooted failure to recognize this fact has undercut all attempts to improve agricultural production in developing countries. And feminist writers and artists are developing a substantial body of literature and art that speaks to different concerns than had been previously addressed.

An example of the way the feminist movement has spread around the globe is the history of the book *Our Bodies Ourselves: A Course By and For Women*, which was originally put together by the Boston Women's Health Course Collective (later the Boston Women's Health Book Collective) in 1971 and published by the New England Free Press, an underground press. It was considered required reading for young women in the United States, because it was the first book written by women that spoke directly to women's concerns, and particularly because it did so through the stories of real women in easily understood language. It was the first stage in a revolution in women's health care in the United States, and it helped bring about profound changes in medical research, which had generally assumed that men were the norm and that separate research on women was unnecessary. It has now sold over four million copies worldwide with numerous translations and adaptations and more of both in process.[15] The most recent edition in English was published in 2005 as *The New Our Bodies Ourselves: A New Edition for a New Era*.

Feminists encourage all human beings to envision the possibility of a society free from sexism, racism, discrimination based on sexual orientation, and all the other ways in which human beings have subjugated other human beings. At present, feminists are divided over exactly how to go about this transformation, and reform feminists are not convinced that such a transformation is either necessary or desirable; but feminism is potentially the most radical of ideologies and the most likely to change the way most of us live today.

Votes for Women

In the twentieth century, women achieved the right to vote in most countries.[16] But this franchise did not translate into many women being elected to office; and although the number slowly rose in most developed countries in the last quarter of the twentieth century, the number of women elected to office has never come close to the percentage of women of voting age in the electorates. Although many arguments are made about both the causes and cures for this situation, one cure that is gaining ground is to set aside a certain number of positions to which only women can be elected. Precedents for this practice set in New Zealand dictate that seats be set aside for Maori, and in India, seats are reserved for the Dalit, or Untouchables.

---

[15] For a history of the book, see Kathy Davis, *The Making of "Our Bodies, Ourselves": How Feminism Travels Across Borders*. Durham, NC: Duke University Press, 2007.

[16] The first country to grant women the vote was New Zealand, which did so in 1893 while still excluding women from running for office; the first country to allow women to run for office was Finland in 1906 with 19 women elected to Parliament in 1907; the United States granted the vote in 1920.

In France, where the practice is called *parity,* a constitutional amendment was passed that states "the law favors equal access for men and women to electoral mandates and elective offices."[17] This amendment is being implemented by requiring that in certain circumstances, political parties must put forward an equal number of men and women as candidates for office. This does not, of course, guarantee election, but it is believed that more women will be elected under this system than have been previously. Anne Phillips (b. 1950) has developed proposals for a similar system designed for Britain.[18] Today, 25 countries allocate access to political power based on gender, either setting aside seats in the legislature or through electoral representation, 15 countries do so based on ethnicity, and 9 do so on the basis of both gender and ethnicity. Also, a growing number of countries practice some form of proportional representation, and such systems almost always produce more minority and women legislators. As of 2007, Sweden had the highest number of women in its legislature with 47.3 percent; the United States had 16.3 percent in the House of Representatives and 16 percent in the Senate.

Feminism and Legal Theory

Catharine A. MacKinnon (b. 1946) developed a legal theory that stresses that male dominance has been accepted in American law.[19] She contends that the male has always been the standard, even if not stated as such, and presents a position generally called *nonsubordination,* which argues for the recognition of women's actual lived experience as opposed to the supposed "objective" model that has turned out to be from the male perspective.

MacKinnon's initial work was on sexual harassment; when she began, harassment was not considered sexual discrimination but merely what should be expected between men and women. It is easy to see that looking at sexual harassment from the point of view of the harassed is essential to seeing the entire picture. MacKinnon's analysis provided the basis for changes in case law and legal codes so that today, sexual harassment is seen as sexual discrimination.[20]

MacKinnon's work to reveal pornography as discrimination based on sex has been much more controversial. She argues that freedom of expression is based on the false assumption of general equality and that gender inequality invalidates negative liberty, or the right of people to be left alone. Thus pornography

---

[17] Sylviane Agacinski, *Parity of the Sexes,* Lisa Walsh, trans. New York: Columbia University Press, 2001: viii.

[18] See Anne Phillips, *Engendering Democracy.* University Park: Pennsylvania State University Press, 1991; and Phillips, *The Politics of Presence.* Oxford: Oxford University Press, 1995.

[19] A parallel movement regarding race, called *critical race theory,* has also developed within legal theory. See Richard Delgado and Jean Stefancic, *Critical Race Theory: An Introduction.* New York: New York University Press, 2001; Richard Delgado and Jean Stefancic, eds., *Critical Race Theory: The Cutting Edge.* Philadelphia, PA: Temple University Press, 2000; and Dorothy A. Brown, *Critical Race Theory: Cases, Materials, and Problems.* St. Paul, MN: West, 2003.

[20] See Catharine A. MacKinnon, *The Sexual Harassment of Working Women.* New Haven, CT: Yale University Press, 1979. See also *Directions in Sexual Harassment Law,* Catharine A. MacKinnon and Reva B. Siegal, eds. New Haven, CT: Yale University Press, 2004.

is not, for MacKinnon, a question of civil liberties but an issue "central to the institutionalization of male dominance."[21] Opponents of MacKinnon's position, which on this issue include many feminists, argue that freedom of the press is too important a negative liberty to be compromised to get rid of pornography, however desirable that might be.

Multiculturalism

Given the emphasis on difference by many feminists, multiculturalism would appear to be an obvious position for feminists to take, and many do. But Susan Moller Okin's (1947–2004) question "Is Multiculturalism Bad for Women?", suggests that accepting multiculturalism may lead to the acceptance of cultures with gender divisions that disadvantage women.[22] Okin's argument poses a serious question for both feminists and multiculturalists. The assertion of universal human rights has been central to the arguments feminists have made that such rights belong equally to both women and men. On the other hand, the recognition of important differences between and among men and women has become central to the argument that equality of rights can go hand in hand with respect for differences among human beings. The problem is that if difference includes cultural differences, then some of those differences include the rejection of equal rights. The valuing of differences can allow difference to be used to undermine gender equality, through the argument that valued differences require differential treatment. Okin contended that equality of rights must not be sacrificed in the name of multicultural respect.

Clearly, as Okin pointed out, multiculturalism poses a major issue for feminists, but the issue is important not just for feminists. As noted throughout this book, in the past all ideologies posited certain universal values; but with the advent of postmodernism, universals of all sorts are now being questioned. The problem, acutely stated by Okin, is how to keep important universals while respecting differences among human beings.[23]

Women of Color The multicultural argument reflects a central, long-standing problem for feminists, particularly in the United States: the fact that most feminists are white. African-American author bell hooks (Gloria Watkins, b. 1952), in her *Ain't I a Woman? Black Women and Feminism* (1981), and the collection of essays *This Bridge Called My Back: Writings by Radical Women of Color* (1983) edited by Cherríe Moraga (b. 1952) and Gloria Anzaldúa (1942–2004), made early statements that the "universal" claims of white feminists did not necessarily apply to black women. The title of the work by bell hooks was taken from the famous

---

[21] Catharine A. MacKinnon, "Pornography," in MacKinnon, *Feminism Unmodified: Discourses on Life and Law.* Cambridge, MA: Harvard University Press, 1987: 146.

[22] For the essay and a number of responses both pro and con, see Susan Moller Okin with respondents, *Is Multiculturalism Bad for Women?* Joshua Cohen, Matthew Howard, and Martha C. Nussbaum, eds. Princeton, NJ: Princeton University Press, 1999.

[23] In her *The Futures of Difference: Truth and Method in Feminist Theory.* Cambridge, England: Polity Press, 1999, Susan J. Hekman argues that it is necessary to find a middle ground between the erasure of difference and the emphasis on difference.

speech "Ain't I a Woman?" (1851), given by Sojourner Truth (c. 1797–1883) at a women's rights convention, which illustrates that the issue is not a new one.

Third World Feminism The multicultural issue, seen through a different lens, is one that continues to be a problem within feminism: the position of women in the Third World. The extent of the problem can be seen in the fact that far fewer girls than boys are born because "excess" girls are either aborted or killed at birth; and far fewer girls survive to maturity than boys because poverty-stricken families feed boys more and they feed them more often, and boys are more likely to get medical care than girls. It has been estimated that at least 100 million women are "missing" worldwide.[24]

Many Western feminists, such as Okin, point to the obvious mistreatment of women in the Third World, the Taliban being only the most glaring case, and argue that the Western model of individual rights is the appropriate solution. On the other hand, both a growing number of Western feminists and many Third World feminists see this as an attempt to impose Western, and particularly American, values where they are not appropriate.[25]

And women in the Third World are not at all happy with the way they are discussed by some Western feminists, who seem to think that Western women should be able to speak for them. Thus, as with the question of race, separate and sometimes antagonistic feminisms have developed among Third World and indigenous women. Both sides in this issue are trying to find common ground, and much progress has been made, but considerable misunderstanding and distrust still exists.

Reproductive Rights

All feminists share a concern with freeing women from unwanted child bearing. This concern has been called *reproductive rights,* the right of a woman to control her own body, or, more recently, *reproductive freedom* in an attempt to separate it from the narrow, legal concept of rights. For most feminists this means that all methods of birth control should be available and either free or inexpensive and, because no system of birth control is 100 percent effective, that safe, and affordable abortions should be available to all women. For a few radical feminists, this means the end of biological motherhood and the development of artificial means of reproduction; but for most feminists, it means the transformation of society to allow full participation by women. Most feminists envision a remodeling of all institutions of socialization so that all human beings can participate fully in all life activities as they freely and independently choose.

There is a difference among feminists on this issue: Some assume that men are capable of the changes needed; others argue that a much more radical transformation

---

[24] See Amartya Sen, *The Argumentative Indian: Writing on History, Culture and Identity.* New York: Farrar, Straus & Giroux, 2005: 225.

[25] For a forceful argument against Western feminist hegemony, see Chilla Bulbeck, *Reorienting Western Feminisms: Women's Diversity in a Postcolonial World.* Cambridge, England: Cambridge University Press, 1998. For a broader consideration of these issues that includes both the arguments against Western dominance and for women in the Third World taking control of their own lives, see Marjorie Agosín, ed., *Women, Gender and Human Rights: A Global Perspective.* New Brunswick, NJ: Rutgers University Press, 2001.

of social institutions, with a resulting change in men, is necessary before men can participate fully in raising children. They argue that without this change, increased male participation in child rearing will only reduce women's power.

Third Wave Feminism

Feminism in the United States is usually described as having experienced two "waves" and is now in its third wave. The first wave occurred in the early part of the twentieth century, when women first got the right to vote. The second wave was the rapid growth of and attention to feminism in the 1980s and 1990s. Much literature sees the waves as generational, with a certain amount of tension between mothers and daughters, thought of as both biological and intellectual; thus the "daughters" of each new wave reject the concerns and approaches of their "mothers" in the previous wave. The waves can also be seen as responses to the differing issues that women have faced at these times.

Third wave feminism is characterized by much more consciously extending the concerns raised by feminism to gay and lesbian issues, postcolonial issues, and racial issues. The inclusion of postcolonial issues reflects an awareness that globalization is a feminist issue, as well as an economic and political one. Third wave feminists are likely to say that feminism today is much less of a political movement than second wave feminism; it is more cultural and local, which may reflect the influence of postmodernism with its emphasis on viewing the world from specific standpoints.

Some third wave feminists distinguish between what they call "victim" feminism, which they equate with the second wave, and "power" or "equality" feminism, which they use to refer to themselves. The idea is that feminists in the second wave presented themselves as victims of patriarchy, but those in the third wave see themselves in a position to make real equality possible.

Postfeminism The term *postfeminism* is used quite frequently, but it is used in different, even contradictory, ways, and therefore it is a word to avoid. In the media, the term *postfeminism* is often used to refer to what are sometimes called "ladettes," or young women who act similarly to men, and this is presented as meaning going out to get drunk and have sex with whomever is available. Feminists wanted sexual freedom, but the "ladette" culture has turned sex into a commodity, and most feminists find this troubling. On the other hand, postfeminism is also used in a way that relates it to postmodernism and the instability of identity, which brings it close to Queer Theory, discussed in Chapter 12.

The Sex Industry

Sex work is a recognized category of work, and prostitution, a subcategory of sex work, is legal in many countries on the assumption that both prostitutes and their clients will be safer and healthier if the prostitutes—and one should remember that both men and women work as prostitutes—can have legally enforceable contracts requiring defined hours, pay, health care, trade unions, and so forth. The legalization of prostitution is quite controversial among feminists, with strongly expressed positions both for and against.

One of the arguments for legalization relates to a significant worsening of the position of women in certain parts of the world. The argument is that where prostitution is legal and regulated, it is harder for organized crime to control it and the women involved. One of the effects of the collapse of communism in Russia and some of the formerly communist countries of eastern Europe is that organized crime has become very powerful. The rampant poverty that came with the end of communism has made it easy to prey upon poor women, by either kidnapping them or by tricking them into believing that they are going to a job in western Europe or the United States, and then selling them into prostitution with threats to kill family members in the home country if they try to escape. Although police task forces are working on the problem in all the countries involved, they have had little effect.

A related area of concern is the growth of child-sex tourism, particularly in Southeast Asia. Children, mostly girls but also many boys, are either kidnapped or they are sold by their parents because they cannot afford to feed them. Male tourists come primarily from Europe, Japan, and the United States, and under pressure from feminist groups, a number of countries have passed laws that make it possible to prosecute the men in their home countries for crimes committed in other countries. Although some have been successfully prosecuted, the trade continues to grow.

Conclusion

The effect of the ideas and policies inspired by feminism have been profound, and the lives of both women and men have changed as a result, both in the developed world and, to a growing extent, in the developing world.

SUGGESTED READING

Some Classic Works

Brownmiller, Susan. *Against Our Will: Men, Women, and Rape.* New York: Simon & Schuster, 1975. Reprinted, New York: Fawcett Columbine, 1993.

Daly, Mary. *Beyond God the Father: Toward a Philosophy of Women's Liberation.* Boston: Beacon Press, 1973. Reprinted, Boston: Beacon Press, 1985.

Davis, Angela Y. *Women, Race, and Class.* New York: Random House, 1981. Reprinted, London: Women's Press, 2001.

De Beauvoir, Simone. *The Second Sex.* H. M. Parshley, trans. and ed. New York: Knopf, 1952. Reprinted, New York: Knopf, 1993. Originally published as *Le Deuxième Sexe.* Paris: Gallimard, 1949.

Firestone, Shulamith. *The Dialectic of Sex: The Case for Feminist Revolution.* New York: Morrow, 1970.

Friedan, Betty. *The Feminine Mystique.* New York: W. W. Norton, 1963. Reprinted, New York: W. W. Norton, 2001.

Gilligan, Carol. *In a Different Voice: Psychological Theory and Women's Development.* Cambridge, MA: Harvard University Press, 1982. Reprinted Cambridge, MA: Harvard University Press, 1993.

Greer, Germaine. *Female Eunuch.* London: MacGibbon & Kee, 1970. Reprinted, London: Harper Perennial, 2006.

hooks, bell [Gloria Watkins]. *Ain't I a Woman: Black Women and Feminism.* Boston: South End Press, 1981. Reprinted, Boston: South End Press, 2007.

Millett, Kate. *Sexual Politics.* Garden City, NY: Doubleday, 1970. Reprinted, New York: Simon & Schuster, 1990.

Moraga, Cherríe, and Gloria Anzaldúa, eds. *This Bridge Called My Back: Writings by Radical Women of Color.* Expanded and enlarged 3rd ed. Berkeley, CA: Third Woman Press, 2001.

Morgan, Robin, ed. *Sisterhood Is Powerful: An Anthology of Writings from the Women's Liberation Movement.* New York: Random House, 1970.

Pateman, Carole. *The Sexual Contract.* Stanford, CA: Stanford University Press, 1988.

Solanas, Valerie. *SCUM Manifesto.* Edinburgh, Scotland: AK Press, 1996. Originally published by the author, New York, 1967.

Books and Articles

Agosín, Marjorie, ed. *Women, Gender and Human Rights: A Global Perspective.* New Brunswick, NJ: Rutgers University Press, 2001.

Antrobus, Peggy. *The Global Women's Movement: Origins, Issues and Strategies.* London: Zed Books, 2004.

Anzaldúa, Gloria E., and AnaLouise Keating, eds. *This Bridge We Call Home: Radical Visions for Transformation.* New York: Routledge, 2002.

Badinter, Elisabeth. *Dead End Feminism.* Julia Borossa, trans. Malden, MA: Polity Press, 2006. Originally published in 2003 in French as *Fausse route.* The author, a leading French feminist, argues that in the 1990s, feminism lost its way, turning into a blame culture rather than a force for social change.

Breines, Winifred. *The Trouble Between Us: An Uneasy History of White and Black Women in the Feminist Movement.* Oxford, England: Oxford University Press, 2006.

Brock, Ann Graham. *Mary Magdalene, The First Apostle: The Struggle for Authority.* Cambridge, MA: Harvard Theological Studies, 2003. A consideration of why some canonical and noncanonical texts describe Mary Magdalene as one of the apostles of Christ while others reject that label.

Bryson, Valerie. *Feminist Political Theory: An Introduction.* 2nd ed. Basingstoke, England: Palgrave Macmillan, 2003. Most of the book is a history of feminist theory from the seventeenth century to the present.

Butler, Judith. *Gender Trouble.* London: Routledge, 1990. Reprinted with a new "Preface 1999" (vii–xxvi). New York: Routledge, 1999. One of the earliest texts of Queer Theory.

————. *Bodies That Matter: On the Discursive Limits of 'Sex'.* New York: Routledge, 1993. Early work of Queer Theory.

Chaudhuri, Maitrayee, ed. *Feminism in India.* London: Zed Books, March 2005.

Chesler, Phyllis. *The Death of Feminism: What's Next in the Struggle for Women's Freedom.* New York: Palgrave Macmillan, 2005. Argues that feminism has lost its focus, in part by becoming too academic, in part by adopting multiculturalism, and in part by being simplistically left-wing.

Chilton, Bruce. *Mary Magdalene: A Biography.* New York: Doubleday, 2005.

Christ, Carol P. *Rebirth of the Goddess: Finding Meaning in Feminist Spirituality.* Reading, MA: Addison-Wesley, 1997. Reprinted, New York: Routledge, 2004.

Code, Lorraine, ed. *Encyclopedia of Feminist Theories.* London: Routledge, 2000.

Cole, Catherine M., Takyiwaa Manuh, and Stephen F. Miescher, eds. *Africa After Gender?* Bloomington: Indiana University Press, 2007.

Collins, Patricia Hill. *Black Feminist Thought: Knowledge, Consciousness, and the Politics of Empowerment.* Boston, MA: Unwin Hyman, 1990. Revised tenth anniversary ed., New York: Routledge, 2000.

Donaldson, Laura E., and Kwok Pui-lan, eds. *Postcolonialism, Feminism, and Religious Discourse.* New York: Routledge, 2002.

El Saadawi, Nawal. *The Hidden Face of Eve: Women in the Arab World.* Translated and edited by Sherif Hetata. London: Zed Books, 1980. New ed., London: Zed Books, 2007.

Evans, Judith. *Feminist Theory Today: An Introduction to Second-Wave Feminism.* London: Sage, 1995.

Feminist Theology Vol. 1:1 to the present (Founded 1992).

Gamble, Sarah, ed. *The Routledge Companion to Feminism and Postfeminism.* London: Routledge, 2001.

Gauch, Suzanne. *Liberating Shahrazad: Feminism, Postcolonialism, and Islam.* Minneapolis: University of Minnesota Press, 2007. Known as Scheherazade in the West and Shahrazad to Arabic speakers.

Graham, Elaine. "Feminist Theology, Northern." In *The Blackwell Companion to Political Theology.* Peter Scott and William T. Cavanaugh, eds. Malden, MA: Blackwell, 2004: 210–226.

Haddad, Yvonne Yazbeck, Jane I. Smith, and Kathleen M. Moore. *Muslim Women in America: The Challenge of Islamic Identity Today.* Oxford, England: Oxford University Press, 2006.

Halley, Janet. *Split Decisions: How and Why to Take a Break from Feminism.* Princeton, NJ: Princeton University Press, 2006. Argues that the serious differences among theories of sexuality are a good thing, and that there is no need for a single, overarching theory. Examines a wide range of feminist theories.

Haraway, Donna. *Simians, Cyborgs, and Women: The Reinvention of Nature.* New York: Routledge/London: Free Association, 1991.

Hearon, Holly E. *The Mary Magdalene Tradition: Witness and Counter-Witness in Early Christian Communities.* Collegeville, MN: Liturgical Press, 2004. A study of the context of the various tales about Mary Magdalene.

Henry, Astrid. *Not My Mother's Sister: Generational Conflict and Third-Wave Feminism.* Bloomington: Indiana University Press, 2004.

Heywood, Leslie L., ed. *The Women's Movement Today: An Encyclopedia of Third Wave Feminism.* 2 vols. Westport, CT: Greenwood, 2006.

hooks, bell [Gloria Watkins]. *Talking Back: Thinking Feminist, Thinking Black.* Boston: South End Press, 1989.

Isherwood, Lisa, ed. *The Good News of the Body: Sexual Theology and Feminism.* New York: New York University Press,

2000. U.K. ed. Sheffield, England: Sheffield Academic Press, 2000.

Jain, Devaki. *Women, Development, and the UN: A Sixty-Year Quest for Equality and Justice.* Bloomington: Indiana University Press, 2005.

Jeffreys, Sheila. *Unpacking Queer Politics: A Lesbian Feminist Perspective.* Cambridge, England: Polity, 2003.

Johnson, Janet Elise, and Jean C. Robinson, eds. *Living Gender After Communism.* Bloomington: Indiana University Press, 2007. Case studies of gender issues in eastern Europe and the former Soviet Union.

Journal of Feminist Studies in Religion Vol. 1:1 to the present (Founded 1985).

Kaplan, Temma. *Taking Back the Streets: Women, Youth, and Direct Democracy.* Berkeley: University of California Press, 2004.

Kerr, Joanna, Ellen Sprenger, and Alison Symington, eds. *The Future of Women's Rights: Global Visions and Strategies.* London: Zed Books published in association with The Association for Women's Rights in Development (AWID) and Mama Cash, 2004.

Kwok Pui-lan. "Feminist Theology, Southern." In *The Blackwell Companion to Political Theology.* Peter Scott and William T. Cavanaugh, eds. Malden, MA: Blackwell, 2004: 194–209.

———. *Introducing Asian Feminist Theology.* Cleveland: Pilgrim Press, 2000. U.K. ed. Sheffield, England: Sheffield Academic Press, 2000. A short overview.

———. *Postcolonial Imagination and Feminist Theology.* Louisville, KY: Westminster John Knox Press, 2005.

Labaton, Vivien, and Dawn Lundy Martin, eds. *The Fire This Time: Young Activists and the New Feminism.* New York: Anchor Books, 2004.

Lewis, Reina, and Sara Mills, eds. *Feminist Postcolonial Theory: A Reader.* Edinburgh, Scotland: Edinburgh University Press, 2003. A large collection of reprinted articles.

Lovenduski, Joni. *Feminizing Politics.* Cambridge, England: Polity Press, 2005. A study of the effects of women in politics.

MacKinnon, Catharine A. *Toward a Feminist Theory of the State*. Cambridge, MA: Harvard University Press, 1989.

———. *Only Words*. Cambridge, MA: Harvard University Press, 1993.

———. *Women's Lives, Men's Laws*. Cambridge, MA: Belknap Press of Harvard University Press, 2005.

———. *Are Women Human? And Other International Dialogues*. Cambridge, MA: Harvard University Press, 2006. Collection of essays.

Mai, Mukhtar with Marie-Thérèse Cuny. *In the Name of Honour*. Linda Coverdale, trans. London:Virago, 2007. Indian woman gang-raped by order of her village tribal council.

Merchant, Carolyn. *The Death of Nature: Women, Ecology, and the Scientific Revolution*. San Francisco: Harper & Row, 1980.

Merry, Sally Engle. *Human Rights and Gender Violence:Translating International Law into Local Justice*. Chicago: University of Chicago Press, 2006.

Morland, Iain, and Annabelle Willox, eds. *Queer Theory*. New York: Palgrave Macmillan, 2005.

Nathanson, Paul, and Katherine K.Young. *Legalizing Misandry: From Public Shame to Systemic Discrimination Against Men*. Montreal, QC, Canada: McGill-Queen's University Press, 2006. Includes a response to critics of their *Spreading Misandry* (2001).

———. *Spreading Misandry:The Teaching of Contempt for Men in Popular Culture*. Montreal, OC, Canada: McGill-Queen's University Press, 2001.

Nussbaum, Martha C[raven]. *Women and Human Development:The Capabilities Approach*. Cambridge, England: Cambridge University Press, 2000. Includes a detailed list of "Central Human Functional Capabilities" that can provide the basis for an analysis of the situation of any group in any country (pp. 78–91).

O'Beirne, Kate. *Women Who Make the World Worse and How Their Radical Feminist Assault Is Ruining Our Families, Military, Schools, and Sports*. New York: Sentinel, 2005. An attack on feminism.

Oduyoye, Mercy Amba, and Musimbi R. A. Kanyoro, eds. *The Will to Arise:Women, Tradition, and the Church in Africa*. Maryknoll, NY: Orbis Books, 1992.

Okin, Susan Moller, with respondents. *Is Multiculturalism Bad for Women?* Joshua Cohen, Matthew Howard, and Martha C. Nussbaum, eds. Princeton, NJ: Princeton University Press, 1999.

Parsons, Susan Frank, ed. *The Cambridge Companion to Feminist Theology*. Cambridge, England: Cambridge University Press, 2002.

Phelan, Shane. *Sexual Strangers: Gays, Lesbians, and Dilemmas of Citizenship*. Philadelphia, PA:Temple University Press, 2001.

Phillips,Anne. " 'Really' Equal: Opportunities and Autonomy." *Journal of Political Philosophy* Vol. 14:1 (March 2006): 18–32.

Roth, Benita. *Separate Roads to Feminism: Black, Chicana, and White Feminist Movements in America's Second Wave*. Cambridge, England: Cambridge University Press, 2004.

Ruether, Rosemary Radford, ed. *Women Healing Earth:Third World Women on Ecology, Feminism, and Religion*. Maryknoll, NY: Orbis Books, 1996. U.K. ed. London: SCM Press, 1996.Writings from Africa, Asia, and Latin America on Christian ecofeminism with some material on indigenous religions and the environment.

Sainsbury, Fail. "Feminist Liberation Theology and the Rise of the Celtic Tiger." *Feminist Theology* Vol. 14:2 (January 2006): 255–264. Ireland.

Scanzoni, Letha Dawson, and Nancy A. Hardesty. *All We're Meant to Be: Biblical Feminism for Today*. 3rd revised ed. Grand Rapids, MI:William B. Eerdmans, 1992.

Schaberg, Jane. *The Resurrection of Mary Magdalene: Legends, Apocrypha, and the Christian Testament*. New York: Continuum, 2002. Includes literary criticism, Christian texts, Gnostic and apocryphal texts, and archeology. *Mary Magdalene Understood*. New York: Continuum, 2006 (A version for nonspecialists).

Schlafly, Phyllis. *Feminist Fantasies*. Dallas: Spence, 2003. Feminism viewed from the Right.

Scott, Joan Wallach. *Parité! Sexual Equality and the Crisis of French Universalism*. Chicago: University of Chicago Press, 2005. History and nature of the arguments.

Seely, Megan. *Fight Like a Girl: How To Be a Fearless Feminist*. New York: New York University Press, 2007. Instructions for activists.

Skaine, Rosemarie. *Female Genital Mutilation: Legal, Cultural, and Medical Issues*. Jefferson, NC: McFarland & Co., 2005.

Welchman, Lynn and Sara Hossain, eds. *"Honour": Crimes, Paradigms, and Violence Against Women*. London: Zed Books/ North Melbourne, Vic, Australia: Spinifex Press, 2005.

Websites

Convention on the Elimination of All Forms of Discrimination against Women (CEDAW): http://www.un.womenwatch/daw/cedaw

A Cooperative Skill Bank. Womanshare: http://www.angelfire.com/ar2/womanshare

Feminist Majority Foundation: http://www.feminist.org

Feminists for Animal Rights. An Ecofeminist Alliance: http://www.farinc.org

Michigan Womyn's Music Festival: http://www.michfest.com

National Organization of Women: http://www.now.org

8

Marxism

Karl Marx (1818–1883) and his followers produced communism, one of the dominant ideologies from World War I to the early 1990s. A number of variants have been, or still are, influential intellectually and politically in many parts of the world. This chapter considers the roots of communism in the writings of Marx and Friedrich Engels (1820–1895)[1] and the theoretical structure based on these writings, called *Marxism,* which is still widely respected. And communism has not disappeared; governments that call themselves communist continue to exist in Cuba, China, Vietnam, and Laos. Communist governments under other names continue in a number of the countries of the former Soviet Union and its former satellites, and communist political parties flourish in many parts of the world.

Communism was the result of a line of intellectual and political development from Marx and Engels through V. I. Lenin (b. Vladimir Ilyich Ulyanov, 1870–1924) and others who emphasized the authoritarian and centralist aspects of Marx's thought. An alternative Marxist tradition has always been available that stressed the decentralist and democratic aspects of Marx's thought, but it was a minority position until the collapse of the Soviet Union. This latter tradition,

---

[1] On the Marx–Engels relationship, see Terrell Carver, "The Engels–Marx Question: Interpretation, Identities, Partnership, Politics," in *Engels after Marx.* Manfred B. Steger and Terrell Carver, eds. University Park: Pennsylvania State University Press, 1999: 17–36. On Engels, see J. D. Huntley, *The Life and Thought of Friedrich Engels.* New Haven, CT: Yale University Press, 1991; and Christopher J. Arthur, ed. *Engels Today: A Centenary Appreciation.* London: Macmillan/New York: St. Martin's Press, 1996.

and Marx's insights into social relations in general and the effects of capitalism in particular, explain Marx's continuing importance. Marxism is a powerful tool for understanding social relations and change, and many thinkers still find the Marxist critique of capitalism to contain considerable truth.

KARL MARX AND FRIEDRICH ENGELS

To understand the branches of the Marxist tradition, it is essential to look first at the philosophic basis found in the thought of Karl Marx and Friedrich Engels, and then to turn to the developments and changes made by others.

Alienation: The Young Marx

In his twenties Marx wrote a number of works that are controversial to this day. Most writers now argue that these early writings are central to any understanding of Marx and that later writings develop and grow out of the themes of the early writings. Those who stress the early writings argue that authoritarian communism lost sight of the human concerns that motivated Marx and that are central to these early writings.

The central concept in these early writings is alienation, particularly found in the work known as *The Economic and Philosophic Manuscripts of 1844* (first published in full in 1932). *Alienation* refers to a relationship between two or more people or parts of oneself in which one is cut off from, a stranger to or alien to, the others. It has been a major theme in modern literature, in works such as Albert Camus's (1913–1960) *The Stranger* (1942; *The Outsider* in the United Kingdom), Jean-Paul Sartre's (1905–1980) *Nausea* (1938) and *No Exit* (1945), and Samuel Beckett's (1906–1989) *Waiting for Godot* (1952), to name four of the best-known depictions of various forms of alienation.

For Marx, alienation meant something more specific. He argued that in capitalism, for reasons that will become apparent later, individuals become cut off from—out of tune with—themselves, their families and friends, and the products of their labor. They are not and cannot be whole, fully developed human beings in a capitalist society.[2]

For Marx, private property and alienation are intimately linked, because the most basic form of alienation is alienated labor, or labor that is sold as an object. A worker sells her or his strength, effort, skill, and time; so for much of the worker's life—someone else has purchased the use of the worker. And in Marx's time, this was usually a minimum of 12 to 14 hours a day, 6 or 7 days a week. Although we think now in terms of much more limited work time, such conditions still exist in much of the world, and even in the United States; many white-collar workers find it necessary to work such hours, and many blue-collar workers hold two jobs.

---

[2] For extended commentaries, see István Mészáros, *Marx's Theory of Alienation*. London: Merlin Press, 1970; Bertell Ollman, *Alienation,* 2nd ed. Cambridge, England: Cambridge University Press, 1976; and Adam Schaff, "Alienation as a Social and Philosophical Problem," *Social Praxis* Vol. 3:1–2 (1975): 7–26.

Alienated labor produced an alienation of self; no longer whole human be-ings, workers could not establish full human relationships with others, who were in the same situation. This is the human meaning of capitalism for Marx: people cut off from self, others, and work. It is this condition that Marx was determined to change; it was the reason for his writings and his revolutionary activity.

Marx's Critique of Capitalism

The Marxian analysis of society and the forces operating in it is a commentary on and condemnation of industrial capitalism. Marx argued both that capitalism was the most progressive economic system developed so far and that capital-ism was an essential stage in the development of socialism. Marx also attributed most of the ills of contemporary society to the capitalist system. Many evils were inherent in developing industrialism, and Marx was not the only one to point them out. His comments are interesting, though, because they indicate a great deal about Marx and how he viewed the world, and much of the appeal of Marxism is found in these criticisms of the industrial system.

For Marx, economic relationships are the foundation of the entire social system; therefore his economic criticism must be considered first. For Marx, the most fundamental fact of life is that people must produce goods before they can do anything else. They must also reproduce themselves, but they cannot even do that unless they are capable of feeding themselves. Thus material production or economic relationships are basic to all life.

The primary points in Marxian economics are the *labor theory of value,* the *doctrine of subsistence wages,* and the *theory of surplus value.* Marx used *value* in the sense of real costs in labor; nothing else was considered. In other words, the value— not the price—of any manufactured object was based on the amount of labor time consumed in producing it.

Marx argued that nothing had value without labor. Neither capital nor land is of any value until labor is added. This is the *labor theory of value.* An individual has to work a certain number of hours or days to produce enough to provide a living. Marx assumed that the capitalist would pay workers only enough to keep them alive, a *subsistence wage.* Marx made this assumption for the following reasons:

1. There was a surplus of laborers and no need to pay more.

2. He could not conceive of the capitalist paying more than absolutely necessary.

3. The capitalist would be faced with a series of economic crises that would make it impossible for the capitalist to pay more.

In addition, Marx believed that the profit of the capitalist was taken from the amount produced over and above the wages paid the worker. This is the theory of *surplus value,* which can be used to explain more fully the doctrine of subsistence wages. As capitalists replaced workers with machines, sometimes called *dead labor*, they would have to reduce wages to keep up their rate of profit, because profit came only from surplus value extracted from labor. The capitalist would also be able to reduce wages, because replacing workers with machines produces a pool of unemployed workers who must compete for whatever wages

Karl Marx (1818–1883) was the father of modern communism. His work as a philosopher, political thinker, and economist has made him one of the most influential thinkers of all time. Born in Germany, Marx spent much of his life in England studying contemporary society and actively working for revolution. In association with Friedrich Engels (1820–1895), he published their famous call for revolution, *Manifesto of the Communist Party,* in 1848. Marx published the first volume of his study of contemporary economics, *Capital,* in 1867; Engels undertook the publication of the other volumes. Today, every word that Marx wrote is carefully studied by a wide range of scholars and revolutionists for clues to his thought.

the capitalists choose to pay. Of course, the real reason that capitalists are constantly pushing down wages is to maximize profits, and Marx was certainly aware of that fact.

Hence Marx's major economic criticism revolved around the exploitation of the majority, the *proletariat* or workers, by the minority, the *bourgeoisie* or capitalists. His concern was not purely economic but also centered on the extent to which the system kept proletarians from ever fulfilling their potential as individuals. It was impossible for them to improve themselves in any way, and they were denied education and were thereby kept from any real understanding of their deplorable position.

At the same time, Marx noted that the growing need for literate workers meant that some had to be educated and that education had the potential of teaching some proletarians about their situation; those workers then might teach others, thus undermining bourgeois dominance. The same thing happened in the Third World, when the colonial powers started to educate some of the colonized to fill jobs that required literate workers; these same workers became part of the successful overthrow of colonial regimes.

The state was the tool of the dominant class, the bourgeoisie, and was used to suppress, violently if necessary, any attempt by the proletariat to better themselves. To Marx and most other radical theorists of the day, the *state* referred to all the officials—such as the police, the army, bureaucrats, and so forth—who could be, and were, used to suppress workers. In addition, Marx contended that as long as the bourgeoisie were the dominant class, the government would be its tool and could not be made responsive to the needs of other classes. Marx always saw the state or the government as the tool of the dominant class, whatever class that might be, and he believed the state would so remain as long as there was more than one class.

For many radicals the state is the epitome of evil, the symbol of all that is bad about society. This is particularly true among the anarchists and will be discussed further in the chapter on anarchism (Chapter 9), but it is also true of Marx and some of Marx's followers, particularly those prior to Lenin. This notion probably developed because the state—through the bureaucracy, the police, and the army—controls the forces regularly used to oppose workers' demands. The history of the labor movement in the United States, for example, reveals the frequent use of the police, the army, and the National Guard to put down strikes and break up demonstrations.[3] Thus Marx's ultimate goal, full communism, has no state, and in this he is similar to the anarchists.

The religious system was also in the hands of the dominant class, the bourgeoisie, and Marx said religion was used to convince the proletariat that if they obeyed the state and their bosses, they would be rewarded in another life. This is what Marx meant by his famous statement that "religion is the opiate of the people." The proletariat is lulled into accepting being oppressed in this life by the vision of heaven. This life might well be harsh, but if the workers can stand it for a brief time, they will be rewarded in the next life. Marx believed religion kept workers from actively seeking to change the system. In this way, the religious system was a major focus of Marx's criticism of contemporary society. He saw religion used by the dominant class, the bourgeoisie, to hold the proletariat in its downtrodden position. As a result, Marx made many scathing attacks on religion and argued that the future society in which the proletariat would rule would have no need for religion. At the same time, Marx argued that religion contains the highest expression of the human ethical sense. The fact that the institution of the church and the beliefs of the masses were used to control people did not mean that Marx rejected all aspects of religious belief.

The state and the religious system were both part of what Marx called the *superstructure,* not fundamental economic structures of society but a reflection of economic relations that would change as these relations changed. Thus, as class antagonism was overcome, both the state and religion would begin to disappear.

Marx argued that the capitalist system degraded workers in all of their relationships. Because they had to fight against others of their own class for bare subsistence, they could never hope to establish any sort of valid relationship with another person. For example, Engels wrote bitterly of the effect capitalism had on marriage and the family. To him, the family system of his day was a repetition of the class struggle. The husband symbolized the bourgeoisie and the wife the proletariat. The contemporary marriage system under capitalism was monogamy supplemented by adultery and prostitution, and it could not change

---

[3] For studies from differing viewpoints, see John R. Commons et al., *History of Labor in the United States.* 4th ed. New York: Kelly, 1955; and Louis Adamic, *Dynamite: The Story of Class Violence in America.* Revised ed. New York: Viking Press, 1934.

until capitalism ceased to exist. This marriage system had originated as an institution of private property at about the same time private property in land and goods originated. It developed to ensure that a man's property would be handed on to his sons. The only way this could be done was to endow the sons of one woman with a particular legal status. This did not limit the man's relationships with other women; it supposedly limited the wife's relationships with other men. In practice, as shown by the incidence of adultery, this latter proscription did not work. It failed because of "individual sex–love." Sometime after the development of monogamous marriage, there developed the tendency to find one sex–love partner and no other. This could, of course, occur after marriage, and it explained the existence of adultery. It also provided the basis for the true monogamous marriage, which Marx believed would develop after the revolution.[4]

It is easy to see how many of Marx's criticisms of capitalism stemmed from the concerns found in his early writings. He was also impressed by Engels's description of the position of industrial workers in *The Condition of the Working Class in England* (1845), which depicted the extreme poverty in which the workers lived and the dehumanizing lives they led as mere extensions of the machines they tended. Thus both Marx and Engels saw capitalism as destroying the humanity of the workers and the bourgeoisie, because wage slavery was degrading to both buyer and seller. Marx and Engels set out to understand capitalism, to destroy it, and to found a new, better world in its place.

Materialism

For Marx, general theoretical positions must always be related to the concrete, material world and vice versa. Questions of theory are never separated from practice; they are always closely related.

The basis of Marx's philosophy is found in the influence of the conditions of life on people. Although Marx did not develop the basis of this notion thoroughly himself, he once spelled out in capsule form the fundamental thesis, saying it "served as the guiding thread in my studies." Although the jargon is a bit difficult to follow, it is best to have this statement in Marx's own words; it thoroughly summarizes his basic ideas. The meaning will become clear later.

> In the social production of their means of existence men enter into definite, necessary relations which are independent of their will, productive relationships which correspond to a definite state of development of their material productive forces. The aggregate of these productive relationships constitutes the economic structure of society, the real basis on which a juridical and political superstructure arises, and to which definite forms of social consciousness correspond. The mode of production of the material means of existence conditions the whole process of social, political, and intellectual life. It is not the consciousness of men that determines their existence, but, on the contrary, it is their social condition that determines

---

[4] Engels discussed the family at length in *The Origin of the Family, Private Property, and the State*. Harmondsworth, England: Penguin, 1985. For a modern Marxist commentary, see Juliet Mitchell, *Women's Estate*. Baltimore, MD: Penguin, 1971.

their consciousness. At a certain stage of their development the material productive forces of society come into contradiction with the existing productive relationships within which they had moved before. From forms of development of the productive forces these relationships are transformed into their fetters. Then an epoch of social revolution opens. With the change in the economic foundation the whole vast superstructure is more or less rapidly transformed.[5]

The fundamental point, which is a truism today, is that how people think is greatly affected by how they live. As was noted in Chapter 1, the whole socialization process is the means by which an individual takes on the values of his or her society. The point made there was that an individual—by her or his position in life economically, socially, and so forth, and by family and religious background, educational experiences, and such daily influences as the mass media—is presented with a picture or a group of pictures of the world that helps form his or her basic value system. In other words, the way an individual lives does quite clearly affect how she or he thinks.

But the point generally accepted today is not quite the same as the point Marx was making. Marx argued that the forms taken by the law, religion, politics, aesthetics, philosophy, and so forth—the *superstructure*—are largely determined by the economic structure and processes of society.

Marx is often with considerable truth called an *economic determinist,* and taken at face value that is the meaning of the phrase "their social condition . . . determines their consciousness." But earlier in the same passage, Marx uses the word *conditions* instead of *determines.* In the simplest formulation, for Marx there is a cause-and-effect relationship between the economic structure of society and the superstructure. However, Marx thought in terms of interactions, not simple cause-and-effect relationships. In this case, economic structure and superstructure interact continuously, with changes in one producing changes in the other, back and forth constantly. Marx's analysis is of a continuing process of change with all aspects of both the economic structure and the superstructure constantly interacting. The economic structure is the driving force of social and intellectual change, but it is not a simple cause-and-effect relationship.

The distinction here is subtle but important: For Marx, economic relationships are the most important factor determining the social forms produced at any time and place; but these economic relationships interact with aspects of the superstructure, opening up possibilities for changes in economic relationships that will then further changes in the superstructure and so on. Today, based mostly on the original insights of Marx, we tend to say that economic relationships are among the most important factors influencing the social and intellectual forms produced, but they are not always the most important factors.

In developing his materialistic approach, Marx was attacking a school of German philosophy known as *idealism.* Its major exponent was Georg Wilhelm Friedrich Hegel (1770–1831), and it was particularly against Hegel that Marx

---

[5] Karl Marx, "Preface," in *A Contribution to the Critique of Political Economy,* N. T. Stone, trans. Chicago: Charles H. Kerr, 1913: 11–12.

directed his attack. Hegel's ideas and the diverse influence they had on Marx are a complex subject and cannot be explored thoroughly here. But some attempt at explanation must be made, because Hegel's influence on Marx, both in what Marx accepted and what he rejected, was so great. Hegel's basic proposition, from Marx's viewpoint, was the existence of an "Absolute Spirit"— sometimes Hegel called it "God"—that gradually revealed more and more of itself in the form of higher and higher stages of human freedom. In Hegel's philosophy, the ideal and the material, or *concrete* as he called it, were intimately connected, but not as cause and effect. The two were closely bound together, each influencing the other, even though ultimately the ideal was more important than the material.

Marx directed his main attack against Hegel's idealism. As Marx put it, he set Hegel on his feet by emphasizing the material rather than the ideal. Marx, of course, stressed economic relationships in his definition of the material, rather than physical nature. By stressing the material, Marx was able to argue that his position was scientific—Marx's approach is often called *scientific socialism*[6]— because matter, the material, is subject to objective scientific analysis and laws; it behaves in a predictable manner. Marx was one of the first to say that economics could be treated scientifically, that it followed certain laws. He also contended that history followed certain patterns and that these patterns could be discovered and projected into the future. Marx did not claim he could predict the future with certainty; he simply stated that, if conditions continued as they were at the present, certain things would probably happen in the future. If conditions changed, which they did (Marx had argued that they probably would not), the future would be different. Because they did change even within his lifetime, some of Marx's positions changed. Finally, it must be noted that Marx believed history was moving not only to a different stage but also to a better one.

Dialectical Materialism   The pattern Marx found in history, which he thought was a basic tool of analysis, was the dialectic. Hegel, too, had argued that history was moving to different and better stages, and he also used the dialectic as his basic tool of analysis.

Marx's position is sometimes referred to as *dialectical materialism*. The *dialectic* seems to have originated in ancient Greece as a means of attaining truth through a process of questions and answers. In answer to an original question—such as the meaning of courage, beauty, justice, or the like—a position is stated. The questioner then criticizes this position through the question-and-answer process until an opposite or significantly different position is taken. Then, by a continuation of the process, an attempt is made to arrive at the truth contained in both positions until all are satisfied that the correct answer has been reached. The most famous illustrations of this process can be found in the dialogues of Plato.

Marx took the dialectic from Hegel, who argued that all ideas develop through this dialectical process of thesis (first position), antithesis (second position), and synthesis (truth of the opposites), which then becomes a new thesis and

---

[6] The best statement of his argument is still Friedrich Engels *Socialism: Utopian and Scientific* (1880). Many editions are available.

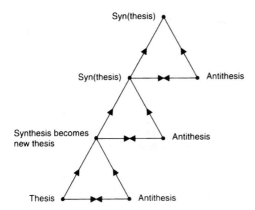

FIGURE 8.1 The Dialectic

thus continue the process. An illustration (see Figure 8.1) shows us something of what both Hegel and Marx are saying. Starting at the bottom with the original thesis (first position), we see its "opposite" antithesis (second position). This opposition is not one of complete difference: it is produced from the thesis in one of two ways, which are spelled out in the first two laws of the dialectic.

1. *The transformation of quantity into quality.* Changes in degree gradually produce a change in quality or kind. The usual example is the change in water from a solid (ice) to a liquid to a gas. The changes Hegel had in mind were more basic, say H_2O (water) to H_2O_2 (hydrogen peroxide). In this process the combination of oxygen and hydrogen first produces H_2O, which is totally different from either hydrogen or oxygen. The continued addition of oxygen produces H_2O_2, which is again different.

2. *Unity or identity of opposites.* Contradictions in the thesis become the antithesis. Thus the opposites are actually similar, because they are composed of similar elements. In addition, the thesis and antithesis become unified, differently, in the synthesis. This unification of thesis and antithesis is produced through the third law of the dialectic.

3. *Negation of the negation.* Contradictions continue to accumulate until another qualitative change occurs and the synthesis is reached. The synthesis, or the unity of the opposites, is a qualitative change, as was the original step from the thesis to the antithesis. In other words, a new position is reached that is not simply the combination of the thesis and antithesis. In a similar way, chemists sometimes speak of synthesizing a new product from two or more products. Thus water (H_2O) is a synthesis of two parts hydrogen with one part oxygen to produce a product that is significantly different from the original components. The synthesis is then treated as a new product, and the process continues in the same manner.

These three laws are often neglected or slighted by students of Marx; but, as we will see later, they help provide an understanding of the pattern taken by his analysis of history. Marx did not attempt to apply the dialectic systematically to the material world. Some of his followers, such as Engels and Lenin, tried to

Vladimir Ilyich Lenin (b. Vladimir Ilyich Ulyanov, 1870–1924) was a follower of Karl Marx. He is remembered primarily as the leader of the successful Bolshevik section of the Communist Party of the Soviet Union and as the first leader of the USSR, which he headed from the time of the Russian revolution in 1917 until his death. He was a major theorist of revolution as well as one of its successful practitioners. His books *What Is to Be Done?* (1902) and *One Step Forward, Two Steps Back* (1904) presented the case for a highly disciplined body of revolutionists as the only approach to a successful revolution. His *Imperialism: The Highest Stage of Capitalism* (1916) and *State and Revolution* (1918) were his major contributions to Marxist theory.

view nature as changing dialectically and spoke vaguely of scientific laws operating dialectically, but their attempts were not very successful.[7]

The general form of the dialectic is the interaction and intermingling of ideas, beliefs, and positions, not the specific form used here as an example. The dialectic is a way of understanding the constant interaction that characterizes the world. For a particularly relevant example, none of the ideologies presented here is, by itself, an accurate reflection of the world; but on the other hand, each of them has something valuable to contribute to the understanding of how people think and behave. Ideological positions constantly interact in the world and are changed by that interaction. This complex, constant interaction and change are a more accurate description of the dialectic.

Historical Materialism   Marx applied the dialectic to his interpretation of history, but for all of the use of the terms *Historical Dialectical* and *Dialectical Materialism* by his followers, Marx did not use those terms himself.[8] Because any change in the economic system is reflected in changes in the entire superstructure, Marx argued that it would be possible to interpret all history from this perspective. He also contended it might be possible to make some general statements about the future on the same basis, arguing that history contains patterns that will in all probability continue into the future. Thus an understanding

---

[7] For a modern consideration, see Richard Levins and Richard Lewontin, *The Dialectical Biologist.* Cambridge, MA: Harvard University Press, 1985.

[8] See Shlomo Avineri, *The Social and Political Thought of Karl Marx* Cambridge, England: Cambridge University Press, 1968. "Much of what is known as 'Marxist materialism' was written not by Marx but by Engels, in most cases after Marx's own death. Students sometimes forget that Marx himself never used the terms 'historical materialism' or 'dialectical materialism' for his systematic approach." (p. 65)

of history should make it possible to argue that if conditions remain the same, certain things are likely to take place in the future.

Although Marx contended that economics is an exact science and is basic to an understanding of his scientific socialism, he nowhere clearly and unambiguously defined the most important element in his economics: the *modes of production*. Most of the time, these consist of (1) available natural resources and (2) productive techniques. At times Marx includes the organization of production as a third element, but this is more properly part of the superstructure.

Natural resources become available as we learn how to use them. Human knowledge is basic to both of the modes of production; this illustrates the interactive nature of Marx's materialism. Tools and knowledge grow together, each improvement in tools adding to knowledge, and each improvement in knowledge making it possible to improve tools. Through this process more natural resources become available for use, and techniques of production change.

As humans learn the uses of natural resources, their modes of production change, and they begin to develop more tools and manufacturing processes. They begin to produce pottery or weave baskets; they learn to form metals into tools and weapons. These changes in turn lead to further changes in both the modes of production and the superstructure.

Changes in productive techniques are brought about because previous changes were made. In other words, each development sets the stage for a further development. Also, major changes in productive techniques, such as the shift from herding to agriculture, produce comprehensive changes in the organization and belief system of society. In the case cited, Marx is right. If we look at any civilization where we know the pattern, we can see, for example, that the change from herding to agriculture was accompanied by new political, religious, and social systems as different activities became important. Although the change from herding to agriculture is an obvious case in which major changes in productive techniques do alter the organization of a society, and specifically the political system of that society, Marx is probably correct in assuming that any such change significantly modifies society. It is again obviously true that the change from a predominantly agricultural society to a predominantly industrial society has produced many far-reaching changes in contemporary society, and many argue that similar far-reaching changes will occur as production becomes more and more highly automated.

Part of the superstructure is a set of relations of production, or property relations. These constitute the second key to Marx's theory of history. *Property relations* in Marx's terminology refer to the ownership of the means of production: land, factories, and so on. These property relations change more slowly than do the modes of production, and thereby a conflict is formed that can be solved only by a change in the property relations. This point is important for an understanding of Marx's analysis of the changes in history and his criticism of contemporary society. Marx argued that property relations evolve more slowly than modes of production, and property relations will not change to meet changing needs. Because his analysis states that property relations are a product of the modes of production, it is clear that the property relations must change to meet the new modes of production rather than the reverse. But in the meantime, tension persists between the modes of production and the property relations, and these cannot be resolved until the more slowly changing property relations have changed.

This tension produces conflict within society and is a primary reason for Marx's prediction of a revolution and his certainty that the proletariat will win. According to Marx, property owners will not be willing to give up their ownership, even though that is dictated by a change in the modes of production. At the same time, they ultimately must give up such ownership because of the change in the modes of production. Thus one can see in operation the three laws of the dialectic mentioned earlier: the transformation of quantity into quality in the changes in the modes of production; the unity of opposites in the growing contradiction between the economic foundation and the superstructure; and finally, the negation of the negation in arriving at the new synthesis of modes of production and superstructure.

In addition, Marx uses the dialectic in his concept of progress to higher and higher, or better and better, stages of society. This is an aspect of the idea of progress, or the notion that the human race and society are inevitably moving to better things. An extremely popular idea in Marx's time, the idea of progress has fallen into disrepute today.

Some believers in progress did think the world was constantly getting better, and the human race had nothing to do with it. They argued that the world was moving in a straight line from some primitive state to some ultimate, perfect society in which everything would be good and beautiful; all people had to do was wait, and things would get better. But most believers in progress did not accept this formulation. They believed that the world, although improving, constantly fell away from the line of progress into some sort of corruption; and then only by great effort, perhaps a revolution, could the world be brought back onto the correct path.

People could affect the path taken by the world in its gradual betterment, either toward good or evil. Marx seems to have assumed the world would gradually get better in spite of whatever humans did, but he contended that through concerted action, people make a tremendous difference in the speed of improvement. Thus humanity's position would improve, but knowledgeable people such as Marx were in a position to recognize the direction that must be taken to achieve this.

The Class Struggle

A central part of Marxism is the *class struggle,* a hypothesis Marx used to explain change. The class struggle is produced by the contradiction between the modes of production and the relations of production. Marx said that in the mid-nineteenth century, the means of production were controlled by the bourgeoisie. This class did little if any work but reaped immense profits from its control of the means of production. The actual labor was done by the proletariat. The modes of production required the proletariat, but did not, according to Marx, require the bourgeoisie; therefore, a struggle between these two classes resulted. For Marx there was no question concerning the result—the proletariat was necessary, the bourgeoisie was not. Although both he and later Marxists applied the theory of class struggle to all history, Marx argued that the best example of class struggle existed in the mid-nineteenth century, when society was clearly split into these two classes: the bourgeoisie (capitalists) and the proletariat (workers).

It is important to clearly understand the nature of classes and of these two classes in particular. Classes are economic groups ordered according to their relationship to the nonhuman powers of production and to each other. The proletariat is the class that makes its living from the sale of its labor power. The bourgeoisie owns the productive resources on which the proletariat works. The bourgeoisie makes its living primarily from profit, interest, and rent, although it may earn some of its income from wages paid for managerial work and for coordinating risk-taking ventures.

Many other smaller classes existed, but they were generally irrelevant to the unfolding conflict. In addition, Marx had a few problems with the manner in which he included certain groups within the class system. For example, he was always unclear as to exactly where the peasantry fit within his system. He often included the peasantry in a group loosely known as the *petite* (small) *bourgeoisie,* because they were landowners. At other times he split his definition of the peasantry into a variety of groups, ranging from the bourgeoisie to the proletariat, but he was never sure exactly where to place peasants who owned their land and worked it themselves. Marx added at the bottom of his classification scheme another class called the *lumpenproletariat,* which was composed of the dregs of society who made no contribution to production. Marx never clarified whether it would be possible to include this group within the proletariat itself, but one would assume from his writings that he thought that at some point after the revolution, it would be possible to incorporate the lumpenproletariat into the proletariat in the same way the bourgeoisie was to be incorporated. For Marx in the nineteenth century, however, the most important classes were the proletariat and the bourgeoisie.

Revolution

The class struggle will, according to Marx, ultimately produce a revolution; and Marx worked for that revolution, arguing that we must move beyond simply understanding society to changing it. Marx was a revolutionary because he believed a revolution was both necessary and inevitable. The revolution would develop as a result of a series of crises capitalism was to experience. These failed to appear as regularly or as seriously as Marx had expected, and thus the revolution did not develop, although some contemporary Marxists prefer to say it has not yet developed as anticipated.

In a small book titled *Imperialism: The Highest Stage of Capitalism* (1916), Lenin attempted to show why these crises failed to occur as predicted. He argued that by colonizing and exploiting underdeveloped countries, the capitalists were temporarily able to stave off the crises. Colonial exploitation made it possible to pay workers slightly better by providing capitalists with (1) cheap raw materials, (2) cheap labor, and (3) markets for manufactured goods and excess capital. Lenin believed imperialism merely postponed the revolution; it did not put it off permanently, but it lulled the proletariat into believing revolution will not be necessary.

This position is particularly relevant today, and some Marxists say that Lenin's analysis was correct, with the results only now developing. Cheap raw materials were provided for Western factories, and higher wages were paid in the West by exporting exploitation to the colonies, where very low wages were paid. Today Third World countries are beginning to control their own resources, such as oil, and are insisting on high prices, in part because of past exploitation. Some contemporary Marxists believe capitalism will now experience the crises that Marx predicted and that Lenin argued had been put off temporarily through imperialism. According to this argument, the capitalist system will collapse, and the revolution will come. So far this has not happened, and the price of raw materials has fluctuated dramatically. Marxists argue that this is only temporary and caused by the capitalists, who still control the markets for raw materials. And, Marxists argue, capitalists continue to control the labor market, as can be seen by the regular movement of jobs to countries with lower labor costs. For example, India, which became the world hub of call centers, is now outsourcing some of these jobs to countries with lower wage scales, including back to some parts of the United States.

In discussing the Marxian approach to revolution, it is instructive to distinguish between two different types of revolution: political and social. Political revolution takes place when political power is seized by the proletariat. Social revolution takes place later, first through changes made in society's property relations, and then as the superstructure adjusts to these changes.

Although he allowed for the possibility of peaceful change, Marx thought the political revolution would probably be violent for two reasons: First, he argued that achieving synthesis would be sudden, thus the gradualness implicit in peaceful change was ruled out by the dialectic. Second, the bourgeoisie would never agree to its disappearance as a class and would force the proletariat into a violent revolution.

Marx was a revolutionary. He believed revolution was necessary and good, and throughout his life, he was involved in groups that tried to bring about revolutions in various countries. He was expelled from a number of countries for his activities. But it was his followers, particularly Lenin and Mao Zedong (1893–1976), who developed the tactics for and led successful communist revolutions.

Lenin Lenin's contribution was the development of the revolutionary party, an organizational weapon in the struggle to overthrow capitalism. Lenin argued that such a party was necessary, because the proletariat was incapable of recognizing its role as the revolutionary class, whereas the party provided this necessary consciousness. As one scholar stated, "The party is conceived as the organization, incarnation, or institutionalization of class consciousness."[9] The party would be made up of those who had achieved this consciousness and had also become professional revolutionists. In the popular phrase, the party was to be the "vanguard of the proletariat"; it would point the way and lead the proletariat to its

---

[9] Alfred G. Meyer, *Leninism*. New York: Praeger, 1962: 31–33.

goal. The party would bring together the divided masses of workers and would express what they truly felt but could not express. It would mold them and unify them into a force for change.

Individual members of the proletariat would be unlikely to recognize their historic role. They would be much too busy attempting to stay alive to be concerned with class questions. In addition, few would ever identify themselves as class members. Thus it would be left up to those who became aware, the party members, to prepare for the great role the proletariat would play.

The importance of Lenin's party is found in the idea of the professional revolutionary and in the organizational principle of *democratic centralism*. The party would be composed of a small, conspiratorial group of professional revolutionists. But because no revolution could succeed without the support of, or at least little direct opposition from, the largest part of the population of a country, Lenin believed the party should develop contacts throughout the society as a whole. This meant party members would need a variety of organizational skills: They would have to be experts at agitation and propaganda. Because they had to be able to establish and maintain a vast network of "front" organizations, they would have to be expert administrators. Ideally, before the revolution, the majority of the population should be organized into a variety of these groups, which would also provide the basis for organization once the revolution succeeded. In addition, the party members would have to prepare constantly for the revolution, because it would come only when the masses suddenly revolted against their oppressors.

The party might light the spark to set the masses afire, but the spark could come from anywhere at any time, and the party had to be ready to ride the revolution into power. The theory of the spark was important to Lenin. One of his newspapers was called *The Spark* (*Iskra*), and he often referred to the necessity of some incident igniting the masses. Lenin believed it was possible for the party to produce the necessary conditions for a revolution, but he believed it was impossible to be absolutely sure when the revolution would come. So the party always had to be prepared for the revolution to come at an unexpected time, perhaps even at a time that was not favorable to the party.

The principle of organization that makes all this possible is *democratic centralism,* which combines free discussion with centralized control and responsibility. Before any decision is made by the party, there should be complete freedom to dissent; after the decision is made, it must be accepted unanimously. Lenin believed this principle could work, because all party members started from a position of agreement regarding goals. In practice, freedom of discussion was often forgotten. Democratic centralism would also serve as the principle of organization in the period immediately following the revolution.

As a technique of revolutionary organization, democratic centralism has important characteristics. In planning a revolution, care must be taken to organize in order to be able to act at a moment's notice. Everyone must also be able to act in a completely concerted manner without disagreements or squabbles over what is to be done now and what is to be done later, or arguments about the correct techniques of taking over the government, or who is to do this or that at a particular moment. Complete agreement is essential among the revolutionists, over both the techniques of the revolution and the organization of society immediately after it succeeds. Democratic centralism provides this by giving the leaders complete control over the actions of the revolutionists and at the same time allowing all members of the party to participate freely and openly in the process of reaching the appropriate decisions. Still, democratic centralism has usually been used in ways that stressed centralism.

Mao Zedong   Other Marxist theorists have also contributed to the tactics of revolution. For example, Mao Zedong's theory of guerrilla warfare is also an organizational weapon. Mao's theory can be divided into two parts: the strictly military principles and some political principles derived from one of the military principles. Militarily, Mao developed what are now the commonly recognized principles of guerrilla warfare. These stress a hit-and-run approach, fighting only when fairly certain of victory, and keeping constant pressure on the enemy.[10] According to Mao, this style of fighting requires a territorial base where the guerrillas will be virtually free from attack so they will be able to rest, train, and so on. To achieve this, they must have the positive support of the people in the area. This support is gained by (1) establishing a peasant government, (2) allowing the peasants to redistribute the land, and (3) helping the peasants in whatever rebuilding activities they undertake. The territorial base will provide food, people, and—perhaps most important— experience in organization. The network of tunnels used by the Vietcong during the Vietnam War provided a similar resting place. Thus Mao's theory of guerrilla warfare fulfills the same function as Lenin's theory of the revolutionary party. Mao's tactics are designed for the same purposes as Lenin's strategies.

Marx had said that revolution required an *industrial* proletariat. But the revolutions brought about by both Lenin and Mao took place in countries that were primarily agricultural; this was particularly the case in China. Lenin still argued that he was sparking a proletarian revolution and worked to develop a base of industrial workers. Although Mao believed that China needed to industrialize quickly, he knew that no industrial proletariat existed and changed his analysis to include the peasantry.

Dictatorship of the Proletariat

Marx envisioned a brief transitional period after the revolution, known as the *dictatorship of the proletariat*. This stage was to be characterized by consolidation of proletarian power through the gradual disappearance of the bourgeoisie and the minor classes as they became part of the proletariat.

The bourgeoisie and the members of other classes would be given jobs that would, over time, change their outlook and make them good members of the proletariat. During the dictatorship of the proletariat, the superstructure would change to adjust to the socialist mode of production. Loosely, the dictatorship of the proletariat would have the following characteristics:

1. Distribution of income according to labor performed
2. Gradual disappearance of classes

---

[10] Mao Zedong, *Selected Works*. Beijing: Foreign Language Press, 1961: 4, 161–62.

3. The state in the hands of the proletariat

4. Increasing productivity

5. Increasing socialist consciousness—people work with few incentives

6. Increasing equality

7. A command economy

8. The economy managed by the state

All of these characteristics were expected to change fairly rapidly, and the dictatorship of the proletariat was to be brief. In practice, no country that has followed Marx's ideas has moved beyond the dictatorship of the proletariat. Contrary to Marx's vision, this "transitional" period does not seem to focus on the economic system; as practiced, it is based on the political system with all else as superstructure.

Marx refused to make specific predictions about the future. He argued that people who had been shaped by new experiences would create the new social forms of the future. Except in the most general sense, those socialized in the old, bad society could have no notion of what the new, better society would look like; therefore, Marx never described the dictatorship of the proletariat in any detail. In addition, the dictatorship of the proletariat was to be a short transitional period and would be characterized more by change than by stable institutions. Still, it is possible to say something about the society of the dictatorship of the proletariat, because Marx gave enough suggestions to allow some elaboration on the eight points listed previously.

During the dictatorship of the proletariat, the state, as always, is the tool of the dominant class, in this case the proletariat. The state is used to achieve a number of related goals. First, the economic system is reorganized; the means of production must be taken from the capitalists and made property of the state. The state must also establish a new way of administering the means of production, so the economy is kept running and goods are produced, distributed, and consumed. As part of this process, workers all become employees of the state: public employees paid by the state on the basis of the quantity and quality of the work they perform, just as they had been by the previous owners. These previous owners and all other members of the bourgeoisie and the other classes are gradually absorbed into the proletariat. They are given jobs, and working for a living resocializes them into the proletariat's way of thought and belief.

These show the operation of a command economy, managed by a state in the hands of the proletariat; distribution of income is on the basis of work performed, and with the gradual disappearance of classes, greater productivity follows—because more workers are available, and there is no unproductive bourgeoisie and no profit. As a result, equality increases, and people become more aware of their roles in society and require fewer incentives to work.

The dictatorship of the proletariat represents a unified view of a society in a period of transition. All these factors must be thought of as in a state of change. Some things will change quickly, others more slowly. In practice, of course, a command economy was established that was managed by the state, but in no communist country has the state ever been in the hands of the proletariat, and none of the other changes have occurred. No communist country has even come close to the goals of the dictatorship of the proletariat, let alone the next, final stage: full communism.

Full Communism

The changes in contemporary communism brought about by the fusion of nationalism, the early writings of Marx, and existentialism have given rise to a resurgence of utopian thinking by Marxists. But they have not significantly changed the characteristics of Marx's ideal system, full or pure communism. Full communism has the following characteristics:

1. Distribution of income according to need, no longer according to labor performed.
2. No classes.
3. The state withers away.
4. Very high productivity, so that there is plenty for all.
5. High socialist consciousness—people work without incentives.
6. More equality but not absolute equality.
7. No money.
8. A command economy.
9. The economy managed by a free and equal association of producers.
10. The differences between occupations disappear, so that there is no social distinction between town and country.
11. Each person does about as much physical as intellectual labor.
12. The system, as Stalin was the first to show, is worldwide.[11]

Full communism is the goal of the entire system—the utopia or better society toward which all else is aimed. Its general characteristics are not much different from the utopias created by a variety of other socialists throughout the centuries, but some of these characteristics are worth further mention.

The similarities and differences between full communism and the dictatorship of the proletariat can be seen by comparing this list with the one in the previous section. The command economy still exists, but it is no longer controlled by the state. Marx was primarily concerned with abolishing exploitation, and in full communism, there are no exploiters, only workers. With the exploiters gone and the people working without incentives, there should be plenty so that all can be rewarded according to need.

The most direct effect of a change to full communism would be on the social stratification and mobility systems. Because classes would no longer exist and no distinction would be made among types of labor, social stratification would be minimal. In the classless or single-class society, no basis would exist for any significant distinctions among people. *Significant* for Marx meant economic;

---

[11] Adapted slightly and reprinted by permission of the author and the publishers from P. J. D. Wiles, *The Political Economy of Communism*. Cambridge, MA: Harvard University Press, © 1962, by Basic Blackwell & Mott Ltd., 332–333.

he did not foresee a complete leveling. Individual differences would remain, but they no longer would be detrimental to the individual or the society, as they had been under capitalism and all the other socioeconomic systems preceding it. Occupational mobility would be increased greatly, because an individual would be able to move freely among positions.

Marx envisioned other significant changes in the social system. There would, of course, be no religion. Education would be available for all. All crime would disappear, because there would be no reason for it. With the coming of full communism, prostitution and adultery would disappear, and the monogamous family would become a reality. A Marxist scholar has suggested that under full communism, a change from personal housekeeping functions, such as cooking and cleaning, to public or communal services would free women to choose among occupations in the same way men can.[12]

With the coming of the classless society, the state would no longer be necessary and would disappear. It would be replaced by "the administration of things," which means the economic system would have to be organized, and somebody would have to administer it. It would be administered by "a free and equal association of producers" with the authority to direct, according to the needs of the people, what should be produced, in what amounts, and how it should be distributed. This "free and equal association of producers" could conceivably take a wide variety of forms, depending on the size of the territory and the complexity of the industries within the territory. Most such associations would undoubtedly take some pattern similar to the following: A committee would be selected, probably by election, that would collect data on the productive capacity of the region and the needs of the people. The committee would establish priorities and goals for the various manufacturing plants, farms, and craft industries. This assumes an economy based on abundance, and thus it would be more concerned with collecting accurate data on needs than with establishing priorities. The process would be continuous, and certainly the composition of the committee would change periodically. The committee would hold no coercive power, still assuming abundance, and would merely administer the economy.

This is the goal of Marxism. Many communists today believe full communism will never come. Others believe it is still possible. But whichever position you take, full communism illustrates some of the appeal communism has had and will continue to have in the future.

ALTERNATIVE MARXIST TRADITIONS

As mentioned earlier, an alternative tradition within Marxism emphasizes the decentralist and humanitarian aspects of Marx's thought. These alternative traditions provide the basis for the continuation of Marxism as a creative and useful social theory. The line of authoritarianism that Lenin developed was successful only

---

[12] E. G. Balagushkin, "The Building of Communism and the Evolution of Family and Marital Relations," *Soviet Sociology* 1 (Winter 1962–63): 43. Originally published in 1962 in *Voprosy Filosofii*. For some similar early U.S. plans, see Dolores Hayden, *The Grand Domestic Revolution: A History of Feminist Designs for American Homes, Neighborhoods, and Cities*. Cambridge, MA: MIT Press, 1981.

after an intellectual and political struggle, and even Lenin regularly expressed reservations about the direction he took. But the centralization of authority that took place under Joseph Stalin (b. Iosif Vissarionovich Dzhugashvili, 1879–1953) became the model for all communist countries and could be justified within the writings of Marx and Lenin. Lenin had rejected Stalin as his successor, but Stalin won the struggle for power after Lenin's death.

Those who lost the early struggle with Lenin, however, remained influential in Western Europe. The first stage of development of an alternative Marxism can be seen in the debate between Eduard Bernstein (1850–1932) and Rosa Luxemburg (1870–1919).

Eduard Bernstein

Bernstein argued, in a work variously translated as *Evolutionary Socialism* and *The Preconditions of Socialism* (1899), that capitalism was more adaptable than Marx had thought, and, as a result, evolution from capitalism to socialism was possible. This position, called *revisionism,* led to the development of democratic socialism (see Chapter 5) and poses one of the central dilemmas for revolutionaries: whether to encourage or discourage reform. If reform is successful, the revolution is delayed; but opposing reform is likely to lose support from those who care more for immediate improvement than for a possible revolution. Bernstein's analysis gave strong support to those advocating reform.

Rosa Luxemburg

Luxemburg was one of Bernstein's strongest opponents. In her *Social Reform and Revolution* (1899), she argued that revolution was essential. She advocated mass strikes as the best route to the revolution, but she explicitly rejected Lenin's notion of a centralized revolutionary party, believing that such a party would undermine the creativity of the workers.

Other opponents of the emphasis on centralism emerged in various countries. Three of the most important were Antonio Gramsci (1891–1937) of Italy, György Lukács (1885–1971) of Hungary, and Anton Pannekoek (1873–1960) of the Netherlands.

Antonio Gramsci

Gramsci advocated democracy within factories. For example, he proposed that each factory be organized into workshops and each workshop into work crews based on similar skills. Each work crew would elect a delegate. These delegates would meet and elect an executive committee; and, in a federal structure above the individual factories, elected representatives from the various factories in the area would meet in a variety of groupings. This system is democratic centralism with the emphasis on democracy, and it has similarities with the idea of workers' control, which we discuss in the next chapter.

Also, Gramsci rejected what he saw as Marx's overemphasis on materialism, particularly rejecting dialectical materialism. In this he was similar to György Lukács. (See also the discussion of Gramsci's concept of *hegemony* in Chapter 1.)

György Lukács

In his book *History and Class Consciousness* (1923), which was rejected by orthodox Marxists of the time, Lukács stressed the need to recognize the role of human creativity in bringing about social change. He argued, against what came to be called *vulgar Marxism,* that human beings can think and act freely, independent of their material and class positions. Lukács is often given credit for the rebirth of Marxist philosophy in the late twentieth century and is seen as a forerunner of post-Marxism.

Anton Pannekoek and Council Communism

Marxists such as Gramsci and Pannekoek provided the basis for the continuation of an alternative Marxist tradition among Western European and American Marxist theoreticians. Pannekoek suggested that full communism be taken seriously and that there be no governing authority, arguing that workers would achieve freedom and security only when they controlled the means of production directly, rather than through the state. The councils he proposed would not be able to require obedience from the people. In this Pannekoek was close to the type of federal communist anarchism described by Pyotr Kropotkin and discussed in the next chapter.

The Frankfurt School

The Frankfurt Institute for Social Research was founded in 1923, and under the leadership of Max Horkheimer (1895–1973) and Theodor Adorno (1903–1969), it became the foremost center in the West for Marxist research. The school is most noted for the development of *critical theory,* a general theory that views society from the point of view of the need to change it; it intended to show how modern society functions but also at what cost to human lives. Marx saw himself as always being both a social theorist and a revolutionary, someone who believed in the need to transform society. In his famous "Eleventh Thesis on Feuerbach," he even emphasized that change was more important than theory: "The philosophers have only *interpreted* the world in various ways; the point is to *change* it."[13] Thus the Frankfurt School followed Marx's example in advocating social change. But, most importantly for the contemporary relevance of Marxism, the Frankfurt School dropped class as the primary driver of history, recognizing that no single factor can be used in such an analysis.

The most influential members of the Frankfurt School have been Herbert Marcuse (1898–1979) and Jürgen Habermas (b. 1929). Marcuse combined the insights of Marx with those of Sigmund Freud to develop a vision of a nonrepressive society in his *Eros and Civilization* (1955) and *One-Dimensional Man* (1964). He greatly influenced the New Left. Habermas has focused on the concept of rationality as the basis of his theory. He has worked to develop a broad concept of rationality as a means of criticizing contemporary culture and as the foundation

---

[13] Karl Marx, "Theses on Feuerbach," in Karl Marx and Friedrich Engels, *Collected Works.* New York: International Publishers, 1976; 5:5. [Emphasis in the original.]

for positive social change. In doing so he developed a theory of communicative action that he used to critique the concept of modernity, while keeping those parts of modernity that he considered most valuable: universal rationality and morality. In his most recent work, he explores the tension between law as a means of achieving stability and its normative role in each society. He argues that *discursive* or *deliberative democracy,* in which there is a continuing process of discussion involving substantial parts of the population, will overcome this tension.

Ernst Bloch

Ernst Bloch (1885–1977) was a German Marxist philosopher who emphasized the utopian aspects of Marxism. In his magnum opus *Das Prinzip Hoffnung* (*The Principle of Hope,* 1959) and in other works, Bloch explored the various manifestations of hope in human history. He argued that the desire for betterment must be brought back to the center of Marxist thought as the real engine of social change. With the translation of his works into English, Bloch's writings are beginning to influence contemporary Marxist thought. Bloch also influenced the development of Liberation Theology.

CURRENT TRENDS

Communism has disappeared as the official ruling force in Eastern Europe and the former Soviet Union. Although modified, it still exists in China, Cuba, Vietnam, and Laos, and among numerous parties and groups throughout the world, including dominant parties with new names but the same leaders in parts of Eastern Europe and the former Soviet Union. But in general, communism as we have known it is coming to an end. It seems appropriate to ask what happened.

The central problem is that the supposedly short-lived dictatorship of the proletariat, during which the various capitalist classes were to become one class, has become a permanent dictatorship in the name of the proletariat but not actually of the proletariat. As Milovan Djilas (1911–1995) pointed out in *The New Class* (1955), communism simply replaced capitalist bosses with bureaucratic bosses, who ruled in their own interest rather than in the interest of the proletariat. Some have actually called communism *state capitalism.*

Other problems included the fact that it is almost impossible to manage all the details of an economy from the center. As a result, many inefficiencies were built into the Soviet economy, gradually developing into total breakdown. On the other hand, central planning and control worked extremely well in rebuilding the Soviet Union after World War II and in building a space program; we should not forget that the Soviet Union put the first person into space.

While Marxism and communism are no longer among the most important ideologies, they have certainly not disappeared. A number of countries are still communist, and Marxism is considered by many to be an important way of understanding human relations. The specifics are changing; in particular, class is no longer central to Marxist analysis, being at the minimum complemented by ethnicity, gender, and race.

The Relevance of Marxism Today

In the past few years, a small body of work has developed exploring the current situation of Marxism, particularly as a tool of social analysis. Most commentators see the greatest relevance of contemporary Marxism in the application of Marx's insight into capitalist exploitation to contemporary economic relationships in capitalism. For some, this analysis is particularly relevant to the Third World and neocolonialism. For others, it is most important for understanding developed capitalist societies, such as the United States, which most people are convinced have demonstrated the success of capitalism and the failure of Marxism. Marxists, to the contrary, argue that capitalism has succeeded only in convincing people of its success, not in overcoming exploitation. They point to the problems of contemporary American society, in which the distance between the rich and the poor continues to grow and many find it necessary to work two jobs to earn enough to maintain the standard of living they believe they need. As a result, many work the same long hours today that they did in Marx's time. And although in many marriages, both spouses choose to work outside the home, many couples feel that both spouses must work, even though they would prefer that one of them stay at home with the children. In these ways and others, contemporary Marxist theorists contend that Marxism is still a relevant tool of analysis.[14]

The three schools of thought regarding Marxism today are often labeled *post-Marxism, analytical Marxism,* and *ecological Marxism.*

Post–Marxism   The two forms of post–Marxism, generally called *post*-Marxism and post-*Marxism,* differ in their emphases, but the end results are not that different. *Post*-Marxism simply rejects Marxism as a way of thinking and uses whatever insights Marxists may have had without adopting a "Marxist" way of thinking. Jean-François Lyotard (1924–1998) was an early *post*-Marxist who is best known for his exposition of postmodernism.[15]

The major theorists of post-*Marxism* are Ernesto Laclau (b. 1935) and Chantal Mouffe (b. 1943), whose book *Hegemony and Socialist Strategy: Towards a Radical Democratic Politics* (1985) was an early challenge to Marxism as usual. Post-*Marxism* grafts developments in poststructuralism, deconstruction, postmodernism, and feminism onto Marxism.

Analytical Marxism   Analytical Marxism is particularly associated with Jon Elster (b. 1940) and John Roemer (b. 1945). These two apply the methodology of analytical philosophy and contemporary economic theory to Marxism in an admixture that produces a complex, economically sophisticated form of market socialism.

Ecological Marxism   Ecological Marxism tends to focus on a critique of the capitalist mode of production's negative impact on the environment. In this way,

---

[14] For discussions of the applicability of Marxism to a wide range of topics, see Andrew Gamble, David Marsh, and Tony Tant, eds. *Marxism and Social Science.* Urbana: University of Illinois Press, 1999.

[15] On Marxism and postmodernism, see Terrell Carver, *The Postmodern Marx.* University Park: Pennsylvania State University Press, 1998.

it might be considered little different from such critiques advanced from within capitalism by environmentalists. But ecological Marxism, or *ecosocialism* as some prefer to call it, has had a political impact, particularly in Europe, with so-called Red–Green alliances. In Germany such an alliance was able to form a national government for awhile.

Marxism and Globalization

In general, Marxists take the position that globalization equals the spread of capitalism to the detriment of workers in both developed and developing countries and the environment. They also argue that rather than showing the strength of capitalism, globalization shows its weakness in an increasingly desperate search for cheaper and cheaper labor, made necessary by rising wages in formerly low-wage areas. A case can be made for both sides. Capitalists argue that the increase in wages is the result of the spread of capitalism; Marxists actually agree but say that such a pattern fits Marx's argument that once capitalism is fully developed, it must inevitably collapse.

Some Marxists take a different approach to globalization, saying that the development of a worldwide market gives rise to international agreements to protect workers. While such agreements do exist,[16] they are rarely enforced.

Movements away from Marxism

The inability of capitalism to rapidly overcome the failures of communist regimes has caused many people in former communist countries to regret the passing of communism and vote for the former communists, usually under new names. Although no informed person expected capitalism to quickly correct communism's legacy, many people believed it would, and self-serving anticommunists oversold capitalism. The required restructuring of the economies involved means that many people are significantly worse off than they were under communism: jobs have been lost, pensions have been radically reduced by inflation, and social services and health care that people relied on have disappeared. Thus it is no surprise that former communists are being elected to office.

Another reason for the difficulties encountered in the transition from communism is the lack of certain aspects of a civil society in the former communist countries. Such countries have no tradition of meaningful elections, no private banking system, and no nonstate social institutions like the Red Cross/Red Crescent, Scouts, the National Organization of Women, and so forth. Thus people in these countries traditionally turn to the state for most of their social activities, and all the needed new practices and organizations take time to grow.

Both Russia and China appear to be without a dominant ideology at present, but both have kept the authoritarian part of the authoritarian state socialism, or state capitalism, definition of communism. In both, and for all of the apparent privatization, the state still dominates politically and economically.

---

[16] For some such agreements, see the sections on freedom of association and employment at http://www.unhchr.ch/html/intlinst.htm.

Russia When the Soviet Union disintegrated, the Russian economy was a mess; it was rapidly privatized, and many of the most important industries came under the control of the family and friends of then-President Boris Yeltsin (1931–2007). Rampant corruption made some people fabulously wealthy, while the majority of the population was made much poorer than they had been under communism, even in its last stages. Organized crime grew rapidly, and the "Russian mafia" has now spread to many other countries, including the United States.

Due to poverty, the birth rate dropped precipitously, and many Russians left the country. Alcohol and drug abuse became a serious problem and continues to be, particularly among men; this has led to a high mortality rate, and there are now 15 percent fewer men than women in Russia. As a result of the combination of these factors, Russia is one of the few countries with a falling population.

In 1999 Yeltsin appointed Vladimir Putin (b. 1952) Prime Minister and then acting President of the Russian Federation, and Putin was elected to the post the next year, served the two terms allowed him under the Russian constitution, and then chose Dimitri Medvedev (b. 1965) to be his successor. Medvedev was duly elected in 2008 in a deeply flawed election that probably still reflected the wishes of the electorate, the flaws resulting primarily from the desire to have the win be by a landslide. Medvedev then appointed Putin as Prime Minister, so it is likely that Putin remains the most powerful person in Russia, at least for the time being.

Due to its gas and oil reserves, Russia is now rich; the budget is balanced, money has been put aside in case the price of oil drops, and wages are rising. Land has been privatized, the last sector of the economy to be. The government has regained control of most of the major sectors of the economy, while the companies remain officially private, and those who had controlled them have either fled the country—often taking billions of dollars with them—or are in prison. Many companies from outside Russia that had invested in the Russian companies have either lost their investment or agreed to local control.

Social services disintegrated and have not recovered; extreme cuts have been made in higher education, and paying for good grades is now common. The Russian Orthodox Church has regained its position as the official church and has used its power to limit the activities of other churches, but Russia is not now a particularly religious country, and church attendance is very low. Corruption remains rampant throughout the economy, and though Putin does not appear to have enriched himself, those who are now getting rich all support him.

The media is under the control of the central government, the courts do what they are told, the political opposition cooperates with those in power, and election results are generally known in advance. All of this is the same as before the collapse of communism.

China In the People's Republic of China, the word *communism* is still used, and the entire political structure is dominated by the Communist Party, whose primary purpose is to hold on to power. There appears to have been widespread privatization in China, but property rights are at best unclear, and the idea of private property is not entrenched in the Chinese legal system.

China is a huge country, and except for the large cities—and often even there—regional and local officials have used their position to enrich themselves, as has the Chinese military, which owns many factories. The Chinese economy appears to be growing at an incredible rate, fueled largely by a construction boom in the cities and the ability to export cheap goods: cheap because labor costs are extremely low, and because almost no environmental or safety regulations exist—and the ones that do can simply be ignored.

As in Russia after the end of Communism, some people in China have become immensely wealthy; whereas more, perhaps even the majority, are currently worse off in many cases, particularly in the countryside, with many falling into abject poverty. But much of the apparent wealth is based on loans that are unlikely to be repaid; and the government has tried, with only limited success, to force banks to improve the quality of their loans. Thus, the entire system depends on continued rapid growth; and because the internal Chinese market is potentially so huge, if most of the Chinese people become consumers, the growth can be sustained for some time. But so far only a tiny percentage of the Chinese population has an income level that allows them to consume much more than the basics, and even those are consumed at low levels.

China has a resource base—its immense population—that, like Russia's oil and gas, may allow it to solve its problems; but the size of the population and the country are also part of China's problem. Regional and local officials are able to simply ignore both the central government and the law; corruption is a huge problem both in government and in the new private enterprises, and so far the central government has managed to prosecute only a few corrupt officials. If found guilty—and it is not an impartial court system—such officials are usually executed.

Marxism, much modified, will remain an important tool of social analysis. And Marxism as a belief system has certainly not disappeared, although it appears unlikely that it will recover as a major ideology in the near future.

SUGGESTED READING

Classic Works

Bernstein, Eduard. *Evolutionary Socialism: A Criticism and Affirmation.* Edith C. Harvey, trans. New York: Schocken Books, 1961. As *The Preconditions of Socialism.* Henry Tudor, trans. and ed. Cambridge, England: Cambridge University Press, 1993. Both are translations of *Die Voraussetzungen des Sozialismus und die Aufgaben der Socialdemokratie.* Stuttgart, Germany: J. H. W. Dietz, 1899.

Bloch, Ernst. *The Principle of Hope.* Neville Plaice, Stephen Plaice, and Paul Knight, trans. Three vols. Oxford, England: Basil Blackwell, 1986. Originally published as *Das Prinzip Hoffnung.* Three vols. Berlin: Aufbau-Verlag, 1955–1959.

Debray, Régis. *Revolution in the Revolution? Armed Struggle and Political Struggle in Latin America.* Bobbye Ortiz, trans. New York: Monthly Review Press, 1967.

Djilas, Milovan. *The New Class: An Analysis of the Communist System.* New York: Harcourt Brace Jovanovich, 1955.

Engels, Friedrich. *The Origin of the Family, Private Property, and the State* (1884).

———. *Socialism: Utopian and Scientific* (1880).

Gramsci, Antonio. *The Modern Prince and Other Writings.* New York: International Publishers, 1957.

Kolakowski, Leszek. *Main Currents of Marxism.* P. S. Falla, trans. Three vols. Oxford, England: Clarendon Press, 1978.

Lenin, V. I. *Imperialism: The Highest State of Capitalism: A Popular Outline.* Moscow: Foreign Language Press, 1953. Originally published in 1916.

———. *State and Revolution.* London: Penguin, 1992. Originally published in 1918.

———. *What Is to Be Done?* London: Penguin, 1988. Originally published in 1902.

Lukács, György. *History and Class Consciousness: Studies in Marxist Dialectics.* Rodney Livingstone, trans. Cambridge, MA: MIT Press, 1971.

Luxemburg, Rosa. *The Accumulation of Capital.* Agnes Schwarzschild, trans. New York: Monthly Review Press, 1964.

Marcuse, Herbert. *An Essay on Liberation.* Boston: Beacon Press, 1969.

Marx, Karl. *Capital* (1867). There are three volumes, but only the first volume is well known.

———. *Economic and Philosophic Manuscripts of 1844* (first published in 1932).

——— and Friedrich Engels. *The Communist Manifesto* (1848).

Pannekoek, Anton. *Workers' Councils.* San Francisco: AK Press, 2003. Originally published in Dutch in 1946.

Books and Articles

Budgen, Sebastian, Stathis Kouvelakis, and Slavoj Žižek, eds. *Lenin Reloaded: Towards a Politics of Truth.* Durham, NC: Duke University Press, 2007.

Burkett, Paul. *Marxism and Ecological Economics: Toward a Red and Green Political Economy.* Leiden, The Netherlands: Brill, 2006. Quite technical.

Cohen, G. A. *If You're an Egalitarian, How Come You're So Rich?* Cambridge, MA: Harvard University Press, 2000.

Collier, Andrew. *Marx.* Oxford, England: Oneworld, 2004. Good introduction.

Cowling, Mark, ed. *The Communist Manifesto: New Interpretations.* New York: New York University Press, 1998.

Devenney, Mark. *Ethics and Politics in Contemporary Theory: Between Critical Theory and Post-Marxism.* London: Routledge, 2004. Quite technical.

Djilas, Milovan. *Fall of the New Class: A History of Communism's Self-Destruction.* Vasilije Kalezic, ed. New York: Knopf, 1998.

Foster, John Bellamy. *Marx's Ecology: Materialism and Nature.* New York: Monthly Review Press, 2000.

Gramsci, Antonio. *Letters from Prison.* Lynne Lawner, trans. and ed. New York: Harper & Row, 1973.

———. *Pre-Prison Writings.* Richard Bellamy, ed. Cambridge, England: Cambridge University Press, 1994.

———. *Selections from Political Writings (1910–1920).* Quinton Hoare and John Mathews, eds. London: Lawrence & Wishart, 1977.

———. *Selections from Political Writings (1921–1926).* Quinton Hoare, ed. Minneapolis: University of Minnesota Press, 1978.

Harnecker, Marta. *Rebuilding the Left.* Janet Duckworth, trans. London: Zed Books, 2007. A contemporary Marxist argument on how to revitalize the anticapitalist movement.

Howorth, David. "Post-Marxism." In *New Political Thought: An Introduction,* Adam Lent, ed. London: Lawrence & Wishart, 1998: 126–142.

Johnson, Janet Elise, and Jean C. Robinson, eds. *Living Gender After Communism.* Bloomington: Indiana University Press, 2007. Case studies of gender issues in eastern Europe and the former Soviet Union.

Laclau, Ernesto, and Chantal Mouffe. *Hegemony and Socialist Strategy: Towards a Radical Democratic Politics.* Winston Moore and Paul Cammack, trans. 2nd ed. London: Verso, 2001.

Lin, Chun. *The Transformation of Chinese Socialism.* Durham, NC: Duke University Press, 2006.

Macdonald, Bradley J. *Performing Marx: Contemporary Negotiations of a Living Tradition.* Albany: State University of New York Press, 2006.

Marx, Karl, and Friedrich Engels. *Collected Works.* 50 vols. New York: International Publishers, 1975–2004.

Mitrany, David. *Marx Against the Peasant: A Study in Social Dogmatism.* London: George Weidenfeld & Nicolson, 1951.

Negri, Antonio. *The Politics of Subversion: A Manifesto for the Twenty-First Century.* Trans. James Newell. 2nd ed. Cambridge, England: Polity, 2005. "Preface to the New Edition." Allan Cameron, trans. (pp. ix–xv).

Ollman, Bertell. *Dance of the Dialectic: Steps in Marx's Method.* Urbana: University of Illinois Press, 2003.

Outhwaite, William, and Larry Ray. *Social Theory and Postcommunism.* Malden, MA: Blackwells, 2005.

Pei, Minxin. *China's Trapped Transition: The Limits of Developmental Autocracy.* Cambridge, MA: Harvard University Press, 2006.

Perry, Elizabeth J., and Merle Goldman, eds. *Grassroots Political Reform in Contemporary China.* Cambridge, MA: Harvard University Press, 2007.

Rethinking MARXISM. Vol. 1 to the present (Founded 1988).

Rush, Fred, ed. *The Cambridge Companion to Critical Theory.* Cambridge, England: Cambridge University Press, 2004.

Sim, Stuart. *Post-Marxism: An Intellectual History.* London: Routledge, 2000.

———, ed. *Post-Marxism: A Reader.* Edinburgh, Scotland: Edinburgh University Press, 1998.

Smith, Tony. *Globalisation: A Systematic Marxian Account.* Leiden, The Netherlands: Brill, 2006.

Tormey, Simon, and Jules Townshend. *Key Thinkers From Critical Theory to Post-Marxism.* London: Sage, 2006.

Wang, Hui. *China's New Order: Society, Politics, and Economy in Transition.* Theodore Huters, ed. Cambridge, MA: Harvard University Press, 2003.

Wilde, Lawrence, ed. *Marxism's Ethical Thinkers.* Basingstoke, England: Palgrave, 2001.

Websites

Communist Party of America: http://www.cpusa.org

The Marxism Mailing List: http://www.marxmail.org

Marxist Internet Archive: http://www.marxists.org/archive

9

Anarchism and
Libertarianism

Although its roots reach back to classical Greece, anarchism emerged as a major modern ideology at about the same time as Marxism. The word *anarchy* means without a chief or ruler, or rule by no one; but today it suggests disorder or chaos, and people connect it to violent protests. As a result, the words *anarchy* and *anarchist* are used indiscriminately to condemn protesters, whether or not any among the protesters are anarchists. This dual perception of anarchism originated in the nineteenth century along with the first statements by modern anarchist theorists.

Today, forms of anarchism exist on the far Left and far Right of the political spectrum. Although anarchism is traditionally identified with the Left, a variant rooted in mid–nineteenth-century America, *anarcho-capitalism,* is generally identified with the Right.

An offshoot of anarchism that developed mostly in the second half of the twentieth century, *libertarianism* or *minimalism*, which many see as a variant of capitalism, is also generally identified with the Right, although Left libertarians have recently attacked the social agenda of the Right libertarians in the United States. Because its followers have been involved in the political process, libertarianism rests on the border between anarchism and some form of democracy; but its roots, particularly in the United States, are clearly in the anarchist tradition; therefore I discuss it here, rather than treating it as another subtype of democracy.

PRINCIPLES OF ANARCHISM

The ideology we call *anarchism* has a variety of forms and includes a number of different ideas. Most studies of anarchism have focused on a select group of men: Prince Pyotr Kropotkin (1842–1921), Pierre-Joseph Proudhon (1809–1865), Mikhail Bakunin (1814–1876), Count Leo Tolstoy (1828–1910), Max Stirner (1806–1856), William Godwin (1756–1836), and William Morris (1834–1896), who rejected the label. Lesser-known figures include Errico Malatesta (1853–1932), Élisée Reclus (1830–1905), Benjamin Tucker (1854–1939), and Josiah Warren (1798–1874). Today anarchists and scholars of anarchism recognize the significant contribution made to the anarchist movement and anarchist theory by women. Emma Goldman (1869–1940) is generally recognized as the most important, but women have always been involved in all aspects of anarchism.

An approach focusing on individual anarchists, although valid, is just as likely to result in a misunderstanding of the similarities and differences among anarchists. The approach here, therefore, is to select those parts of the anarchist tradition that are most important today while striving to maintain a balanced presentation.

Kropotkin once defined *anarchism* as

> the name given to a principle or theory of life and conduct under which society is conceived without government—harmony in such a society being obtained, not by submission to law or by obedience to any authority, but by free agreements concluded between the various groups, territorial and professional, freely constituted for the sake of production and consumption, as also for the satisfaction of the infinite variety of needs and aspirations of a civilized being.[1]

Anarchism is, then, a political philosophy that says no group in society should be able to coerce anyone. Such a society should contain a wide variety of groups that reflect the interests of its members. Anarchists differ somewhat on the relationships among these groups and on the importance of particular groups, but most would agree with this definition. As another anarchist, Alexander Berkman (1870–1936), stated, "Anarchism teaches that we can live in a society where there is no compulsion of any kind. A life without compulsion naturally means liberty; it means freedom from being forced or coerced, a chance to lead the life that suits you best."[2] Anarchists envision a peaceful, free life without rules and regulations. Of course, opponents of anarchism believe the result would be chaos rather than a peaceful, noncoercive society.

The basic assumption of anarchism is that power exercised by one person or group over another causes most social problems. As one anarchist says, "Many people say that government is necessary because some men cannot be trusted to look after themselves, but anarchists say that government is harmful because no man can be trusted to look after anyone else,"[3] and all anarchists would agree with this statement.

---

[1] Peter Kropotkin, "Anarchism," *Encyclopaedia Britannica,* 11th ed. New York: Encyclopaedia Britannica Co., 1910, Vol. 1: 914.

[2] Alexander Berkman, *ABC of Anarchism,* 3rd ed. London: Freedom Press, 1964: 10.

[3] Nicolas Walter, *About Anarchism.* London: Freedom Press, 1969: 6. Originally published as *Anarchy* 100, vol. 9 (June 1969).

Prince Pyotr (Peter) Kropotkin (1842–1921) was born into the Russian aristocracy but became the most important anarchist thinker of all time. Kropotkin's ideas originated during a long trip to Siberia as a geographer and naturalist. Intending to demonstrate a "struggle for survival" and "survival of the fittest," he found instead cooperation and what he came to call "mutual aid." He published his findings in a series of essays between 1890 and 1896 and then collected them as *Mutual Aid* (1902). His argument that cooperation rather than competition is the basis of evolution became the foundation of all his thought. From this position he contended that anarchism, not Marxism, was scientific. After escaping from a Russian prison, he spent most of his life in western Europe, primarily in England where he published his most famous books, *The Conquest of Bread* (1892), *Memoirs of a Revolutionist* (1898–1899), and *Fields, Factories and Workshops* (1899). He returned to Russia after the revolution in 1917 but quickly came into conflict with Lenin, whom he criticized for centralizing power.

They contend that power corrupts, and that human beings are capable of organizing their affairs without anyone exercising authority over others. This does not mean there will be no order in society; it means that people will cooperatively produce a better system than one based on power relations. "Given a common need, a collection of people will, by trial and error, by improvisation and experiment, evolve order out of chaos—this order being more durable than any kind of externally imposed order."[4] This order—this organization—will be better designed for human needs than any imposed system could be because it will be "(1) voluntary, (2) functional, (3) temporary, and (4) small."[5]

Each of these points is important for an understanding of anarchism. First, basic to all anarchism is the voluntary nature of any association. Second, an association will develop only to fill a fairly specific need and thus will be designed to fill that need alone. Third, it will therefore disappear after the need is met. Finally, it must be small enough so people can control it rather than be controlled by it. Many examples of such organizations, such as the cooperatives discussed in Chapter 5, exist today.

All anarchists agree that it is possible to replace a coercive society with voluntary cooperation, and "the essence of anarchism, the one thing without which it is not anarchism, is the negation of authority over anyone by anyone."[6] Or as another theorist put it, "Nobody is fit to rule anybody else. It is not alleged that people are

---

[4] Colin Ward, "Anarchism as a Theory of Organization," *Anarchy* 62, Vol. 6 (April 1966): 103.

[5] Ward, "Anarchism," 101. See also Terry Phillips, "Organization—The Way Forward," *Freedom* Vol. 31. (August 22, 1970): 3.

[6] Walter, *About Anarchism*, 8.

perfect, or that merely through his/her natural goodness (or lack of same) he/she should (or should not) be permitted to rule. Rule as such causes abuse."[7]

Beyond this, anarchism divides loosely into two categories: (1) collectivist, with emphasis on the individual within a voluntary association of individuals; and (2) individualist, with emphasis on the individual separate from any association. The former is sometimes divided into communist anarchism and anarcho-syndicalism; the latter is usually divided into individualist anarchism and anarcho-capitalism. In each case, though, the similarities are more important than the differences.

Collectivist Anarchism

Communist anarchism, traditionally associated with Kropotkin, is the most developed and comprehensive anarchist theory. It starts, as does all anarchism, with the assumption that coercion in any form is bad. As the solution to the problem of order in a society without a government, it suggests establishing a series of small, voluntary communes or collectives, somewhat like the intentional communities or communes discussed in Chapter 5. In communist anarchism, these small communities would join together into a federation to deal with any common problems. As George Woodcock (1912–1995) wrote, "The village would appoint delegates to the regional federations, which in their turn would appoint delegates to the national federations. No delegate would have the power to speak for anything but the decisions of the workers who elected him and would be subject to recall at any time."[8] Woodcock goes on to say that the delegates would be elected for a short period, and although expenses might be paid, delegates would receive exactly the same salary as they would at their regular jobs. In this way, the anarchist delegate is a very restricted representative.

Anarcho-syndicalists take essentially the same approach, except that they refer specifically to the work situation, particularly industrial work. The basic principles are:

1. Each industry (*industry* includes all those involved in such activities as erecting buildings, manufacturing automobiles, etc.) is organized into a federation of independent syndicates.

2. The workers in each industry control that industry.

3. Policy questions and questions of relations among syndicates are handled by a coordinating council.

Syndicalism originated as part of the trade union movement in France, but most anarcho-syndicalists today view trade unions as conservative, arguing that they fail to support workers against both management and government.

The central element of anarcho-syndicalism is workers' control,[9] the position that workers should be making workplace decisions, rather than managers who

---

[7] Albert Meltzer, *Anarchism, Arguments For and Against*. Edinburgh: AK Press, 1996: 19.

[8] George Woodcock, *New Life to the Land*. London: Freedom Press, 1942: 26.

[9] There is a vast literature on workers' control. For a sampling, see Ken Coates and Tony Topham, eds., *Workers' Control*. London: Panther Books, 1970; and *Anarchy* 2, Vol. 1 (April 1961).

are not in contact with the actual work. Anarcho-syndicalists argue that putting workers in control will enable them to produce more, thus lessening the problem of the allocation of scarce goods. In addition, anarcho-syndicalists contend that workers' control acts as a work incentive. Workers meet to resolve workplace problems and the issues that arise in any industry; then representatives of each industry assemble to administer the economic life of the entire country. The key word here is *administer.*

This is the same as Friedrich Engels's statement that in the final stage of communism, the government of people will become the administration of things, and it is the position held by all collectivist anarchists: People will no longer be governed. They will be free from government, but they will participate in administering the economic life of the country. The contention is that there need be no such thing as a political decision. The administration of things should be a fairly simple and mechanical operation that does not give rise to many conflicts. Of course, we are now aware that administration is not free of politics, which is one of the reasons anarchists insist that the power given anyone is temporary and that any representative is subject to immediate removal.

The differences between communist anarchism and anarcho-syndicalism are not great. Anarcho-syndicalism is more directly concerned with the organization of industry than is communist anarchism, but both arrive at fundamentally the same conclusions. Both accept the notion that the people in a given area should administer that area for the benefit of society as a whole. It is assumed that everyone will work and participate to some degree in the economic life of the society. Both believe that if coercion is removed, a viable society can develop.

Both stress the need for some way of developing cooperation among communities or industries. Although the focus of most studies of anarchist thought has been on individual freedom, anarchists have always argued that it is not possible to stop there. The primary focus of collectivist anarchism is not the isolated individual, but an individual within a noncoercive society. Anarchists recognize that the small community or industry is not sufficient and that cooperation among communities and industries is necessary to produce enough goods in sufficient diversity.

In anarcho-syndicalism, to give each individual the goods necessary for life, a high degree of cooperation must exist among industries to provide an efficient distribution system for the goods produced. The only way to handle this is through cooperation by the workers within the various industries. To some extent, this is simply a form of enlightened self-interest, because each worker needs the products of a wide variety of industries. Therefore, all workers will cooperate, because they all need the products of each and every industry. Anarcho-syndicalists believe this cooperation can develop readily once coercion disappears. To achieve this, government and capitalism must go.

The abolition of capitalism is a central concern for most anarchists, because they believe capitalists exploit workers in about the same ways Marx believed they did. Collectivist anarchists argue for common ownership of the means of production and distribution of goods according to need. Getting rid of government and capitalism raises the question of means, which raises the question of violence. Anarchists believe that no established authority will simply give up without a fight; therefore, revolution is likely to be the means of change.[10] But some anarchists are deeply bothered by the connection with violence, and a strong current of pacifist anarchism is associated with thinkers like Leo Tolstoy and Mohandas K. Gandhi (1869–1948). Other anarchists accept the connection with violence, believing that only through violent revolution will significant change be possible.

Anarcho-capitalists, discussed shortly, believe that collective systems exploit the best workers. Collectivist anarchists respond that capitalism exploits all workers. To put it in perspective, let us look at the individualist position.

Individualist Anarchism

The individualist anarchist recognizes nothing above his ego and rebels against all discipline and all authority, divine or human. He accepts no morality and when he gives himself to the feelings of love, friendship, or sociability, he does so because it is a personal need, an egoistic satisfaction—because it pleases him to do it.[11]

Essentially the position of individualist anarchism is as just stated: individuals determine for themselves, out of their own needs and desires, what is right for them. Max Stirner, generally thought of as the major exponent of individualist anarchism, even applies this to murder.[12]

Individualist anarchists do not completely reject cooperation, because cooperation is essential for the fulfillment of some human needs. But they contend that only the individualist is capable of genuinely forming a voluntary association with others. And such an association is not an end in itself but merely useful for a temporary purpose.

Individualist anarchists argue against collective ownership of goods, but not all are convinced that capitalism is better. Here we find a major split in the ranks of individualist anarchists: Some reject both capitalism and socialism and are not convinced that either system is valid. On the other hand, there are anarcho-capitalists.

Anarcho-Capitalism

Anarcho-capitalists contend that the only form of economic life compatible with individualism is capitalism. Usually their approach is connected with a view of life similar to that of the social Darwinist: both see life as a struggle for survival and hold that a socialist economic system supports those who do not deserve to survive. Anarcho-capitalists take the position that all essential social services can be better operated privately for profit than by any government or community; and they do mean *all* essential services, including the police and the military.

---

[10] For a discussion, see Vernon Richards, ed., *Violence & Anarchism: A Polemic.* London: Freedom Press, 1993.

[11] Enzo Martucci, "Individualist Amoralism," *Minus One,* no. 16 (November–December 1966): 5, J.-P.S. trans. From *L'Unique,* no. 37.

[12] See Max Stirner [Johann Kasper Schmidt], *The Ego and His Own,* David Leopold, ed. Steven T. Byington, trans. Cambridge, England: Cambridge University Press, 1995: 167–168.

In the United States, one of the earliest anarcho-capitalists was Lysander Spooner (1808–1887), who argued for the abolition of slavery on anarchist grounds and, after the Civil War, wrote tracts opposing all government. In the U.S. today most anarcho-capitalism and libertarianism stems from Ayn Rand (1905–1982), whose novels *Anthem* (1938), *Fountainhead* (1943), and *Atlas Shrugged* (1957) and many essays became the most popular expressions of these positions.[13] Less well known, but generally considered the ablest advocate of anarcho-capitalism, was Murray Rothbard (1926–1995), whose *For a New Liberty* (1973, republished in 1985 with the subtitle *The Libertarian Manifesto*), *Ethics of Liberty* (1982), and numerous other books were uncompromising defenses of the inviolability of private property. His works constitute a consistent moral defense of anarcho-capitalism. The successor to Rothbard is Llewellyn H. Rockwell (b. 1944), founder and president of the Ludwig von Mises Centre, currently the most important center of anarcho-capitalist advocacy and research.

LIBERTARIANISM

Closely related to anarcho-capitalism is libertarianism, sometimes called *minimalism* because some theorists include a role for government. Probably the best-known libertarian/minimalist text is *Anarchy, State, and Utopia* (1974)[14] by Robert Nozick (1938–2002). Nozick once argued for a minimal government, saying, "Our main conclusions about the state are that a minimal state, limited to the narrow functions of protection against force, theft, fraud, enforcement of contracts, and so on is justified; that any more extensive state will violate persons' rights not to be forced to do certain things, and is unjustified; and the minimal state is inspiring as well as right."[15] According to Nozick, an ideal system would consist of a number of small communities whose members agree on a particular way of life; many different communities would allow a wide variety of ways of living. But in 1989 Nozick at least partially backed away from his earlier stance, saying, "The libertarian position I once propounded now seems to me seriously inadequate, in part because it did not fully knit the humane considerations and joint cooperative activities it left room for more closely into its fabric."[16] As a result, Nozick has undermined the most sophisticated and well worked-out defense of libertarianism, but since his 1989 statement was so general, we do not really know whether he was rejecting all or only part of his previous position, let alone which part.

---

[13] On Rand's popularity, see Jerome Tuccille, *It Usually Begins with Ayn Rand.* New York: Stein and Day, 1971.

[14] For discussions of this book, see Jeffrey Paul, ed., *Reading Nozick: Essays on Anarchy, State, and Utopia.* Totowa, NJ: Rowman & Littlefield, 1981; and J. Angelo Corlett, ed., *Equality and Liberty: Analyzing Rawls and Nozick: Property, Justice, and the Minimal State.* Stanford, CA: Stanford University Press, 1991.

[15] Robert Nozick, *Anarchy, State, and Utopia.* New York: Basic Books, 1974: ix.

[16] Robert Nozick, "The Zigzag of Politics," in Nozick, *The Examined Life: Philosophical Meditations.* New York: Simon & Schuster, 1989: 186–187.

In the United States, one form taken by libertarianism is the Libertarian Party, a political party supporting candidates for office who pledge to severely reduce government. The "Preamble" to the "National Platform of the Libertarian Party" adopted in 2006 says, in words unchanged from previous platforms, "As Libertarians, we seek a world of liberty; a world in which all individuals are sovereign over their own lives, and no one is forced to sacrifice his or her values for the benefit of others."[17] In its "Statement of Principles," the 2006 platform says that individuals should be free to do as they choose as long as they do not "forcibly interfere with the right of others to do the same."[18] And the platform stresses that government power must be strictly limited. In particular, governments should not "violate the rights of any individual" with a particular emphasis on the individual's rights of speech or press.[19] The platform specifies many areas in which government should not be involved, such as the use of drugs, alcohol, consensual sexual relations—both heterosexual and homosexual—pornography, and gambling.

The platform is deeply concerned with the economy, but less so than in previous platforms. Again the stress is on what government should not do. Social welfare should be eliminated, as should corporate welfare. All service monopolies created by governments, such as the postal service, should be eliminated. The appropriate role for government in the economy is "to protect property rights, adjudicate disputes, and provide a legal framework in which voluntary trade is protected." Along the same lines, government should "support the prohibition of robbery, trespass, fraud, and misrepresentation."[20] In all cases government activity should be the least possible to achieve the desired result: thus the use of the word *minimalism* to describe this position.

ANARCHIST SOCIAL THOUGHT

Both anarchism and libertarianism have a central critique of contemporary society: they both reject control by any group but particularly by the organized group we call the *state*, or government. On the positive side, both anarchists and libertarians argue that people are capable of creating a better society under conditions of freedom. They diverge to some extent on the mechanisms of cooperation in this better society. Libertarians stress the free market and contractual relations between and among individuals and groups. In this, although they would not take the argument nearly as far, they are closer to individualist anarchists than to collectivist anarchists. Collectivist anarchists generally expect cooperation to operate on the basis of consensus among individuals and among groups.

Anarchist theory has developed mostly as a series of commentaries on specific areas of life believed to be coercive that could be improved by providing

---

[17] 2006 Libertarian Party Platform: http://www.lp.org/issues/platform_all.

[18] Ibid.

[19] Ibid.

[20] Ibid.

a free atmosphere. The ultimate goal is a truly free life in a community that weaves together the various ways of being free.

Anarchist theories of education are widely respected and have been put successfully into practice in many different countries, with the best known probably the Summerhill school in England, founded in 1921 by A. S. Neill (1883–1973) and still doing very well.[21] Anarchists believe that education today destroys freedom, creativity, and learning. They want an education directed to the needs of the individual child, whatever those needs may be; and this cannot be found, they contend, in the highly organized, overly complex system we have today. It can be found only in small groups educating for freedom. Anarchists believe that children, given the freedom to choose and the encouragement to follow their own bent, will gradually find distinct interests and will apply to those interests the tremendous energies children can develop. Children will learn more this way than by traditional methods.

The anarchist believes that much of what we are taught in our schools is irrelevant to our lives; we waste many years attempting to learn things that will never interest us or be of any use to us. A child should be encouraged to look at the world and interpret it on her or his own rather than being given answers. This approach to education puts a tremendous burden on parents and teachers: Teachers must develop a close relationship with each child to be able to understand the child's changing interests and to suggest ways in which the child might best fulfill them. This must be done without too much direction. Parents must be capable of giving their children freedom and must not control them too much.

Related to this approach is the homeschooling movement, in which parents educate their children at home rather than exposing them to public education. For some parents the motivation is religious; for some it is concern over the quality of education; and for others it centers on educating their children for freedom.[22] Thus homeschooling has produced some odd partnerships among people with very different motivations to defend the right to remove their children from public schools and educate them at home (not in a private school).

Anarchists believe human beings are willing and able to help each other and that our best instincts are destroyed by the present organization of society. They believe, as did Marx, that true love between individuals is impossible, or virtually impossible, under contemporary conditions. They believe a system that rejects sexual relationships outside the sanction of church or state destroys the possibility of developing what Marx called the love–sex relationship. The anarchist does not insist on or reject monogamous marriage; they simply contend that such questions should be left to individual decisions. People must be free to live their lives as they choose.

There is no anarchist proscription of or support of religion, and considerable debate takes place among anarchists over the question of religious affiliation.

[21] See, for example, Herbert Read, *The Education of Free Men*. London: Freedom Press, 1944; A. S. Neill, *Summerhill: A Radical Approach to Child Rearing*. New York: Hart Publication, 1960; Neill, *A Dominie's Log*. 1915; London: Hogarth Press, 1986; Ivan D. Illich, *Deschooling Society*. London: Calder; New York: Harper & Row, 1971; and Peter Buckman, ed., *Education without Schools*. London: Souvenir Press, 1973.

[22] See the list of homeschooling websites at the end of this chapter.

Emma Goldman (1869–1940), also known as "Red Emma," was a leading anarchist, lecturer, popularizer of the arts, and agitator for birth control, women's rights, and free speech. Born in Russia, she emigrated to the United States in 1885. In 1889 she moved from Rochester, New York, to New York City, where she met Johann Most (1846–1906) and Alexander Berkman (1870–1936) and became active with them in anarchist circles. In 1892 she and Berkman attempted to assassinate industrial leader Henry Clay Frick (1849–1919). She edited the journal *Mother Earth* (1906–1917) and wrote a number of books, including *Anarchism and Other Essays* (1911), *The Social Significance of Modern Drama* (1914), and *Living My Life* (1931). She was involved in most radical activities in the United States until she was deported as an undesirable alien in 1919. After her deportation, she traveled in the Soviet Union and wrote *My Disillusionment with Russia* (1923) and *My Further Disillusionment with Russia* (1924), both of which discussed the authoritarian nature of the Soviet government. After leaving Russia she continued her career as a radical agitator through involvement in the Spanish civil war.

Many say that such affiliation is incompatible with anarchism, while others argue that it depends on the type of organization or church. Still others, including Catholic anarchists such as Dorothy Day (1897–1980) and Ammon Hennacy (1893–1970), who left the church shortly before he died, have argued that faith in the doctrines of the church did not affect them as anarchists. They hold that the church speaks only on matters of faith and morals; outside these areas, Catholic anarchists consider themselves free of the church. The Catholic anarchist is merely a special case of contemporary anarchism. Individuals such as Day and Hennacy, who accepted an authoritarian religion and at the same time considered themselves anarchists, were merely accepting the dictates of the church in one part of their lives—that part dealing with questions of religious faith. As long as this acceptance is restricted to religious and perhaps moral questions, it does not necessarily affect the social and political positions of the anarchist. Today Dorothy Day's Catholic Worker Movement continues mostly in North America devoted to assisting those at the very bottom of the social ladder. In cities drop in centers provide people shelter and assistance in getting off alcohol and drugs. Those who make progress are then offered places in communities in the country where they will face less temptation and can regain their health. Church authorities who opposed Day during her lifetime have recently suggested that she be considered for sainthood.

Anarchism will probably always remain a minor ideology. Although unlikely to ever succeed in this world, it is the ideology that has the most faith in people. It believes, more than any other ideology does, that people are capable of freedom and cooperation. As Colin Ward (b. 1924) wrote, "Anarchism in all its guises is an assertion of human dignity and responsibility."[23]

---

[23] Colin Ward, *Anarchism in Action*. 2nd ed. London: Freedom Press, 1982: 143.

CURRENT TRENDS

In the last quarter of the twentieth century, a number of creative anarchist thinkers have published innovative applications of anarchist theory to current issues of public policy. The most important of these writers is Colin Ward, a freelance writer who has been particularly concerned with transportation policy, housing and town planning, environmental policy, and architecture. Alex Comfort (1920–2000) is best known for his book *The Joy of Sex* (1972); Comfort believed that a free sexuality is essential to the ability of people to act freely in other areas. Later he contributed substantially to anarchist theory in the area of aging.

Recently, in *Social Anarchism or Lifestyle Anarchism* (1995), Murray Bookchin (1921–2006) argued that anarchism is in serious danger of losing its value, because many anarchists are what he calls "lifestyle anarchists" rather than being seriously involved in trying to change social policy. Lifestyle anarchists are, according to Bookchin, committed to individual autonomy rather than to a collective vision of social freedom for all. The issue Bookchin raises is important: Many people who believe in anarchism do not think that a fully anarchist society is possible. As a result, they try to live their own lives as freely as possible, but with little or no concern for others. But unless anarchism remains a major critic of contemporary social and political policy, it will lose all claim to be taken seriously as a living ideology.

Bookchin, who will also be discussed in Chapter 13, is a critic of contemporary technology and an advocate of what he calls "social ecology." He writes that "social ecology 'radicalizes' nature, or more precisely, our understanding of natural phenomena, by questioning the prevailing marketplace image of nature from an ecological standpoint. . . ." He goes on to say that it replaces the consumption approach to nature with "an ethics of freedom rather than domination" that comes from an understanding of nature as an interactive, participatory system.[24]

Anarchism and Globalization

Anarchism has been making headlines in the recent past. Those producing the violence at the World Trade Organization (WTO) meeting in Seattle in 1999; the Group of 8 (G-8) summit in Genoa, Italy, in 2001; and at other economic and political meetings designed to foster globalization have identified themselves as anarchists and, in a few cases, have worn black clothes and carried the black flag symbolic of anarchism. Most protesters tried to distance themselves from these anarchists, but officials, particularly in Genoa, used the anarchists as an excuse for a violent attack on all the protesters.

As noted earlier, anarchists have long had an ambivalent attitude toward the use of violence. Many anarchists have argued that violence is most often ineffective and commonly counterproductive. It may give the violent demonstrators the feeling that they are personally doing something about the evil they oppose, and it certainly gets the attention of the media—these days this is the main reason for its use; but it rarely changes policy and frequently produces a backlash against the position being advocated.

---

[24] Murray Bookchin, *The Modern Crisis.* 2nd rev. ed. Montreal, QC, Canada: Black Rose Books, 1987: 55.

The supporters of violence as a tool contend that it is the only way to get the attention of the media, who without it would ignore the opposition at such meetings. Indeed, violence staged for the cameras, often with the collusion of the media, is a regular feature of demonstrations. Violence is also used by the ignored powerless simply as an expression of frustration. Those whose beliefs fall outside the dominant ideologies and paradigms of the countries in which they live rarely have ways to be heard. They may come to believe that the only way to get attention is to throw a stone through the window of a shop, attack the police, or trash a city center.

There is some merit to the argument. When a protester in Genoa was killed by a police officer, the G-8 leaders all said that they were responsive to the concerns expressed by the protesters and that they were actually trying to solve the problems the protesters raised. The protesters' response was that they wanted action, not talk, and that the leaders would not even have said they were aware of the issues without the protests. Therefore, both peaceful and violent protesters will be at future meetings.

TAZ, or Temporary Autonomous Zones

An important development within anarchism is what Hakim Bey (b. Peter Lamborn Wilson, 1945) calls *temporary autonomous zones (TAZ)* and what George McKay (b. 1950) called *do-it-yourself (DiY) culture*. Both labels suggest a free space in which people can temporarily create the life they want—where one can, briefly, be free.

The edited collection *DiY Culture* (1998) uses the peace camps, or long-term protests against military bases and construction projects in the United Kingdom, as one example of an instance in which free communities have been established. Other examples include New Age Travelers and Rainbow Gatherings.[25] A much more temporary version of a free community are the "raves," or music and dance festivals, that occur somewhat spontaneously, mostly by word of mouth, in urban and rural settings; these usually last for one night. In Britain, a collective creates them; in the United States, raves are often quasi-commercial enterprises.

TAZ opens up a space in which it is possible for believers to live their beliefs for a while. Julia "Butterfly" Hill lived in a tree for two years to prevent its being cut down; a few of the women protesting the placement of nuclear missiles at Greenham Common Air Base stayed for years, but most were there for short periods. Musical festivals like Woodstock are short-lived but still provide a different space for a short time. A lesbian music camp and some lesbian communes are re-created each summer (other lesbian communes are permanent); women who attend say that they are able to truly be themselves at that time, whereas they cannot be the rest of the year.

For some, the temporary can become permanent. New Age Travellers are noticed only when they gather in groups for one of their periodic festivals.

---

[25] Richard Lowe and William Shaw, *Travellers: Voices of the New Age Nomads.* London: Fourth Estate, 1993; Michael I. Niman, *People of the Rainbow: A Nomadic Utopia.* Knoxville: University of Tennessee Press, 1997.

Although for some the Rainbow Gatherings are a once-a-year festival, others travel from gathering to gathering, which now occur both regionally and worldwide.

These people used to be called "dropouts," although most of them prefer to say that they "dropped in" to a better life. But the most common way anarchism is practiced is through individual life choices; for example, to teach in a school in which pupils are given freedom as opposed to teaching in a traditional, hierarchical public or private school.[26]

LETS, or Local Exchange and Trading Systems

An example of TAZ is *LETS,* or *local exchange and trading systems,* in which "a number of people get together to form an association. They create a unit of exchange, choose a name for it, and offer each other goods and services priced in these units. Offers and wants are listed in a directory, which is circulated periodically to members. Members decide whom to trade with and how much trading they want to do."[27] There are many LETS groups, ranging from child care groups, in which parents in a neighborhood exchange child care so that they can sometimes have a night out; to Womanshare in New York City, which has created a "skill bank" in which each woman gains credit for the work she contributes;[28] to local currency schemes, like Ithaca HOURS, BloomingHours, the Maine Time Dollar Network, and Bread Hours in the San Francisco Bay area.[29] Hundreds of such groups exist today.

All of the forms of TAZ are growing in number, although the greatest growth seems to be in LETS groups. Few of the people involved in any of the TAZ groups are self-consciously anarchists, but they have chosen to structure a part of their lives in ways that they see as enhancing their freedom.

SUGGESTED READING

Some Classic Works

Bakunin, Mikhail. *God and the State.*
New York: Mother Earth Press, 1916.
Reprinted, Mineola, NY: Dover, 1970.
No translator given.

Berkman, Alexander. *ABC of Anarchism.*
3rd ed. London: Freedom Press, 1964.
Reprinted, New York: Dover, 2005.

Bey, Hakim [Peter Lamborn Wilson].
T. A. Z. The Temporary Autonomous Zone,
Ontological Anarchy, Poetic Terrorism.
Brooklyn, NY: Autonomedia, 1991.
2nd revised ed. with a new Preface.
Brooklyn, NY: Autonomedia, 2003.

Bookchin, Murray. *Post-Scarcity Anarchism.*
2nd ed. Montreal: Black Rose Books, 1986.

Debord, Guy. *The Society of the Spectacle.*
Donald Nicholson-Smith, trans. New
York: Zone Books, 1994. Originally
published in French in 1967.

---

[26] Colin Ward describes DiY culture (although he does not call it that) at work in a community in "Anarchy in Milton Keynes," *The Raven,* no. 18 (5:2) (April–June 1992): 116–131.

[27] Harold Sculthorpe, "LETS: Local Exchange and Trading Schemes," *The Raven,* no. 31 (8:3) (Autumn 1995): 237.

[28] http://www.angelfire.com/ar2/womanshare.

[29] See the list of LETS websites at the end of this chapter.

Freire, Paulo. *Pedagogy of the Oppressed.* Myra Bergman Ramos, trans. 30th anniversary ed. New York: Continuum, 2000.

Godwin, William. *Enquiry Concerning Political Justice and Its Influence on Morals and Happiness.* R. E. L. Priestley, ed. 3 vols. Toronto: University of Toronto Press, 1946. Originally published in 2 vols. London: Printed for G. G. J. and J. Robinson, 1793. Recent reprint edited by Isaac Kramnick. New York: Penguin, 1976.

Goldman, Emma. *Anarchism and Other Essays.* New York: Mother Earth Press, 1910. Reprinted, New York: Dover, 1969.

———. *Living My Life.* 2 vols. New York: Alfred A. Knopf, 1931. Reprinted, New York: Penguin, 2006.

Kropotkin, Peter. *The Conquest of Bread.* New York: Putnam's, 1907. Reprinted as *The Conquest of Bread and Other Writings.* Marshall Shatz, ed. Cambridge, England: Cambridge University Press, 1995.

———. *Fields, Factories and Workshops.* London: Swan Sonnenschein, 1901. Reprinted, New York: Benjamin Blom, 1968.

———. *Fields, Factories and Workshops Tomorrow.* Colin Ward, ed. London: George Allen & Unwin, 1974.

———. *Kropotkin's Revolutionary Pamphlets.* Roger N. Baldwin, ed. New York: Vanguard Press, 1927. Reprinted, New York: Dover, 1970.

———. *Memoirs of a Revolutionist.* New York: Houghton Mifflin, 1899. Reprinted, James Allen Rogers, ed. Garden City, NY: Doubleday, 1962.

———. *Mutual Aid: A Factor of Evolution.* New York: McClure Philips, 1902. Reprinted, Mineola, NY: Dover, 2006.

Malatesta, Errico. *Anarchy.* 8th ed. Vernon Richards, trans. London: Freedom Press, 1949. Also translated by Michael de Cossart. Liverpool, England: Department of History, University of Liverpool, 1988.

Neill, A. S. *Summerhill: A Radical Approach to Child Rearing.* New York: Hart Publications, 1960. Reprinted, New York: Penguin, 1990.

Nozick, Robert. *Anarchy, State, and Utopia.* New York: Basic Books, 1974.

Proudhon, Pierre-Joseph. *What Is Property? An Inquiry into the Principle of Right and of Government.* Donald R. Kelley and Bonnie G. Smith, ed. and trans. Cambridge, England: Cambridge University Press, 1994. Originally published in 1840 as *Qu'est-ce que la propriété?*

Read, Herbert. *The Philosophy of Anarchism.* London: Freedom Press, 1940.

Stirner, Max [Johann Kasper Schmidt]. *The Ego and His Own.* David Leopold, ed. Steven T. Byington, trans. Cambridge, England: Cambridge University Press, 1995.

Tolstoy, Leo. *The Law of Love and the Law of Violence.* Mary Koutouzow Tolstoy, trans. London: Anthony Blond, 1970.

Tucker, Benjamin R. *Individual Liberty: Selections from the Writings of Benjamin R. Tucker.* C. L. S., ed. New York: Vanguard Press, 1926. Reprinted, Millwood, NY: Kraus, 1973.

Ward, Colin. *Anarchy in Action.* 2nd ed. London: Freedom Press, 1982.

Books and Articles

Anarchist Studies Vol. 1:1 to the present (Founded 1993)

Anarchy, nos. 1–114 (1960–1970).

Anderson, Benedict. *Under Three Flags: Anarchism and the Anti-Colonial Imagination.* London: Verso, 2005.

Antliff, Allan, ed. *Only A Beginning: An Anarchist Anthology.* Vancouver, BC, Canada: Arsenal Pulp Press, 2004.

Avrich, Paul. *Anarchist Portraits.* Princeton, NJ: Princeton University Press, 1988.

———. *Bakunin & Nechaev.* London: Freedom Press, 1974.

———. *The Modern School Movement: Anarchism and Education in the United States.* Princeton, NJ: Princeton University Press, 1980.

Barnett, Randy E. *Restoring the Lost Constitution: The Presumption of Liberty.* Princeton, NJ: Princeton University Press, 2004. Argument against both the history of judicial interpretations of the Constitution and those who insist on interpretation on the basis on the original intent of the founders. From a libertarian perspective.

Berneri, Camillo. *Peter Kropotkin: His Federalist Ideas.* London: Freedom Press, 1942.

Bey, Hakim [Peter Lamborn Wilson]. *Immediatism.* Edinburgh: AK Press, 1994. Originally published as *Radio Sermonettes.* New York: Libertarian Book Club, 1992.

———. *Millennium.* Brooklyn, NY: Autonomedia/Dublin, Ireland: Garden of Delight, 1996.

Bookchin, Murray. *Anarchism, Marxism, and the Future of the Left: Interviews and Essays, 1993–1998.* San Francisco: AK Press, 1999.

———. *The Modern Crisis.* 2nd rev. ed. Montreal, QC, Canada: Black Rose Books, 1987.

———. *Social Anarchism or Lifestyle Anarchism: An Unbridgeable Chasm.* San Francisco: AK Press, 1994.

Brooks, Frank H., ed. *The Individualist Anarchists: An Anthology of "Liberty" (1881–1908).* New Brunswick, NJ: Transaction, 1994.

Call, Lewis. *Postmodernism Anarchism.* Lanham, MD: Lexington Books, 2002.

Carter, April. *The Political Theory of Anarchism.* London: Routledge & Kegan Paul, 1971.

Cayley, David. *The Rivers North of the Future: The Testament of Ivan Illich as Told to David Cayley.* Toronto, On, Canada: Anansi, 2005.

Chan, Andy. "Violence, nonviolence, and the concept of revolution in anarchist thought." *Anarchist Studies* Vol. 12.2 (2004): 103–123.

Christie, Stuart. *Granny Made Me an Anarchist.* London: Simon & Schuster, 2004.

Curran, Giorel. *21st Century Dissent: Anarchism, Anti-Globalization and Environmentalism.* New York: Palgrave Macmillan, 2006.

de Cleyre, Voltairine. *Selected Works of Voltairine de Cleyre.* Alexander Berkman, ed. New York: Mother Earth Press, 1914.

Franks, Benjamin. "Postanarchism: A Critical Assessment." *Journal of Political Ideologies* Vol. 12:2 (June 2007): 127–145.

Freire, Paulo. *Pedagogy of the City.* Donaldo Macedo, trans. New York: Continuum, 1993. Interviews that Freire gave while head of the school system in São Paulo, Brazil.

———. *Pedagogy of Freedom: Ethics, Democracy, and Civic Courage.* Patrick Clarke, trans. Lanham, MD: Rowman & Littlefield, 1998.

———. *Pedagogy of Hope: Reliving Pedagogy of the Oppressed. With Notes by Ana Maria Araújo Freire.* Robert R. Barr, trans. New York: Continuum, 1999.

———. *Pedagogy of Indignation.* Boulder, CO: Paradigm Publications, 2004. No translator given.

Gladstein, Mimi Reisel. *The Ayn Rand Companion.* Westport, CT: Greenwood Press, 1984. Revised and expanded as *The New Ayn Rand Companion.* Westport, CT: Greenwood Press, 1999.

Glassgold, Peter, ed. *Anarchy! An Anthology of Emma Goldman's Mother Earth.* Washington, D.C.: Counterpoint, 2001.

Goodway, David. "The Anarchism of Colin Ward." In *Richer Futures: Fashioning a New Politics.* Ken Worple, ed. London: Earthscan, 1999: 3–20. The entire book honors Ward's career.

———. *Anarchist Seeds beneath the Snow: Left-Libertarian Thought and British Writers from William Morris to Colin Ward.* Liverpool, England: Liverpool University Press, 2006.

———, ed. *For Anarchism: History, Theory, and Practice.* London: Routledge, 1989.

Gordon, Uri. "Anarchism Reloaded." *Journal of Political Ideologies* Vol. 12:1 (February 2007): 29–48.

Graham, Robert, ed. *Anarchism: A Documentary History of Libertarian Ideas. Volume One: From Anarchy to Anarchism (300 CE to 1930).* Montreal, QC, Canada: Black Rose Books, 2005.

Guérin, Daniel, ed. *No Gods No Masters.* Paul Sharkey, trans. 2 vols. Edinburgh: AK Press, 1998.

Harding, Thomas. *The Video Activist Handbook.* London: Pluto Press, 1997. 2nd ed. London: Pluto Press, 2001.

Hennacy, Ammon. *The Book of Ammon.* Author: 1965.

————. *The One-Man Revolution in America.* Salt Lake City, UT: Ammon Hennacy Publications, 1965.

Herzog, Don. "Romantic Anarchism and Pedestrian Liberalism." *Political Theory* Vol. 35:3 (June 2007): 313–333.

Horowitz, Irving Louis, ed. *The Anarchists.* New Brunswick, NJ: Aldine Transaction, 2005. "Introduction to the Transaction Edition" (xi–xx).

Illich, Ivan. *Celebration of Awareness: A Call for Institutional Revolution.* Garden City, NY: Anchor Books, 1971.

————. *Deschooling Society.* New York: Harper & Row, 1971. Reprinted, London: Marion Boyars, 1996.

————. *The Right to Useful Unemployment and Its Professional Enemies.* London: Marion Boyars, 1978.

————. *Tools for Conviviality.* London: Calder & Boyars, 1973.

————, Irving Kenneth Zola, John McKnight, Jonathan Caplan, and Harley Shaiken. *Disabling Professions.* London: Marion Boyars, 1977.

Jordan, Tim. *Activism! Direct Action, Hacktivism and the Future of Society.* London: Reaktion Books, 2002.

Kinna, Ruth. *Anarchism: A Beginners Guide.* Oxford, England: OneWorld, 2005. Good basic introduction.

Loomis, Mildred J. *Decentralism: Where It Came From—Where Is It Going?* Montreal, QC, Canada: Black Rose Books, 2005.

Machen, Tibor R. *Libertarianism Defended.* Aldershot, England: Ashgate, 2006.

Marshall, Peter H. *Demanding the Impossible: A History of Anarchism.* London: HarperCollins, 1992. Revised ed. with an epilogue, London: Harper Perennial, 2008. This is currently the most important history of the subject.

Mbah, Sam, and I. E. Igariwey. *African Anarchism: The History of a Movement.* Tucson, AZ: See Sharp Press, 1997.

O'Hara, Craig. *The Philosophy of Punk: More Than Noise.* 2nd ed. Edinburgh, Scotland: AK Press, 1999.

Purkis, Jonathan, and James Bowen, eds. *Changing Anarchism: Anarchist Theory and Practice in a Global Age.* Manchester, England: Manchester University Press, 2004.

————, eds. *Twenty-first Century Anarchism: Unorthodox Ideas for a New Millennium.* London: Cassell, 1997.

Raddon, Mary-Beth. *Community and Money: Men and Women Making Change.* Montreal, QC, Canada: Black Rose Books, 2003. On Local Exchange and Trading Systems.

Raimondo, Justin. *An Enemy of the State: The Life of Murray Rothbard.* Amherst, NY: Prometheus Books, 2000.

Rand, Ayn. *Anthem.* London: Cassell, 1938. 1st U.S. ed. Los Angeles, CA: Pamphleteers, 1946. Expanded 50th anniversary ed., New York: Dutton, 1995.

————. *Atlas Shrugged.* New York: Random House, 1957. 35th anniversary ed. New York: Dutton, 1992.

————. *Capitalism, the Unknown Ideal.* With additional articles by Nathaniel Branden, Alan Greenspan, and Robert Hessen. New York: New American Library, 1966.

————. *For the New Intellectual: The Philosophy of Ayn Rand.* New York: Random House, 1961.

————. *The Fountainhead.* Indianapolis: Bobbs-Merrill, 1943. Reprinted, New York: Plume, 2005.

————. *The Virtue of Selfishness: A New Concept of Egoism.* With additional articles by Nathaniel Branden. New York: New American Library, 1964.

————. *We the Living.* New York: Random House, 1959. 60th anniversary ed. New York: Signet, 1996.

Richards, Vernon, ed. *Violence & Anarchism.* London: Freedom Press, 1993.

Rockwell, Llewellyn H. *Speaking of Liberty.* Auburn, AL: Ludwig von Mises Centre, 2003.

————, ed. *Irrepressible Rockwell: The Rothbard-Rockwell Report. Essays of Murray N. Rothbard.* Burlingame, CA: Center for Libertarian Studies, 2000.

Rothbard, Murray. *The Ethics of Liberty.* Atlantic Highlands, NJ: Humanities Press, 1982.

————. *For a New Liberty: The Libertarian Manifesto.* Rev. ed. New York: Collier Books, 1978.

Roussopoulos, Dimitrios I., ed. *The Anarchist Papers*. 3 vols. Montreal, QC, Canada: Black Rose Books, 1986–1990.

Stevens, Mitchell L. *Kingdom of Children: Culture and Controversy in the Home-schooling Movement*. Princeton, NJ: Princeton University Press, 2001.

Stringham, Edward P., ed. *Anarchy and the Law: The Political Economy of Choice*. New Brunswick, NJ: Transaction Publishers, 2007. A large (698 page) collection primarily, but not solely, from the perspective of anarcho-capitalism.

Suissa, Judith. *Anarchism and Education: A Philosophical Essay*. London: Routledge, 2006.

Tullock, Gordon, ed. *Explorations in the Theory of Anarchy*. Blacksburg: Center for the Study of Public Choice, Virginia Polytechnic Institute and State University, 1972.

———, ed. *Further Explorations in the Theory of Anarchy*. Blacksburg, VA: University Publications, 1974.

Uricchio, William. "Beyond the Great Divide: Collaborative Networks and the Challenge to Dominant Conceptions of Creative Industries." *International Journal of Cultural Studies* Vol. 7:1 (March 2004): 79–90. Peer-to-peer networks similar to LETS.

Vallentyne, Peter, and Hillel Steiner, eds. *Left Libertarianism and Its Critics: The Contemporary Debate*. London: Palgrave, 2000.

———. *The Origins of Left Libertarianism: An Anthology of Historical Writings*. London: Palgrave, 2000.

Vaughan, Mark, ed. with contributions from Tim Brighouse, Zoë Neill Readhead, and Ian Stronach. *Summerhill and A.S. Neill*. Maidenhead, England: Open University Press, 2006. Much of the book is made up of extracts from Neill's *Summerhill*.

Walter, Nicolas. *The Anarchist Past and Other Essays*. David Goodway, ed. Nottingham, England: Five Leaves, 2007.

Ward, Colin. *Anarchism: A Very Short Introduction*. Oxford, England: Oxford University Press, 2004.

———. *Housing: An Anarchist Approach*. London: Freedom Press, 1982.

———. *Social Policy: An Anarchist Response*. Rev. ed. London: Freedom Press, 2000.

——— and David Goodway. *Talking Anarchy*. Nottingham, England: Five Leaves, 2003. Interview.

White, Stuart. "Making anarchism respectable? The social philosophy of Colin Ward." *Journal of Political Ideologies* Vol. 12:1 (February 2007): 11–28.

Wolff, Robert Paul. *In Defense of Anarchism*. New York: Harper & Row, 1970. Reprinted, Berkeley: University of California Press, 1998.

Woodcock, George. *Anarchism: A History of Libertarian Ideas and Movements*. Peterborough, ON, Canada: Broadview Encore Editions, 2004. Last edition during the author's lifetime was 1986, and this edition reprints that one.

Websites

A-Infos: http://www.ainfos.org

Anarchy Archives: http://dwardmac.pitzer.edu/Anarchist_Archives/index.html

Anarchist Yellow Pages: http://www.ayp.subvert.info

Catholic Worker Movement: http://www.catholicworker.org

Institute for Humane Studies: http://www.theihs.org

Institute for Social Ecology: http://www.social-ecology.org

Libertarian Party: http://www.lp.org

Libertarian Party of Canada/*Parti Libertarien du Canada*: http://www.libertarian.ca

Ludwig von Mises Institute: http://www.mises.org

Summerhill: http://www.summerhillschools.co.uk

LETS

Bread Hours—What you need, when you need it: http://www.breadhours.org

E. F. Schumacher Society, Local Currency Groups: http://www.schumachersociety.org/local_currencies.html

Ithaca Hours Local Currency: http://www.ithacahours.org

LETSystems The Home Page: http://www.gmlets.u-net.com

Transaction Net: LETS—Local Exchange Trading Systems: http://www.transaction.net/money/lets

Vancouver—LETS development: http://www.alternatives.com/lets

A Cooperative Skill Bank. Womanshare: http://www.angelfire.com/ar2/womanshare

Homeschooling

A to Z Home's Cool Homeschooling Website: http://homeschooling.gomilpitas.com

Classical Christian Homeschooling: http://www.classicalhomeschooling.org

Classical Homeschooling Magazine: http://www.classicalhomeschooling.com

Home School Legal Defense Association (HSLDA): http://www.hslda.org/Default.asp?bhcp=1

Homefires, The Journal of Homeschooling Online: http://www.homefires.com

Homeschoolzone: http://www.homeschoolzone.com

Montessori Homeschooling: http://www.montessori.edu/homeschooling.html

National Home Education Research Institute (NHERI): http://www.nheri.org

10

Fascism and National Socialism

ascism developed early in the twentieth century in France and Italy, and the first successful fascist movement was in Italy in the 1920s. National socialism developed in Germany in the 1930s, and the movements in Germany and Italy before World War II provided the ideological basis for later movements. They are similar enough to be called one ideology, with national socialism one of a number of varieties of fascism.

For the generation that lived through World War II, the words *fascism, national socialism,* and *Nazism* raise indescribably horrible pictures of brutality and inhumanity. Today the words *fascist* and *Nazi* are too often used loosely to refer to any authoritarian countries and individuals, but such loose usage obscures both the history and the fact that fascist and national socialist movements based on, and similar to, the earlier movements exist today in many countries, including the United States.

THE THEORETICAL BASE

Although the emphasis can vary, the following seven ideas are found in almost all fascist and national socialist writing:

1. Irrationalism
2. Social Darwinism
3. Nationalism

4. Glorification of the state

5. The leadership principle

6. Racism

7. Anticommunism

The first two are basic themes that are rarely explicitly stated. All seven concepts are interrelated but can be separated for analysis. A recent commentator argues that antifeminism should be added to this list.[1]

Irrationalism

In the nineteenth and early twentieth centuries, reason and science were the central tenets of liberal and Marxist approaches to social change, and irrationalism specifically rejects those approaches and replaces them with myth, emotion, and hate. National socialism in particular has an affinity for astrology, the occult, and various pseudo-sciences, and that affinity continues into contemporary neo-Nazi movements.[2]

The basic assumption is that humans are not rational beings, and they need not be reasoned with; they can only be led and manipulated. Other ideologies take note of the irrational aspects of human psychology and behavior, but only fascism and national socialism emphasize the irrational and treat it as a central part of the ideology.

The emphasis in national socialism is on myths of blood (racism) and soil (nationalism) and on violence as a constant, normal part of political life. When it was in power in Germany, those who did not fit its image of racial purity were executed; Jews, homosexuals, Gypsies or Roma, and the physically or mentally disabled were specifically targeted.

Paradoxically, racial hatred and intense nationalism are part of the appeal of fascism and national socialism. For those who are insecure—financially, socially, or emotionally—an appeal based on racial hatred and intense nationalism that promotes a feeling of worth in members as being a superior race or nation, one that identifies other people as inferior, can be very effective. Fascism and national socialism give a sense of belonging, superiority, and security to those who feel cut off, inferior, or insecure.

Social Darwinism

Social Darwinism is the name generally given to social theories that view life as a struggle for survival within each species, as well as between species. The key to success is the "survival of the fittest"—a phrase first used by Herbert Spencer

---

[1] Kevin Passmore, *Fascism: A Very Short Introduction.* Oxford, England: Oxford University Press, 2002: 31.

[2] See Nicholas Goodrick-Clarke, *The Occult Roots of Nazism: Secret Aryan Cults and Their Influence on Nazi Ideology. The Ariosophists of Austria and Germany, 1890–1935.* New York: New York University Press, 1992; Goodrick-Clarke, *Hitler's Priestess: Savitra Devi, the Hindu–Aryan Myth, and Neo-Nazism.* New York: Oxford University Press, 2000; and Goodrick-Clarke, *Black Sun: Aryan Cults, Esoteric Nazism, and the Politics of Identity.* New York: New York University Press, 2001.

(1820–1903) in his *Principles of Biology* (1864) after reading *On the Origin of Species by Means of Natural Selection* (1859) by Charles Darwin (1809–1882). Darwin had argued that life evolved by species successfully adapting to conditions so that some were able to reproduce most effectively. A simple example would be that white bears were most successful in breeding in arctic areas, and brown bears were most successful in breeding in forest areas; so two different species of bear emerged by adapting to life in those areas.

While Darwin had focused on adaptation by different species, social Darwinists apply the idea to each species. In other words, rather than seeing change as coming about through successful adaptation by different species, they see a struggle for survival *within* each species. Fascists and national socialists have applied this to the human species, arguing that nations and races have to compete to survive.[3] Arguing against the social Darwinists, Pyotr, or Peter, Kropotkin (1842–1921), who was discussed in the previous chapter, argued in his book *Mutual Aid* (1902) that considerable evidence exists for cooperation within species.

Nationalism

Nationalism, discussed in Chapter 2, is basic to both fascism and national socialism: the nation is based on ethnicity, generally called *race* by national socialists, and the boundaries of the nation are defined by language. In this view, if a majority—or even a substantial minority—of the people in an area speak German or Italian, that area should become part of Germany or Italy Still, as we shall see later, just speaking the language is not enough, particularly for national socialists; individuals must also be of the correct ethnic background to be part of a nation.

The ideal fascist individual does not really exist apart from his or her existence in the nation. An individual is one small part of the nation, and the individual and the nation are inseparable. Individuals should not be able to conceive of themselves as distinct entities separate from the nation; ideally, people should be completely wrapped up in the nation, although not all fascists feel this strongly.

For the national socialist, nationalism and racism are so closely connected that they form one concept rather than two. For example, among the basic principles on which the national socialists in Germany intended to reform the legal system, race is considered the most important:

> The legal protection of the race, which has created a new concept of nationality [*Volkszugehörigkeit*], is consciously put in first place, for the most significant historical principle which has been established by the victory of National Socialism is that of the necessity for keeping race and blood pure. All human mistakes and errors can be corrected except one: "the error regarding the importance of maintaining the basic values of a nation."

---

[3] For further analysis of the role of social Darwinism in National Socialism, see Hajo Holborn, "Origins and Political Character of Nazi Ideology," *Political Science Quarterly* Vol. 74 (December 1964): 542–554.

The purpose of this legal protection of the basic value of *race* must be the prevention for all time of a further mixture of German Blood with foreign blood, as well as the prevention of continued procreation of racially unworthy and undesirable members of the people.[4]

In the middle of the twentieth century, many fascists distanced themselves from national socialism on the issue of race. But contemporary fascism tends to have a strong concern with ethnicity, which is treated in terms similar to race.

The mechanism by which the nation is enhanced is the state, and the physical boundaries of the nation and the state should be the same. Thus, if areas of the nation are outside the state, they should become part of the state. Benito Mussolini (1883–1945) wrote that the state is the carrier of the culture and spirit of the nation; that it is the past, present, and future; that it represents the "immanent conscience of the nation"; and that it educates the citizens in all the virtues.[5] And he said, "The keystone of the Fascist doctrine is the conception of the State, of its essence, of its functions, its aims. For Fascism the State is absolute, individuals and groups relative."[6] The nation is embodied in the state, and therefore the state must be glorified.

Glorification of the State

The state, as Mussolini said, is the carrier of the culture and spirit of the people and the driving force that welds the people together. It must, therefore, be strong; it must have the power necessary to achieve its goals. The people collectively are the locus of emotion, and the state is the structure through which that emotion is expressed. The theory of the state as presented by fascists and national socialists combines these two notions into the idea of an organic or corporate state. The state, at least as seen by Adolf Hitler (1889–1945), is a "rigid formal organization," and the people are, or the nation is, a "living organism."[7]

In this context, the word *organic* means "social groups as fractions of the species receive thereby a life and scope which transcends the scope and life of the individuals identifying themselves with the history and finalities of the uninterrupted series of generations."[8] Put somewhat differently, this means society, represented by the state, is a separate entity with a life or existence at once different from, and greater than, the life of any individual. This also means—and

---

[4] Otto Gauweiler, *Rechtseinrichtungen und Rechtsaufgaben der Bewegung.* Munich: Zentralverlag der NSDAP, Franz Eher, Nachfolger, 1939; trans. in *National Socialism: Basic Principles. Their Application by the Nazi Party's Foreign Organization, and the Use of Germans Abroad for Nazi Aims,* prepared in the Special Unit of the Division of European Affairs by Raymond E. Murphy, Francis B. Stevens, Howard Trivers, and Joseph M. Roland. Washington, D.C.: GPO, 1943: 208–209.

[5] Benito Mussolini, "The Doctrine of Fascism," in Mussolini, *Fascism: Doctrine and Institutions.* New York: Howard Fertig, 1968: 27–28.

[6] Mussolini, "Doctrine of Fascism," 27.

[7] Adolf Hitler, *The Speeches of Adolf Hitler, April 1922–August 1939,* Norman H. Baynes, ed. London: Oxford University Press, 1942, Vol. 1:178, speech of September 1930.

[8] Alfredo Rocco, "The Political Doctrine of Fascism," D. Bigongiari, trans. *International Conciliation,* no. 223 (October 1926): 402. Some fascists reject the idea that they are presenting the "organic theory of the state."

this is the important point—that the life of the individual is less important than the life of the society.

This is illustrated by the "folkish" state expressed by Hitler in his book *Mein Kampf:* "Thus, the highest purpose of a *folkish* state is concern for the preservation of those original racial elements which bestow culture and create the beauty and dignity of a higher humanity."[9] This folkish state is a racial state; only the members of the true Aryan race may participate, but they participate only in the sense of giving of themselves to the state. They do not govern. The folkish state, then, is a state based on racial purity and on ideas of soil—myths of racial content connected with the particular history of the German nation. Here race and nationalism, blood and soil, are combined. An understanding of national socialism as it developed in Germany cannot be separated from an understanding of race and nationalism and the combination of the two in a folkish state.

Mussolini said the state is the source of the life of the people of all generations that compose it.[10] The state is owed supreme loyalty by the individuals who live in it, but the state is also something more than what these somewhat mechanical notions imply. It is also a "spiritual" unit, but this "spiritual" side is closely related to the authority controlling the state. The state "enforces discipline and uses authority, entering into the soul and ruling with undisputed sway."[11] It does this through the leadership principle.

The Leadership Principle

The state is the mechanism for enforcing fascist beliefs, and the state is run on the *leadership principle,* or *Führer principle,* under which each subordinate owes absolute obedience to his or her immediate superior; everyone is ultimately subordinate to the absolute leader, the Führer, which was Hitler's title. Mussolini's title was *Il Duce,* which also means "the leader." This hierarchy of leaders with a single, absolute leader at the top is an important characteristic of fascism and national socialism. The leader is expected to reflect the collective will of the people, but the leader's will is, by definition, the same as the collective will. "His will is not the subjective individual will of a single man, but the collective national will."[12] Therefore, the leader's authority is absolute. Hitler and Mussolini were both charismatic leaders: the word *charismatic* comes from *kharisma,* meaning "favor" or "divine gift". Both were able to attract people by sheer force of personality, and few fascist movements have survived the death of the leader.

The Führer principle on which Hitler based his power and organization seems, on the surface, to be complicated. But it is similar to the notion of a representative as embodying the will of the constituency, discussed in Chapter 4. Hitler, as leader, was the representative of the German nation and the Aryan race

---

[9] Adolf Hitler, *Mein Kampf,* Ralph Manheim, trans. Boston: Houghton Mifflin, 1943: 394. Emphasis in the original.

[10] Mussolini, "Doctrine of Fascism," 11–12.

[11] Mussolini, "Doctrine of Fascism," 14.

[12] Ernst Rudolf Huber, *Verfassungsrecht des grossdeutschen Reiches.* Hamburg, 1939: 195; translated and quoted in *Readings on Fascism and National Socialism.* Denver, CO: Alan Swallow, 1952: 75.

Adolf Hitler (1889–1945) was founder and leader of the National Socialist German Workers' Party, chancellor (1933–1945), and head of state (1934–1945) of Germany. He was the leading figure of the Nazi movement and is still venerated as such by Nazis everywhere. He was violently nationalist and anti-Semitic and author of one of the classic texts of national socialism, *Mein Kampf* (1925–1927). The swastika on Hitler's uniform is the symbol of national socialism. Standing next to him is Benito Mussolini (1883–1945). In this picture Mussolini is giving the Nazi salute. Mussolini, known as *Il Duce* (the Leader), ruled Italy from 1922 until shortly before his death.

in that he embodied within himself all the aspirations of the people. This does not mean that Hitler followed the will of the people, but that he, by embodying their will, was capable of *rightly* interpreting it. This is the key to the whole Führer principle—the Führer is the only one capable of rightly interpreting the will of the people. When the Führer speaks, he represents what the people truly want. In this sense he is virtually infallible, and this is clearly how Hitler viewed himself: Hitler as Führer could do no wrong.

But no one person, even a Führer, can rule an entire country; even an absolute ruler needs some apparatus to enforce rules. This apparatus is the party. Party members are separate from and have power over the rest of the population. Some clearly recognizable sign, such as a uniform, usually identifies them. Finally, there is a corps within the party, an elite within the elite, to check on the rest of the party. The two groups that served this function within the National Socialist German Workers' Party, the official name of Hitler's party, were the SA (*Sturmabteilung*) and the SS (*Schutzstaffel*). Hitler defined the task of the SA as follows: "The SA on behalf of our German people must educate the young German in mind and body so that he becomes a man hard as steel and ready to fight. Out of hundreds of thousands of individuals it must forge one united, disciplined, mighty organization."[13] The party was the effective ruling mechanism. But as Hitler said, "Every member of the Party has to do what the leader orders."[14]

The word *totalitarian*, which implies total control, emerged in the 1920s and 1930s as a way of characterizing governments in Italy under fascism and then Germany under national socialism. It was later extended to the Soviet Union under communism, particularly to the regime of Joseph Stalin. It refers to a

---

[13] Adolf Hitler, "Introduction to the Service-Order of the SA," quoted in Hitler, *Speeches,* Vol. 1:169.

[14] Hitler, *Speeches,* Vol. 1:459, speech of May 21, 1930.

government that controls or attempts to control the totality of human life and completely subordinates the individual to the state.[15]

The party plays a role similar in fascism and national socialism to that of the Communist Party as described by Lenin, as discussed in Chapter 8. The party is the vanguard of the nation or the race, rather than of the proletariat, but the general notion is the same. The party is the forerunner of the new order to come, and for the national socialist, this new order is based on race.

Racism

Probably the single best-known part of national socialism is its racism.[16] The words *racism* and *racist* were first used in the 1930s to refer to the beliefs of the national socialists, and they reflect the belief that the human species can be subdivided into *races,* or subgroups with similar cultural and/or physical characteristics, and that one of these races is superior to the others. The most extreme forms of racism see what they call races, never clearly defined, as different species; to them, the so-called "inferior" races are not really human. Modern science provides no support for the idea of races within the human species.[17]

For national socialism, racism represents the underlying current of social Darwinism and is a mechanism of social control: by destroying Jews and others targeted by the regime—primarily Roma (the word Gypsies use to describe themselves) and homosexuals—they instilled fear in the Germans, and they also instilled pride in the Germans' so-called racial heritage. Nazi policy stressed both negative and positive eugenics.[18] Negative eugenics aims at keeping those perceived to be unfit from having children; positive eugenics aims at encouraging those thought to be fit to have many children.

Hitler believed that what he variously called the Aryan, Nordic, white, or sometimes German race was the strongest. He contended that the domination of one "race" over others was good for all, because it was natural and founded on reason. But it must be remembered that the social Darwinian struggle for survival, as interpreted by the national socialists, requires the elimination of the dominated races.

The racial policies of Hitler were not limited to extermination and breeding. They included the belief that all that is good in culture stems from the Aryan race and that Germany, therefore, as the representative of the Aryans had the best

---

[15] For different perspectives on the concept of totalitarianism, see Carl J. Friedrich, Michael Curtis, and Benjamin R. Barber, *Totalitarianism in Perspective: Three Views.* New York: Praeger, 1969.

[16] The best study is Claudia Koonz, *The Nazi Conscience.* Cambridge, MA: Belknap Press of Harvard University Press, 2007.

[17] For the history of the concept and current understandings of race, see Bernard Boxill, ed., *Race and Racism.* Oxford, England: Oxford University Press, 2001; George M. Fredrickson, *Racism: A Short History.* Princeton, NJ: Princeton University Press, 2002; Joseph L. Graves, Jr., *The Emperor's New Clothes: Biological Theories of Race at the Millennium.* New Brunswick, NJ: Rutgers University Press, 2001; and Paul C. Taylor, *Race: A Philosophical Introduction.* Cambridge, England: Polity, 2004.

[18] The word *eugenics* was coined in 1883 by Francis Galton (1822–1911). Its original meaning referred only to what came to be called *positive eugenics,* or the science of producing of the best offspring, particularly in humans.

cultural heritage of the Western world and would have an even better culture in the future. One of Hitler's great loves was the operas of Richard Wagner (1813–1883), because Wagner's operas could be seen as operas of the folkish state that represented the myths of blood and soil that were so important to Hitler. In particular, they represented what he saw as a high point in German culture—an illustration that the Germans had a great culture, and particularly that Wagner, as a representative of German culture, seemed to agree with some of the ideas put forth by Hitler. Therefore, Hitler was able to present national socialism as a logical outgrowth of German culture and the German nation.

The relationship of the state to racism is seen in *Mein Kampf,* where Hitler wrote, "The state is a means to an end. Its end lies in the preservation and advancement of a community of physically and psychically homogeneous creatures."[19] The effect of racism on other aspects of the society is obvious. Social stratification would be based on racial purity and party membership plus positive support for the regime and contributions to the country. In addition, the racist ideology would control marriage, and the desire to control the minds of children would dictate control of the family system. Along these lines, German women of the correct racial type were encouraged to have many children. As Joseph Goebbels (1897–1945) put it, "The mission of woman is to be beautiful and to bring children into the world."[20] German women were also supposed to be athletic, and they were to refrain from wearing makeup and such things as smoking in public, which were thought to detract from their femininity. But above all, they were to have children. The educational system, the family, and religion were all used to develop the correct values in children. Parents were to teach their children the true national socialist ideals from birth. National socialism also contended that God supported it; thus religion was used for the same purpose.[21]

Anticommunism

One aspect of fascism and national socialism that made both acceptable to many was their anticommunism. As one scholar of fascism put it, "Before all else, it was anticommunist. It lived and throve on anticommunism."[22] Since communism presented itself as based on reason, this was an aspect of fascism's antirationalist approach and its general rejection of the modern world, and it was a part of fascism's appeal.[23]

---

[19] Hitler, *Mein Kampf,* 393.

[20] Joseph Goebbels, quoted in Mosse, *Nazi Culture: Intellectual, Cultural, and Social Life in the Third Reich.* New York: Grosset & Dunlap, 1966: 41. A good introduction to the socialization process is Fritz Brennecke, *The Nazi Primer: Official Handbook for Schooling the Hitler Youth,* Harwood L. Childs, trans. New York: Harper & Brothers, 1938; New York: AMS Press, 1972.

[21] On religion under national socialism, see Richard Steigmann-Gall, *The Holy Reich: Nazi Conceptions of Christianity, 1919–1945.* Cambridge, England: Cambridge University Press, 2003.

[22] H. R. Trevor-Roper, "The Phenomenon of Fascism," in S. J. Woolf, ed., *European Fascism.* New York: Vintage Books, 1969: 24.

[23] See, for example, Alastair Hamilton, *The Appeal of Fascism: A Study of Intellectuals and Fascism 1919–1945.* New York: Macmillan, 1971.

THE ECONOMIC SYSTEM

The economic theory of fascism and national socialism was never developed systematically, and there were marked differences in the countries involved. Even though *socialism* is part of the name *national socialism,* and Mussolini was originally a socialist, neither fascism nor national socialism was actually socialist. National socialism began from that position, but it quickly changed as it gained the support of capitalists.[24] Probably the best statement of the general economic theory of national socialism is this:"All property is common property. The owner is bound by the people and the Reich [government] to the responsible management of his goods. His legal position is only justified when he satisfies this responsibility to the community."[25] Thus property was held privately, but it had to be used as the government dictated or it would be confiscated. Even though an individual may have temporary control of some economic good—land, capital, or whatever—this control must serve the interests of the collective nation or race, as interpreted by the Führer, or the control must be terminated.

A major concern in fascism and national socialist economic theory is to establish economic self-sufficiency. For fascism and national socialism to achieve their goals, the countries involved must be self-sufficient; they must not depend on other countries for supplies.[26] All the stress on the nation, the state, the race, and the people would lose considerable force if these entities were dependent on other nations, states, races, and peoples.

The economic system of fascism includes the idea of state-controlled *syndicates.* The state creates all economic organizations, as the Labour Charter of April 21, 1927, says: "Work in all its forms—intellectual, technical and manual—both organizing or executive, is a social duty. On this score and only on this score, it is protected by the State. From the national standpoint the mass of production represents a single unit; it has a single object, namely, the well-being of individuals and the development of national power."[27] All economic organization under fascism is ultimately controlled by the state and is designed to include both workers and employers in the same organization; this is called *corporatism,* or the *corporate economy.* In this way, the state is made superior to every part of the economy. The syndicates are designed to ensure that production continues as long as the state requires it. The right to strike is taken away from the workers, but at the same time, the syndicate, operating as an arm of the state, has the power to set wages; thus the syndicate acts as a policymaking arm of the state in economic affairs. As in Germany, the Fascist Party in Italy with Mussolini at the head had ultimate power. In many ways, the syndicates were merely administrative arms of the Fascist Party and of Mussolini rather than having any real power to

---

[24] On this point, see Martin Broszat, *German National Socialism 1919–1945,* Kurt Rosenbaum and Inge Pauli Boehm, trans. Santa Barbara, CA: CLIO Press, 1966: 22–24.

[25] Huber, *Verfassungsrecht,* 372–373, quoted in *Readings on Fascism,* 91.

[26] See the discussion in Paul M. Hayes, *Fascism.* London: George Allen & Unwin, 1973: 89–105.

[27] "The Labour Charter," in Benito Mussolini, *Four Speeches on the Corporate State.* Rome: "Laboremus," 1935: 53.

make decisions. The leadership principle was not abrogated in Italy; it was maintained, and the syndicates acted as lower-level leaders following the dictates of the supreme leader.

CURRENT TRENDS

Neofascism

In the past few years, fascism and national socialism have revived in a number of countries, including Germany, Italy, the United Kingdom, Russia, a number of the countries of the former Soviet Union, China, and the United States.[28] In Italy parties associated with fascism have made substantial electoral gains. In Germany direct reference to national socialism is rare, but opposition to immigration has produced groups that are quite similar to early national socialists. This is particularly true in the former East Germany, where the unification of Germany has produced substantial unemployment and poverty in contrast to the obvious wealth of the former West Germany. In the United States, a number of groups, most fairly small, either identify with national socialism through the use of its traditional symbols, mostly the swastika, or they support social and political traditions closely associated with national socialism.

Although these small groups clearly exist, most of the extreme Right political movements are not necessarily fascist; these were discussed under the heading "The Extreme Right" in Chapter 6. If we take the seven points with which the chapter began, most of the movements are anticommunist, racist, and nationalist, but they generally do not stress the other four points. Because anticommunism, racism, and nationalism are the most important of the seven, there is certainly a close affinity between the contemporary extremist groups and fascism, and perhaps that is enough for us to use the word *neofascism* to describe them. Such groups are particularly strong in Austria, Germany, the United Kingdom, and the United States. They are also emerging in Russia, other states of the former Soviet Union, and China.[29]

Some groups in the United States are clearly fascist, and others explicitly align themselves with national socialism. The former leader of the National Alliance, William L. Pierce (1933–2002), was once an associate of George Lincoln Rockwell (1918–1967), the longtime leader of the American Nazi Party, which still exists, together with other U.S. groups that explicitly align themselves with national socialism. The National Alliance, which has gone through a number of conflicts since Pierce's death, continues in part because it controls a number of white racist music companies and supports white racist music festivals. It is also closely connected to "skinhead" groups.

---

[28] A. James Gregor, *Phoenix: Fascism in Our Time.* New Brunswick, NJ: Transaction, 1999. See also Peter Davies and Derek Lynch, eds., *The Routledge Companion to Fascism and the Far Right.* London: Routledge, 2002.

[29] In a recent book, one of the most important scholars of fascism argues that most groups identified as such today are incorrectly labeled; see A. James Gregor, *The Search for Neofascism: The Use and Abuse of Social Science.* Cambridge, England: Cambridge University Press, 2006.

In Europe the issue that seems to most attract people to the neofascist ranks is immigration. The focus of the neofascist Right in the United States was, until recently, race, with anti–Semitism still particularly important, followed by internationalism, the power of the Federal Reserve and the Internal Revenue Service, and the perceived desire of the central government to restrict the freedoms of dissenters on the Right. But in the past couple of years, immigration is a growing concern, with a particular focus on Muslims.

Another issue of interest to neo-Nazi groups around the world is a revival in the Nazi interest in eugenics, brought about in part by the possibility of genetic engineering and cloning. They see the possibility of these new or potential technologies being used for racist purposes.

SUGGESTED READING

Some Classic Works

Gentile, Giovanni. *Origins and Doctrine of Fascism with Selections from Other Works*. A. James Gregor, trans. and ed. New Brunswick, NJ: Transaction Publishers, 2002.

Hitler, Adolf. *Mein Kampf.* Ralph Manheim, trans. Boston: Houghton Mifflin, 1943.

Mussolini, Benito. *Fascism: Doctrine and Institutions.* Rome: Ardita, 1936. Reprinted New York: Howard Fertig, 1968.

———. *Four Speeches on the Corporate State.* Rome: "Laboremus," 1935. No translator given.

———. *My Autobiography.* New York: Scribner, 1928. No translator given. Reprinted, Mineola, NY: Dover, 2006.

Rocco, Alfredo. "The Political Doctrine of Fascism." D. Bigongiari, trans. *International Conciliation,* no. 223 (October 1926): 393–415.

Books and Articles

Barkun, Michael. *Religion and the Racist Right: The Origins of the Christian Identity Movement.* Revised ed. Chapel Hill: University of North Carolina Press, 1997.

Blinkhorn, Martin, ed. *Fascists and Conservatives: The Radical Right and the Establishment in Twentieth-Century Europe.* London: Unwin Hyman, 1990. Primarily concerned with the first half of the twentieth century.

Brennecke, Fritz. *The Nazi Primer: Official Handbook for Schooling the Hitler Youth.* Translated by Harwood L. Childs. New York: Harper & Brothers, 1938; Reprinted, New York: AMS Press, 1972.

Browning, Christopher with contributions by Jürgen Matthäus. *The Origins of the Final Solution: The Evolution of Nazi Jewish Policy September 1939–March 1942.* Lincoln: University of Nebraska and Yad Vashem, Jerusalem, 2004.

Burrin, Philippe. *Nazi Anti-Semitism: From Prejudice to Holocaust.* Janet Lloyd, trans. New York: New Press, 2005. Evolution of the policies that led to the Holocaust.

Davies, Peter, and Derek Lynch, eds. *The Routledge Companion to Fascism and the Far Right.* London: Routledge, 2002.

Dobratz, Betty A., and Stephanie L. Shanks-Meile. *"White Power, White Pride!": The White Separatist Movement in the United States.* New York: Twayne, 1997.

Durham, Martin. *Women and Fascism.* London: Routledge, 1998.

Gregor, A. James. *Giovanni Gentile: Philosopher of Fascism.* New Brunswick, NJ: Transaction, 2001.

———. *Interpretations of Fascism.* New Brunswick, NJ: Transaction, 1997.

———. *Mussolini's Intellectuals: Fascist Social and Political Thought.* Princeton, NJ: Princeton University Press, 2005. Important argument that fascism had a reasoned social and political theory.

————. *Phoenix: Fascism in Our Time.* New Brunswick, NJ: Transaction, 1999.

————. *The Search for Neofascism: The Use and Abuse of Social Science.* Cambridge, England: Cambridge University Press, 2006.

Griffin, Roger. *Modernism and Fascism: The Sense of a Beginning under Mussolini and Hitler.* Basingstoke, England: Palgrave Macmillan, 2007. Argues against many commentators that fascism did not reject modernism.

————. *The Nature of Fascism.* New York: St. Martin's Press, 1991.

Guenther, Irene. *Nazi Chic? Fashioning Women in the Third Reich.* Oxford, England: Berg, 2004.

Harootunian, Harry. "The Future of Fascism." *Radical Philosophy*, no. 136 (March/April 2006): 23–33. Argument regarding the relationship between capitalism and fascism.

Hitler, Adolf. *Hitler's Second Book: The Unpublished Sequel to Mein Kampf.* Krista Smith, trans. Gerhard L. Weinberg, ed. New York: Enigma Books, 2003.

————. *The Speeches of Adolf Hitler, April 1922–August 1939.* Edited by Norman H. Baynes. 2 vols. London: Oxford University Press, 1942.

Kallis, Aristotle A., ed. *The Fascism Reader.* London: Routledge, 2003.

Kaplan, Jeffrey, ed. *Encyclopedia of White Power: A Sourcebook on the Radical Racist Right.* Walnut Creek, CA: AltaMira Press, 2000.

Koonz, Claudia. *The Nazi Conscience.* Cambridge, MA: Belknap Press of Harvard University Press, 2003. An important study tracing the racial practices.

Kuntz, Dieter, ed. *Deadly Medicine: Creating the Master Race.* Washington, D.C.: United States Holocaust Memorial Museum, 2004.

Passmore, Kevin. *Fascism: A Very Short Introduction.* Oxford, England: Oxford University Press, 2002.

Paulicelli, Eugenia. *Fashion Under Fascism: Beyond the Black Shirt.* Oxford, England: Berg, 2004.

Paxton, Robert O. *The Anatomy of Fascism.* New York: Alfred A. Knopf, 2004.

Pfaff, William. *The Bullet's Song: Romantic Violence and Utopia.* New York: Simon & Schuster, 2004.

Redles, David. *Hitler's Millennial Reich: Apocalyptic Belief and the Search for Salvation.* New York: New York University Press, 2005.

Sargent, Lyman Tower, ed. *Extremism: A Reader.* New York: New York University Press, 1995.

Shenfield, Stephen D. *Russian Fascism: Traditions, Tendencies, Movements.* Armonk, NY: M.E. Sharpe, 2001.

Simonelli, Frederick J. *American Fuehrer: George Lincoln Rockwell and the American Nazi Party.* Urbana: University of Illinois Press, 1999.

Steigmann-Gall, Richard. *The Holy Reich: Nazi Conceptions of Christianity, 1919–1945.* Cambridge, England: Cambridge University Press, 2003.

Viereck, Peter. *Metapolitics: The Roots of the Nazi Mind.* Rev. and enl. ed. New York: Capricorn Books, 1965.

Wolin, Richard. *The Seduction of Unreason: The Intellectual Romance with Fascism from Nietzsche to Postmodernism.* Princeton, NJ: Princeton University Press, 2004.

Websites

American Nazi Party: http://www.americannaziparty.com

Libertarian National Socialist Green Party: http://www.nazi.org

National Alliance: http://www.natall.com

11

☙

Islamic Political Ideologies

The religion of Islam has become a major political force in the contemporary world.[1] *Islam* is an Arabic word meaning "submission," specifically submission to the will of God, or *Allah* in Arabic; *Muslim* means "one who submits."[2] Islam is the second largest world religion, after Christianity, with about a billion adherents. Muslims live mostly in a wide belt from Senegal on the west coast of Africa, east to Indonesia on the western edge of the Pacific Ocean, reaching south into sub-Saharan Africa and north into the southern part of the former Soviet Union. Although many equate Islam with the Arab Middle East, only about 18 percent of Muslims are Arabs, and most Muslims do not speak or read Arabic. About 50 countries are predominantly Islamic, with Indonesia the largest. In addition, Muslim communities are growing throughout the rest of the world, including the United States and Europe.

---

[1] Islamic political thought has not yet been studied much in the West. The following sources in English include works both for the beginner and for someone wanting some depth. Good places for the neophyte to start are Aziz Al-Azmeh, "Islamic Political Thought," in *Blackwell Encyclopedia of Political Thought,* David Miller, ed. Oxford, England: Blackwell Reference, 1987: 249–253; and Phil Marfleet, "Islamist Political Thought," in *New Political Thought: An Introduction,* Adam Lent, ed. London: Lawrence & Wishart, 1998: 89–111. The best and most recent systematic study is Antony Black, *The History of Islamic Political Thought: From the Prophet to the Present.* New York: Routledge, 2001.

[2] In Arabic—the language in which the Islamic holy book, the Qur'an was written—the words used are *Muslim* (singular masculine), *Muslima* (singular feminine), *Muslimûn* (plural masculine), and *Muslimât* (plural feminine). *Islamists is Islamiyyûn* (plural masculine) and is used only in that form. The Qur'an does not use *Islamiyyûn;* it uses *Muslimûn* or *Mu'minûn* (Believers).

Similarities of belief among Muslims allow us to identify a community of believers, just as similarities of belief exist among the widely divergent sects of Christianity. Just like Christianity, Islam is not a single, unified religion. It has a number of subgroups, and there is no final authority in Islam to settle disputes. In fact, although there have been attempts to create greater unity, at least nationally, the leader of each mosque is quite independent.

The most important division is between the Sunni, who represent about 85 percent of all Muslims, and the Shiite, who include most of the rest; but a number of smaller sects exist both within and outside of the two major groups. Equally important, just as in Christianity, are significant differences in Islamic practice from country to country, mosque to mosque, and individual to individual.

For most of the twentieth century, Islam was not a significant political force in world affairs. Most Islamic countries were attempting to modernize and join the developed world. Four things changed this:

1. The establishment of the state of Israel in 1948, on land then occupied by Palestinians, united Islamic countries that had been previously divided.

2. The rapid rise in the price of oil made some poor countries suddenly rich.

3. The Iranian revolution, combined with Iranian attempts to foment revolution in other Islamic countries, led to a much greater focus on Islam both in the Middle East and elsewhere.

4. The process of decolonization and the connected revitalization of national cultures revived divisions in Islam that had lain dormant during the colonial period.

Many Muslims reject modernization and Westernization, seeing it as corrupting basic Islamic values. Many different labels—such as *Islamic fundamentalism*, *Islamic revivalism*, and *re-Islamization*—have been used to describe this movement, but recently *Islamism* has come to be the most widely accepted term.[3]

BELIEFS

A few points about religious belief are necessary as background to help understand Islam. Islam is unified by its faith in Allah, the holy book the *Qur'an* (*Koran*), and the teachings of its prophet, Muhammad (570–632). Islam sprang from the same roots and the same geographic area as Christianity and Judaism, and Islam accepts the Jewish prophets and Jesus as great religious teachers who

---

[3] *Fundamentalist* was the preferred term for some time, but it simply refers to going back to the fundamentals of the faith and was never really accurate. Also, while there are fundamentalist currents in Christianity, Hinduism, and Judaism as well as Islam, the word was first used in 1920 to describe debates within Protestantism in the United States. See Gabriel Almond, R. Scott Appleby, and Emmanuel Sivan, *Strong Religion: The Rise of Fundamentalisms around the World* (Chicago: University of Chicago Press, 2003: 14–17) for a discussion of the word. See also Malise Ruthven, *Fundamentalism: The Search for Meaning* (Oxford: Oxford University Press, 2004).

were forerunners to Muhammad. Islam, like both Judaism and Christianity, is monotheistic. Christians, Jews, and Muslims are all thought of as "People of the Book," although, of course, the books are different.

Every pious Muslim must perform the five "pillars" of Islam:

1. In a lifetime the believer must at least once say, "There is no god but God and Muhammad is the messenger of God," in full understanding and acceptance.
2. The believer must pray five times a day: at dawn, noon, midafternoon, dusk, and after dark.
3. The believer must give alms or charity generously.
4. The believer must keep the fast of Ramadan, the ninth month of the Muslim year.
5. The believer must once make the pilgrimage (*hajj*) to Mecca in Saudi Arabia (in Arabic, *Makkah-tul-Mukarramah*, usually shortened to *Makkah*, but *Mecca* is still used outside Islam).

A sixth pillar is sometimes included, the *jihad*, usually thought of in the West as denoting holy war but actually meaning "to struggle," signifying that believers must struggle with themselves and their communities to be good Muslims and to proselytize to enlarge the Muslim community.[4] Today *jihad* is being used by radical Islamic sects specifically to describe a holy war against the West, but this meaning is rejected by the overwhelming majority of Muslims.

Beyond these basic beliefs and duties, the believer refers for guidance to the *Shari'a* (path or way), the religious law.[5] Islamic law gives both legal and moral guidance and has provided an additional point of reference for the widely divergent cultures represented by the many Islamic countries. For radical Muslims, one central goal is the adoption of the *Shari'a* as the law of the land. Of course, any law requires interpreters, and who is to interpret the law is a basis for disagreement within Islam. Many Islamic countries can be thought of as theocratic societies—*theo* means "god," *kratos* means "rule"—in which there is no separation of church and state, and politics is subordinate to religion.

Islamic law is derived from the *Qur'an*, the *Sunna* (life) of the Prophet Muhammad, legal reasoning, and the consensus of the community.[6] It is more like a set of moral and ethical principles than what Westerners today think of as law, although it can be considered similar to customary law. It was, and in many Muslim countries is, interpreted and applied by a variety of courts and officials. In addition, in most countries the *Shari'a* was gradually supplemented and, in the eyes of some, supplanted by laws designed to address changing economic and political conditions.

---

[4] John L. Esposito, *Islam: The Straight Path*, expanded ed. New York: Oxford University Press, 1991: 93.

[5] Esposito, Islam: *The Straight Path*, 75–76.

[6] Esposito, Islam: *The Straight Path*, 79–85.

HISTORY

It is impossible to understand contemporary Islam without a little history. The major division in Islam relates to the leaders of Islam after Muhammad's death. Most Islamic groups accept that the first four *caliphs* (successors) were correctly chosen. The dispute involves the line of succession after the fourth caliph. The Sunni believe that the caliphs that followed Ali were correctly chosen and believe that consensus should be the basis for the choice of successor. The Shiites believe that divine appointment should be the basis for the choice of successor. The main Shiite sect, the Twelvers (believers in the Twelfth Imam), believe that the correct succession was through the fourth caliph's descendants by his wife Fatima, Muhammad's daughter, through a line of infallible imams—beginning with Ali ben Abi Talib, the fourth caliph, and his two sons to the Twelfth Imam, who disappeared while still a boy. The Twelvers believe that the Twelfth Imam is waiting for the right time to return, and that he will overthrow oppression and bring justice to the earth.

Undoubtedly the most politically important of the other sub-groups of Islam today are the Wahhabi, who have ruled Saudi Arabia since 1932; they consider Salafism or Wahhabism—a name its adherents reject—a purified form of Islam. The movement became politically important through Muhammad bin Abd al-Wahhab (1703–1792), a clan leader influenced by Ibn Taymiyya (1263–1328), a Sunni thinker who argued for a strict interpretation of the *Qu'ran*. Salafism

UPI /Bettmann

The Great Mosque, or *Haran*, at Mecca, Saudi Arabia, is the spiritual center of Islam. At the center of the mosque is the Kaaba or Caaba, the most sacred sanctuary in Islam. Mecca and the mosque are the destination of the *hajj*, or the pilgrimage that every Muslim is required to make in his or her lifetime. The towers are minarets, and from them a *muezzin* calls the faithful to prayer five times a day.

is influential in the Emirates on the Arabian Peninsula; the Caucasus, particularly in Chechnya; and Central Asia. Another important group within Islam are the Sufis, a mystical sect found throughout Islam; numerous smaller sects also exist.

Islam has gone through a variety of periods of change and division; the Shiites in particular have splintered into a number of sects. The Sunni have followed one of two paths: literalists and those trying to break away from the texts. Literalism is based on the belief that the Qur'an is the unaltered word of God, and the success of the literalists has narrowed the Sunni canon.

As with most other colonized areas, Islamic countries went through a process of combined acceptance and rejection of Western values and practices. While it was clear that Western technology allowed colonization to take place and was useful, perhaps even necessary, a deep division occurred over the acceptance of Western values, particularly those related to individual freedom and equality.

ISLAM TODAY

Politically, Islam is deeply divided between those who accept modernization and those who reject it. In the West today, we mostly hear about the latter. The primary issue is not technology but the attitudes and beliefs of the West, and there is great pressure to reject Western beliefs and attitudes even while encouraging the use of modern technologies.

Islamic Liberalism or Modernism

In the nineteenth and early twentieth centuries, Islam went through a lengthy transformation similar to the changes Christianity experienced in the seventeenth through nineteenth centuries. Specifically, Islamic liberal thinkers accepted the notion of historical change and, in particular, the idea that Islamic texts could be reinterpreted to meet changing conditions. The key texts of Islam have undergone critical analysis by scholars throughout the history of Islam, but today that sort of analysis tends to remain with academics and does not penetrate the mosques. There are no seminaries of the "higher criticism," which in U.S. Christianity undertook detailed analyses of the text of the Bible.

Islamic liberals argue for the reconciliation of reason and faith, religious freedom within Islam, recognition that religious practices need to change to meet changed conditions, the need for educational reform to take advantage of Western science and technology, democracy, and the desirability of greater equality for women. For quite some time and in many countries, Islamic liberalism was dominant, but in the second quarter of the twentieth century, a shift began to take place. Based on the experience of colonialism, Islamic liberalism was rejected as too Western, and the identification of Islamic liberalism with the West and colonialism provided the ideological basis for the emergence of Islamism.

Islamic thought has no concept of individual freedom or rights.[7] The emphasis is on the community of believers rather than the individual. An Islamic government is expected to provide the internal and external security that will allow the believer to worship and earn a living. But these are not rights that an individual can claim against a government. The process of government is dependent on the *Shari'a,* which means that religious teachers and interpreters are very powerful.

But the ideas of freedom, rights, and equality proved appealing to some believers, and groups of Westernizers, Islamic liberals, Islamic socialists, and advocates of women's rights addressed those issues, and in practice the ideals of Islam have been challenged. Islamic liberalism or modernism survives as a strong intellectual force throughout Islam, and in movements that stem from the earlier liberal period, but it has made compromises with Islamism.[8]

Intellectually, Islamic liberalism or modernism centers on democratization and what Western intellectuals and a growing number of Islamic scholars see as related issues, freedom and equality, the latter particularly as it relates to the status of women. Although they approach the question from a number of different angles, many Islamic scholars argue that democracy, with its attendant elections and the loss and gain of power, is completely acceptable within Islam as a way of fulfilling the traditional obligation that rulers have to consult widely.[9] One commentator notes that the Qur'an does not specify a form of government but requires "pursuing justice through cooperation and mutual assistance (49:13, 11:119); establishing a nonautocratic, consultative method of governance; and institutionalizing mercy and compassion in social interactions (6:12, 6:54, 21:107, 27:77, 29:51, 45:20)."[10]

In Egypt the movement started by Gamal Abdel Nasser (1918–1970) still exists but is much less important than it once was, even though the current leaders of Egypt see themselves as the heirs of Nasser. Nasserism was essentially secular but used Islamic symbols. In Libya, Colonel Mu'ammar Gadafi (al-Qaddafi, b. 1942) established a highly idiosyncratic version of Islam expressed in his *Green Book* (three volumes, 1975 to 1980). Gadafi hides a dictatorship behind most of the policies of Islamic liberalism. In Syria, the Baath Party, founded in 1940 by Michel Aflaq (1910–1989), a Christian, and Salah al-Din Bitar (1912–1980), a Muslim, is essentially secular, although it uses Islamic symbols. It rejects both capitalism and communism because both are based on materialism; economically the Baath Party is socialist. Its greatest emphasis, though, is on Arab nationalism and the desirability of a single Arab nation, and it finds Islamic origins for this position.

---

[7] Montgomery Watt, *Islamic Political Thought: The Basic Concepts*. Edinburgh: Edinburgh University Press, 1968: 96. The Arab version of the "Universal Declaration of Human Rights" differs from the English version and has more exceptions; see Ann Elizabeth Mayer, *Islam and Human Rights: Tradition and Politics,* 2nd ed. Boulder, CO: Westview Press/London: Pinter Publishers, 1995.

[8] See, for example, Charles Kurzman, ed., *Liberal Islam: A Sourcebook*. New York: Oxford University Press, 1998.

[9] See, for example, Azzam Tamimi, ed., *Power-Sharing Islam?* London: Liberty for Muslim World Publications, 1993, particularly the essays by Rachid Ghannouchi, Muhammad Salim Al-Awa, and Hassan Al-Alkim.

[10] Khaled Abou El Fadl, *Islam and the Challenge of Democracy. A Boston Review Book,* Joshua Cohen and Deborah Chasman, eds. Princeton, NJ: Princeton University Press, 2004: 5. The numbers in parentheses refer to passages in the *Qur'an.*

Islamism

In the West, Islamism is usually associated with the Shiites, but it is also strong among the Sunni. Although significant differences exist between Sunni and Shiite Islamists, major agreements exist as well. In particular, all Islamists want to reestablish the *Shari'a,* which they believe will result in an Islamic theocracy and full realization of the ideal Islamic community.

The intellectual grounding of Islamism is usually traced to Ayatollah Ruhollah Khomeini (1903?–1989), Abu al-A'la al-Mawdudi (1903–1979), and Sayyid Qutb (1906–1966). Qutb is best known for the concept of *jahiliyya,* which originally referred to the period of "ignorance" or "barbarism" that existed before Muhammad preached in Arabia. Qutb used *jahiliyya* to refer to the present day, explicitly to the influence of the West. Although these Islamists had serious differences, they all wanted to create theocracies in which Allah delegated political power to the current rulers. In other words, all temporal power was to be held in the name of Allah, and the leader was to be responsible to Allah for his (none of them could conceive of a woman as a ruler) use of that power.

The Muslim Brotherhood The fact that Islamism can combine modernization with rejection of Westernization is demonstrated best by the Muslim Brotherhood, *al-Ikhwan al-Muslimun*, the first major Islamist movement, founded in 1928 in Egypt by Hasan al-Banna (1906–1949). The Muslim Brotherhood, which became one of the most powerful movements ever within Islam and still exists today, emphasizes both a return to Islamic traditions and scientific and technical education. The Muslim Brotherhood also argues for major social and economic reforms within the framework of Islam. In addition, the Brotherhood seeks the unification of all Muslims.

Politics For Muslims, Allah is the only legislator; any earthly ruler is only to ensure that God's laws are practiced. Therefore, any such ruler is an administrator, not a lawgiver. Sunni and Shiite Islamists disagree on who should rule. The most extreme Sunni believe that a caliph, or successor, should administer the divine law. Shiite Islam requires the presence of the *Mahdi,* or Twelfth or Hidden Imam, for the correct government to be established. In his absence a monarch or sultan who rules with the consent of the *ulama*—religious teachers, or those who are learned in the divine law—is the best possible solution.

A legislature composed of the *ulama* operating with the advice of an *imam* (leader) can replace the monarch or sultan, but that legislature is still subordinate to the *Shari'a.* In Iran the Ayatollah Khomeini argued that the clergy were the appropriate rulers, and that the most preeminent among the clergy—that is, the most learned, just, and pious—should hold the highest office, that of deputy to the Hidden or Twelfth Imam. Khomeini saw himself in that role and was accepted as such, and this arrangement is part of the Iranian constitution, with a supreme religious leader and a body of clergy outside the legislature able to overrule legislative action. But without Khomeini, although they still effectively rule, acceptance of the decisions by the clergy has been harder to achieve.

Social Organization The traditional, patriarchal family with the man as its head is at the center of the Islamic community. A Muslim man may have up to four wives as long as he can support them. Under the law the testimony of two women is equal to that of one man. However, the Qur'an gives women specific rights. Most important, women can hold and inherit property, although these rights have been frequently violated and some Islamists would like them limited. But women are to function only in the private sphere; only men are to act publicly.

In traditional Islam, which the Islamists want to see reestablished, equality between women and men is impossible—the concept is meaningless. According to one scholar's interpretation, the functions of men and women could be divided into privileges and duties. Men have the privileges of social authority and mobility and the duty of economic responsibility.[11] Women have three privileges:

1. "A woman in traditional Islamic society does not have to worry about earning a living."
2. "A woman does not have to find a husband for herself."
3. A woman "is spared direct military and political responsibility." Her primary duty "is to provide a home for her family and to bring up her children properly."[12]

The Taliban In September 2001, Americans suddenly became aware of the Taliban (spelled Taleban in the U.K.), an obscure sect of Islam closely related to Salafism, which then ruled most of Afghanistan. The word *taliban* means "student," and the movement is sometimes called the *Religious Students' Movement.* The goal of the Taliban was to create a pure Islamic state in Afghanistan under its founder and leader, Mullah Mohammad Omar Akhund (b. circa 1959).

Although mostly representing the Pashtuns, the largest ethnic group in Afghanistan, the Taliban was initially very popular, because it brought relative peace to a country that had been at war with its neighbors and within itself since 1978. The Soviet Union invaded Afghanistan in 1979 and was finally forced to withdraw in 1988, at which time a struggle for power among various factions within Afghanistan began. With the ultimate goal of abolishing all contemporary political boundaries and reestablishing the rule of the caliphs, the Taliban captured the capital, Kabul, in 1996 and began to enforce its very narrow interpretation of the Islamic rule of law—one in which women must wear the *burqa,* a dress that covers them completely from head to toe, and men must grow beards. Women in particular were severely restricted in that few were allowed to work or be educated, and with almost no women doctors, their access to health care was almost nonexistent.[13]

After the 2001 U.S. invasion of Afghanistan, the Taliban leaders escaped and many remain in hiding either in Afghanistan or in a remote part of neighboring Pakistan. Some areas of Afghanistan are only nominally under the rule of the central government in Kabul, and the Taliban has reestablished its authority in some areas.

---

[11] Seyyad Hossein Nasr, *Ideals and Realities of Islam,* 2nd ed. London: George Allen & Unwin, 1975: 112.

[12] Nasr, *Ideals and Realities of Islam,* 112–113.

[13] For some of the actual rules, see "A Sample of Taliban Decrees Relating to Women and Other Cultural Issues, after the Capture of Kabul, 1996," in Ahmed Rashid, *Taliban: Militant Islam, Oil, and Fundamentalism in Central Asia.* New Haven, CT: Yale University Press, 2000: 217–219.

ISLAM IN THE UNITED STATES

Islam has deep roots in the United States and is growing rapidly, with somewhere around five million adherents—about the same as Lutherans and Mormons—with estimates ranging from one and a half to seven million. These came mostly from south Asia, rather than the Middle East, and 90 percent of Arab Americans are Christian.

Muslims were among the earliest explorers and settlers in North America, but significant numbers began to arrive in the late 1800s, with later waves of immigrants in the periods 1947 to 1960 and 1967 to the present. As a result, there are Islamic communities in the United States that are over 100 years old.

In addition, many African Americans converted to Islam. This movement began early in the twentieth century, partially as a result of the racism of mainstream Christian denominations that were unwilling to accept African-American members. This also led to the creation of many African-American Christian denominations, most of which still exist.

But the greatest growth of Islam among African Americans was in the 1950s and 1960s with the development of the Nation of Islam under the leadership of Elijah Muhammad (1897–1975) and Malcolm X (1925–1965). It continues today in a variety of groups that emerged from the Nation of Islam. About 30 percent of the Muslims in America today are African American, and two African-American converts to Islam have been elected to the U.S. House of Representatives, Keith Ellison (b. 1963), elected from Minnesota in 2006, and André Carson (b. 1974) of Indiana, elected in 2008 to fill the remainder of his grandmother's term after she died.

Immigrant Islam

Islam is among the fastest-growing religions in both Europe and the United States. Although estimates of the number of Muslims in the United States vary widely and are considered unreliable, more Muslims live in the United States than in a number of Islamic countries in the Middle East. In the United States, Islam tends to center on local mosques, which generally operate quite independently, although there are the beginnings of a number of regional and countrywide federations of mosques, mostly based on the country of origin of the immigrant community attending.[14] At present, there are over 2000 mosques in the United States.

Because many Islamic students come to the United States to attend university, there are also a number of Muslim student groups, the Muslim Student

---

[14] On Islam in America, see Yvonne Yazbeck Haddad and Jane Idleman Smith, *Mission to America* (Gainesville: University Press of Florida, 1993), which discusses Islamic groups in America outside the mainstream; Haddad and Smith, eds., *Muslim Communities in North America* (Albany: State University of New York Press, 1994), a collection of essays on many specific Muslim communities in the United States and Canada; Haddad, ed., *The Muslims of America* (New York: Oxford University Press, 1991); Gilles Kepel, *Allah in the West: Islamic Movements in America and Europe*, Susan Milner, trans. (Stanford, CA: Stanford University Press, 1997); Michael A. Koszegi and J. Gordon Melton, eds., *Islam in North America: A Sourcebook* (New York: Garland, 1992); Jane I. Smith, *Islam in America* (New York: Columbia University Press, 1999); and Earle H. Waugh, Sharon McIrvin Abu-Laban, and Regula Burckhardt Qureshi, eds., *Muslim Families in North America* (Calgary: University of Alberta Press, 1991).

Association being the largest. There are also a number of immigrant communities based around specific Islamic sects.[15] The largest and best established of these are the Sufis.

American Muslims have the same experiences as immigrants of other faiths, including discrimination and harassment. In response, some return to the home country, sometimes with the idea of building an Islamic state; others work to establish Islamic communities in the United States, so that it will be possible to live an Islamic life within its boundaries; and yet others assimilate. As with other immigrants, the second and third generations tend toward the third option, but often with the desire to reconnect with their national and religious roots.[16] An indication of the adjustment to U.S. conditions is that women now head the boards of some mosques in the United States. It is, of course, entirely possible that the attacks on Muslims in the United States since September 11, 2001, will produce future terrorists from people who were once good, loyal American citizens—until they and their fellow Muslims were targeted by U.S. ethnic nationalists.

Most immigrant U.S. Muslims are integrating into American society. Muslim religious leaders preach on television in the United States and throughout the Muslim world and appeal to young, upwardly mobile Muslims; they say there is nothing wrong with being successful and enjoying life, and that this can be done while remaining a good, observant Muslim. And 24-hour Islamic telephone and Internet services provide answers to questions regarding what is acceptable in both American and Islamic cultures, and they provide both matchmaking and marriage counseling services. Those giving the answers differ significantly so that it is possible to choose services that are more or less strict, more or less integrationist. Islamic Americans face the same issues as other Americans, but within the teachings of Islam; for example, how does a successful and busy Islamic couple, who are both employed, fulfill the Islamic injunction to care for elderly parents? In the past the answer was simple: they were cared for by the wife, who did not go out to work. Today, care in nursing homes, which would have been unthinkable before, is no longer unusual.

African-American Islam

African Americans have been affiliated with Islam since at least 1913, when the Moorish American Science Temple was founded in Newark, New Jersey. But African-American Islam is most commonly identified with the Nation of Islam, better known as the *Black Muslims*—a direct response to the conditions in U.S. inner cities in the second half of the twentieth century. As taught by Elijah Muhammad, the Nation of Islam combined traditional Islamic teachings with

---

[15] For a list of Islamic organizations in North America, see the Suggested Reading and "A Directory of Islamic Organizations and Centers in North America," in Koszegi and Melton, *Islam in North America*, 291–395. For a list of Internet sources (though be aware that many of these will have changed), see Smith, *Islam in America*, 225–226.

[16] On the immigrant experience, see Yvonne Yazbeck Haddad and Adair T. Lummis, *Islamic Values in the United States: A Comparative Study*. New York: Oxford University Press, 1987; Haddad and John L. Esposito, eds. *Muslims: The New Generation*. New York: Continuum, 2000.

an interpretation of the African-American experience in the United States that saw whites as the Devil.

After the death of Elijah Muhammad and the assassination of Malcolm X, who, after a pilgrimage to Mecca, rejected the racial message of the Nation of Islam, the movement fragmented. One of Elijah Muhammad's sons, Warith Deen Mohammad (b. 1933), rejected the racial message of his father, decentralized the organization, changed its name to the American Muslim Mission, and encouraged African-American Muslims to join mainstream Islam. The best-known contemporary descendent of the Nation, Louis Farrakhan (b. 1933), kept both the name and centralized structure of the Nation of Islam and, although not consistently, has kept at least some of its racial message.[17]

CURRENT TRENDS

Looked at internationally, Islam today is remarkably diverse, with advocates of capitalism and socialism, authoritarianism and democracy, feminism and anti-feminism all within its boundaries. And a number of issues are slowly changing the political dimensions of Islam, particularly in the West.

Rereadings of the Qur'an

There have always been those who have argued that the Qur'an has either been misread or that it requires a more sophisticated reading than it usually receives. Today, the former position is taken by most Islamic feminists, and it is taken by the overwhelming majority of Muslims who say that Islamists deliberately misread the Qur'an; the latter position is taken by the wide range of thinkers who fall under the rubric of Islamic liberals or modernists.

Political Rereadings   There are many thinkers who argue that the Qur'an does not exclude adaptation to the modern world. Here I shall briefly look at three of these thinkers, Mahmoud Mohamed Taha (1909–1985), Ziauddin Sardar (b. 1951), and Tariq Ramadan (b. 1962).

Taha was a Sudanese political leader and theologian, a significant figure in Sudan's independence movement, a founder of the Sudanese Republican Party, and an advocate for liberal reform after independence. He was executed by the Sudanese government for his political activities. As a theologian Taha argued that there are in effect two Qur'ans: one from when Islam was under physical attack and one from when it was at peace. He contended that too much emphasis was put on the former, that the latter was a truer reflection of Muhammad's position, and that understanding the historical situation relative to different parts

---

[17] On the Nation of Islam, see Essien Udosen Essien-Udom, *Black Nationalism: A Search for Identity in America*. Chicago: University of Chicago Press, 1962; Mattias Gardell, *In the Name of Elijah Muhammad: Louis Farrakhan and the Nation of Islam*. Durham, NC: Duke University Press, 1996; C. Eric Lincoln, *The Black Muslims in America*. Boston: Beacon Press, 1973; and Vibert L. White, Jr., *Inside the Nation of Islam: A Historical and Personal Account by a Black Muslim*. Gainesville: University Press of Florida, 2001.

of the Qur'an shows that its true message is democratic. For Taha, the Qur'an advocates universal human rights, tolerance, equality, and freedom.

Sardar takes the position that because new questions arise that require answers, each generation must read the Qur'an afresh. He argues for the reconciliation of Christianity, Islam, and Judaism, contending that their fundamental positions on ethical questions are similar. He is particularly interested in the ways that science and technology can be used to overcome the problems that all humanity faces. And he notes that Islamic science was initially far in advance of Western science and provided the basis for much of what developed in the West. He argues that the suppression of science in Islamic countries by colonial regimes set Islam back significantly and provided the conditions that allowed the development of Islamism.

Ramadan is the most conservative of the three in that he calls for a strict reading of the Qur'an, but he argues that this can be done while also creating a European Islam, just as there are now African and Asian variants of Islam. He argues for a Western Islam tied to the classic roots of Islam, and he says that Western Islam is beginning to influence Muslims throughout the entire Islamic world.

For Ramadan the social message of Islam includes the following:

1. The right to life and the minimum necessary to sustain it
2. The right to family
3. The right to housing
4. The right to education
5. The right to work
6. The right to justice
7. The right to solidarity or the right to participate in social life[18]

Ramadan argues that both Muslims and non-Muslims need to recognize that we all have multiple identities and learn to separate what is religious from what is cultural. His message to immigrant Muslims is that they can and should be both believers and full citizens of their adopted countries with the emphasis on being both, insisting that there is no need to choose between being a good Muslim and being a good citizen.

The arguments of Ramadan, and a growing number of Islamic theorists and theologians, for an Islam that fits the West illustrates the revival of Islamic modernism in a form that aims at remaining true to Islam while adjusting to the West. And the message to the West is a reminder that both groups can and should learn from and enrich each other.

Islamic Feminism   Those arguing for a different position for women within Islam point out that men have dominated theological studies, as they had in all other religions, and that they interpreted the text of the Qur'an in ways favoring male dominance and local practice. They contend that the passages in the

---

[18] Tariq Ramadan, *Western Muslims and the Future of Islam*. Oxford: Oxford University Press, 2004: 149–152 (In italics in the original). Ramadan had been hired to teach at Notre Dame but had his visa revoked just days before he and his family were to move to the United States from Switzerland.

Qur'an used to support male dominance are about obedience to Allah, not to husbands and fathers, and that the passages used to justify the various clothing restrictions imposed on women are actually about sexual modesty. They say that the text of the Qur'an and Islam during Muhammad's life support equality between men and women, not dominance and submission.

Men and women worship separately in mosques, as they do in Orthodox Jewish synagogues and some Protestant sects, but this practice has been challenged recently. For example, Amina Wadud (b. 1952), an African-American Muslim convert to Islam, led a mixed gender congregation in prayer March 18, 2005, and has continued to do so throughout the world. While she has been condemned for doing this, the fact that so many Islamic groups invite her to do so suggests that room for greater equality is opening up.

An illustration of the status of women in some Islamic countries—and how far they have to go—is the fact that the government of Saudi Arabia has just announced that by the end of 2008, women will be allowed to drive for the first time. A few women have defied the old law and have been arrested for the crime of driving. The current law has the side effect that many offices close for a period in the afternoon so that the men can leave work to pick up their children from school. It is possible that the economic effect of having to close offices may be a more important reason for the proposed change than any desire to improve the status of women.

CURRENT ISSUES

A number of issues have arisen—particularly in Europe, regarding the position of Islam in contemporary Western society—that illustrate conflicts within Islam and between Muslims and the countries to which they have immigrated. Some of these issues have produced violent conflict. But it is also important to note that conflict labeled as "Islamic violence" is sometimes based on socioeconomic issues. For example, the "Islamic" violence in the poor areas of France was not carried out by recent immigrants but by young third, fourth, and fifth generation French citizens, few of whom spoke any language other than French, who had no jobs and no hope of ever getting any job.

The Cartoon Controversy An issue that raised serious questions for Muslims everywhere, especially in the Western countries to which many had migrated, was the publication in Denmark of a series of derogatory cartoons depicting Muhammad. Muslims objected strenuously and sometimes violently to their publication, with the violence mostly but not exclusively in the Middle East. The first publication of the cartoons had gone largely unnoticed and this reprinting of the cartoons was a deliberate insult to Islam. But the Islamic reaction was orchestrated by a Muslim cleric who spread information about the cartoons to those people and places he knew would be most insulted. In the name of freedom of the press, the cartoons were reprinted around the world. When people were arrested in February of 2008 for threatening to kill the cartoonist, the cartoons were reprinted. The question arises whether the multiple reprintings of the cartoons and their display on TV and the Internet are an appropriate use of freedom of the press, a deliberate exacerbation of the insult, or simply a means of selling more papers or getting more viewers. The Islamists who used the cartoons to depict an insensitive West that had to be rejected were very happy to have them reprinted and shown; they could argue that this made their point clear.

Murder in Holland   The Netherlands (Holland) prides itself on its tolerance. While this is partly national myth, it has been challenged in the early twenty-first century primarily with regard to immigration and particularly to the place of Muslims in Dutch society, in which they are a significant minority. In 2002, Pim Fortuyn (Wilhelmus Simon Petrus Fortuijn, b. 1948), a gay, right-wing, anti-Islamic, anti-immigration activist, was murdered by an animal rights activist who justified the murder on the basis of what he saw as the scapegoating of Muslims by Fortuyn. This led to followers of Fortuyn winning 17 percent of the seats in the national legislature in the subsequent election. Although their percentage fell in the election that followed that, and they now hold no seats, the election was symbolic of a significant anti-immigrant and anti-Muslim sentiment. In 2004, Theo van Gogh (b. 1957), who had made a film portraying violence against women in Islamic societies, was murdered by a young Muslim man. And Ayaan Hirsi Ali (b. 1969), a Dutch legislator who had emigrated from Somalia and had both written on the same subject and cooperated with van Gogh on the film, received many death threats (she is now attached to the American Enterprise Institute, a conservative think tank in Washington, D.C.). In early 2008, when the Dutch government stopped paying for around-the-clock security and the U.S. government refused pay for it, Hirsi Ali asked the European Union to do so; and she has been granted police protection in all European Union countries.

The Headscarf Controversy   Orthodox Jewish women and women in some Protestant sects are required to cover their hair and dress modestly, which usually means being covered from head to toe. And Roman Catholic nuns used to have to be fully covered except for their faces. In some Islamic traditions, women are required to wear similar clothing, ranging from the *burqa*, which covers the body from head to toe except for a mesh or mask over the face; the *niqab*, which covers the entire face except the eyes; a covering most often called a *hajib*, a large scarf that completely covers the hair; or a simple headscarf. These different practices are often referred to, quite inaccurately, as *veiling*. The majority of Islamic women in non-Islamic countries, and many in Islamic countries, wear no such covering, but many choose to wear some covering as a way of respecting their religion, and they do not see it as a symbol of inferiority.[19]

   In France and Turkey, France being traditionally Roman Catholic but officially secular and Turkey being Muslim but legally secular, significant controversies have arisen over headscarves. France has banned the use of any obvious

---

[19] On the issue, see Fadwa El Guindi, *Veil: Modesty, Privacy, and Resistance*. Oxford, England: Berg, 1999; and Joan Wallach Scott, *The Politics of the Veil*. Princeton, NJ: Princeton University Press, 2007.

religious symbols in schools, and although the rule includes such Christian symbols as large crosses, it is clearly aimed at the scarves worn by some Islamic girls. Turkey, which is both Islamic and secular, has for some years banned the wearing of such scarves in its legislative assembly, and it removed one duly elected member because she wore one.

In Turkey the issue caused a constitutional crisis, because the military, which sees itself as the protector of the secular state, removed from office a government that proposed legislation to remove the ban. In the next election, the party proposing the legislation won a clear majority and has since passed a law lifting the ban. This has resulted in huge protests, and in early 2008, the law was being challenged in the courts.

It is difficult to generalize about Islam on this issue. For example, in March 2001, I flew from New Zealand to Europe and back on Air Malaysia, and I spent a few hours in each direction waiting in the airport in Kuala Lumpur. Malaysia is an Islamic country, and one of the most striking things in the airport was that women, both those working in the airport and those traveling, wore clothes that ranged from blue jeans and short skirts to complete coverings, including the *niqab* and *burqa*.

Shari'a Law An issue that reemerges regularly is the extent to which Islamic law, or *Shari'a,* should replace the legal codes currently in place. Most of these codes are based on Western models, either left over from colonial times or put into place by the first post-independence governments; putting *Shari'a* in place would serve the dual purpose of rejecting the West and enhancing the Islamic identity of the country. But non-Muslims are afraid that they will lose the rights they had under the previous codes and become an oppressed minority. In Nigeria and a growing number of other countries, this dispute has led to sporadic violence.

In early 2008, Rowan Williams (b. 1950), the Archbishop of Canterbury and the titular head of the Anglican Church, gave a speech and an interview in which he said that the adoption of some aspects of *Shari'a* in the United Kingdom "seems unavoidable." After an extremely strong reaction included calls for his resignation, Williams gave a series of speeches condemning the way *Shar'ia* law was implemented in many countries, particularly regarding women. In his original argument, he noted that Orthodox Jews were allowed to settle certain issues in their own courts and that other adjustments had been made for certain Christian groups; therefore, the same should be possible for Muslims. The reaction to his proposal also led him to warn against the apparently deep-seated anti-Muslim prejudice existing in the West.

Funding of Mosques Another issue is the dominance of the Middle East in training Islamic religious leaders. The typical pattern in founding a mosque in the West is that a small group gets together, often including both men and women, and rotates leading the prayers or chooses a member who is thought to be wise; the group buys a house or some other building and continues the community-based services. Then the group decides it wants a "proper" mosque with an imam. Mosques tend to be funded by Saudi Arabia or other Gulf states, and the imams are mostly trained in the Gulf and brought to mosques around the world. Even if the mosque is funded locally, the imam usually comes from the Arab world, because Saudi Arabia and other Gulf states are willing to both pay to build a mosque almost anywhere in the world and pay the imam. Having trained in the conservative Islam of that region, the imam changes the entire pattern of behavior in the mosque. Islam is multicultural and multilinguistic, but given the Middle Eastern funding, much of the preaching is in Arabic, which is not understood by the average member. I have been told of a mosque where the imam speaks in Arabic, which is translated into the local language (English in this case) by someone who regularly skips those parts of the imam's talk thought to be too radical for the members.

For most people in the West, Islam is still identified with the radical fringe of the religion and with terrorism. In a real sense, this is simply wrong. Islam is a rich and varied religion, and we should not identify one small part of it as the whole. At the same time, it is hard for most people in the West, who know little or nothing about Islam, to get beyond the daily news and understand that such events represent groups that are rejected by the majority of believers.

SUGGESTED READING

Some Classic Works

Ahmad, Jalal Al-E. *Gharbzadegi (Weststruckness)*. John Green and Ahmad Alizadeh, trans. Lexington, KY: Mazdâ Publishers, 1982. Reprinted with the title *Occidentosis: A Plague from the West*. Berkeley, CA: Mizan Press, 1984.

Banisadr, Asbolhassan. *The Fundamental Principles and Precepts of Islamic Government*. Mohammad R. Ghanoonparvar, trans. Lexington, KY: Mazdâ Publishers, 1981.

El Saadawi, Nawal. *The Hidden Face of Eve: Women in the Arab World*. Sherif Hetata, trans. and ed. London: Zed Books, 1980. New ed. London: Zed Books, 2007.

Khomeini, Ayatollah Sayyed Ruhollah Mousavi. *Islam and Revolution*. Hamid Algar, trans. Berkeley, CA: Mizan Press, 1981.

———. *Islamic Government*. Joint Publications Research Service, trans. New York: Manor Books, 1979.

The Koran. With Parallel Arabic Text. N. J. Dawood, trans. London: Penguin Books, 1990.

Malcolm X. *The Autobiography of Malcolm X*. New York: Grove Press, 1965. Reprinted New York: Penguin, 2001.

Taha, Mahmoud Mohamed. *The Second Message of Islam*. Abdullahi Ahmed An-Na'im, trans. Syracuse, NY: Syracuse University Press, 1987. A Sudanese who argued that the Shari'a needed to be revised based on different foundational texts. He was executed in 1985.

Books and Articles

Abbas, Tahir, ed. *Muslim Britain: Communities Under Pressure*. London: Zed Books, 2005.

Abdo, Geneive. *Mecca and Main Street: Muslim Lives in America After 9/11*. New York: Oxford University Press, 2006.

Abou El Fadl, Khaled. *The Great Theft: Wrestling Islam from the Extremists*. San Francisco, CA: HarperSanFrancisco, 2005. A moderate Muslim arguing against the extremists, particularly Salafism.

———. *Islam and the Challenge of Democracy*. Joshua Cohen and Deborah Chasman, eds. Princeton, NJ: Princeton University Press, 2004. Includes responses by 11 people and a reply. Argues that the Shari'a includes the rule of law and limited government, two fundamental principles of democracy, but other parts of democracy are harder to fit within it.

Abu-Hamdiyyah, Mohammad. *The Qur'an: An Introduction*. London: Routledge, 2000.

Afzal-Khan, Fawzia, ed. *Shattering the Stereotypes: Muslim Women Speak Out.* Northampton, MA: Olive Branch Press, 2005. Includes fiction and nonfiction.

Ahmad, Khurshid. *Islam: Its Meaning and Message*. 2nd ed. Leicester, England: The Islamic Foundation, 1976. Conservative; includes articles by some of the founders of Islamism, including Qutb and Mawdudi.

Ahmed, Akbar. *Journey into Islam: The Crisis of Globalization*. Washington, D.C.: Brookings Institution Press, 2007. Traces a research team on a visit to a number of Islamic countries and a range of groups within those countries. Important for students in that the team includes two undergraduates, a man and a woman, whose perspectives and experiences are highlighted.

Al-Rasheed, Madawi. *Contesting the Saudi State: Islamic Voices from a New Generation*. Cambridge, England: Cambridge University Press, 2007.

Alagha, Joseph Elie. *The Shifts in Hizbullah's Ideology: Religious Ideology, Political Ideology, and Political Program*. Leiden, The Netherlands: Amsterdam University Press, 2006. History from 1978 to 2005.

An-Na'im, Abdullahi Ahmed. *African Constitutionalism and the Role of Islam*. Philadelphia: University of Pennsylvania Press, 2006.

Baker, Raymond William. *Islam without Fear: Egypt and the New Islamists*. Cambridge, MA: Harvard University Press, 2003. Liberal Islam.

Barlas, Asma. *"Believing Women" in Islam: Unreading Patriarchal Interpretations of the Qur'an*. Austin: University of Texas Press, 2002. Argues that the Qur'an is radically egalitarian and antipatriarchal.

———. "Women's Readings of the Qur'ān." In *The Cambridge Companion to the Qur'ān*. Jane Dammen McAuliffe, ed. Cambridge, England: Cambridge University Press, 2006: 255–271. Argues that the Qur'an provides the basis for gender equality and that the inequality in Muslim countries is the result of

male dominance of interpretation and their desire to give particular traditional practices religious justification.

Bayat, Asef. *Making Islam Democratic: Social Movements and the Post-Islamic Turn*. Stanford, CA: Stanford University Press, 2007.

Black, Antony. *The History of Islamic Political Thought: From the Prophet to the Present*. New York: Routledge, 2001.

Blank, Jonah. *Mullahs on the Mainframe: Islam and Modernity among the Daudi Bohras*. Chicago: University of Chicago Press, 2001. A community of Sh'ite Muslims in south Asia, with members throughout the world who balance traditional Islam and the modern world.

Bonner, Michael. *Jihad in Islamic History: Doctrines and Practice*. Princeton, NJ: Princeton University Press, 2006.

Bonney, Richard. *Jihād: From Qu'rān to bin Laden*. Houndsmill, England: Palgrave Macmillan, 2004. Detailed discussion of the concept.

Bowen, John R. *Why the French Don't Like Headscarves: Islam, the State, and Public Space*. Princeton, NJ: Princeton University Press, 2007.

Brown, Daniel. *A New Introduction to Islam*. Malden, MA: Blackwell, 2004.

Brumberg, Daniel. *Reinventing Khomeini: The Struggle for Reform in Iran*. Chicago: University of Chicago Press, 2001. Argues that Khomeini was sufficiently vague that all the current factions can legitimately draw from him.

Bunzl, Matti. *Anti-Semitism and Islamophobia: Hatreds Old and New in Europe*. Chicago, IL: Prickly Paradigm Press, 2007. An essay and six responses and the responses of the author of the essay.

Burr, J. Millard, and Robert O. Collins. *Alms for Jihad: Charity and Terrorism in the Islamic World*. Cambridge, England: Cambridge University Press, 2006.

Charfi, Mohamed. *Islam and Liberty: The Historical Misunderstanding*. London: Zed Books, 2005. Argues for a tradition of liberty within Islam.

Cook, Michael. *Forbidding Wrong in Islam*. Cambridge, England: Cambridge University Press, 2001. This is a summary for the general reader of his *Commanding Right and Forbidding Wrong in Islamic Thought*. Cambridge, England: Cambridge University Press, 2000.

————. *The Koran: A Very Short Introduction*. Oxford, England: Oxford University Press, 2000.

————. *Understanding Jihad*. Berkeley: University of California Press, 2005. A thorough analysis of the concept both historically and in current usage.

cooke, miriam, and Bruce B. Lawrence, eds. *Muslim Networks from Hajj to Hip Hop*. Chapel Hill: University of North Carolina Press, 2005. The book was published with the name lowercased.

Curtis, Edward E., IV. "Islamism and Its African American Muslim Critics: Black Muslims in the Era of the Arab Cold War." *American Quarterly* Vol. 59:3 (September 2007): 683–709.

DeLong-Bas, Natana J. *Wahhabi Islam: From Revival and Reform to Global Jihad*. New York: Oxford University Press, 2004.

Devji, Faisal. *Landscapes of the Jihad: Militancy Morality and Modernity*. Ithaca, NY: Cornell University Press, 2005. U.K. ed. London: C. Hurst & Co., 2005. Addresses the meanings of *jihad*.

Donohue, John J., and John L. Espositio, eds. *Islam in Transition: Muslim Perspectives.* 2nd ed. New York: Oxford University Press, 2007.

Esposito, John L. *The Oxford Encyclopedia of the Modern Islamic World*. 4 vols. New York: Oxford University Press, 1995.

————. *What Everyone Needs to Know about Islam*. Oxford, England: Oxford University Press, 2003. Questions and short answers.

————, ed. *The Oxford History of Islam*. New York: Oxford University Press, 1999.

————, and John O. Voll. *Makers of Contemporary Islam*. Oxford, England: Oxford University Press, 2001.

Ess, Josef van. *The Flowering of Muslim Theology*. Jane Marie Todd, trans. Cambridge, MA: Harvard University Press, 2006.

Fluehr-Lobban, Carolyn, ed. *Against Islamic Extremism: The Writings of Muhammad Sa'id al-'Ashmawy*. Gainesville: University Press of Florida, 1998. The writings of a secularist former chief justice of the High Court of Cairo, who opposes politicizing Islam and violence as a political tool. Al-'Ashmawy calls himself a humanist.

Foltz, Richard C., Frederick M. Denny, and Azizan Baharuddin, eds. *Islam and Ecology: A Bestowed Trust*. Cambridge, MA: Harvard University Press for the Center for the Study of World Religions, Harvard Divinity School, 2003. Collection of essays arguing that Islam is ecologically sensitive. The argument is that the Prophet prohibited wastefulness, which led to many rulings on water management that could be extended to other resources. Others argue that sustainability is a basic tenet. The Prophet encouraged planting trees, even on doomsday.

Furnish, Timothy R. *Holiest Wars: Islamic Mahdis, Their Jihads, and Osama bin Laden*. Westport, CT: Praeger, 2005. *Mahdi* means "messiah."

Gauch, Suzanne. *Liberating Shahrazad: Feminism, Postcolonialism, and Islam*. Minneapolis: University of Minnesota Press, 2007. Known as *Scheherazade* in the West and *Shahrazad* to Arabic speakers.

Gerges, Fawaz A. *The Far Enemy: Why Jihad Went Global*. Cambridge, England: Cambridge University Press, 2005. Tactics of the jihadists in recruiting supporters.

Gomez, Michael A. *Black Crescent: The Experience and Legacy of African Muslims in the Americas*. Cambridge, England: Cambridge University Press, 2005. Includes experience in both North and South America.

Haddad, Yvonne Yazbeck. *Muslims in the West*. Oxford, England: Oxford University Press, 2002.

————, and John L. Esposito, eds. *Muslims on the Americanization Path?* Atlanta: Scholars Press, 1998.

————, and Jane Idleman Smith, eds. *Muslim Minorities in the West: Visible and Invisible*. Walnut Creek, CA: Alta Mira, 2002.

————, and Kathleen M. Moore. *Muslim Women in America: The Challenge of Islamic Identity Today*. Oxford, England: Oxford University Press, 2006.

Hafez, Mohammed M. *Manufacturing Human Bombs: The Making of Palestinian Suicide Bombers.* Washington, D.C.: United States Institute of Peace Press, 2006.

————. *Why Muslims Rebel: Repression and Resistance in the Islamic World.* Boulder, CO: Lynne Rienner, 2003. Argues that Islamist activism is a response to being repressed.

Hammond, Andrew. *What the Arabs Think of America.* Oxford, England: Greenwood World Publishing, 2007.

Hammoudi, Abdellah. *A Season in Mecca: Narrative of a Pilgrimage.* Pascale Ghazaleh, trans. New York: Hill and Wang, 2006. Originally published as *Une saison à La Mecque.* Paris: Éditions du Seuil, 2005.

Hansen, Hendrik, and Peter Kainz. "Radical Islamism and Totalitarian Ideology: a Comparison of Sayyid Qutb's Islamism with Marxism and National Socialism." *TMPR: Totalitarian Movements and Political Religions* Vol. 8:1 (March 2007): 55–76.

Hirschkind, Charles. *The Ethical Soundscape: Cassette Sermons and Islamic Counterpublics.* New York: Columbia University Press, 2006.

Hirsi Ali, Ayaan. *The Caged Virgin: A Muslim Woman's Cry for Reason.* Jane Brown, trans. London: Free Press, 2006. Originally published in Dutch in 2004.

————. *Infidel.* London: Free Press, 2007. The life story of a woman from Somalia who became a member of the parliament of the Netherlands and attracted many death threats from Islamists.

Hussain, Zahid. *Frontline Pakistan: The Struggle with Militant Islam.* London: I.B. Tauris, 2007.

Inayatullah, Sohail, and Gail Boxwell, eds. *Islam, Postmodernism and Other Futures: A Ziauddin Sardar Reader.* London: Pluto Press, 2003.

Kabbani, Shaykh Muhammad Hisham. *The Approach of Armageddon? An Islamic Perspective. A Chronicle of scientific break-throughs and world events that occur during the last days, as foretold by Prophet Muhammad.* Washington, D.C.: Islamic Supreme Council of America (ISCA), 2003.

Kamrava, Mehran, ed. *The New Voices of Islam: Reforming Politics and Modernity: A Reader.* Berkeley: University of California Press, 2006. U.K. ed. London: I.B. Tauris, 2006. Important collection of reformist Islamic thinkers from many different countries.

Karsh, Efraim. *Islamic Imperialism: A History.* New Haven, CT: Yale University Press, 2006.

Keddie, Nikki R. with a section by Yann Richard. *Modern Iran: Roots and Results of Revolution.* Updated ed. New Haven, CT: Yale University Press, 2006.

Kelsay, John. *Arguing the Just War in Islam.* Cambridge, MA: Harvard University Press, 2007.

Kepel, Gilles. *The War for Muslim Minds: Islam and the West.* Pascale Ghazaleh, trans. Cambridge, MA: The Belknap Press of Harvard University Press, 2004.

Klausen, Jytte. *The Islamic Challenge: Politics and Religion in Western Europe.* Oxford, England: Oxford University Press, 2005. Based on interviews with European Muslims who have chosen to become involved in the local political process.

Küng, Hans. *Islam: Past, Present and Future.* John Bowden, trans. Oxford, England: Oneworld, 2007. Massive (767 page) discussion of Islam by a major liberal Roman Catholic theologian.

Kurzman, Charles, ed. *Liberal Islam: A Sourcebook.* New York: Oxford University Press, 1998.

Laborde, Cécile. "Female Autonomy, Education and the *Hijab*." *CRISPP: Critical Review of International Social and Political Philosophy* Vol. 9:3 (September 2006): 351–377.

————. "Secular Philosophy and Muslim Headscarves in Schools." *Journal of Political Philosophy* Vol. 13:3 (September 2005): 305–329.

Lahoud, Nelly. *Political Thought in Islam: A Study in Intellectual Boundaries.* London: RoutledgeCurzon, 2005.

————, and Anthony H. Johns, eds. *Islam in World Politics.* New York: Routledge, 2005.

Lawrence, Bruce, ed. *Messages to the World: The Statements of Osama bin Laden.* James Howarth, trans. London: Verso, 2005.

LeVine, Mark. *Why They Don't Hate Us: Lifting the Veil on the Axis of Evil*. Oxford, England: Oneworld Publications, 2005. An argument, with examples, that the West is not hated in the Islamic world. He argues that both sides need to understand the cultures of the other, and he points out that Muslim youth know much more about the West than the West does about them. Unusual personal accounts of performing with young Muslim hip hop, jazz, and rock musicians in the Middle East.

Levitt, Matthew. *Hamas: Politics, Charity, and Terrorism in the Service of Jihad*. New Haven, CT: Yale University Press, 2006.

Lynch, Marc. *Voices of the New Arab Public: Iraq, al-Jazeera, and Middle East Politics Today*. New York: Columbia University Press, 2006.

Mahmood, Saba. *Politics of Piety: The Islamic Revival and the Feminist Subject*. Princeton, NJ: Princeton University Press, 2005. An important study from a feminist perspective of women as active participants in Islamism. In some ways this parallels similar involvement by right-wing women in activities that seem to be antiwoman.

Mahmoud, Mohamed A. *Quest for Divinity: A Critical Examination of the Thought of Mahmud Muhammad Taha*. Syracuse: Syracuse University Press, 2007.

Majid, Anouar. *Freedom and Orthodoxy: Islam in the Post-Andalusian Age*. Stanford, CA: Stanford University Press, 2004. Rejects the "clash of civilizations" theory and argues for one diverse human community in which people are reattached to their local cultures while being connected to the entire world.

Martin, Vanessa. *Creating an Islamic State: Khomeini and the Making of a New Iran*. New ed. London: I.B. Tauris, 2003. On Khomeini's political theory. Strong, centralized government capable of ensuring an Islamic state (theocracy).

Maurer, Bill. *Mutual Life, Limited: Islamic Banking, Alternative Currencies, Lateral Reason*. Princeton, NJ: Princeton University Press, 2005. Combines Islamic banking with its avoidance of interest and the development of local area currencies.

————. *Pious Property: Islamic Mortgages in the United States*. New York: Russell Sage Foundation, 2006.

Mayer, Ann Elizabeth. *Islam and Human Rights: Tradition and Politics*. 4th ed. Boulder, CO: Westview Press, 2007.

McAuley, Denis. "The Ideology of Osama Bin Laden: Nation, Tribe and World Economy." *Journal of Political Ideologies* Vol. 10:3 (October 2005): 269–287.

McAuliffe, Jane Dammen, ed. *The Cambridge Companion to the Qur'ān*. Cambridge, England: Cambridge University Press, 2006.

Metcalf, Barbara. "Piety, Persuasion and Politics: Deoband's Model of Social Activism." In *The Empire and the Crescent: Global Implications for a New American Century*. Aftab Ahmad Malik, ed. Bristol, England: Amal Press, 2003: 156–174. The Deoband movement is the basis of the Taliban.

Mir-Hosseini, Ziba, and Richard Tapper. *Islam and Democracy in Iran: Eshkevari and the Quest for Reform*. London: I.B. Tauris, 2006. Hasan Yousefi Eshkevari (b. 1949) is an Iranian Islamic cleric who has argued for greater democracy. This volume includes some of his writings, as well as a commentary.

Mozaffari, Mehdi. "What is Islamism? History and Definition of a Concept." *TMPR: Totalitarian Movements and Political Religions* Vol. 8:1 (March 2007): 7–33.

Musallam, Adnan A. *From Secularism to Jihad: Sayyid Qutb and the Foundation of Radical Islamism*. Westport, CT: Praeger, 2005.

————. *Sayyid Qutb: The Emergence of the Ilsamicist, 1939–1950*. 2nd ed. Jerusalem: PASSIA The Palestinian Academic Society for the Study of International Affairs, 1997.

Nakash, Yetzhak. *Reaching for Power: The Shi'a in the Modern Arab World*. Princeton, NJ: Princeton University Press, 2006.

Nasr, Vali. *The Shia Revival: How Conflicts within Islam Will Shape the Future*. New York: W.W. Norton, 2006.

Noe, Nicholas, ed. *Voice of Hezbollah: The Statements of Sayyed Hassan Nasrallah*. Ellen Khouri, trans. London: Verso, 2007. Covers material from 1986 to 2006.

Noorani, Abdul Gafoor Abdul Majeed. *Islam and Jihad: Prejudice versus Reality*. London: Zed Books/Dhaka, Bangladesh: University Press/Bangkok, Thailand: White

Lotus/Black Point, NS, Canada: Fernwood/Cape Town, South Africa: David Philip, 2002. An argument, aimed at a general audience, that rejects the Islamist approach to jihad. Includes as appendices the "Universal Islamic Declaration of Human Rights" (133–141) and "The Protection of Human Rights in Islamic Criminal Justice" (142–144).

Norton, Augustus Richard. *Hezbollah: A Short History*. Princeton, NJ: Princeton University Press, 2007.

Phares, Walid. *The War of Ideas: Jihad Against Democracy*. New York: Palgrave Macmillan, 2007.

Qassem, Naim. *Hizbullah: The Story from Within*. Dalia Khalil, trans. London: Saqi, 2005.

Ramadan, Tariq. *Islam, the West and the Challenges of Modernity*. Said Amghar, trans. Leicester, England: The Islamic Foundation, 2001. Argues that Muslims can function in the modern world without losing their faith or identity as long as the West does not impose the ideology of modernism, which he equates with Westernization, on them.

———. *Western Muslims and the Future of Islam*. Oxford, England: Oxford University Press, 2004.

Rogerson, Barnaby. *The Heirs of the Prophet Muhammad and the Roots of the Sunni-Shia Schism*. London: Little, Brown, 2006.

Rostami-Povey, Elaheh. *Afghan Women: Identity and Invasion*. London: Zed Books, 2007.

Rouse, Carolyn Moxley. *Engaged Surrender: African American Women and Islam*. Berkeley: University of California Press, 2004.

Roy, Olivier. *Globalized Islam: The Search for a New Ummah*. New York: Columbia University Press in association with the Centre d'Etudes et de Recherches Internationales, Paris, 2004. Argument for a modernized Islam.

———. *Secularism Confronts Islam*. George Holoch, trans. New York: Columbia University Press, 2007. Originally published in French in 2005.

Ruthven, Malise. *Islam in the World*. 3rd ed. London: Granta, Books, 2006.

———. *Islam: A Very Short Introduction*. Oxford, England: Oxford University Press, 1997.

Sachedina, Abdulaziz. *The Islamic Roots of Democratic Pluralism*. Oxford, England: Oxford University Press, 2001.

Sadri, Mahmoud, and Ahmad Sadri, eds. and trans. *Reason, Freedom, and Democracy in Islam: Essential Writings of 'Abdolkarim Soroush*. Oxford, England: Oxford University Press, 2000. Tries to combine reason and faith, spiritual authority, and political liberty.

Safi, Omid, ed. *Progressive Muslims on Gender, Justice, and Pluralism*. Oxford, England: Oneworld, 2003.

Sardar, Ziauddin. *Desperately Seeking Paradise: Journeys of a Sceptical Muslim*. London: Granta Books, 2004.

Scott, Joan Wallach. *The Politics of the Veil*. Princeton, NJ: Princeton University Press, 2007.

Shehadeh, Lamia Rustum. *The Idea of Women in Fundamentalist Islam*. Gainesville: University Press of Florida, 2003. Discusses the treatment of women by a number of the most important Islamist theologians. Argues that for all their differences, the subtext is political power.

Shore, Zachary. *Breeding Bin Ladens: America, Islam, and the Future of Europe*. Baltimore, MD: Johns Hopkins University Press, 2006.

Sonbol, Amira El-Azhary, ed. *Beyond the Exotic: Women's Histories in Islamic Societies*. Syracuse, NY: Syracuse University Press, 2005. Essays on Islam and women from the beginning to the present.

Soueif, Ahdaf. *Mezzaterra: Fragments from the Common Ground*. London: Bloomsbury, 2004. U.S. ed. New York: Anchor Books, 2005. Collection of political and literary essays by a woman, born and raised in Egypt, who has lived most of her life in England. Argues that throughout history, cultures have overlapped more than they have conflicted.

Taji-Farouki, Suha, and Basheer M. Nafi, eds. *Islamic Thought in the Twentieth Century*. London: I.B. Tauris, 2004.

Tibi, Bassam. "The Totalitarianism of Jihadist Islam and its Challenges to Europe and Islam." *TMPR: Totalitarian Movements and Political Religions* Vol. 8:1 (March 2007): 35–54.

Tripp, Charles. *Islam and the Moral Economy: The Challenge of Capitalism*. Cambridge, England: Cambridge University Press, 2006.

Turner, Richard Brent. *Islam in the African American Experience*. 2nd ed. Bloomington: Indiana University Press, 2003.

Wadud, Amina. *Inside the Gender Jihad: Women's Reform in Islam*. Oxford, England: Oneworld Publications, 2006.

Wadud-Muhsin, Amina. *Qur'an and Woman*. 2nd ed. New York: Oxford University Press, 2001.

White, Vibert L. Jr. *Inside the Nation of Islam: A Historical and Personal Account by a Black Muslim*. Gainesville: University Press of Florida, 2001.

Wild, Stefan. "Political interpretations of the Qur'ān." In *The Cambridge Companion to the Qur'ān*. Jane Dammen McAuliffe, ed. Cambridge, England: Cambridge University Press, 2006: 272–289. General overview.

Wright, Lawrence. *The Looming Tower: Al-Qaeda and the Road to 9/11*. New York: Alfred A. Knopf, 2006.

Zeitlin, Irving M. *The Historical Muhammad*. Cambridge, England: Polity, 2007.

Zia, Khan Hussan. *Muslims and the West: A Muslim Perspective*. Bloomington, IN: AuthorHouse, 2005. Some history and commentary on recent events by a Muslim from Pakistan.

Websites

Central Asia Institute. Building schools open to all in Pakistan and Afghanistan: http://www.ikat.org

Islamicity. News, shopping, and contact site for African-American Muslims: http://www.islamicity.com

Islamophobia Watch: http://www.islamophobia-watch.com

Liberal Islam: http://www.unc.edu/~kurzman/LiberalIslamLinks.htm

Osama bin Laden, World Islamic Front Statement: http://www.fas.org/irp/world/para/docs/980223-fatwa.htm

Tariq Ramadan: http://www.tariqramadan.com. Can be read in English or French.

Ziauddin Sardar: http://www.ziauddinsardar.com

Muslim Organizations in the United States

Al Islam: The Official Website of the Ahmadiyya Muslim Community: http://www.alislam.org

American Muslim Alliance (AMA): http://www.amaweb.org

American Muslim Council (AMC): http://www.amcnational.org

Council on American-Islamic Relations (CAIR): http://www.cair.com

Dar al Islam. Building Bridges with the American Community and among the Muslims of America: http://www.daralislam.org

Islam America: http://www.islamamerica.org

Islamic Assembly of North America: http://www.iananet.org

Islamic Center of North America: http://www.icofa.com

Islamic Circle of North America (ICNA): http://www.icna.org

Islamic Society of North America (ISNA): http://www.isna.net

Moorish Science Temple of America, Inc.: http://www.moorishsciencetempleofamericainc.com

Muslim Public Affairs Council (MPAC): http://www.mpac.org

Muslim Students' Association National: http://www.msanational.org

Nation of Islam: http://www.noi.org

Triangle Sufi Center. International Sufi Movement, America: http://www.universalsufism.com

12

✣

Liberation Theologies

Liberation Theology began as a movement within the Roman Catholic Church in Latin America and is now a worldwide movement found within most Christian denominations. For all their differences, these theologies agree on the central role of the poor and the oppressed and the need for committed action to achieve their liberation. Thus Liberation Theology is explicitly and consciously a political movement that challenges economic and political oppression, as well as the acceptance of such oppression by religious hierarchies.

The first stage of any liberation movement is the recognition of oppression. Thus every one of the liberation theologies discussed here began with a critique of the current power structure, identifying who were the oppressed and who were the oppressors and how the oppressed were being oppressed. When a person is born with or without power, that situation appears normal, and it can be hard to grasp the realities of power relationships. Thus, critique of the power structure and the communication of the critique are essential first steps.

Liberation Theology is based on the message that Jesus was and is a liberator. It brings "the good news of liberation" from unjust social structures, the power of fate, and the burden of personal sin and guilt through divine mercy and the action of people to transform their own lives. It requires commitment from its adherents to the effort to prepare the way, and it brings hope that the Kingdom of God can be created on earth.

As a movement Liberation Theology struggled to define itself: against the opposition of most of the church hierarchy in the areas where it developed; and against the opposition of the papacy, both under Pope John Paul II (1920–2005;

elevated to the papacy in 1978) and Pope Benedict XVI (b. 1927; elevated to the papacy in 2005). Pope Benedict, then Cardinal Ratzinger, was head of the Congregation of the Doctrine of Faith—the body designed to ensure that church teachings are correctly followed—during the period that Liberation Theology was most actively condemned. From these roots Liberation Theology spread to Protestantism and to Africa, Asia, Ireland, and the United States. Today, because of the continuing opposition of the Roman Catholic Church, Liberation Theology is most dynamic in Protestantism, particularly in Asia and Africa and in Black and Womanist theologies in the United States, rather than Catholicism.

Women have spoken of the need to "engender" Liberation Theology and have largely succeeded in doing so; as a result, a feminist Liberation Theology is flourishing throughout the world. Coordination among liberation theologies is provided by the Ecumenical Association of Third World Theologians (EATWOT) founded in 1980.

Liberation Theology has a conflicted relationship with European theology, which provided some of its ideas and early thinkers. Particularly outside Latin America, the European—or in the United States the white—character of theology is seen as a problem to be overcome. This is so because European/white theology has ignored or, to some degree, opposed the concerns of the poor, minorities, colonized peoples, and women. As Tissa Balasuriya (b. 1924), a Sri Lankan priest and theologian, put it, "We find that many elements in the Christian teachings are not relevant to us."[1]

Liberation Theology developed as a response to the poverty found in Latin America. The phrase "the preferential option for the poor," which means that all actions should be judged on whether or not they help the poor, is one of the identifying marks of Liberation Theology and has had a major impact on Christian thinking throughout the world. As one writer recently said, "The preferential option for the poor has been one of the most significant developments in theology and the church in the twentieth century, signaling a broad shift in theological sensitivities."[2]

The Roman Catholic Church, the dominant Christian church in Latin America, was identified with the rich and powerful and was having difficulty providing priests for rural areas, where most of the poor lived. As a result, those who were concerned with these problems began, first in Brazil as early as the late 1950s, to encourage community-based organizations—later called *base communities, base Christian communities,* or *base ecclesial communities*—to provide for their own religious needs.

As the movement developed, intellectuals began to look for theological and theoretical justification and for any earlier attempts to deal with such problems. They found the French worker–priest movement, in which French priests worked in factories so that they could experience the lives of the people more completely

---

[1] Tissa Balasuriya, "Toward the Liberation Theology of Asia," in *Asia's Struggle for Full Humanity: Toward a Relevant Theology.* Papers from the Asian Theological Conference, January 7–20, 1979, Wennappuwa, Sri Lanka, Virginia Fabella, ed. Maryknoll, NY: Orbis Books, 1980: 19. The author is a Sri Lankan priest.

[2] Joerg Rieger, "Introduction: Opting for the Margins in a Postmodern World," in *Opting for the Margins: Postmodernity and Liberation in Christian Theology,* Joerg Rieger, ed. New York: Oxford University Press, 2003: 3.

and therefore better understand their needs. And they found Western Marxism with its concern for the poor. The worker–priest movement helped encourage priests to work in communities as equals with laypeople. Marxism, but particularly the so-called Marxist–Christian dialogue of the late 1960s, provided a theory that could be integrated with the theological movements that produced the Ecumenical Council of 1962–1965, better known as *Vatican II,* with its emphasis on modernizing the Church and making it more responsive to laypeople. Vatican II also stressed collective responsibility in the Church, which fit well with the community organizations that Liberation Theology was developing.

A well-known theologian, Leonardo Boff (b. 1938), argued that Liberation Theology developed as and where it did because Latin Americans are both poor and Christian. As Boff and his brother Clodovis Boff (b. 1944) wrote, "We can be followers of Jesus and true Christians only by making common cause with the poor and working out the gospel of liberation."[3] The poor are, for the Boffs, "the Disfigured Son of God,"[4] and the poor include not just the economically deprived but all of the oppressed. This extension of the idea of the poor became the basis for the worldwide growth of Liberation Theology.

THE MARXIST–CHRISTIAN DIALOGUE

In 1965 French Roman Catholic Marxist Roger Garaudy (b. 1913) published a book titled *From Anathema to Dialogue: The Challenge of Marxist–Christian Cooperation.*[5] The publication of this book began a long-lasting debate on the degree to which Marxists and Christians could learn from each other or even actively cooperate. The basis of the developing dialogue was the writings of the young Marx (discussed in Chapter 8), which focused on human alienation and the dehumanizing effects of capitalist society. These writings attracted theologians with similar concerns, and some Marxists found in Christianity both a deep concern with the oppressed and a message of hope for the future in this life. As a result, both Marxists and Christians began to consider what they could say to each other without losing the essential characteristics of their beliefs.

Much of the Marxism found in Liberation Theology came through Ernst Bloch (1885–1977; discussed in Chapter 8). A Marxist who spent much of his life in what was then East Germany, Bloch argued that Christianity had a tremendous radical potential, and theologians within Liberation Theology found that Marx's emphasis on the poor resonated with their concerns and the needs of the people. Thus Christian theologians and Marxist theorists found common ground.[6]

---

[3] Leonardo Boff and Clodovis Boff, *Introducing Liberation Theology,* Paul Burns, trans. Maryknoll, NY: Orbis Books, 1987: 7.

[4] Boff and Boff, *Introducing Liberation Theology,* 31.

[5] Garaudy converted to Islam in 1982 and is now known both for his books extolling Muslim culture and his 1995 book denying the Holocaust, for which he was tried and fined.

[6] For a statement on the relations between Christian thinkers and Marxists, see Andrew Collier, *Christianity and Marxism: A Philosophical Contribution to Their Reconciliation.* London: Routledge, 2001.

For Liberation Theology the connection to Marxism is found in accepting that Marx made major contributions to our understanding of capitalism and helped illuminate the position of the poor in modern society, but Marx is seen to have been limited by his rejection of God. Thus "Marx (like any other Marxist) can be a companion on the way . . . but he can never be the guide, because 'You have only one teacher, the Christ' (Matt. 23:10)."[7]

In addition to Marx, one of the most important nontheological sources of Liberation Theology is the work of the Brazilian Paulo Freire (1921–1997), particularly his *Pedagogy of the Oppressed* (1970). Freire advocated what he called *conscientization,* or consciousness-raising (also discussed in Chapter 7), a process in which the oppressed become aware of their oppression through participation in group discussion with others in similar circumstances. Anarchists also claim Freire as an important theorist, and he is best known as an educational theorist who successfully headed the school system in São Paulo, Brazil.

Most conservatives within the Roman Catholic Church reject Liberation Theology. Although at one point Pope John Paul II condemned Liberation Theology, he later accepted some of its positions. The current pope, Benedict XVI, while on a trip to Brazil in May 2007, used the central phrase of Liberation Theology, "preferential option for the poor," but he used it to reject the need for Liberation Theology.

THE PRINCIPLES OF LATIN AMERICAN LIBERATION THEOLOGY

Liberation Theology arose out of the dialogue just described. It has also been said that "Liberation theology was born when faith confronted the injustice done to the poor."[8] In broad outline, the position of Liberation Theology is as follows:

1. The church should be concerned with poverty.
2. The church should be concerned with political repression.
3. The church should be concerned with economic repression.
4. Priests should become actively involved in trying to solve these problems.
5. Priests should move beyond general activity to
   a. Direct political action, and, possibly,
   b. Direct involvement in attempts to change political and economic systems, even by actual participation in revolutionary activity.[9]
6. *Base communities,* or communities that include both religious (priests and nuns) and laypeople, should be established. These communities should be designed to overcome the division between religious and laypeople.

---

[7] Boff and Boff, *Introducing Liberation Theology,* 28.

[8] Boff and Boff, *Introducing Liberation Theology,* 3.

[9] Camilo Torres (1929–1966) was a priest who took the political messages to heart and became an active revolutionary. For his writings, see *Revolutionary Priest: The Complete Writings and Messages of Camilo Torres,* John Gerassi, ed. New York: Random House, 1971.

The Roman Catholic Church specifically rejects item five and is not sure about item three. Pope John Paul II once rejected item six but later accepted it in some circumstances.

One of the earliest theorists of Liberation Theology was Gustavo Gutiérrez (b. 1928) of Chile, and his *Theology of Liberation* (1971, English trans. 1973) was the first work to bring together the elements of Liberation Theology. Gutiérrez argued, based on Freire and Bloch, that the Church must recognize the positive function of the idea of utopia. In this context, the idea of utopia includes both condemnation of the evils of the present and affirmation of the possibilities of the future. As Gutiérrez put it,

> The theology of liberation attempts to reflect on the experience and meaning of the faith based on the commitment to abolish injustice and to build a new society; this theology must be verified by the practice of that commitment, by active, effective participation in the struggle which the exploited social classes have undertaken against their oppressors. Liberation from every form of exploitation, the possibility of a more human and more dignified life, the creation of a new man—all pass through this struggle.[10]

Liberation Theology, in common with a number of other movements in the 1960s and 1970s, stressed consciousness-raising, the direct participation of the people, and socialism. But Liberation Theology is different in that it is first and foremost a theology, and its political and economic message is founded on the mission of Christ.

One early spiritual leader who is thought to have truly followed Christ's message, to whom the Liberation Theologians look for inspiration, is St. Francis of Assisi (1182–1226), who insisted on the absolute poverty of his followers.[11] St. Francis posed a serious problem for the established Church of his time; among other things, he took the vow of poverty more seriously than was acceptable. For the Church the vow meant that although the Church could own property, the individual could not; but St. Francis and his followers begged for their food every day with nothing kept for the next day, as do many Buddhist monks today, particularly in Southeast Asia. For Liberation Theology, poverty like that chosen by St. Francis is to be honored, and the poverty that is at issue in their theology is not chosen but is, in fact, they argue, imposed by a social structure that the established church both benefits from and supports.

Base Communities

In a phrase reminiscent of Karl Marx's statement, "The philosophers have only *interpreted* the world in various ways; the point is to *change* it,"[12] Leonardo Boff

---

[10] Gustavo Gutiérrez, *A Theology of Liberation: History, Politics, and Salvation*, 15th anniversary ed., Sister Caridad Inda and John Eagleson, trans. and ed. Maryknoll, NY: Orbis Books, 1988: 174.

[11] Leonardo Boff, *Saint Francis: A Model for Human Liberation*, John W. Diercksmeier, trans. New York: Crossroad Press, 1982.

[12] Karl Marx, "Theses on Feuerbach," in *Karl Marx and Friedrich Engels, Collected Works.* New York: International Publishers, 1976, 5: 5. Original emphasis.

wrote, "More important than to see and to judge is to act."[13] And in Latin America, part of acting was the establishment of base communities, or base ecclesial communities, where, in the absence of priests, the laity took responsibility for their own religious activity. This led to them identify social, economic, and political needs of central importance and to organize themselves to meet those needs. Such communities both aided consciousness raising and provided a setting where people learned to take control of their own lives.

In 1979 Latin American bishops met at Puebla, Mexico, and recognized base communities as an important new form of both evangelizing and liberating the poor and oppressed.[14] Base communities have also become central to the development of Liberation Theology in the Philippines, where it is known as the *Theology of Struggle*.[15]

Leonardo Boff described a typical community as follows:

> The base ecclesial community is generally made up of fifteen to twenty families. They get together once or twice a week to hear the Word of God, to share their problems in common, and to solve those problems through the inspiration of the Gospel. They share their comments on the biblical passages, create their own prayers, and decide as a group what their tasks should be. After centuries of silence, the People of God are beginning to speak. They are no longer just parishioners in their parish; they have their own ecclesiological value; they are recreating the Church of God.[16]

Such activity, which resonates with the Protestant Reformation, is, of course, potentially dangerous for a hierarchical church. In South America many of Liberation Theology's most prominent exponents have left the church, or, as they say, they have been forced out. Others have left South America for teaching posts in North America and Europe, where they are no longer directly involved with the activities of the movement they helped establish. But many of the activities fostered by Liberation Theology still exist because the problems still exist. Poverty is still a major problem, and the church continues to have serious difficulties finding enough priests to meet even the minimal needs of parishes. Thus, base communities still exist where laypeople fill religious functions, and where the community provides support for its own members. But Liberation Theology has largely disappeared from the theological schools and universities in Latin America, and teachers who show signs of leanings toward Liberation Theology are removed.

In Ireland, for a time the European center of a ground-level Liberation Theology, the shift from being one of the poorest countries in Europe to being

---

[13] Boff, *Saint Francis*, 87.

[14] *Puebla and Beyond: Documentation and Commentary,* John Eagleson and Philip Scharper, ed. Maryknoll, NY: Orbis Books, 1979: 211.

[15] See Kathleen M. Nadeau, *Liberation Theology in the Philippines: Faith in a Revolution.* Westport, CT: Praeger, 2002.

[16] Leonardo Boff, Church: *Charism and Power—Liberation Theology and the Institutional Church,* John W. Diercksmeier, trans. (New York: Crossroad Press, 1985:), 125–26. From Church: Charism and Power—Liberation Theology and the Institutional Church by Leonardo Boff, trans. John W. Diercksmeier. English translation © 1985 by T. C. P. C. Reprinted by permission of The Crossroad Publishing Company.

one of the richest combined with active suppression of any sign of Liberation Theology resulted in Liberation Theology being virtually eliminated from the country. Within Catholicism, Liberation Theology appears to be most dynamic in the Philippines.

PROTESTANT LIBERATION THEOLOGY

Although Liberation Theology originated within the Roman Catholic Church, it moved to Protestantism and may now be most dynamic within Protestant denominations in the United States and the Third World with significant movements in both Africa and Asia. A leftist evangelical Protestant Liberation Theology movement even exists in the United States. The People's Christian Coalition, known as the Sojourners, published the journal *Post American* from 1971 to 1975, which became *Sojourners Magazine* from 1976 to 2000; it has simply been called *Sojourners* since 2001.

One way of thinking about the issue of how Christ can speak for various minorities is to think about the way Christ is depicted. The representations of Christ that I grew up with showed an Anglo-Saxon male, and I can recall a friend's mother feeling insulted by a Christmas card that depicted Christ as Semitic. For liberation theologies, the representations of my childhood exclude the overwhelming majority of Christians, who are not Anglo-Saxon males. For them, Christ must be black, female, Asian, and so forth; Christ must be whoever is oppressed; for them Christ and Christianity are liberating because Christ spoke for the oppressed as one of the oppressed.

Black Liberation Theology in the United States

From the perspective of the United States, the most interesting development is the spread of Liberation Theology within African American Protestantism. James H. Cone (b. 1938), certainly one of the most important theologians of the twentieth century, was the first exponent of Black Theology, a distinct movement which predated the emergence of Liberation Theology in Latin America. For a time, Cone kept his distance from Latin American Liberation Theology, because it was rooted in Roman Catholicism and because he saw its proponents as white and insensitive to racial questions. But Cone recognized the commonalities between his position and theirs. As a result, he has been a key figure internationally in bringing together the various strands of Liberation Theology, and he helped introduce Asian Liberation Theology to U.S. theologians and Black Theology to both Latin American and Asian theologians. Through his work, Latin American Liberation theology was sensitized to racial questions. And Cone recognized weaknesses in his own initial analysis, particularly regarding women and class, and he has worked to overcome them.

Cone stresses that Black Theology derives from the lived experiences of African Americans in racist America and their experiences in the black church. He calls white theology *ideology* and means it negatively, saying, "Christ *really* enters into our world where the poor, the despised, and the black are, disclosing that he

James H. Cone (b. 1938) is the Charles A. Briggs Distinguished Professor of Systematic Theology at Union Theological Seminary. His book *A Black Theology of Liberation* (1970) founded the school of thought now known as *Black Theology.* Over the years, he has enriched his thought by incorporating work by theologians from North America, Africa, Asia, and Latin America, including black women theologians. Later editions of *A Black Theology of Liberation* (1986 and 1990) illustrate the evolution of his thought. His books *Black Power and Black Theology* (1969, new ed. 1989); *The Spirituals and the Blues* (1972); *God of the Oppressed* (1975, revised ed. 1997); *For My People: Black Theology and the Black Church* (1984); *Speaking the Truth: Ecumenism, Liberation, and Black Theology* (1986); *My Soul Looks Back* (1986); and *Martin and Malcolm and America: A Dream or a Nightmare?* (1991) reflect his growing stature as both a theologian and a cultural critic.

is with them, enduring their humiliation and pain and transforming oppressed slaves into liberated servants. Indeed, if Christ is not *truly* black, then the historical Jesus lied."[17] This strong language emphasizes Black Theology's alienation from the dominant theological culture in Europe and North America, in which Christ is always depicted as white. Black Theology, like all liberation theologies, emphasizes that Christ spoke for the oppressed, not the rich and powerful.

Currently the best-known exponent of Black Liberation theology is Dwight N. Hopkins, Professor of Theology at the University of Chicago Divinity School. Hopkins, drawing explicitly on Gutiérrez, argues, "Indeed, we need the preferential option for the poor more than ever these days because postmodernity includes an intensification of worker exploitation, racial oppression, discrimination against women, and sexual-identity exclusion."[18]

He bases the "Liberation of the Least" on Matthew 25:31–46, in which Christ says (in verses 34–40, RSV),

> Come, O blessed of my Father, inherit the kingdom prepared for you from the foundation of the world; for I was hungry and you gave me food, I was thirsty and you gave me drink, I was a stranger and you welcomed me, I was naked and you clothed me, I was sick and you visited me, I was in prison and you came to me. . . . Truly, I say to you, as you did it to one of the least of these my brethren, you did it to me.

---

[17] James H. Cone, *God of the Oppressed.* New York: Seabury Press, 1975: 136. Emphasis in the original.

[18] Dwight N. Hopkins, "More Than Ever: The Preferential Option for the Poor," in *Opting for the Margins: Postmodernity and Liberation in Christian Theology,* Joerg Rieger, ed. New York: Oxford University Press, 2003: 138.

Sheila Turner, Atlanta, GA

Womanist Theology

As indicated, Cone was criticized for ignoring gender issues, and although he responded positively to the criticisms, African-American women have developed a variant of Black Liberation Theology known as Womanist Theology. *Womanist* comes from Alice Walker's (b. 1944) *In Search of Our Mothers' Gardens* (1983).[19] Womanist theologians argue, as did Cone, that "Christ is Black. That is to say, Christ has Black skin and features and is committed to the Black community's struggle for life and wholeness."[20] They argue that African-American women must free themselves from their own acceptance "of sexist oppression, the black man's acceptance of patriarchal privilege, and the white woman's acceptance of white racist privilege."[21] Womanist theologians also argue, as do most feminists, that liberation must be for all peoples regardless of race, gender, and ethnicity. A Roman Catholic variant of Womanist theology directed at Latina women is called *Mujerista* theology and was founded by Ada María Isasi-Díaz (b. 1943).

Asian Theologies of Liberation

This section will examine three Asian liberation theologies: Korean Minjung theology, Dalit theology in India, and Asian feminist theology that has developed in a number of countries. In most Asian countries, Christianity arrived with colonialism, and in most Asian countries, Christianity is not the dominant religion. Christians are a tiny minority, less than 3 percent of the population in Asia as a whole, and Christian practice is often influenced by indigenous religions. As a result, Asian theologians of liberation try to respect and learn from local traditions.

Minjung Theology In Korea the colonial power was Japan, so Christianity was seen from the beginning in more liberatory terms than in most Asian countries, and now Korea is one of the most Christian countries in Asia. Japan recognized the potential of Christianity and banned the books of *Exodus* and *Daniel* in the Bible as potentially subversive.

Although Minjung derives from a nineteenth century movement against the Japanese, Minjung theology is a Korean Liberation Theology that emerged initially within the Korean Methodist Church in the 1970s in response to oppression by the Korean government. The central theologian of Minjung theology was Ahn Byung-mu (1922–1996). Minjung is Korean, derived from the Chinese *min,* meaning "people," and *jung,* meaning "mass"; but the word cannot be easily translated into English.[22] Minjung theology is millenarian,

---

[19] Alice Walker, "Womanist," in *In Search of Our Mothers' Gardens: Womanist Prose.* San Diego: Harcourt Brace Jovanovich, 1983.

[20] Kelly Brown Douglas, *The Black Christ.* Maryknoll, NY: Orbis Books, 1994: 106–107.

[21] Marcia Y. Riggs, *Awake, Arise, and Act: A Womanist Call for Black Liberation.* Cleveland: Pilgrim Press, 1994: 2.

[22] David Suh Kwang-sun, "A Biographical Sketch of an Asian Theological Consultation," in *Minjung Theology: People as the Subjects of History.* Commission on Theological Concerns of the Christian Conference of Asia (CTC-CCA), ed. Revised ed. Maryknoll, NY: Orbis Books; London: Zed Books, 1983: 16.

believing that the Kingdom of God will be established on earth in the near future.[23]

Minjung refers to the common people oppressed by an elite: "Minjung are the people of God, and their experience of suffering owing to the injustice of the ruling group has to be eliminated from this world. Therefore, the act of liberation becomes the central focus of Minjung theology. Moreover, the realization of the fruits of liberation produces the establishment of the Messianic Kingdom or the Reign of God on earth."[24] The key concepts of Minjung are *Han* and *Dan*. "*Han* is the feeling of resentment, depression, repressed anger, helplessness, just indignation, and so forth, which is combined with a desire for a better future."[25] *Dan* is a more complex and more clearly political concept that refers to the ability to overcome *Han* with the help of God by breaking through the repression that creates *Han*. Thus, using different concepts, Minjung theology is quite similar to Latin American Liberation Theology. It focuses on the poor and repressed and fashions a theology that energizes people to help themselves and thereby overcome their situation. It is different from Latin American Liberation Theology in being millenarian and in relying on local congregations rather than base ecclesial communities. A women's movement has also developed within Minjung to address the specific oppression of Korean women.

Dalit Theology Still better known outside India as the "untouchables," the Dalit or "broken ones" are at the bottom of the highly structured Indian system of social stratification. Their oppression has been recognized to the extent that there are seats reserved in the Indian parliament for Dalit based on population. The perceived libratory potential of Christianity can be seen in the fact that a high percentage of Indian Christians are Dalits. In some cases this has led to further oppression, because the development of a militant Hinduism called *Hinduvata* has mostly been directed against Muslims; this has led to the murders of recent converts to Christianity. Just as Christ has been represented as black or female, in Dalit theology Christ is Dalit, one of the oppressed who can therefore speak to and for the oppressed.

Asian Feminist Theology Asian feminist theology is an aspect of the feminist theology mentioned in Chapter 7, but Asian women see themselves as the Minjung of the Minjung or the Dalit of the Dalit, meaning the oppressed of—and by—the oppressed. In addition, in Asia and Africa, feminism has often been seen as a middle-class white movement that only benefits women in the developed world; ignorant of colonial, racial, and even class oppression, such feminism

---

[23] There are various millennialisms, which are generally divided into those who believe that the millennial period will come before or after Armageddon, the final battle between good and evil: but many complications and disagreements exist among the divisions.

[24] Jung Young Lee, "Minjung Theology: A Critical Introduction," in *An Emerging Theology in World Perspective: Commentary on Korean Minjung Theology,* Jung Young Lee, ed. Mystic, CT: Twenty-Third Publications, 1988: 11.

[25] Michael Amaladoss, S. J., *Life in Freedom: Liberation Theologies from Asia.* Maryknoll, NY: Orbis Books, 1997: 4.

Kwok Pui-lan (b. 1952) is the William F. Cole Professor of Christian Theology and Spirituality at the Episcopal Divinity School in Cambridge, Massachusetts and the foremost expert on Asian feminist theology.

often includes the oppression of women by women. The Ecumenical Association of Third World Theologians has had to recognize the fact that many of its own members, male and female, are antifeminist.

Feminist theology sees itself as emerging from the real life experiences of women, and the experiences of Asian women are not the same as the experiences of women in the developed West or Africa or Latin America. Such experiences are not even the same throughout Asia. Probably most important from the point of view of Christian theology, many women live in a world that is not Christian, a world that is Buddhist, Confucian, Hindu, Islamic, and Shinto, and in which any number of indigenous religions are active. Indigenous religions are also important in Africa and Latin America, but in both those areas, Christianity is better established. And some of these religions have traditionally valued women more highly than Christianity did and have recognized a special role for women's spirituality, which was given a much lower status in most Christian denominations.

In part due to the role women's spirituality plays in it, ecofeminism has become an integral part of Asian feminist theology. The foremost person writing on Asian feminist theology, Episcopalian theologian Kwok Pui-lan (b. 1952), has also written on ecology and feminism.

LIBERATION THEOLOGY IN AFRICA

Contemporary Christian theology in Africa can be divided into theologies focusing on liberation, most obviously in South Africa and now emerging in Zimbabwe, and theologies focusing on inculturation, found throughout the rest of Christian Africa. *Inculturation* means that indigenous African religious practices have been grafted onto Christian theology, just as has happened in parts of Asia. This has generally been easier within Protestantism but is also found in Roman Catholicism. Liberation Theology took hold in South Africa because it provided a response to Apartheid, the extreme oppression of the black majority by the white majority.[26] The best known of the South African Liberation Theologians is Allan Boesak (b. 1946), who in *Farewell to Innocence* (1976, English trans. 1977) argued that African theology, Latin American Liberation Theology, Black Theology in the United States, and Black Theology in Africa are all expressions of the same fundamental theology of liberation. The growth of Liberation Theology in Zimbabwe is undoubtedly a reflection of the extreme poverty and political repression that exists there. As one Zimbabwean theologian recently wrote, citing Exodus 3:7 and Luke 4:18–19, "... the divine revelation in history is focused on the liberation of the suffering, the poor, the dispossessed and the oppressed. ..."[27] As with most other areas, a women's movement exists within African Liberation Theology, the organizational face of which is the Circle of Concerned African Theologians.

CURRENT TRENDS

The Ecumenical Association of Third World Theologians (EATWOT) provides a recurring venue for dialogue among theologians from Africa, Asia, the Caribbean, Latin America, the Pacific Islands, and North America. They are trying to address how Protestants and Roman Catholics, men and women of all colors, ethnicities, and nationalities, can forge a common understanding within Christianity of a common theology of liberation. Liberation Theology is as active today as at any time in the past.

The Catholic Worker Movement

In the United States, the Catholic Worker Movement (discussed in Chapter 9) now identifies itself with Liberation Theology. Given the movement's tradition of working with the poorest of the poor, specifically alcoholics and drug addicts, the affinity with Liberation Theology is obvious. But the movement also appears to be reemphasizing its connection to the Roman Catholic Church while continuing its social and political activity. Even though some members of the Church's hierarchy still oppose it, Catholic Worker centers exist throughout the United States, and this could signal a strengthened Roman Catholic Liberation Theology within the United States to parallel the still strong Black Liberation Theology.

Ecology and Globalization

Recently a few theologians have begun to integrate ecology into Liberation Theology, again appealing to the image of St. Francis of Assisi, who is often depicted

---

[26] For a discussion of both trends, see Emmanuel Martey, *African Theology: Inculturation and Liberation*. Maryknoll, NY: Orbis Books, 1993.

[27] Gwinyai Muzorewa, "Some Thoughts on African Liberation: From Independence to True Liberation—Parts I and II." *The Other Journal: An Intersection of Theology and Culture*, Vol. 6 (August 8, 2005) http://www.theotherjournal.com. Accessed March 20, 2008.

preaching to the birds. Other theologians have added a specific critique of globalization to the mix, arguing that although the rhetoric of globalization suggests inclusion, its practice excludes the poor and minorities and destroys the environment.[28]

Queer Theology

An addition to the range of liberation theologies, one that has both vehement supporters and strong opponents, is being variously called *gay and lesbian theology,* or *Queer Theology.* The latter is more accurate, both because gays and lesbians disagree fundamentally regarding central aspects of the theology, and because "gay and lesbian" puts sexual identity to the fore, and "queer" is both more inclusive and rejects single identities. Such an approach—and this is accepted by some feminists—sees gender as performance, something that is both self-made and socially constructed. In other words, although we are born with certain bodily characteristics, the gendered character of our personalities is only partly biological.

In one sense, the extension of Liberation Theology in this direction is unremarkable; it is simply the extension of the idea of a theology for the oppressed to another oppressed group. But given the status of anyone other than heterosexuals within most Christian denominations, it may seem odd to see the beginnings of a coherent set of ideas being recognized, if not necessarily accepted, by some respected theologians.

As with other liberation theologies, Queer Theology emerged from the real lives of real people who found themselves unwanted in most Christian churches. Religious experience and the desire for an active spiritual life is not limited to heterosexuals, so the excluded searched for and then created a theology that spoke directly to their own lives. And in Liberation Theology, they found voices speaking out for others who had been ostracized and oppressed within their churches. To the language of Liberation Theology, they add the language and concepts of Queer Theory, creating a consciously transgressive theology.

Conclusion

Although Liberation Theology has been weakened in the areas where it first emerged, it is a flourishing religious/ideological movement within Christianity that has a core set of values with different details, depending on the particular oppressed group concerned. Most versions of Liberation Theology make it clear that all oppressed groups should experience the "preferential option." For them God plays no favorites but wants liberation for all, and Christ was a radical seeking justice for all people. People cannot simply sit back and wait to be saved but must struggle for salvation, both in religious terms and from oppressive regimes, whether economic, political, or religious—the last being particularly important, because many institutional churches have lost the real message of Christ.[29]

---

[28] Among Leonardo Boff's books are *Ecology and Liberation: A New Paradigm,* John Cumming, trans. Maryknoll, NY: Orbis Books, 1995; and *Cry of the Earth, Cry of the Poor.* Philip Berryman, trans. Maryknoll, NY: Orbis Books, 1997.

[29] For a discussion of these agreements among the liberation theologies, see Lisa Isherwood, *Liberating Christ: Exploration of the Christologies of Contemporary Liberation Movements.* Cleveland: Pilgrim Press, 1999: 16–20.

SUGGESTED READING

Some Classic Works

Boff, Leonardo. *Jesus Christ Liberator: A Critical Christology for Our Times.* Patrick Hughes, trans. Maryknoll, NY: Orbis Books, 1981.

———. *Saint Francis: A Model for Human Liberation.* John W. Diercksmeier, trans. Maryknoll, NY: Orbis Books, 1982.

Cleage, Albert B., Jr. *The Black Messiah.* New York: Sheed & Ward, 1968.

Cone, James H. *A Black Theology of Liberation.* 20th anniversary ed. Maryknoll, NY: Orbis Books, 1990.

Dussel, Enrique. *History and Theology of Liberation: A Latin American Perspective.* John Drury, trans. Maryknoll, NY: Orbis Books, 1975.

Gutiérrez, Gustavo. *The Power of the Poor in History: Selected Writings.* Robert R. Barr, trans. Maryknoll, NY: Orbis Books, 1983.

———. *A Theology of Liberation: History, Politics, and Salvation.* 15th anniversary ed. Maryknoll, NY: Orbis Books, 1988.

———. *We Drink from Our Own Wells: The Spiritual Journey of a People.* Matthew J. O'Connell, trans. 20th anniversary ed. Maryknoll, NY: Orbis Books, 2003.

Hopkins, Dwight N[athaniel]. *Down, Up, and Over: Slave Religion and Black Theology.* Minneapolis, MN: Fortress Press, 2000.

———. *Heart and Head: Black Theology— Past, Present, and Future.* New York: Palgrave, 2002.

———. *Introducing Black Theology of Liberation.* Maryknoll, NY: Orbis Books, 1999.

Isasi-Díaz, Ada María. *En la Lucha/In the Struggle: Elaborating a Mujerista Theology.* 10th anniversary ed. Minneapolis, MN: Fortress Press, 2004.

Míguez Bonino, José. *Doing Theology in a Revolutionary Situation.* Philadelphia: Fortress Press, 1975. Published in the U.K. as *Revolutionary Theology Comes of Age.* London: SPCK, 1975.

Roberts, J[ames] Deotis. *A Black Political Theology.* Philadelphia, PA: Westminster Press, 1974.

———. *Liberation and Reconciliation: A Black Theology.* Revised ed. Maryknoll, NY: Orbis Books, 1994. 2nd ed. Louisville, KY: Westminster John Knox Press, 2005. Notes that "the sexism in the first edition is offensive to the present writer" (xiv).

Segundo, Juan Luis. *Liberation of Theology.* John Drury, trans. Maryknoll, NY: Orbis Books, 1976.

Williams, Delores S. *Sisters in the Wilderness: The Challenges of Womanist God-Talk.* Maryknoll, NY: Orbis Books, 1993.

Books and Articles

Althaus-Reid, Marcella, and Lisa Isherwood. "Thinking Theology and Queer Theory." *Feminist Theology.* Vol. 15:3 (May 2007): 300–314.

Althaus-Reid, Marcella. *Indecent Theology: Theological Perversions in Sex, Gender and Politics.* London: Routledge, 2000.

———. *The Queer God.* London: Routledge, 2003. Focuses on South America; the author is originally from Argentina.

Battle, Michael, ed. *The Quest for Liberation and Reconciliation: Essays in Honor of J. Deotis Roberts.* Louisville, KY: Westminster John Knox Press, 2005.

Boesak, Allan [Aubrey]. *Farewell to Innocence: A Socio-Ethical Study on Black Theology and Black Power.* Maryknoll, NY: Orbis Books, 1977.

Boff, Leonardo. *Cry of the Earth, Cry of the Poor.* Philip Berryman, trans. Maryknoll, NY: Orbis Books, 1997.

———. *Ecclesiogenesis: The Base Communities Reinvent the Church.* Robert R. Barr, trans. Maryknoll, NY: Orbis Books, 1986.

———. *Ecology and Liberation: A New Paradigm.* John Cumming, trans. Maryknoll, NY: Orbis Books, 1995. Originally published in Portuguese.

———. *Way of the Cross—Way of Justice.* John Drury, trans. Maryknoll, NY: Orbis Books, 1980.

———, and Clodovis Boff. *Introducing Liberation Theology.* Paul Burns, trans. Maryknoll, NY: Orbis Books, 1987.

———, and Virgil Elizondo, eds. *Ecology and Poverty: Cry of the Earth, Cry of the*

Poor. London: SCM Press/Maryknoll, NY: Orbis Books, 1997.

Commission on Theological Concerns of the Christian Conference of Asia (CTCCCA), ed. *Minjung Theology: People as the Subjects of History.* Revised ed. Maryknoll, NY: Orbis Books; London: Zed Books; Singapore: Christian Conference of Asia, 1983.

Cone, James H. *Black Theology and Black Power.* 20th anniversary ed. San Francisco: Harper & Row, 1989.

————. *God of the Oppressed.* Revised ed. Maryknoll, NY: Orbis Books, 1997.

————. *Martin and Malcolm and America: A Dream or a Nightmare?* Maryknoll, NY: Orbis Books, 1991.

————. *Risks of Faith: The Emergence of a Black Theology of Liberation, 1968–1998.* Boston: Beacon Press, 1999.

————. *The Spirituals and the Blues: An Interpretation.* New York: Seabury Press, 1972. Reprinted, Maryknoll, NY: Orbis Books, 1991.

————, and Gayraud S. Wilmore, eds. *Black Theology: A Documentary History, 1966–1979.* 2nd revised ed. Maryknoll, NY: Orbis Books, 1993.

————, eds. *Black Theology: A Documentary History, 1980–1992.* Maryknoll, NY: Orbis Books, 1993.

Copeland, M. Shawn. "Black Political Theologies." In *The Blackwell Companion to Political Theology.* Peter Scott, and William T. Cavanaugh, eds. Malden, MA: Blackwell, 2004: 271–287. The article is a political statement as well as a description.

Davis, Kortright. *Emancipation Still Comin': Explorations in Caribbean Emancipatory Theology.* Maryknoll, NY: Orbis, 1990.

de Vries, Hent, and Lawrence E. Sullivan, eds. *Political Theologies: Public Religions in a Post-secular World.* New York: Fordham University Press, 2006. Large collection (796 pages) of original and reprinted articles.

Donaldson, Laura E., and Kwok Pui-lan, eds. *Postcolonialism, Feminism, and Religious Discourse.* New York: Routledge, 2002.

Douglas, Kelly Brown. *The Black Christ.* Maryknoll, NY: Orbis Books, 1994.

Dussel, Enrique. *Philosophy of Liberation.* Aquilina Martinez, and Christine Morkowsky, trans. Maryknoll, NY: Orbis Books, 1985.

Ecumenical Association of Third World Theologians. *Voices from the Third World.* A biannual publication founded December 1978.

Fabella, Virginia, and R. S. Sugirtharajah, eds. *Dictionary of Third World Theologies.* Maryknoll, NY: Orbis Books, 2000. U.K. ed. as *The SCM Dictionary of Third World Theologies.* London: SCM Press, 2003. A very good collection of short introductory essays on both a wide range of Christian and indigenous theologies and the concepts they use.

————, M.M. and Sun Ai Lee Park, eds. *We Dare to Dream: Doing Theology as Asian Women.* Hong Kong: Asian Women's Resource Centre for Culture and Theology/Manila, Philippines: The Asian Office of the Women's Commission of the Ecumenical Association of Third World Theologians (EATWOT), 1989. Reprinted, Maryknoll, NY: Orbis Books, 1990.

Gilkes, Cheryl Townsend. *"If It Wasn't for the Women . . .": Black Women's Experience and Womanist Culture in Church and Community.* Maryknoll, NY: Orbis Books, 2001.

Goss, Robert [E]. *Jesus Acted Up: A Gay and Lesbian Manifesto.* New York: Harper Collins, 1993. The author is a former Jesuit priest.

————, and Mona West, eds. *Take Back the Word: A Queer Reading of the Bible.* Cleveland: Pilgrim Press, 2000.

Hebblethwaite, Margaret. *Base Communities: An Introduction.* London: Geoffrey Chapman, 1993.

Hopkins, Dwight, ed. *Black Faith and Public Talk: Critical Essays on James H. Cone's Black Theology and Black Power.* Maryknoll, NY: Orbis, 1999.

————. "Theologies in the U.S.A." *Voices from the Third World.* Vol. 28:1 (June 2005): 27–37. Political statement.

Isasi-Díaz, Ada María. *Mujerista Theology: A Theology for the Twenty-First Century.* Maryknoll, NY: Orbis Books, 1996.

Isherwood, Lisa. *Liberating Christ: Exploration of the Christologies of Contemporary Liberation Movements.* Cleveland: Pilgrim Press, 1999.

Kee, Alistair. *The Rise and Demise of Black Theology.* Aldershot, England: Ashgate, 2006. A wide-ranging attack on all forms of black theology.

Kwok, Pui-lan. *Discovering the Bible in the Non-Biblical World.* Maryknoll, NY: Orbis Books, 1995.

———. *Introducing Asian Feminist Theology.* Cleveland: Pilgrim Press, 2000. U.K. ed. Sheffield, England: Sheffield Academic Press, 2000. A short overview.

———. *Postcolonial Imagination and Feminist Theology.* Louisville, KY: Westminster John Knox Press, 2005.

Loughlin, Gerard, ed. *Queer Theology: Rethinking the Western Body.* Malden, MA: Blackwell, 2007.

Muzorewa, Gwinyai H. "African Liberation Theology." *Journal of Black Theology in South Africa.* Vol. 3:2 (November 1989): 52–70.

———. "Some Thoughts on African Liberation: From Independence to True Liberation—Parts I and II." *The Other Journal: An Intersection of Theology and Culture,* Vol. 6 (August 8, 2005). http://www.theotherjournal.com.

Nadeau, Kathleen M. *Liberation Theology in the Philippines: Faith in a Revolution.* Westport, CT: Praeger, 2002.

Oduyoye, Mercy Amba, and Musimbi R.A. Kanyoro, eds. *The Will to Arise: Women, Tradition, and the Church in Africa.* Maryknoll, NY: Orbis Books, 1992.

Petrella, Ivan. *The Future of Liberation Theology: An Argument and Manifesto.* Aldershot, England: Ashgate, 2004. Reprinted, London: SCM Press, 2006.

Argues that Liberation Theology needs reinvention.

Pieris, Aloysius. "Political Theologies in Asia." In *The Blackwell Companion to Political Theology.* Peter Scott, and William T. Cavanaugh, eds. Malden, MA: Blackwell, 2004: 256–270. Asian Third World Theology or Asian Theology of Liberation (pp. 256–263); Minjung (263–265, 369–370); Dalit (265–267, 270), Asian feminist theology (267–270).

Rowland, Christopher, ed. *The Cambridge Companion to Liberation Theology.* Cambridge, England: Cambridge University Press, 1999.

Ruether, Rosemary Radford. *Gaia & God: An Ecofeminist Theology of Earth Healing.* San Francisco: HarperSanFrancisco, 1992.

———, ed. *Women Healing Earth: Third World Women on Ecology, Feminism, and Religion.* Maryknoll, NY: Orbis Books, 1996. U.K. ed. London: SCM Press, 1996. Writings from Africa, Asia, and Latin America on Christian ecofeminism with some material on indigenous religions and the environment.

Stuart, Elizabeth. *Gay and Lesbian Theologies: Repetitions with Critical Difference.* London: Ashgate, 2002. Argues that such theologies have reached a dead end, and the only way forward is by both gays and lesbians and the churches finding areas of compromise.

Wilmore, Gayraud S. *Black Religion and Black Radicalism: An Interpretation of the Religious History of African Americans.* 3rd ed., revised and enl. Maryknoll, NY: Orbis Books, 1998.

Websites

Ecumenical Association of Third World Theologians (EATWOT): http://www.eatwot.org

Liberation Theology at Believe Religious Information Source Website: http://mb-soft.com/believe/txn/liberati.htm

Mujerista Theology: http://www.users.drew.edu/aisasidi/Definition1.htm

Sabeel Ecumenical Liberation Theology Center, Jerusalem: http://www.sabeel.org

13

Environmentalism

T his chapter briefly examines the origins and development of what is variously called *ecologism, environmentalism, Green politics,* the *Green Movement,* or *Green political thought.* Here it is simply called *environmentalism,* because that is what it is most often called in the United States. In Europe the word *environmentalism* reflects a fairly conservative approach, rather like the word *conservationism* does in the United States. Thus European thinkers tend to use words like *ecologism,* which have not caught on in the United States. One aspect of environmentalism, animal rights, has become important recently both philosophically and politically.

In 2004 environmentalism was recognized with the awarding of the Nobel Peace Prize to Kenyan environmental activist Wangari Maathai (b. 1940) for her "fight to promote ecologically viable social, economic, and cultural development in Kenya and Africa" in a "holistic approach to sustainable development that embraces democracy, human rights and women's rights in particular."[1] Her organization, the Green Belt Movement, had planted over 30 million trees, providing fuel, food, shelter, and income, creating employment, and improving soil and watersheds. Maathai also developed a program of citizen education to teach the connections between environmental degradation and the other problems facing Africa, and she has worked to encourage people, women in particular, that their individual actions make a difference.

---

[1] http://.nobelpeaceprize.org/eng_lau_announce2004.html. Accessed April 10, 2008.

Also, in 2007 Al Gore (b. 1948) and the United Nation's Intergovernmental Panel on Climate Change shared the Nobel Peace Prize for their work regarding the problem of climate change and global warming. In his speech to accept the prize, Rajendra K. Pachauri (b. 1940), the Chair of the U.N. panel, said the award recognized "three important realities":

1. The power and promise of collective scientific endeavour, which, as demonstrated by the IPCC, can reach across national boundaries and political differences in the pursuit of objectives defining the larger good of human society.

2. The importance of the role of knowledge in shaping public policy and guiding global affairs for the sustainable development of human society.

3. An acknowledgement of the threats to stability and human security inherent in the impact of a changing climate and, therefore, the need for developing an effective rationale for timely and adequate action to avoid such threats in the future.[2]

For most people the impact of environmentalism is not found in a radical rethinking of the place of human beings in the biosphere but in smaller things, like recycling, buying canned tuna certified as having been caught using methods that do not harm dolphins, eating more organic foods, increasing awareness of the importance of clean air and water and the problems related to climate change. Others focus on specific issues, such as the treatment of animals, genetically modified foods, or the protection of whales. The environmental movement has changed the way many people shop and deal with their rubbish, but its greatest impact has been on the lives of activists who devote their entire lives to some aspect of the movement. At the same time, radical environmentalism represents the beginning of an entirely new way of conceptualizing the world, one that moves human beings off center stage and puts the biosphere, of which humanity is only a small part, at the center.

Many countries have Green political parties; the first were founded in Australia and New Zealand in 1972. Such parties have elected members to various local and regional legislative bodies, national legislative bodies, and the European Parliament of the European Union. Green political parties are uncommon in North America. Ralph Nader (b. 1934) ran for president in 2000 as the candidate of the Green Party, but he received only 2.7 percent of the votes cast and was either blamed for or credited with Al Gore losing the presidency while winning the popular vote. The Green Party did not renominate Nader; in 2004, they ran a candidate, and Nader ran as an independent; together they received a lower percentage of the total vote than Nader had in 2000. Green parties do better at the local or state level, but as with most so-called third parties in the United States, their greatest influence is in bringing issues to public attention and having these issues taken up by one of the two major parties.

Environmentalism is found primarily in the developed North (including Australia and New Zealand in the South but generally excluding Japan) and is

---

[2] http://nobelprize.org/cgi-bin. Accessed April 10, 2008.

beginning to be felt in the rest of the world. Many, but not all, thinkers in the Third World argue that although they would like to encourage environmentally sound policies, they cannot afford to; they see environmentalism as a luxury that only the developed world can afford. However, the environmental movement is beginning to convince some of them that environmentalism is good economic policy and considerable political and economic pressure is being put on Third World countries to change. A case in point is that China was trying to find ways of cutting its extreme pollution before the Beijing Olympics in 2008.

ORIGINS

In North America two major sources have coalesced in the development of environmentalism. One source is the conservationism that developed in the United States as a result of such works as *Silent Spring* (1962), by Rachel Carson (1907–1964), and out of concern about the effects of overpopulation, stemming from such works as *The Population Bomb* (1968) by Paul Ehrlich (b. 1932). The controversial report *The Limits to Growth,* published in 1972, argued that constant economic growth was unsustainable.

The other main source is the environmental theorists and activists who give the movement its belief system, and it is possible to follow the careers and writings of major figures of this second source back to the ferment of the 1960s. In North America, protests against the Vietnam War, nuclear weapons, and nuclear power broadened awareness of how these issues interact with political power and social conflict. There was a strong concern with self-sufficiency and a "back-to-the-land" component to some of the movements of the 1960s and 1970s. In the United States, the immensely successful series *The Whole Earth Catalog* (1968–1981) and the related *CoEvolution Quarterly* (1974–1984) were evidence of this. A new edition of *The Whole Earth Catalog* was published in 1994, and the *CoEvolution Quarterly* continued as the *Whole Earth Review* until 1996, when it became *Whole Earth,* which was published through 2003. Similar books and journals were published in Europe, Canada, Australia, and New Zealand.

In Europe the development of the movement was similar, but the failed revolutions of 1968 in Czechoslovakia and France were of central importance, followed by the campaign against nuclear weapons, a growing recognition of the cross-national effects of pollution, and an early awareness that political and economic systems were centrally involved in the existing environmental problems as well as in any possible solutions. The key difference is that in in addition to the interest or pressure groups that were established in North America, in Europe political parties were formed and ran in elections.

A slightly different path involving the same issues can be traced in the writings of major theorists of environmentalism, such as André Gorz (1923–2007), Ivan Illich (1926–2002), and Murray Bookchin (1921–2006). These theorists usually started from a position of general radicalism and then focused more and more on ecological issues.

Environmentalism also has more remote origins that are difficult to define precisely. In North America these origins can be found in the writings of early environmentalists such as Henry David Thoreau (1817–1862), a writer whose *A Week on the Concord and Merrimack Rivers* (1849) and especially *Walden, or Life in the Woods* (1854) are imbued with a sensuous love of nature and a political rebelliousness that are echoed in many contemporary works; and John Muir (1838–1914), who successfully campaigned for forest reserves and national parks and is now a "patron saint" of radical environmentalists.

Ecotopia

In 1975 Ernest Callenbach (b. 1929) self-published a novel, *Ecotopia,* that was to become the classic ecological utopia, particularly after it was republished in 1977 in a mass-market edition.[3] *Ecotopia* also produced a small body of related literature.[4]

Ecotopia is a fictitious country formed out of the northwestern United States—Washington, Oregon, and Northern California—with the story of the revolution that led to this successful secession told in Callenbach's *Ecotopia Emerging* (1981). The story is set in 1999, when a reporter visits Ecotopia for the first time since the 1980 secession, and his description of a train trip in *Ecotopia* is a good example of what environmentalists hope to achieve:

> Their sentimentality about nature has even led the Ecotopians to bring greenery into their trains, which are full of hanging ferns and small plants I could not identify. (My companions however reeled off their botanical names with assurance.) At the end of the car stood containers rather like trash bins, each with a large letter—M, G, and P. These, I was told, were "recycle bins." It may seem unlikely to Americans, but I observed that during our trip my fellow travelers did without exception dispose of all metal, glass, or paper and plastic refuse in the appropriate bin. That they did so without the embarrassment Americans would experience was my first introduction to the rigid practices of recycling and re-use upon which Ecotopians are said to pride themselves so fiercely.[5]

The principles behind Callenbach's description and the rest of the utopia he presents in *Ecotopia* include closeness to nature, illustrated by the plants inside the train; knowledge of the natural world, as shown by the passengers' ability to name the plants; and recycling.

---

[3] Ernest Callenbach, *Ecotopia: The Notebooks and Reports of William Weston.* Berkeley, CA: Banyan Tree Books, 1975; New York: Bantam Books, 1977.

[4] See Ernest Callenbach, *Ecotopia Emerging.* Berkeley, CA: Banyan Tree Books, 1981; and Callenbach, *The Ecotopian Encyclopedia for the 80s: A Survival Guide for the Age of Inflation.* Berkeley, CA: And/Or, 1980. See also Judith Clancy, *The Ecotopian Sketchbook: A Book for Drawing, Writing, Collaging, Designing, Thinking About, and Creating a New World, Based on the Novel Ecotopia by Ernest Callenbach.* Berkeley, CA: Banyan Tree Books, 1981.

[5] Callenbach, *Ecotopia,* 9–10. Reprinted by permission of the author.

Photographs of Earth taken from outer space make the point that all human beings inhabit a single planet. Such photographs have struck a chord in many people and have encouraged them to become aware of themselves as part of an international community. In addition, Earth as seen from outer space has a fragile beauty that has helped fuel the recognition that ecological and environmental concerns cross all national borders.

NASA

THE PRINCIPLES OF ENVIRONMENTALISM

Different but closely related versions of the fundamental principles of environmentalism have been spelled out by many groups and individuals. One of the most detailed is the Earth Charter, which specifies what it calls "four broad commitments"; it then lays out twelve points, with subpoints necessary to meet the commitments. These commitments are as follows:

1. Respect Earth and Life in all its diversity.

2. Care for the community of life with understanding, compassion, and love.

3. Build democratic societies that are just, participatory, sustainable, and peaceful.

4. Secure Earth's bounty and beauty for present and future generations.[6]

The striking thing about this and all the other similar statements is the emphasis in the third point on issues that go well beyond the environment narrowly defined. For example, the key values of the U.S. Green Party are:

1. Grassroots Democracy

2. Social Justice and Equal Opportunity

3. Ecological Wisdom

4. Non-Violence

5. Decentralization

6. Community-Based Economics and Economic Justice

7. Feminism and Gender Equity

---

[6] http://www.earthcharter.org. Accessed April 25, 2008.

8. Respect for Diversity

9. Personal and Global Responsibility

10. Future Focus and Sustainability[7]

And Lester W. Milbrath (b. 1925) has argued that there is a "new environmental paradigm" that includes a "high valuation on nature"; compassion toward other peoples, generations, and species; planning to avoid technology that is not environmentally sensitive; limiting growth; and, most important for the development of a new ideology, a new social paradigm and a new politics. The latter will require, among other things, greater participation, simpler living, cooperation, public versus private solutions to many issues, and a greater emphasis on worker satisfaction.[8]

Although basic similarities exist, positions differ within environmentalism. Here we will look briefly at three of these different positions—ecosocialism, ecofeminism, and Deep Ecology.

ECOSOCIALISM

André Gorz

André Gorz argued that *"the ecological movement is not an end in itself but a stage in the larger struggle."*[9] That larger struggle is the one against capitalism. Gorz was a Marxist who influenced the development of environmental concerns within Marxism (see the discussion in Chapter 8). He rejected the centralism of the dominant Marxist tradition and used Marx's philosophy to argue for a way of life no longer dominated by work. He wanted a simpler lifestyle based on production limited to socially necessary goods. Everyone would work, but they would work less and at more satisfying jobs. To the extent possible, necessary but repetitive work would be replaced by automated machinery, a position that many environmentalists reject.

Gorz also contended that ecology cannot produce an ethic, another argument widely rejected by environmentalists. With the existence of journals such as *Environmental Ethics* (founded 1979) and *Ethics and the Environment* (founded 1996), Gorz clearly lost that part of the argument. He also contended that ecology should be seen as a "purely scientific discipline" that "does not necessarily imply the rejection of authoritarian technological solutions."[10]

Most environmentalists argue that ecology does produce an ethic, one that requires the rejection of "authoritarian technological solutions." But Gorz's argument was based on the fact that many environmentalists accept the possibility of using highly technological means to solve some of the world's pollution problems.

---

[7] http://gp.org/tenkey.html. Acessed April 25, 2008.

[8] Lester W. Milbrath, "Environmental Beliefs and Values," in *Political Psychology.* San Francisco: Jossey-Bass, 1986: 100.

[9] André Gorz, *Ecology as Politics,* Patsy Vigderman and Jonathan Cloud, trans. Boston: South End Press, 1980: 3. Original emphasis.

[10] Gorz, *Ecology as Politics,* 17.

Thus, while the left wing of environmentalism rejects his position and argues for an ethic that is antitechnological, those to Gorz's right generally accept his conclusion and support the use of technology to solve problems brought about by technology while generally rejecting his Marxism.

Murray Bookchin

Murray Bookchin was an anarchist theorist (see the discussion of him in Chapter 9), an ecological theorist, and an activist. Bookchin described what he calls "an ecological society" as one that "would fully recognize that the human animal is biologically structured to live with its kind, and to care for and love its own kind within a broadly and freely defined social group."[11] His *Ecology of Freedom* (1982) and *Toward an Ecological Society* (1980) describe what a society based on many of the sort of principles outlined in the Earth Charter and elsewhere would look like. It would be radically decentralized, participatory, and would have overcome hierarchy; it would include respect for each individual and the planet.

ECOFEMINISM

Ecofeminism mostly springs from the part of feminism that views women as more in tune with nature than men, and it begins with the assertion that our ecological problems stem from the male notion of dominance, which is reflected in the technological approach of theorists like Gorz.[12] Not all self-described ecofeminists are women, and many of their positions are widely accepted by other environmentalists.

An interesting example of the sensibility found in ecofeminism is found in Ursula K. Le Guin's short story "She Unnames Them" (1985), in which Eve is depicted as freeing the animals from Adam's domination by unnaming them—that is, giving them back their own identities rather than those imposed by Adam's names.

Ecofeminists tend to accept what is called the *Gaia hypothesis,* which was originated by James Lovelock (b. 1919) and sees the Earth as a self-regulating entity analogous in many ways to a living organism, which must be nourished and protected rather than exploited. Many ecofeminists see this as part of a belief in what they call the Goddess, a revived religious idea that in some ways is close to nature worship.[13] Others see it as part of Christianity but with a recognition of a special women's spirituality, and it now plays a significant role in Asian feminist

---

[11] Murray Bookchin, *The Ecology of Freedom: The Emergence and Dissolution of Hierarchy.* Palo Alto, CA: Cheshire Books, 1982: 318.

[12] For collections, see Irene Diamond and Gloria Feman Orenstein, eds., *Reweaving the World: The Emergence of Ecofeminism.* San Francisco: Sierra Club Books, 1990; and Heather Eaton and Lois Ann Lorentzen, eds., *Ecofeminism and Globalization: Exploring Culture, Context, and Religion.* Lanham, MD: Rowman & Littlefield, 2003.

[13] See, for example, Carol P. Christ, *Rebirth of the Goddess: Finding Meaning in Feminist Spirituality.* New York: Routledge, 1999; and Christ, *She Who Changes: Re-imagining the Divine in the World.* London: Palgrave Macmillan, 2003.

theology, as was mentioned in the previous chapter. Non-Christian religious developments of ecofeminism are found in Wicca and the closely related New Age feminist paganism, which see witchcraft as a spiritual system close to pantheism, and, in the New Age version, worship the Goddess or venerate female deities.

Ecofeminists are thus using age-old traditions, combined with new understandings contributed by feminism and environmentalism, to give birth to a different way of viewing the relationship between the human race and the rest of the natural world. They are close to the most controversial part of the environmental movement, Deep Ecology, but they contend that Deep Ecology has missed the point—that our problems stem specifically from the masculine worldview rather than from the more general human-centeredness that Deep Ecology identifies as their source.

DEEP ECOLOGY

The single most controversial movement found within environmentalism today is Deep Ecology—a term coined in 1972 by the Norwegian philospher Arne Naess (b. 1912)—and sometimes called *biocentrism*. It is controversial because it places the rest of nature above humans. In other words, it is acceptable to damage human interests and even human beings in order to protect nature. One of its popularizers, Dave Foreman (b. 1946), the founder of Earth First! puts it as follows: "This philosophy states simply and essentially that all living creatures and communities possess intrinsic value, inherent worth. Natural things live for their own sake, which is another way of saying they have value. Other beings (both animal and plant) and even so-called 'inanimate' objects such as rivers and mountains are not placed here for the convenience of human beings."[14]

The "deepness" of Deep Ecology lies in its rejection of the emphasis on human beings; there are "deeper" values that emphasize the entire biosphere. Nature is not for human use; it has value in and of itself and has rights that need to be protected against human beings. Nature is the standard, and human beings are the problem.

Clearly such a position is not acceptable to many environmentalists. For example, Murray Bookchin attacked Deep Ecology in his *Remaking Society* (1989), arguing that the whole approach of biocentrism is wrongheaded. He contended that it simply reverses the domination of nature by humanity to the domination of humanity by nature and says that the goal should be balance, not domination.

In 1984, Arne Naess and George Sessions (b. 1938) spelled out eight principles to form a platform of Deep Ecology:

1. The flourishing of human and nonhuman life on Earth has intrinsic value. The value of nonhuman life forms is independent of the usefulness these may have for narrow human purposes.

2. Richness and diversity of life forms are values in themselves and contribute to the flourishing of human and nonhuman life on Earth.

---

[14] Dave Foreman, *Confessions of an Eco-Warrior.* New York: Harmony Books, 1991: 26–27.

3. Humans have no right to reduce this richness and diversity except to satisfy vital needs.

4. Present human interference with the nonhuman world is excessive, and the situation is rapidly worsening.

5. The flourishing of human life and cultures is compatible with a substantial decrease of the human population. The flourishing of nonhuman life requires such a decrease.

6. Significant change of life conditions for the better requires change in policies. These affect basic economic, technological, and ideological structures.

7. The ideological change is mainly that of appreciating *life quality* (dwelling in situations of intrinsic value) rather than adhering to a high standard of living. There will be a profound awareness of the differences between big and great.

8. Those who subscribe to the foregoing points have an obligation directly or indirectly to participate in the attempt to implement the necessary changes.[15]

Supporters of Deep Ecology are willing to make two points that most other environmentalists are unwilling to make: that the world's population must be reduced and that the developed world must be willing to significantly reduce its standard of living. In "Population Reduction: An Ecosophical View" (written in 1987), Naess says "The flourishing of human life and cultures is compatible with a substantial decrease of human population. The flourishing of nonhuman life requires such a decrease."[16] A simple point illustrates the problem: If China, with its current population, were to develop to the same level as is found in the developed world today, it would take *all* the world's resources. Since China is rapidly developing, this is becoming a serious issue.

NEO-LUDDITES AND THE UNABOMBER

In April 1996, Theodore J. Kaczynski (b. 1942) was arrested and identified as the so-called Unabomber, who had assembled a number of bombs that killed or injured leading figures in industry and technology. During the bombing campaign, the Unabomber published a manifesto justifying his actions and calling for a return to a more natural, less technological way of life.[17] He and others like him have sometimes been called *neo-Luddites* after Ned Lud (or Ludd), a workman

---

[15] See Arne Naess, *Ecology, Community, and Lifestyle: Outline of an Ecosophy,* David Rothenberg, trans. and ed. Cambridge, England: Cambridge University Press, 1989: 29. Reprinted by permission. Original emphasis. See also Naess, "The Deep Ecology 'Eight Points' Revisited." In *Deep Ecology for the Twenty-First Century.* George Sessions, ed. Boston, MA: Shambhala, 1995: 213–221.

[16] Arne Naess, "Population Reduction: An Ecosophical View." In *Deep Ecology of Wisdom: Explorations in Unities of Nature and Cultures. Selected Papers.* Harold Glasser and Alan Drengson, eds. in cooperation with the author and with assistance from Bill Devall and George Sessions. Vol. X of *The Selected Works of Arne Naess.* 10 vols. Dordrecht, The Netherlands: Springer, 2005: 275.

[17] For the Unabomber Manifesto, see http://www.soci.niu.edu/~critcrim/uni/uni.txt.

who broke stocking frames (mechanical knitting machines) in 1779 because he was convinced that the newly introduced machines were taking away jobs. In the early nineteenth century, a group of workmen calling themselves Luddites broke up textile machinery for the same reason, and contemporary neo-Luddites, like the Unabomber, are also taking direct action against the forces that they see destroying the environment.

MONKEYWRENCHING

In environmentalism in the United States, civil disobedience, or direct action, is frequently called *monkeywrenching* after Edward Abbey's (1927–1989) novels *The Monkey Wrench Gang* (1975) and *Hayduke Lives!* (1990), which describe a group of environmental activists who destroy things they believe are damaging the environment. The Deep Ecology group Earth First! follows the precepts of Abbey's novels, as do those who free animals from experiments or from battery farms, where animals are kept closely penned for life.

The people who are sometimes called *ecowarriors* contend that they are trying to break down the wall between the human and the nonhuman. It is their aim to protect biodiversity through direct action, particularly direct action that will play well to the media. There is no central organization in the groups that practice monkeywrenching; they act either individually or in small groups. A number of ecowarriors practice what they preach by living in voluntary poverty.[18] Many in the environmental movement respect the ecowarriors and monkeywrenching, even though they do not believe monkeywrenching to be a good tactic politically.

A famous case was that of Butterfly (Julia Hill, b. 1974), who lived in a tree she called Luna for 738 days—over two years—to protest logging. This act of monkeywrenching was at least partially successful in that she saved Luna and some other old-growth forest.[19]

ANIMAL RIGHTS

An aspect of the environmental movement that has produced some of the most extreme forms of monkeywrenching, to the extent that a number of groups advocating it have been labeled terrorists, is animal rights. Do animals have rights, and, if so, what are they?

On the whole, environmentalists accept the notion that animals have rights at roughly the same level as human beings—that is, at a minimum they have the right to be treated in the way that humans call *humane*. Others argue that animals have more rights, including the right not to be exploited by human beings. This

---

[18] See Rik Scarce, *Eco-Warriors: Understanding the Radical Environmental Movement.* Chicago: Noble Press, 1990: 5–6.

[19] See Julia Butterfly Hill, *The Legacy of Luna: The Story of a Tree, a Woman, and the Struggle to Save the Redwoods.* New York: HarperCollins, 2000.

Najlah Feanny/Corbis

Peter Singer (b. 1946) is the Ira W. DeCamp Professor of Bioethics at the University Center for Human Values, Princeton University. He is author of *Animal Liberation: A New Ethics for Our Treatment of Animals* (1975); he is credited with beginning the modern animal rights movement and was the first director of the Center for Human Bioethics at Monash University in Australia. He has authored and coauthored several books: *Democracy and Disobedience* (1973, 1994), *Practical Ethics* (1979), *The Reproduction Revolution, Should the Baby Live? Rethinking Life and Death* (1995), *One World: The Ethics of Globalization* (2002), and *The President of Good & Evil: The Ethics of George W. Bush* (2004).

position translates into vegetarianism and the rejection of the use of animals in scientific experimentation. Vegetarianism first became a significant movement in the late nineteenth and early twentieth centuries, primarily for health rather than animal rights reasons.[20]

Animal rights are controversial for some environmentalists, because they think the issue detracts from what they consider more important questions, such as reducing the actual degradation of the environment. But groups such as the Animal Liberation Front (most active in the United Kingdom) and People for the Ethical Treatment of Animals (PETA) believe that animals have the exact same rights as human beings, and these groups are willing to use violence against humans to further their position, and they act on their beliefs. For example, in the United Kingdom in 2004, under threat from animal rights activists, Cambridge University decided not to build an animal research laboratory. Oxford University has continued to build one, but a fake letter purporting to be from the chairman was sent to shareholders of the main construction company suggesting that shareholders sell their shares to avoid being targeted by activists. Shares dropped 19 percent, and the company later withdrew from the project. In addition, a company that supplied concrete for the project had its depots around the country vandalized with extensive damage to equipment. As a result, parts of central Oxford are now off limits to a defined list of activists, who the police keep an eye out for.

An indication of the strength of feeling on the part of some animal rights activists is the death of Barry Horne (1952–2001) while on a hunger strike in prison. Horne is considered a martyr to the animal rights cause. And in 2004 Jerry Vlasek, a Los Angeles trauma surgeon and animal rights activist, was reported to have

---

[20] For histories of vegetarianism, see Colin Spencer, *Vegetarianism: A History.* London: Grub Street, 2000 [Originally published as *The Heretic's Feast.* London: Fourth Estate, 1993]; and Karen Iacobbo, and Michael Iacobbo. *Vegetarian America: A History.* Westport, CT: Praeger, 2004.

argued that the lives of millions of animals could be saved by assassinating scientists who use animals in research.

The phrase *animal liberation* was first used April 5, 1973, as a headline for an article by Peter Singer (b. 1946) in *The New York Review of Books.* Today Singer, now a professor of philosophy at Princeton University, says that despite differences, "We share with them [animals] a capacity to suffer, and this means that they, like us, have interests."[21] Singer, probably the best-known advocate of animal rights, argues against *speciesism,* or "the idea that it is justifiable to give preference to beings simply on the grounds that they are members of the species *Homo sapiens,*"[22] saying that arguments in favor of the species are similar to those favoring one race over another, and we now reject racial arguments.[23]

Most environmentalists take a middle ground where animals are concerned, wanting to protect species deemed endangered—a rapidly growing list worldwide—encouraging the reintroduction of species to traditional habitats where they no longer exist, and recognizing that humans regularly upset any balance among animal species so that some species multiply rapidly to the detriment of others. Many environmentalists believe that this last problem requires human intervention to reestablish balance, while Deep Ecologists point out that it simply demonstrates that humans are the problem and cannot therefore be the solution. Law in the United States has generally followed the more conservative approach.[24]

The concern for animals has influenced behavior and public policy. About half as many animals are used in research today as were used in 1970, and it is easy to buy products, such as cosmetics, that used to be tested on animals but are now labeled as not having been tested in this way. And in the European Union, new rules are in place on how animals destined to be food are treated; for example, providing more space for them to live in is one of the new rules.

On the other hand, the World Trade Organization (WTO) does not allow countries to ban importation of products produced by cruel means, even if those means are illegal. For example, the United States was prohibited from barring the importation of tuna caught in Mexico using drift nets, which kill dolphins.

CURRENT TRENDS

Within environmentalism, most issues are relatively unchanging; but environmentalism has been picked up by theorists of other ideologies, such as political Islam, Liberation Theology, and Marxism, in which it previously played little or no role. In particular, most religions have developed a significant concern with environmentalism.

---

[21] Peter Singer, "Animal Liberation at 30," *New York Review of Books* (May 15, 2003): 23.

[22] Singer, "Animal Liberation at 30," 23.

[23] Singer, "Animal Liberation at 30," 23–24.

[24] Specific laws of importance where animals are concerned include the National Environmental Policy Act of 1969 (83 Stat. 852), the Marine Mammal Protection Act of 1972 (86 Stat. 1027), and the Endangered Species Act of 1973 (87 Stat. 884). For the main laws, see http://www.epa.gov/epahome/laws.htm.

ENVIRONMENTALISM AND RELIGION

As illustrated by the well-known story of St. Francis preaching to the birds, the Hindu prohibition against killing cows, the vegetarianism of Buddhists, and the rituals used by some Native Americans to thank the animal killed in the hunt for providing food, most religions have a long history of sensitivity to environmental issues. And recently these traditions have been reinvigorated or rediscovered by most religions. Also, as was noted in the previous chapter, environmentalism has become an aspect of most liberation theologies.

While all positions are represented, within Christianity most of the positions taken are roughly in the middle of the environmental spectrum and stress sustainability based on respect for God's creation. Much the same can be said about Islam and Judaism with considerable work being done to find textual bases for environmentalism.[25]

The most extreme form of environmental concern based on religious belief is found in Jainism in India, in which one sect known as the *Shvetambara* wear face masks to avoid harming insects or microbes by breathing them in. Most Jainists do not go this far, but overwhelmingly they are vegetarians or even fruitarians, who eat only fruits, nuts, and milk to avoid harming plants.[26]

BIOREGIONALISM AND BIODIVERSITY

A significant issue is what is called *bioregionalism,* which refers to the recognition that no single policy is appropriate to any political area. Each ecological region has its own unique relationship among land, flora, fauna, and the human inhabitants, and this unique relationship needs to be respected.

In addition, each bioregion is biologically diverse, and environmentalists say that such diversity must be maintained and fostered. The particular target of this concern is monoculture agriculture—the tendency to replace diversity with one cash crop, such as wheat or corn. The classic depiction of a bioregion is Aldo Leopold's (1886–1948) *A Sand County Almanac* (1949). A more recent look at bioregionalism is William Least Heat-Moon's (b. 1939) *PrairyErth* (1991), which examines the history and ecology of Chase County, Kansas, an area of 744 square miles, in great depth.

The problems with bioregionalism begin with defining regions; this is difficult, because subregions overlap and may be different for wind, water, waste, and so on. In addition, political boundaries rarely coincide with bioregions, and bioregions exist within the larger ecological system.

---

[25] See, for example, See Richard C. Foltz, Frederick M. Denny, and Azizan Baharuddin, eds. *Islam and Ecology: A Bestowed Trust.* Cambridge, MA: Harvard University Press for the Center for the Study of World Religions, Harvard Divinity School, 2003.

[26] On the Jain, see http://www.intranet.csupomona.edu/~plin/ews430/jain3.html. Accessed April 28, 2008.

GENETICALLY MODIFIED FOODS

A controversial issue today is genetically modified (GM) foods. Advocates say that such foods are identical to natural foods; that horticulturalists and farmers have used GM through selective breeding for centuries; and that it can radically increase food production, solve the problem of world hunger, and produce new drugs and biofuels. Opponents argue that scientific evidence is not yet established for any of these claims, and that until it is, GM crops should be grown only in carefully controlled experiments or not at all. Particularly in the United Kingdom, groups have been destroying such crops when they can be identified. Proponents argue that Americans have been eating GM foods for over 10 years (few Americans know this) with no known side effects. For the last few years, most large European supermarket chains have required their suppliers to certify that no product contains any GM product; large signs in their stores say that everything is, to the extent possible, GM free. Such actions are much less common in the United States. The same approach is growing in restaurants, some of which put notices on their menus that to the extent possible, the food served is GM free.

Biofuels, crop-based fuels that replace or at least partially replace oil, are high on the agendas of governments around the world; but governments are ignoring serious problems. First, since biofuels generally come from GM crops, the same issues that raise questions for some about such crops apply to biofuels also. Second, significant forest areas are already being destroyed to grow such crops. Third, and probably most important, land used for biofuels cannot be used to produce food. At the beginning of 2008, the European Union announced that it was backing off from its previous strong support for biofuels, primarily because of concern over the world food supply; but the other two problems were part of the reason for the changed policy.

As the interest in biofuels indicates, an issue that is of growing concern is that the world appears to be running out of oil, known as *peak oil;* and oil is the basis for huge sectors of the world economy.

GLOBAL WARMING

Internationally, one issue currently a focus of attention is global warming. The concern here is that human activity appears to be producing a gradual increase in average temperatures around the globe. The first warnings were given in 1980 under President Jimmy Carter, who took them seriously, but he was unable to muster the political support to do anything.[27]

Major global temperature fluctuations have occurred in the past, so some disputes exist over the degree to which the observable changes are part of a "normal" cycle or the direct result of human activity; but scientists now overwhelmingly agree that warming is occurring and that it could be disastrous.

---

[27] For a brief history of the early warnings, see James Gustave Speth, *Red Sky in the Morning: America and the Crisis of the Global Environment.* New Haven, CT: Yale University Press, 2004: 1–9.

The concerns range from significant changes in weather patterns that affect agricultural production to the melting of the polar icecaps (clearly happening) and the flooding of coastal cities that are already below sea level, like New Orleans in the United States and Amsterdam in The Netherlands, as well as cities like New York and London that have not previously been thought vulnerable. For example, some years ago, a barrier was built in the Thames River to protect London from unusually high tides coming up the river, and it has worked successfully so far; but it is now thought that the barrier is neither as large nor as strong as will be needed. Other possible effects include much more severe weather, such as hurricane Katrina, in areas not prepared for such storms, and altered ocean currents that could completely change the climate of countries bordering the currents.

What to do about this phenomenon is in dispute. Some scientists believe that it is already too late or nearly so, but most think that agreements to limit damage to the environment can still work. The United Nations Framework Convention on Climate Change, known as the Kyoto Protocol, agreed to the following objective regarding global warming:

> The ultimate objective of this Convention and any related legal instruments that the Conference of the Parties may adopt is to achieve, in accordance with the relevant provisions of the Convention, stabilization of greenhouse gas concentrations in the atmosphere at a level that would prevent dangerous anthropogenic interference with the climate system. Such a level should be achieved within a time-frame sufficient to allow ecosystems to adapt naturally to climate change, to ensure that food production is not threatened and to enable economic development to proceed in a sustainable manner.[28]

Although the United States withdrew from the agreement and convinced some other countries to do so, the protocol has been signed by enough countries for it to go into effect, and it became legally binding on February 16, 2005.

OTHER DEVELOPMENTS AND TRENDS

The Eco-Village Movement A worldwide movement has recently developed to establish small settlements that integrate human life into the natural environment. Such villages already exist throughout the world. The movement stresses learning about how people throughout the world have successfully adapted to their environments.

"An eco-village is a human scale, full-featured settlement which integrates human activities harmlessly into the natural environment, supports healthy human development, and can be continued into the indefinite future"[29] Eco-villages can be urban or rural, although so far most are rural. Urban eco-villages tend to be neighborhoods that have either collectively decided to transform themselves into a sustainable community or were purposely built as such. Most rural eco-villages

---

[28] http://unfccc.int/resource/convkp.html Article 2. Accessed April 29, 2008.

[29] www://www.gaia.org. Accessed April 29, 2008.

have resulted from changes made to existing villages, but a few have been built from scratch.

Sustainability The central issue for most North American environmentalists is sustainability. Sustainability goes to the heart of the ecological approach in that it sees all aspects of the environment, including human beings, as capable of being balanced so that the environment can be sustained, or kept from being significantly damaged or depleted.

One focus of sustainability is energy policy. The Green Party advocates the elimination of nuclear power and the development of renewable energy sources, like solar and wind power. Renewable energy sources are symbolic of the sustainability ethic, because their use is not supposed to damage or deplete any aspect of the environment. But some problems have arisen: wind farms, for example, are quite noisy, and they have been known to kill migratory birds.

This experience reflects one of the two very different ways wind power has been developed. In most countries, as reflected in the use of the phrase "wind farm," large arrays of many turbines are erected in one place and owned by large companies. In Germany, on the other hand—which produces more electricity from wind power than any other country—one, two, or three turbines are erected and owned by local farmers, a group of individuals, or cooperatives. Such small arrays make relatively little noise and are much less likely to kill migratory birds. Also, being locally owned, they are supported by the local community; whereas the large arrays are often opposed locally, and opposition groups delay construction, sometimes for years, or manage to block construction altogether. One of the reasons Germany has been so successful implementing wind power is because of the approach used.

Sustainability is something that environmentalists argue we can all contribute to, and the most obvious thing that people must do is to recycle. But even this apparently simply action raises a number of issues.

In the past three years, I have lived in cities in three different countries. I am writing this in Wellington, New Zealand, where I can recycle almost everything easily. I am required to purchase official rubbish bags to be used for the garbage that cannot be recycled. These cost about $1.20 each (U.S. dollars) and can easily hold the average family's weekly rubbish. Observation suggests that most people use the system conscientiously, although some do not separate out as much for recycling as they could, and some hire a private waste company to avoid the system. Last year I lived in a suburb of London called Islington, where I could recycle about the same things—with the exception of plastic bags—but where I was also asked to separate food waste for treatment due to the problem of methane from such waste in landfills. Many other London areas do not recycle food waste separately, nor do they cover as much in their recycling program. But the system in Islington ensured that waste that could not be recycled was minimal. Costs were covered through local taxes. Observation suggested that most people used the system. The year before that, I lived in St. Louis, Missouri, where I could recycle much the same as the other places, although plastic bags had to be taken to local grocery stores. Costs were again covered by local taxes. Observation suggested that relatively few people used the system. In all three cities, you are asked to recycle certain things separately—electronic equipment, batteries, paint, used oil, and so on—by taking them to a recycling center, and it is illegal in the European Union to dispose of electronic products in normal waste. The effort involved in taking things to a recycling center means that such material is not always treated as it should be, although in Islington anything bulky, like a TV set, would be picked up simply by calling the local council. As suggested by these examples and the EU regulations, different countries are trying different approaches to managing waste, recycling, and the costs involved. One clear problem is that many disabled and elderly people simply cannot handle the accumulated weight of a week's recyclable material and cannot put it out for collection.[30]

Many places are working to eliminate plastic bags, because most are not recycled and are not biodegradable—and 42 billion were used worldwide in January 2008 alone. Ireland taxed such bags, and usage dropped 94 percent within weeks, but few other places have had much success in even getting legislation passed.

One way that many people are responding to sustainability and GM foods is to try to eat more organically grown foods, although there are deep disagreements over what constitutes "organic." The original idea behind organic farming was that it should be small scale and that the distance from the farmer to the consumer should be short; but except at local farmers' markets, this no longer holds true. Much organic food is raised on huge, corporate-owned farms and trucked cross country to distant markets, or even flown in from another country, which has raised the issue of "food miles." To what extent should we take distance traveled and the resulting fuel use into account in purchasing products? But to illustrate the global nature of issues, not buying food and other products brought in from other countries will damage the already fragile economies of the developing world, a point most environmentalists make.[31]

On the morning that I sat down to write this chapter, the news carried a warning that the plants that are the basis for something like 50 percent of the world's medicine are under threat as a result of environmental damage. Also, two environmental organizations, Greenpeace and the Sea Shepherd Conservation Society, were chasing the Japanese whaling fleet around the waters of the Antarctic in an attempt to stop the slaughter of a thousand whales.[32] Environmental and animal rights issues are at the forefront of the daily news, and more and more people are seeing these issues as central to their world view, either as the primary focus or as an important aspect of a broader belief system.

It should also be noted that the conflict in Darfur has been called the *first* climate change war by the current Secretary-General of the United Nations, Ban Ki-moon (b. 1944), among many others. A drought hit the Darfur region of Sudan in the 1980s and has never really ended. This displaced entire populations of people and set up a conflict over scarcer and scarcer resources. Thus significant, long-term climate change has serious implications for economic and political stability.

---

[30] A number of websites list things citizens can do regarding the environment. See, for example, http://TheWebofHope.com, http://www.redskyatmorning.com, and http://www.handbookforchange.org.

[31] On organic farming, see Albert Howard, *An Agricultural Testament.* Oxford, England: Oxford University Press, 1940.

[32] Greenpeace was founded in 1971 by Canadian environmental activists; Sea Shepherd was founded in 1977 by Paul Watson (b. 1950) who is a hero in monkeywrenching circles. The two organizations often disagree on tactics.

SUGGESTED READING

Environmentalism

Some Classic Works

Abbey, Edward. *The Monkey Wrench Gang.* Philadelphia: J.B. Lippincott, 1975. Reprinted New York: HarperCollins, 2006.

Berry, Wendell. "Think Little." *The Last Whole Earth Catalogue.* Menlo Park, CA: Portola Institute, 1971: 24–25. Influential article.

Bookchin, Murray. *Toward an Ecological Society.* Montreal: Black Rose Books, 1980.

Callenbach, Ernest. *Ecotopia: The Notebooks and Reports of William Weston.* Berkeley, CA: Banyan Tree Books, 1975.

Carson, Rachel. *Silent Spring.* 40th anniversary ed. Boston: Houghton Mifflin, 2002.

Club of Rome. *The Limits to Growth.* 2nd ed. New York: Universe Books, 1974.

Ehrlich, Paul. *The Population Bomb.* Revised and expanded. ed. New York: Ballantine, 1989.

Foreman, Dave. *Confessions of an Eco Warrior.* New York: Harmony Books, 1991.

Gorz, André. *Ecology as Politics.* Patsy Vigderman, and Jonathan Cloud, trans. Boston: South End Press, 1980. U.K. ed. London: Pluto Press, 1983.

Illich, Ivan. *Energy and Equity.* London: Calder & Boyars, 1974.

Leopold, Aldo. *A Sand County Almanac, and Sketches Here and There.* New York: Oxford University Press, 1949. Reprinted, New York: Oxford University Press, 1987.

Naess, Arne. *Ecology, Community and Lifestyle: Outline of an Ecosophy.* David Rothenberg, trans. Cambridge, England: Cambridge University Press, 1989. Originally published in Norwegian in 1976.

Passmore, John. *Man's Responsibility for Nature: Ecological Problems and Western Traditions.* 2nd ed. London: Duckworth, 1980. A classic of environmental theory.

Schumacher E. F. [Ernst Friedrich]. *Small Is Beautiful: A Study of Economics as If People Mattered.* London: Blond and Briggs, 1973.

World Commission on Environment and Development. *Our Common Future* [Known as the *Brundtland Report*]. New York: Oxford University Press, 1987. Beginning of the movement for sustainable growth.

Books and Articles

Abbey, Edward. *Hayduke Lives!* Boston: Little, Brown, 1990.

Attfield, Robin. *Environmental Ethics: An Overview for the Twenty-First Century.* Cambridge, England: Polity, 2003.

Alaimo, Stacy. *Undomesticated Ground: Recasting Nature as Feminist Space.* Ithaca, NY: Cornell University Press, 2000.

Barry, John, and Robyn Eckersley, eds. *The State and the Global Ecological Crisis.* Cambridge, MA: MIT Press, 2005.

Best, Steven, and Anthony J. Nocella, II, eds. *Igniting a Revolution: Voices In Defense of the Earth.* Oakland, CA: AK Press, 2006. Broad ranging collection generally from the Left of the environmental movement.

Binfield, Kevin, ed. *Writings of the Luddites.* Baltimore: Johns Hopkins University Press, 2004.

Bookchin, Murray. *The Ecology of Freedom: The Emergence and Dissolution of Hierarchy.* Palo Alto, CA: Chesire Books, 1982. Reprinted, Oakland, CA: AK Press, 2005.

Broers, Alec. *The Triumph of Technology. The BBC Reith Lectures 2005.* Cambridge, England: Cambridge University Press, 2005. He argues that a "green" position must recognize that that the solution to pollution and other problems caused by technology will necessarily be technological (p. 83).

Bullard, Robert D., ed. *The Quest for Environmental Justice: Human Rights and the Politics of Pollution.* San Francisco, CA: Sierra Club Books, 2005.

Caldecott, Helen. *Nuclear Power is Not the Answer.* London: New Press, 2006. Argues against the use of nuclear power to generate electricity, noting that it is not as "clean and green" as its advocates contend.

Callenbach, Ernest. *Ecotopia Emerging.* Berkeley, CA: Banyan Tree Books, 1981.

———. *Ecotopia: A Pocket Guide.* Berkeley: University of California Press, 1998. Popular guide to environmentalism.

Carter, Neil. *The Politics of the Environment: Ideas, Activism, Policy.* 2nd ed. Cambridge, England: Cambridge University Press, 2007.

Davis, John, ed. *The Earth First! Reader: Ten Years of Environmental Radicalism.* Salt Lake City: Gibbs Smith, 1991.

Dobson, Andrew. *Green Political Thought.* 4th ed. London: Routledge, 2007.

Durant, Robert F., Daniel J. Fiorino, and Rosemary O'Leary, eds. *Environmental Governance Reconsidered: Challenges, Choices, and Opportunities.* Cambridge, MA: MIT Press, 2004.

Dryzek, John, David Downes, Christian Hunold, and David Schlosberg with Hans-Kristian Hernes. *Green States and Social Movements: Environmentalism in the United States, United Kingdom, Germany, and Norway.* Oxford, England: Oxford University Press, 2003.

Eaton, Heather, and Lois Ann Lorentzen, eds. *Ecofeminism and Globalization: Exploring Culture, Context, and Religion.* Lanham, MD: Rowman & Littlefield, 2003.

Eckersley, Robyn. *The Green State: Rethinking Democracy and Sovereignty.* Cambridge, MA: MIT Press, 2004.

Environmental Ethics. Vol. 1:1 to the present (Founded 1979).

Environmental Politics. Vol. 1:1 to the present (Founded 1992)

Ethics and the Environment. Vol. 1:1 to the present (Founded 1996).

Flippen, J. Brooks. *Conservative Conservationist: Russell E. Train and the Emergence of American Environmentalism.* Baton Rouge: Louisiana State University Press, 2006.

Foltz, Richard C., Frederick M. Denny, and Azizan Baharuddin, eds. *Islam and Ecology: A Bestowed Trust.* Cambridge, MA: Harvard University Press for the Center for the Study of World Religions, Harvard Divinity School, 2003.

Fromartz, Samuel. *Organic, Inc.: Natural Foods and How They Grow.* Orlando, FL: Harcourt, 2004.

Gebara, Ivone. *Longing for Running Water: Ecofeminism and Liberation.* David Molineaux, trans. Minneapolis, MN: Fortress, 1999. Theological approach.

Goldstein, Robert Jay. *Ecology and Environmental Ethics: Green Wood in the Bundle of Sticks.* Aldershot, England: Ashgate, 2004. Environmental law.

Gottlieb, Roger S. *A Greener Faith: Religious Environmentalism and Our Planet's Future.* Oxford, England: Oxford University Press, 2006.

———, ed. *This Sacred Earth: Religion, Nature and Environment.* 2nd ed. New York: Routledge, 2004.

Grey, Mary C. *Sacred Longings: Ecofeminist Theology and Globalization.* London: SCM Press, 2003. U.S. ed. as *Sacred Longings: The Ecological Spirit and Global Culture.* Minneapolis, MN: Fortress Press, 2004.

Grim, John A., ed. *Indigenous Traditions and Ecology: The Interbreeding of Cosmology and Community.* Cambridge, MA: Harvard University Press for the Center for the Study of World Religions, Harvard Divinity School, 2001.

Gupta, Joyeeta. *Our Simmering Planet: What to Do about Global Warming.* London: Zed Books/Dhaka, Bangladesh: University Press/Bangkok, Thailand: White Lotus/Halifax, NS, Canada: Fernwood Publishing/Cape Town, South Africa: David Philip/Bangalore, India: Books for Change, 2001.

Guthman, Julie. *Agrarian Dreams: The Paradox of Organic Farming in California.* Berkeley: University of California Press, 2004. Problems of industrial organic farming.

Hawken, Paul. *Blessed Unrest: How the Largest Movement in the World Came into Being and Why No One Saw It Coming.* New York: Viking, 2007. See http:// www.wiserearth.org, which lists over 100,000 organizations.

Heinberg, Richard. *The Party's Over: Oil, War, and the Fate of Industrial Societies.* 2nd ed. with an "Afterword to the Revised Edition" (pp. 263–274). Gabriola Island, BC, Canada: New Society Publishers, 2005.

Hester, Randolph T. *Design for Ecological Democracy.* Cambridge, MA: MIT Press, 2006. Ecological thinking applied to city planning.

Hillel, Daniel. *The Natural History of the Bible: An Environmental Exploration of the Hebrew Scriptures.* New York: Columbia University Press, 2006.

Hitchcock, Darcy, and Marshal Willard. *The Business Guide to Sustainability: Practical Strategies and Tools for Organizations.* London: Earthscan, 2006. A pro-environment, business oriented guidebook.

Howard, Albert. *An Agricultural Testament* Oxford, England: Oxford University Press, 1940. Twentieth century origin of the organic agriculture movement.

Kearns, Laurel, and Catherine Keller, eds. *Ecospirit: Religions and Philosophies for the Earth.* New York: Fordham University Press, 2007. Large collection (644 pages) of primarily original essays.

Kirk, Andrew G. *Counterculture Green: The "Whole Earth Catalog" and American Environmentalism.* Lawrence: University Press of Kansas, 2007.

Kovel, Joel. *The Enemy of Nature: The End of Capitalism at the End of the World.* 2nd ed. London: Zed Books/Halifax, NS, Canada: Fernwood Publishing, 2007.

Pui-lan, Kwok. "Ecology and Christology." *Feminist Theology,* Vol. 15 (May 1997): 113–125.

Lazarus, Richard J. *The Making of Environmental Law.* Chicago: University of Chicago Press, 2004. In the United States.

Lodge, David M., and Christopher Hamlin, eds. *Religion and the New Ecology: Environmental Responsibility in a World in Flux.* Notre Dame, IN: University of Notre Dame Press, 2006. Christian only.

Lyon, Thomas P., and John W. Maxwell. *Corporate Environmentalism and Public Policy.* Cambridge, England: Cambridge University Press, 2004.

Maathai, Wangari Muta. *Unbowed: A Memoir.* London: William Heinemann, 2007. Winner of the 2004 Nobel Peace Prize.

Muir, John. *The Velvet Monkey Wrench.* Santa Fe, NM: John Muir Publications, 1975.

Nadeau, Robert L. *The Environmental Endgame: Mainstream Economics, Ecological Disaster, and Human Survival.* New Brunswick, NJ: Rutgers University Press, 2006.

Naess, Arne. *The Selected Works of Arne Naess.* 10 vols. Dordrecht, The Netherlands: Springer, 2005. Vol. X is entitled *Deep Ecology of Wisdom: Explorations in Unities of Nature and Cultures. Selected Papers.* Harold Glasser, and Alan Drengson, eds., in cooperation with the author and with assistance from Bill Devall and George Sessions.

Norton, Bryan G. *Sustainability: A Philosophy of Adaptive Ecosystem Management.* Chicago: University of Chicago Press, 2005.

Paehlke, Robert C. *Democracy's Dilemma: Environment, Social Equity, and the Global Economy.* Cambridge, MA: MIT Press, 2003.

Parkins, Wendy, and Geoffrey Craig. *Slow Living.* Oxford, England: Berg, 2006.

Robbins, Paul. *Political Ecology: A Critical Introduction.* Malden, MA: Blackwell, 2004. Argues that environmental decisions are always political and that political decisions not directly concerned with the environment still affect it.

Ruether, Rosemary Radford, ed. *Women Healing Earth: Third World Women on Ecology, Feminism, and Religion.* Maryknoll, NY: Orbis Books, 1996. U.K. ed. London: SCM Press, 1996. Writings from Africa, Asia, and Latin America on Christian ecofeminism with some material on indigenous religions and the environment.

Sessions, George, ed. *Deep Ecology for the Twenty-First Century* [Cover adds *Readings on the Philosophy and Practice of the New Environmentalism*]. Boston, MA: Shambhala, 1995. See Arne Naess, "The Deep Ecology 'Eight Points' Revisited" (pp. 213–221). First published in this volume.

Smith, Kimberly K. *African American Environmental Thought.* Lawrence: University Press of Kansas, 2007.

Stein, Rachel, ed. *New Perspectives on Environmental Justice: Gender, Sexuality, and Activism.* New Brunswick, NJ: Rutgers University Press, 2004.

Stern, Nicholas. *The Economics of Climate Change: The Stern Review.* Cambridge, England: Cambridge University Press, 2007.

Talshir, Gayil. *The Political Ideology of Green Parties: From the Politics of Nature to Redefining the Nature of Politics.* London: Palgrave Macmillan, 2002.

Thomson, Jennifer A. *Seeds for the Future: The Impact of Genetically Modified Crops on the Environment.* Ithaca, NY: Cornell University Press, 2007. Originally published as *GM Crops: The Impact and the Potential.* Collingwood, Vic, Australia: CSIRO Publishing, 2006. Generally positive.

Tirosh-Samuelson, Hava, ed. *Judaism and Ecology: Created World and Revealed World.* Cambridge, MA: Harvard University Press for the Center for the Study of World Religions, Harvard Divinity School, 2002.

Trapese Collective, ed. *Do It Yourself: A Handbook for Changing Our World.* London: Pluto Press, 2007. Specific things individuals and small groups can do regarding the environment.

Turner, Fred. *From Counterculture to Cyberculture: Stewart Brand, the Whole Earth Network, and the Rise of Digital Utopianism.* Chicago: University of Chicago Press, 2006.

Weaver, Jace, ed. *Defending Mother Earth: Native American Perspectives on Environmental Justice.* Maryknoll, NY: Orbis Books, 1996.

Animal Rights

Some Classic Works

Singer, Peter. *Animal Liberation.* 2nd ed. New York: New York Review of Books, 1990.

———, ed. *In Defense of Animals: The Second Wave.* Malden, MA: Blackwell, 2006. New edition reflecting the greater radicalism of the animal rights movement.

Books and Articles

Armstrong, Susan J., and Richard G. Botzler, eds. *The Animal Ethics Reader.* London: Routledge, 2003.

Cavalieri, Paola. *The Animal Question: Why Nonhuman Animals Deserve Human Rights.* Catherine Woollard, trans. Revised by the author. Oxford, England: Oxford University Press, 2001.

Franklin, Julian H. *Animal Rights and Moral Philosophy.* New York: Columbia University Press, 2005.

Garner, Robert. *Animal Ethics.* Cambridge, England: Polity, 2005. Overview.

———. *The Political Theory of Animal Rights.* Manchester: Manchester University Press, 2005. Discusses liberalism.

Singer, Peter. "Animal Liberation at 30." *New York Review of Books* (May 15, 2003): 23–26.

———. *The Animal Liberation Movement: Its Philosophy, Its Achievements, and Its Future.* Nottingham, England: Old Hammond, 2000.

Singer, Peter, and Jim Mason. *The Way We Eat: Why Our Food Choices Matter.* Emmaus, PA: Rodale, 2006. U.K. ed. *Eating: What We Eat and Why It Matters.* London: Arrow, 2006.

Sunstein, Cass R., and Martha C. Nussbaum, eds. *Animal Rights: Current Debates and New Directions.* New York: Oxford University Press, 2004.

Websites

Environmentalism

Earth Island Institute: http://www.earthisland.org

Friends of the Earth: http://www.foe.org

Future 500: http://www.globalfutures.org

The Gaia Trust: http://www.gaia.org

Green Alliance: http://www.greenalliance.org.uk

Green Party of the United States: http://www.gp.org

Greenpeace: http://www.greenpeace.org

National Council for Science and the Environment: http://www.ncseonline.org

The Organic Consumers Association: http://www.purefood.org

Sierra Club: http://www.sierraclub.org

Student Environmental Action Coalition: http://www.seac.org

Unabomber Manifesto: http://www.soci.niu.edu/~critcrim/uni/uni.txt

Animal Rights

Animal Concerns Community: http://www.animalconcerns.org

Animal Liberation Front: http://www.animalliberationfront.com

Animal Rights Canada: http://www.animalrightscanada.com

Animal Rights FAQ (includes lists of organizations): http://www.animal-rights.com

Feminists for Animal Rights. An Ecofeminist Alliance: http://www.farinc.org

People for the Ethical Treatment of Animals: http://www.peta.org

The Sea Shepherd Conservation Society: http://www.seashepherd.org

14

Conclusion

Anumber of ideologies have been discussed in this book, and major disagreements and differences of opinion have been described in connection
with all of them. Each has a clear core of beliefs and a number of variants.
In conclusion, it will be instructive to compare these ideologies with regard to
the questions in Chapter 1 and with the various parts of the social system described there. Any comparison must be general but must attempt to avoid being
too broad and therefore meaningless. A number of points will be relevant only to
certain ideologies.

HUMAN NATURE

The first question concerns human nature; thus we ask, (a) What are the basic
characteristics of human beings as human beings? and (b) What effect does human
nature have on the political system? The first question is answered in surpris-
ingly similar ways by all the ideologies except fascism and national socialism. In
Marxism, democracy, anarchism, and feminism we find the position that human
beings are capable of a high degree of community spirit and good feeling toward other humans. Hate and fear are stressed in fascism and national socialism.
Also underlying much of Marxism, democracy, and anarchism is a belief that
humans are fundamentally rational. This is not found in nationalism, fascism,
and national socialism; instead, our irrational side is stressed. Feminism attempts

to recognize both sides. Liberation Theology is also balanced because it recognizes the Christian assumption of original sin but stresses the liberating nature of Christ's message. Both Islam and environmentalism have a mixed view of human nature; people are capable of both great good and great evil. Globalization does not really address the issue.

The question about the effect of human nature on the political system is not answered directly or conclusively by most of the ideologies. In most of the ideologies, the concern is with the effect on people of changes in the political system. This is most obvious in anarchism: the development of a noncoercive society will allow the growth of a better, more sociable human being. In Marxism, the abolition of class will lead to the development of a more cooperative human being. Democracy has the most complex and sophisticated approach. The whole complex of ideas focusing on freedom with limits, representation with regular checks by voters, and general equality is based on the position that each individual is capable of both high-minded self-sacrifice and corruption, and that the human being is an extremely complex creature who cannot be encompassed by a unidimensional system.

ORIGINS

The second set of questions—the origin of society and government or the state—is, on the whole, ignored. I have indicated that both traditional Marxism and certain arguments for democracy discuss these origins, but contemporary political ideologies are not often concerned with such questions for the simple reason that most people view them as irrelevant. People everywhere find themselves in society and ruled by government; therefore, the question of how this came about does not seem important.

Anarchist thinkers, because they reject the notion of government and the state, do consider this question. Generally, the conclusion is that humans at some time or other formed a society for protection. Some anarchists argue that government was also formed out of society for protection or security. Others argue that government came about simply by usurpation on the part of some group. Each argument accepts society as a necessary form of cooperation, whereas government is rejected as unnecessary, and it should, and can, be done away with, because it stifles our ability to cooperate.

OBLIGATION

Questions in the third set, centering on political obligation, are answered by about half the ideologies, with the exceptions being nationalism, globalization, feminism, Liberation Theology, and environmentalism, which ignore the questions as irrelevant to their central concerns. But in some ideologies, such as democracy, the answers are so diverse and varied that it is difficult even to summarize them, although it may be this very complexity that makes democracy so successful.

Why do people obey the government, and why should they? Or, in order to include anarchism, should they obey at all? Anarchism gives the simplest answer: there is no reason why anyone should obey government. For fascists and national socialists, government must be obeyed because it is the government—because the system of leadership demands obedience. People must obey because it is their role to obey. Marxists argue that the dictatorship of the proletariat should be obeyed because it provides security and economic benefits in the period of transition from bourgeois society to a full communist society. At the same time, Marxists contend that the individual living under capitalism has no specific obligation to obey; on the contrary, the proletariat has an obligation to attempt to overthrow capitalism.

Democracy justifies obedience in a variety of ways, some of which are similar to the reasons given in other ideologies. These reasons may be summarized as follows: (1) security, (2) other benefits, (3) requirement by the community justifying obedience, and (4) the ability of citizens to use the system to bring about fundamental change. The fourth reason is, of course, the central characteristic of democracy. Democracy raises other problems with regard to revolution and the possibility of disobedience. Some contemporary democratic theory accepts the idea of disobedience without revolution as a safety value when the system fails to respond the serious problems. Most democratic ideology rejects revolution, because citizens can make changes without one. Islamism is a theocracy with God's will interpreted by the ruler; therefore, the citizen clearly must obey. The other political ideologies of Islam mostly lean to the same answers as found in democracy.

LAW

The fourth set of questions concerns law. All the ideologies, with the exception of anarchism, consider law to be a major means of instituting and maintaining the social norms they support. And even some anarchists see a role for policies and procedures that have been agreed upon by the members of the community. The sources of law, though, differ greatly among the ideologies. In fascism and national socialism, the will of the leader is the source of law. In Marxism, during the dictatorship of the proletariat, law should reflect the needs of the proletariat as the dominant class, but in fact, law generally comes from the political leaders. In all forms of democracy, law should come from the people, either directly or through representatives. An area of difference that affects democracy, as well as most of the other ideologies, is how hard law should be to make and change. For some, law should be easy to make or change to reflect the changing needs of the leadership or the people. For many, fundamental sets of laws or constitutions should be hard to change so as to maintain the social norms established by the ideology or, in many forms of democracy, to protect the liberties of citizens. Liberals believe that it is right to use law to bring about social change; conservatives are less certain this is desirable and stress respect for tradition, which includes respect for the law. The various ideologies of Islam differ on whether or not Islamic law, the *Shari'a,* should become the law of the land and, of equal importance, who should interpret it. Islamism, advocating a theocracy, wants the *Shari'a* established as the law and religious leaders as its interpreters.

LIBERTY

The fifth set of questions concerns liberty. Marxists argue that under full communism, the individual has complete liberty. Under the dictatorship of the proletariat, the individual must have sharply curtailed liberty in order to achieve the transition from capitalism to the dictatorship of the proletariat and then to full communism. Fascists and national socialists consider the question of liberty irrelevant. The individual's freedom, such as it is, is found entirely in giving himself or herself to the state. Anarchism, because it has no government, offers a system of complete liberty except as people choose to limit themselves as part of a cooperative endeavor. Liberation Theology stresses the need to develop liberty as a means of helping the oppressed. There is no concept of freedom in Islamism, but other political ideologies of Islam have begun to develop a notion of liberty.

Democracy again is the most complicated of the ideologies because it provides limited liberty within the system. The problem for democracy is how to maintain a system in which the people are willing and able to limit themselves, both individually and through the legal system, so the liberty of one individual does not infringe on the liberty of another. Democratic capitalists also stress economic freedom. Liberty is central to liberalism but not as important to traditional conservatives.

Almost equally complex is feminism. Reform feminists argue that freedom is all that is really needed, but most feminists are ambivalent. Is pornography acceptable? Is advertising that exploits women acceptable? Hence most feminists, while arguing for the basic freedoms, feel that some limitations may be necessary, particularly to overcome the mental abuse that women suffer.

EQUALITY

The sixth set of questions concerns equality. Clearly fascists and national socialists reject any form of equality. In anarchism all individuals should be equal in most ways, but considerable debate exists among anarchists over whether economic equality is a worthwhile goal. Marxists stress social equality and include political equality in the ideal of full communism. In the period of the dictatorship of the proletariat, social equality would exist, but political equality would not because of the need for strong power at the top. Limited economic equality is a goal of Marxism in that Marxists argue for overcoming the extremes of economic inequality. In democracy, political and legal equality are emphasized; democratic capitalism stresses equality of opportunity, and democratic socialism stresses greater economic equality. Feminists generally favor all forms of equality. Reform feminists would exclude economic equality and stress equality of opportunity. Liberation Theology stresses the need to overcome inequality. Social equality has become a more important focus in a number of ideologies with democracy and feminism particularly concerned with the issue. Islamism assumes a hierarchical society; people are equal in the eyes of God but not in society. The other Islamic ideologies would simply have a less hierarchical society.

COMMUNITY

The seventh set of questions concerns community, which is reemerging as a central concern of some ideologies. In nationalism, developmental socialism, and Islam, community is and always has been a major component of the belief system. In fascism and national socialism, the idea of the nation has elements of community, as does the vision of community-based authority in full communism. And of course, community is at the core of communitarianism. Many of the other ideologies tend to downplay community and stress individual fulfillment.

POWER

The eighth set of questions relates to power. Power for the Marxist varies, depending on whether one is concerned with the dictatorship of the proletariat or full communism. In full communism, power would be spread among all individuals. In the dictatorship of the proletariat, power rests in the hands of a few at the very top of the Communist party. Some thinkers contend that power resides in the party as such, but it is more accurate to see it in the hands of a few. Fascists and national socialists also invest power in the hands of very few people or one individual at the top. Supporters of democracy argue that power is held collectively by all citizens, but it is more accurate to see power in the hands of those actively concerned with the governmental process and working within it. There is no focus on power in anarchism; power is found in each individual. Many feminists argue for the empowerment of women as a means of balancing male power, but others argue for a transformation of our whole notion of power to one based on competence and cooperation rather than dominance. Liberation Theologians argue for empowerment of the poor and oppressed. They want power in the sense of domination replaced with a concept of social or communal power. In Islamism no single attitude about power can be found; Islamists and Islamic liberals differ fundamentally, as do Sunnis and Shiites.

JUSTICE

The next two sets of questions, justice and the end of society or government, may be conveniently collapsed together; because in each ideology, justice will be found by achieving the ends of the ideology or the ends of the society or government. In Marxism, justice is found in the proletariat collectively owning the means of production and distribution. For the democrat, justice is found in the individual citizen, controlling his or her own destiny through the political system with different emphases in democratic capitalism and democratic socialism. For the fascist and national socialist, justice is found in the individual giving up himself or herself willingly and thoroughly to the state. For the anarchist, justice is found in the end of government and the achievement of a society based on the individual, usually within a community. For the feminist and Liberation Theologian, justice is found in a truly free and equal society. In Islamism most believers find justice in the application of the *Shari'a* or Islamic law.

STRUCTURE

The structural characteristics of government are almost irrelevant in nationalism, anarchism, full communism, feminism, and environmentalism. The other ideologies include answers to the questions but not in any way that makes valid generalization possible, except that in democracy, governmental structure is seen as a way of ensuring that power is limited.

RELIGION

Obviously the political ideologies of Islam and the liberation theologies put religion at the center of their belief systems; but Islamism proposes a theocracy, and liberal Islam and the various liberation theologies tend toward separation of church and state with religion playing the central role of establishing the principles on which the state should operate. Marxism and most anarchists reject religion altogether while still appreciating that it contains valuable ethical principles. Fascism and national socialism also reject any political influence of religion, but they both believe that religion could be co-opted to support their beliefs. All the other ideologies have a mixed position regarding the relationship between religion and government, but all of them consider religious principles and ideas of fundamental importance in establishing the content of their beliefs.

In the answers to these questions, we are able to see the variety of positions taken on fundamental political questions. The answers vary considerably from ideology to ideology, but the answers are also sometimes divergent even within a given ideology. This overview gives us some basis for comparing the political aspects of the ideologies. In order to understand more fully the value system in each ideology, we must look at certain other social institutions. Therefore, a second stage of comparing the ideologies must look at these other subsystems of the social system.

SOCIAL STRATIFICATION AND MOBILITY

The first is the social stratification and mobility system. Marxists argue that there will be no social stratification and hence no social mobility system within full communism. Under the dictatorship of the proletariat, the stratification system would be that between the proletariat and the remnants of the classes that are disappearing, like the bourgeoisie and the peasantry. The only form of mobility would be for the bourgeoisie and the peasantry to move into the proletariat.

In practice, however, the dictatorship of the proletariat produced a new social stratification system that established a class of technocrats who operated the government, the Communist party, and the various important institutions of the country. The democratic social stratification and mobility system is in practice based primarily on money and education. The primary means of mobility in the democratic system is also education and money. In fascism and national socialism, stratification is based on race, indications of loyalty to the nation, and service in the party and to the state. Mobility is based on the same standards. In anarchism, there should be no social stratification and hence no mobility system is needed. Feminists are mostly concerned with removing racial, sexual, and gender orientation barriers from the operation of the social mobility system. Liberation Theology is directed at removing barriers to social advancement. Islamism has a highly structured social stratification system based on birth, wealth, and learning. Liberal Muslims question some of the ways Islamic societies are stratified.

SOCIALIZATION

The socialization system is made up of various institutions in society that help give an individual the values of that society. The primary institutions of socialization are the family, the education system, the religious system, and, in modern societies, the mass media. Children gain ideas about life before they are capable of articulating those ideas themselves. They hear their parents give positive or negative connotations to certain words and phrases the children can identify but for which they have no meaning.

Marxists, fascists, and national socialists almost without exception hold that the mass media must be carefully controlled to present a positive picture of the system. Anarchists tend to argue for completely unlimited mass media. Democracy comes close to this, limiting the media only in cases of libel and then only in relatively rare cases, although this varies radically from country to country. Democracies have found a greater problem, though, in the unwillingness of government officials to give the mass media complete information, thus attempting to control the media.

Marxism, fascism, and national socialism also include control of the other institutions of socialization. Marxists argue for control of religion, because religion is seen as a direct threat to the ideology. Fascists and national socialists tend, on the other hand, to view religion as positive support for the nationalism that is so important to those ideologies, and in many cases, the religious system supported fascism and national socialism or at least did not actually oppose them. This remains a controversial issue within the Roman Catholic Church. In anarchism, little concern is given to controlling religion, although in anarchism, one often finds an antipathy toward religion. Many anarchists believe that religion consistently supports the state, and thus religion is opposed to the anarchist philosophy. Most, but not all, democratic ideologies and democratic systems separate the religious system and the political system. At the same time, in democracy religion is often a support for the political system.

In every ideology the educational system is used to directly support the ideology. For all the ideologies, education is the most potent force of socialization; therefore the educational system must be used to support the values of the society or the ideology. On the other hand, only feminism and, to a lesser extent, anarchism say much about changing the family system. It is probably better policy to attempt to imbue parents with the values one wishes to have passed on to the children; if the parents accept the values, they will be automatically passed on to the children. Therefore, it is not really necessary to tamper with the family system. Clearly the greatest concern of Liberation Theology is changing the churches as a means of socialization. It wants to change other mechanisms of socialization also, but churches are its primary target.

Most feminists feel a need for a completely transformed socialization system. Education, the family, religion, and the mass media must not merely be open to women, but they must be changed so that no one will be socialized into submission. In this sense feminism is potentially the most radical of contemporary ideologies.

Religion, the family, and the mosque are the centers of society in Islam; socialization takes place there first, and education plays a central role. For Islamists socialization must be tightly controlled to ensure that that people are given the correct values. Other Muslims are more open to variety and thus are open to less control of the socialization process.

THE ECONOMIC SYSTEM

In each of the ideologies we have discussed, a considerable amount of time has been spent analyzing the economic system. It is not necessary to repeat those arguments here, only to say that each ideology differs regarding the economic system. Marxist Communism combines a state socialist economic system with an authoritarian political system, but other Marxists see the possibility of freer economic and political systems. Democracy combines either a capitalist or a socialist economic system with its political system, although there are variations within each. Fascism and national socialism have authoritarian political systems combined with modified capitalist systems. Developmental socialism is connected to a wide variety of political systems, anarchists are unclear on the appropriate system, and feminists are deeply divided on economic questions. Liberation Theology is primarily concerned with the results of the economic system, not the means, but it is accurate to say that it leans heavily toward socialism. Islamism encourages private property with a religious duty of charity. The advocates of globalization stress a capitalism economic system and free trade in particular; it opponents come from a wide variety of economic positions and are particularly concerned with the effects of globalization.

THE POLITICAL SYSTEM

The political system is the mechanism that makes binding decisions on society, and even an anarchist society would have to make some such decisions. Today almost all ideologies at least pay lip service to democracy; the only exceptions are fascism and national socialism and some positions within Islamism. Arguments center mostly around the degree of democracy, which relates back to the question of power and to what extent it should be representative or participatory.

It is noteworthy that environmentalism, nationalism, and globalization have few positions that fit the categories used here. This fact suggests that environmentalism is still developing the attributes of an ideology and that globalization and nationalism are what Michael Freeden calls "thin" ideologies, which—except for certain core principles—take their characteristics from the other ideologies.

These comments have been very general, but they provide some basis for comparing ideologies. It is important for a student of contemporary political ideologies to understand both the similarities and differences among these ideologies. We do not know what the future holds for any of them, but it is important for us to understand what each of these ideologies accepts so we will be able to evaluate them objectively.

In conclusion, I hope the reader will reflect carefully on the challenges that the variety of belief systems poses for his or her own beliefs. What can be expected of humanity in the future? Are we rational, capable of determining a desirable future and working for it? Or are we irrational, incapable of so choosing or unwilling to work for our goals? Must humans be coerced, or can we cooperate without coercion? Can humanity achieve a meaningful equality, or is equality of any sort an impossible dream? Can humans be free or is freedom a dangerous fantasy? All these questions and many others are continually being answered. We must reflect on the society in which we want to live. We must ask ourselves in what ways we are affected by ideologies. Do we have an ideology? What are its elements? How does it affect us? How do the ideologies held by others affect us? The answers to all these questions will affect how we spend our lives.

Glossary

This glossary provides a short definition of certain terms used in the text to help the reader better understand the discussion. Many terms are discussed at some length, and the reader should refer to the index to locate that discussion. An asterisk identifies indexed terms. Because some words have different meanings in different ideologies, it is important when using the index to follow the word as it appears in each ideology.

Accountability   Various systems in which public officials, both elected and nonelected, are required to give an accounting of their performance in fiscal and other matters.

Al Qaeda   Islamic terrorist group.

Alienation   Estrangement or being cut off.

***Anarchism**   A system of social order achieved without government.

Antiglobalization   Opposition to the perceived dominance of free-market capitalism throughout the world.

Apartheid   An Afrikaans word, now part of most languages, that refers to the extreme form of racial separation practiced in the Republic of South Africa.

Aristocracy   Originally meant "rule by the few best;" it now means "rule by the few," usually with the implication of a hereditary few.

Authority   Legitimate power (*see* Power).

Ayatollah   A Shiite title meaning "sign of God."

Biocentrism   A theory that argues that the biosphere should be the focus of value as opposed to human beings being the focus (called *anthropocentrism*).

Bourgeoisie   In Marxism, refers to the owners of the means of production as contrasted to the proletariat (*see* Proletariat), who have only their labor power to sell. More generally used to refer to the property-owning middle class.

Bureaucracy   The set of nonelected public officials or administrators in any political system.

Burqa   Clothing that covers a woman's body from the top of the head to the ground with only a mesh opening over the eyes.

Caliph   Successor (Sunni Islam).

*Capitalism   Private ownership of the means of production and the organization of production for profit.

Caste   An exclusive, hereditary class. Most often refers to the system found in Hinduism, in which people who are members of specific occupations are separated from other occupations through rigid social divisions that prohibit any kind of contact.

Charismatic leader   A person who is able to gain followers through the force of her or his personality.

Charter schools   Schools established to operate outside the regulation of state and local government to provide an education that fits the needs of specific groups of students.

Civil disobedience   The belief that disobedience to the law (see *Law*) is an appropriate means of forcing a political system to change the law.

Civil society   The set of largely voluntary associations and interactions found in families, clubs, neighborhood associations, and so forth that operate outside the formal political system.

Class   A way of ranking or ordering society. In Marxism the ranking is based on the relationship to the means of production. Other ideologies rank on the basis of wealth, education, racial purity, service to the state, or some other criterion.

*Class struggle   In Marxism, used to describe the fundamental relationship between or among classes and the driving force of social change.

Cohousing   A modern version of cooperative housing in which people own individual houses or apartments and collectively own the land and common buildings.

Colonialism   A system in which one state (see *State*) controls another state for the benefit of the former (see also *Neocolonialism*).

Communal living   A group of people living together in an intentional community. Such communities have a wide range of forms, from charismatic or authoritarian leadership to consensual democracy, and from complete income sharing to complete private ownership.

*Communism   A social and economic system characterized by an authoritarian political system and a state socialist economic system. Originally meant "community of goods" or "goods publicly held" (see also *Full communism*).

Communitarianism   Focus on the community rather than on the individual.

*Community   A sense of common interest.

Consciousness raising   People meeting in small groups to explore their own experiences to learn about the ways they have been oppressed.

*Conservatism   The belief that social change should take place slowly with due account taken of tradition.

Consociational democracy   A system of power sharing in which each significant group in a country is guaranteed a place in the governing bodies and has a veto on some issues.

Cooperation   An economic theory in which people join together to form an economic unit from which they will all benefit.

*Corporatism   Sometimes called *neocorporatism*. The arrangement of political and economic relationships so that power groups in society are actively involved with government in making public policy.

Cosmopolitanism   See *Internationalism*.

Critical theory   A general theory that views society from the point of view of the need to change it.

Dalit   The group in the Indian caste system known as the *Untouchable*. *Dalit* means "the broken ones," and they are at the bottom of the rigid Indian social structure.

Dan   A Chinese word used in Minjung Theology referring to the ability of overcome *Han* with the help of God. See also *Han*.

Decentralization   A system in which power is moved from a central organization to regional centers or from a large group to the small groups that compose it.

Deep Ecology A movement that stresses the importance of the entire biosphere as opposed to only considering the welfare of human beings.

*Democracy A political system characterized by direct or indirect rule by the people (see also *Participatory democracy, Representation,* and *Consociational democracy*).

Democratic centralism A system developed by V. I. Lenin in which discussion within an organization is completely free until a decision is made, at which time all must support the decision.

Democratization The process of developing democratic institutions in societies in which they did not previously exist.

Developmental socialism A theory that proposes to use socialist economic policies to assist the economic development of a country.

Diaspora From a Greek word meaning "dispersion," diaspora originally was used to refer to Jews living outside the Holy Land but is now used to refer to any group with large numbers living outside their traditional homeland.

*Dictatorship of the proletariat In Marxism, the transitional stage after a successful revolution in which society is gradually transformed.

Direct democracy Democracy by citizens rather than by representatives.

Ecofeminism A movement that argues that women are closer to nature than men.

Economic democracy A theory that suggests that some portion of the economy, ranging from individual firms to the entire economy, should be run democratically.

Ecosocialism A movement that combines environmentalism and socialism.

Elitism The belief that society is and/or should be ruled by a small group of powerful people.

*Equality Sameness in some defined way.

*Equality of opportunity The situation that exists when an individual can succeed or fail on the basis of his or her own ability and effort with no artificial barriers to that success or failure.

Essentially contested concepts Concepts over which there are fundamental irreconcilable differences.

Ethnic group A group of people united by race or national origin.

Eugenics The selection or prevention of births to produce a particular type of human being.

Extremism The far Right and the far Left.

False consciousness A phrase within Marxism referring to the results of the class-based socialization process in which an individual gains an incorrect view of the world.

*Fascism Originally referred to the principles of the 1922 Italian anticommunist revolution. Now a general term referring to authoritarian political systems characterized by extreme nationalism (see also *National socialism*).

Federalism The division of political power between a central government and governments representing defined territories within the country. These latter units, called *states* in the United States, may be further divided into smaller units, but these smaller units do not have the same standing as the other two levels of government.

*Feminism An ideology centered on eliminating oppression of all human beings while stressing the importance of women.

Fifth World Used by some to describe those displaced as immigrants or refugees.

Fourth World Two very different meanings are in use today: one refers to indigenous peoples, the other refers to the poorest of the developing countries.

Frankfurt School The school of Marxist thought that developed critical theory (see *Critical theory*).

*Freedom The ability to act without constraint (see also *Liberty* and *Rights*).

Führer German word for "leader." Used in national socialism.

*Full communism The final stage of the Marxist theory of history.

Gaia hypothesis Proposes that our planet functions as a single organism that maintains conditions necessary for its survival.

General strike A strike in which all workers engage at the same time. Generally believed to be a major tactic in a revolution or to put pressure on a government.

Gerrymander A method of drawing legislative districts to ensure victory for one side and defeat for the other.

*Globalization   The process by which the world economy is becoming fully integrated. (see also *Antiglobalization*).

Government   See *Political system*.

Hadith   Sayings of the Prophet Muhammad.

Hajib   A large scarf that completely covers the hair.

Hajj   The pilgrimage to Mecca required at least once of every Muslim.

Han   A Chinese word adopted by Koreans to describe a perceived aspect of and split in their character. It refers, on the one side, to accumulated grievances, resentments, frustrations, and the like that build into a deep-seated sense of being wounded. On the other side, it refers to a self-mockery of these very feelings. See also *Dan*.

Hegemony   A word used by Antonio Gramsci and others to refer to the intellectual and cultural dominance of a class.

*Human nature   The essential characteristics of all human beings.

Idea of progress   The belief that the world is getting continually better. May or may not include a role for human action.

Ideologue   A true believer or one who has an extremely limited view of the world based on an ideology; an unusually strong believer in an ideology.

*Ideology   A value system or belief system accepted as fact or truth by some group. It composed of sets of attitudes toward the various institutions and processes of society.

Imam   Leader (Shiite Islam).

Immigration   Moving to a new country with the intent of establishing permanent residence.

Initiative   A method of bringing a proposed piece of legislation to a vote of the citizenry through a petition signed by citizens.

Internationalism   A belief in the need to unify the entire world in some way; a love of the world.

Jahiliyya   In Islam the period of "ignorance" or "barbarism" before Muhammad preached in Arabia. Used by Sayyid Qutb to refer to the present day.

Jihad   The struggle to follow Islam. Holy war.

Jingoism   Extreme nationalism.

*Justice   Fairness.

*Law   A rule established through an accepted procedure within a community that permits or prohibits certain actions. The system of rules so established.

Levellers   A seventeenth-century British movement favoring political equality.

*Liberalism   A general tendency to accept the ability of human beings to use their reason to reform the social system; a general tendency to accept change as inevitable but controllable; the advocacy of liberty.

*Liberation Theology   Initially described a Roman Catholic movement in South America that combined Marxism and theology in opposition to the oppression of the poor. Now refers to a wide variety of theologies of the oppressed within Christianity.

*Libertarianism   An ideology related to anarchism that advocates a radically reduced role for government. Also known as *minimalism*.

*Liberty   Freedom. Generally used to refer to legally established freedoms, such as civil rights (see also *Rights*).

Luddites   Men who broke up textile machinery in the early nineteenth century because they believed the machines were taking away jobs (see also *Neo-Luddites*).

Lumpenproletariat   The lowest class in the Marxist class analysis.

Majority rule   An electoral system in which 50 percent plus 1 (or more) of those voting win.

Maori   The minority population of New Zealand, which settled there, probably from Polynesia, about a thousand years ago.

Market socialism   Socialism that accepts some aspects of the free market.

*Materialism   The belief that matter or the material—as opposed to spirit, the spiritual, or the ideal—is the determining factor in human life.

Minimalism   See *Libertarianism*.

Monetarism   The belief that control of the money supply is the most important tool for manipulating a national economy and avoiding inflation.

Monkeywrenching   Direct action or civil disobedience to protect the biosphere.

Monopoly   An organization that controls trade in some commodity or a sector of the economy of a country.

Mosque   A building for Islamic worship.

Muslim   An adherent of Islam.

Nation   A people or race with common descent, language, history, and/or political institutions.

*National socialism   An ideology developed in Germany under the leadership of Adolf Hitler emphasizing an authoritarian political system, extreme nationalism, and racism (see also *Fascism*).

Nationalism   An ideology based on love for a nation or patriotism together with demands for action. See also *Patriotism*.

Nationalization of industries   Taking industries into public ownership.

Naturalization   A process by which a citizen of one country becomes a citizen of another country.

Negative liberty   Liberty achieved by limitations on government activity.

*Neocolonialism   A system of economic dominance over a former colony by an industrialized nation (see also *Colonialism*).

*Neoconservatism   The position held by former liberals in the United States who have become fiscal and foreign policy conservatives.

Neocorporatism   See *Corporatism*.

Neofascism   Contemporary versions of fascism found throughout the world but particularly common in France, Germany, and the United States.

*Neoliberalism   The position taken by liberals in the United States who have tried to modify the welfare-state image of liberalism.

Neo-Luddites   Contemporary opponents of technology (see also *Luddites*).

Neutralism   See *Nonalignment*.

New Left   The phenomenon of the so-called Sixties, from 1965 to 1975 in the United States, that tried to revitalize the old Left without making the same mistakes it had.

Niqab   A head covering worn by some Islamic women that covers the entire face except the eyes.

Nonalignment   A stance taken in the Third World in which nations refuse to

identify themselves with either of the major power blocs, hence the name *Third World*.

Ombudsman   A Swedish word that has been adopted into English to refer to a public official whose duties are to protect the rights of citizens against government, particularly bureaucracies.

PR   See *Proportional representation*.

Participation   In democracy, to be actively involved in the political system.

*Participatory democracy   A form of democracy in which individuals who are to be affected by a decision make the decision collectively.

Patriarchy   The system of male dominance that affects all social institutions.

*Patriotism   Love of country (see also *Nationalism*).

Petite bourgeoisie   In Marxist class analysis, the class of small shopkeepers, artisans, and the like who are being pushed down into the proletariat.

Pluralism   In the United States, the political system seen as composed of competing groups.

*Political obligation   The duty to obey the dictates of the political system.

*Political system   Those parts of the social system that have the ability to make authoritative or binding decisions for a territory.

Popular sovereignty   The belief, central to democracy, that ultimate political authority rests with the people.

Positive liberty   Liberty achieved through government support.

Postcolonialism   A contested concept concerned with the social, economic, political, cultural, and psychological conditions created by colonialism and the resistance to it.

Post-Marxism   Two forms of theorizing that have developed to apply the insights of Karl Marx to the contemporary world.

*Postmodernism   A contested concept that rejects universals and emphasizes the multiplicity of viewpoints through which people view the world.

Post-secularism   The belief that a period with little focus on religion has run its course and that religion has now returned as a major focus of life.

*Power   The ability to compel others to act in the way one wishes (see also *Authority*).

Privatization   The movement of activities from public control to private control.

Proletariat   That class in Marxism that has only its labor power to sell (see also *Bourgeoisie*).

Property   Something owned or possessed. Private property is something owned by an individual; public property is something owned collectively.

Proportional representation   A system of election in which individuals are elected on the basis of the proportion of the votes received rather than the majority, as under majority rule.

Queer Theory   A set of ideas based on the view that identities are not fixed.

Qur'an   The Muslim holy book.

Ramadan   The ninth month of the Muslim year. A month of fasting.

Reapportionment   The process of realigning the boundaries of electoral districts to bring them more in balance in the population.

Recall   A mechanism by which an elected official may be removed from office during his or her term through a vote of the electors in the area represented.

Referendum   A process of deciding political questions by the direct vote of the electorate.

Regionalism   The tendency that exists in a number of parts of the world to form economic and sometimes political agreements among states to form larger and more powerful units.

*Representation   A system in which voters choose other individuals to act in their place to make political decisions.

Republic   A state in which political decisions are made by elected representatives.

*Revolution   The process of bringing about radical political and social change, usually violently.

*Rights   Legally defined and enforceable freedoms. More generally, something to which a person is entitled, traditionally divided into natural rights, or rights that are due a person just because of his or her existence as a human being, and civil rights, or rights that are guaranteed by government (see also *Freedom* and *Liberty*).

Rochdale Society of Equitable Pioneers, or Rochdale Pioneers   The mid–nineteenth-century founders of the Cooperative movement.

Salafism   A conservative, puritanical Islamic sect that dominates Saudi Arabia.

Self-governing socialism   See *Self-management*.

Self-management   A type of socialism, sometimes known as *self-governing socialism*, in which workers' control (*see* Workers' control) operates in industry, and decentralized democracy works in government.

Shari'a   Islamic law.

Sikh   An adherent of a monotheistic religion founded in India around 1500.

Skinheads   A subculture group known for their shaved heads and distinctive style of dress (generally jeans, polos, military flight jackets, and boots). They are most often identified with the far Right, but there are antiracist skinheads and apolitical skinheads.

Social construction of reality   A phrase used in Marxism to refer to the socialization process. It means that an individual gains a view of the world based on her or his place in society.

Social Darwinism   The belief that relations among human beings are characterized by a struggle for survival.

*Social mobility   The process by which individuals move up or down in a society's social stratification system.

Social stratification   The system by which a society ranks the people within it (see also *Caste, Class, Equality of opportunity,* and *Social mobility*).

*Socialism   Public ownership of the means of production and distribution. May be highly centralized, as in communism, or very decentralized, as in self-management.

*Socialization   The process by which a society transmits its values from generation to generation.

*Social mobility   The process by which individuals move up or down in a society's social stratification system (see *Social stratification*).

*State   An organized community with its own political system and law.

Sufi   A believer in Sufism, an ascetic and mystical movement within Islam.

Sunna Exemplary behavior of Muhammad.

*Superstructure In Marxism, all those parts of life that are produced by the basic economic relations of society.

*Surplus value In Marxism, the value of goods produced above and beyond that needed to support labor.

Syndicalism A system in which the means of production and distribution are under the control of a federation of trade unions.

Taliban The former rulers of Afghanistan who were a small, extremely conservative sect within Islam. Spelled *Taleban* in the United Kingdom.

Terrorism A form of killing for political purposes. It differs from assassination in that it is frequently directed at nonpolitical targets and groups of people rather than individuals. Its purpose, as implied by the word, is to terrorize the people in a country.

Theocracy Literally, "rule by God." Usually refers to a government in which religious leaders rule directly or indirectly based on their claim of divine authority.

Toleration The recognition and acceptance of differing belief systems, particularly the acceptance of beliefs viewed as wrong.

Totalitarianism An authoritarian government that involves itself in all aspects of society, including the private lives of citizens. The word initially developed to refer to Germany under Hitler and the Soviet Union under Stalin.

Ulama Muslim religious scholar.

Utopia Literally means "no place." Term invented by Thomas More (1478–1535) that now refers to all representations of much better societies.

Utopian socialism Refers to the ideas of a number of nineteenth-century thinkers who proposed ways of changing the world. The phrase was first used by Friedrich Engels (1820–1895) and was meant as criticism.

Welfare The system of contributory and noncontributory pension, health, unemployment, and other benefits and social services funded and regulated by government.

Workers' control Power in the workplace in the hands of workers rather than management; the industrial system produced by such an arrangement.

Workplace democracy Democracy within the working environment.

Biographical Notes

These notes are intended to be a basic identification of those people mentioned in the text. More information on most of them can be found on the Web, but information found on the Web is often biased or inaccurate so care should be used to find the most reliable sources.

Edward Abbey (1927–1989) is revered by radical environmentalists for his fictional portrayals of environmental direct action.

Abigail Adams (1744–1818) was an early advocate of women's rights in the United States and wife of John Adams, the second president.

John Adams (1735–1826) was the second president of the United States.

Jane Addams (1860–1935) was a social settlement worker and peace advocate. She ran Hull House in Chicago from 1889 to 1935 and was awarded the Nobel Peace Prize in 1931.

Theodor Adorno (1903–1969) was one of the founders of the Frankfurt School.

Michel Aflaq (1910–1989) was a founder of the Baath Party.

Ahn Byung-mu (1922–1996) was the leading theologian of Minjung Theology.

Mullah Mohammad Omar Akhund (b. 1959?) is the founder and head of the Taliban movement in Afghanistan.

Ayaan Hirsi Ali (b. 1969) is a Dutch legislator who had emigrated from Somalia and wrote on the mistreatment of women in Islam. She resigned from the legislature in 2006 after questions were raised regarding the accuracy of her original application to enter the country. She is currently associated with the American Enterprise Institute in Washington, D.C.

Dante Alighieri (1265–1321) was an Italian poet best known as the author of the *Divine Comedy* who also contributed to political theory.

Louis Althusser (1918–1990) was a French Marxist philosopher best known as a theorist of ideology who also contributed more widely to late twentieth-century Marxist thought.

Benedict Anderson (b. 1936) is the Aaron L. Binenkorb Professor of International Relations and Director of the Modern Indonesia Program at Cornell University.

Susan B. Anthony (1820–1906) was one of the leaders of the women's suffrage movement.

Gloria Anzaldúa (1942–2004) was a Chicana lesbian feminist activist.

Aristophanes (c. 445–386/80 BCE) was a Greek playwright and satirist.

Mary Astell (1668–1731) was an English author who proposed a separate community of women in her *A Serious Proposal to the Ladies* (1694).

Mikhail Bakunin (1814–1876) was a leading Russian anarchist theorist who spent most of his life in western Europe.

Ban Ki-moon (b. 1944) of South Korea became the Secretary-General of the United Nations in 2006.

Hasan al-Banna (1906–1949) was the founder of the Muslim Brotherhood.

Simone de Beauvoir (1908–1986) was a French author best known for her reflections on the status of women, *Le Deuxième Sexe* (1949; published in English as *The Second Sex* in 1952).

Samuel Beckett (1906–1989) was an Irish playwright who moved to Paris in the 1930s. He is famous for his depictions of alienation, particularly in *Waiting for Godot*. He won the Nobel Prize in Literature in 1969.

Edward Bellamy (1850–1898) was a U.S. author remembered for his best-selling utopian novel *Looking Backward 2000–1887* (1888). A movement for social change was founded to promote Bellamy's ideas and was influential both in the United States and abroad.

Pope Benedict XVI (b. Joseph Ratzinger, 1927) was elevated to the papacy in 2005.

Jeremy Bentham (1748–1832) was the chief advocate of utilitarianism.

Alexander Berkman (1870–1936) was a friend of Emma Goldman and an activist in the American anarchist movement. He spent many years in prison in the United States.

Isaiah Berlin (1909–1997) was a British historian of ideas and a social theorist.

Eduard Bernstein (1850–1932) was a follower of Marx who rejected revolutionary socialism. He was a major Marxist revisionist, arguing for evolutionary socialism and political activity.

Hakim Bey (b. 1945) is a pseudonym of Peter Lamborn Wilson, coeditor of *Autonomedia* and *Semiotext(e)* who has written extensively on Sufism, Persian poetry, and Irish literature. As Bey he is known as one of the foremost theorists of contemporary anarchism.

Homi K. Bhabha (b. 1949) is an Indian-born professor at Harvard University and a major theorist of postcolonialism.

Vinoba Bhave (1895–1982) was an Indian spiritual leader.

Osama bin Laden (b. 1957) is the leader of the worldwide terrorist network Al Qaeda.

Salah al-Din Bitar (1912–1980) was a founder of the Baath Party.

Ernst Bloch (1885–1977) was a German Marxist philosopher best known for his book *Das Prinzip Hoffnung (The Principle of Hope;* 1959).

Allan Aubrey Boesak (b. 1946) is a South African minister, theologian, and activist. He was found guilty of fraud in his use of funds intended for the victims of apartheid and served a year in prison before being released on parole. He is currently Visiting Professor of Theology, Church, and Society at American Baptist Seminary of the West.

Clodovis Boff (b. 1944) is a Servite priest and a professor of theology at the Catholic University of São Paulo. He is the brother of Leonardo Boff.

Leonardo Boff (b. 1938) is Emeritus Professor of Ethics, Philosophy of Religion, and Ecology at the State University of Rio de Janeiro. For 20 years he was Professor of Systematic Theology at the Institute for Philosophy and Theology in Petrópolis, Brazil. He is one of the best-known theologians of Liberation Theology. Boff was a member of the Franciscan order but left after twice being "silenced" (meaning he could not publish) by the Vatican for his writings on Liberation Theology.

Murray Bookchin (1921–2006) was a major anarchist theorist who had recently been a major contributor to environmentalism in the United States.

Bernard Bosanquet (1848–1923) was an English conservative philosopher.

Willy Brandt (1913–1992) was active in German politics throughout the postwar period. He was best known for his period as governing mayor of Berlin, from 1957 to 1966, and as chancellor of the Federal Republic of Germany from 1969 to 1974.

William F. Buckley, Jr. (1925–2008) was a major spokesperson for conservatism in the United States. He founded the *National Review* in 1955 and hosted the television program *Firing Line* from 1966 to 1999.

Warren Buffett (b. 1930) is the CEO of Berkshire Hathaway and one of the trustees of the Bill and Melinda Gates Foundation.

Edmund Burke (1729–1797) is best known as the founder of conservatism.

George W. Bush (b. 1946) was the forty-third president of the United States and was elected to a second term in 2004.

Étienne Cabet (1788–1856) was a French utopian socialist and founder of the Icarian movement, which established a number of communities in the United States.

Ernest Callenbach (b. 1929) is the author of a series of books describing a fictional society that emphasizes ecology.

Albert Camus (1913–1960) was an Algerian-born French novelist and exponent of existentialism who won the Nobel Prize in literature in 1957. He was part of the French Resistance movement during World War II.

André Carson (b. 1974) is an African-American convert to Islam who was elected to the House of Representatives in 2008.

Rachel Carson (1907–1964) was an early writer on environmental issues.

Jimmy [James Edward] Carter (b. 1924) was the thirty-ninth President of the United States, from 1977–1981. Since leaving office, he has been active in promoting democracy worldwide, and he was awarded the Nobel Peace Prize in 2002.

Hugo Chavez (b. 1954) is the controversial president of Venezuela, elected in 1998.

Judy Chicago (b. 1939) is a feminist artist.

Robert Coles (b. 1929) is James Agee Professor of Social Ethics at Harvard and a research psychiatrist for Harvard University Health Services. He was awarded the Medal of Freedom by President Clinton in 1998, is known for his work with underprivileged children, and has written extensively on how children experience the world.

Álvaro Colom Caballeros (b. 1951) is a socialist who was elected president of Guatemala in 2007, calling for Social Democracy with a Mayan face. Guatemala has 23 Mayan ethnic groups that constitute 40 percent of the population. Colom is not Mayan but has been ordained as a Mayan priest and got support from the rural areas where most Mayans live. Guatemala is the poorest country in Latin America.

Alex Comfort (1920–2000) is best known for his books on sexual technique, but his published works include fiction, poetry, anarchist theory, and geriatric psychology.

James H. Cone (b. 1938) is the leading exponent of Black Theology and is Charles A. Briggs Distinguished Professor of Systematic Theology at Union Theological Seminary in New York.

Joseph Conrad (1857–1924) was a Polish-born English novelist.

Sir Bernard Crick (b. 1929) is a professor emeritus of politics at the University of London and was previously professor of political theory at Sheffield University. As a scholar he is best known for his book *In Defence of Politics* (1972 and later editions) and *George Orwell: A Life* (1982). He was knighted for service to citizenship education from his work chairing the Advisory Group on Citizenship in England, which issued the "Crick Report" in 1998.

Robert A. Dahl (b. 1915) is Sterling Professor of Political Science Emeritus at Yale University.

Charles Darwin (1809–1882) was a famous English naturalist who put forth a number of important theses about evolution.

Dorothy Day (1897–1980) was a leader of the Catholic Worker Movement. She was jailed in 1917 for protesting in front of the White House in favor of women's suffrage.

Antoine Louis Claude Destutt, Comte de Tracy (1754–1836) coined the term *ideology*.

Milovan Djilas (1911–1995) was vice president under Josep Tito when Tito originally came to power in 1945. He was expelled from the party in 1954, losing all his government positions, because of articles he had written criticizing the manner in which communism was developing in Yugoslavia. He was jailed in 1956 for writing about the "New Class" of communist elites that shared privileges; he was jailed again, from 1962 to 1966, for publishing *Conversations with Stalin*, which was based on his personal experience.

Ronald Dworkin (b. 1931) is Professor of Philosophy and Frank Henry Sommer Professor of Law at New York University.

Paul Ehrlich (b. 1932) is Bing Professor of Population Studies and President of the Center for Conservation Biology, Stanford University. He was one of the first people in the twentieth century to write about the problems of overpopulation.

Dwight David Eisenhower (1890–1969) was the thirty-fourth president of the United States, from 1953 to 1961. Before becoming president, he was a general in the U.S. Army and one of the leaders of the Allied Forces in World War II, chief of staff of the U.S. Army (1945–1948), and president of Columbia University (1948–1953).

Keith Ellison (b. 1963) is an African-American convert to Islam who was elected to the U.S. House of Representatives in 2006. He is the first Muslim to have been elected to Congress.

Jon Elster (b. 1940) is Robert K. Merton Professor of Social Sciences, Political Science Department, Columbia University, and is known for his work on rational choice theory.

Friedrich Engels (1820–1895) was a friend of and coauthor with Karl Marx.

Amitai Etzioni (b. 1929) is University Professor and Director of the Institute of Communitarian Policy Studies at George Washington University.

Jerry Lewis Falwell (1933–2007) was one of the most important religious leaders supporting political conservatism. He led the *Old-Time Gospel Hour* on radio and later on TV (from 1956). He founded the Lynchburg Christian Academy in Virginia, a day school for kindergarten through high school in 1967, and later founded Liberty University in Lynchburg in 1971. He established the Moral Majority in 1979.

Louis Farrakhan (b. Louis Eugene Walkott, 1933) is the current head of the Nation of Islam.

Shulamith Firestone (b. 1945) is the author of *The Dialectic of Sex* (1970), one of the more radical feminist texts of the period, and a strong advocate of women's reproductive rights.

Henry Ford (1863–1947) established the Ford Motor Company using assembly-line production.

Dave Foreman (b. 1946) is an active environmentalist and was a founder of Earth First! He left Earth First! in 1989 and founded the Wildlands Project, which seekswants to restrict humanity to specific areas.

Pim Fortuyn (b. Wilhelmus Simon Petrus Fortuijn, 1948–2002) was a Dutch gay, anti-immigrant activist murdered by an animal rights activist, who said he did so because of Fortuyn's scapegoating of Muslims.

Charles Fourier (1772–1837) was a French utopian socialist.

Saint Francis of Assisi (b. Giovanni Francesco Bernardone, 1182–1226) was the radical founder of the Franciscan movement and is now recognized in Liberation Theology as an early advocate of the poor.

Michael Freeden (b. 1944) is Professor of Politics and Professorial Fellow, Mansfield College, Oxford University, and is the editor of the *Journal of Political Ideologies.*

Paulo Freire (1921–1997) was a Brazilian social theorist best known for his book *The Pedagogy of the Oppressed* (1972). He is seen as a theorist of both anarchism and Liberation Theology.

Sigmund Freud (1856–1939) was the Austrian founder of psychoanalysis.

Betty Friedan (1921–2006) was a feminist author and lecturer.

Milton Friedman (1912–2006) won the Nobel Prize in Economics in 1976 for his work on monetary theory. He is the best-known conservative economist in the United States and taught economics at the University of Chicago for many years.

Francis Fukuyama (b. 1952) restarted the "end of ideology" debate in 1989. He is Bernard L. Schwartz Professor of International Political Economy at the Paul H. Nitze School of Advanced International Studies, Johns Hopkins University.

Margaret Fuller (1810–1850) was a teacher and writer struggling against the limited roles allowed women during her lifetime.

Mu'ammar Gadafi (b. al-Qaddafi, 1942) took over the leadership of Libya in 1969. He renamed the country the Libyan Arab Republic and led it under various titles until he renounced all titles in 1979. For many years he provided financial support for various terrorist groups and supported most movements opposed to the West. In the last few years, he has begun to establish more positive relations with the West.

Francis Galton (1822–1911) is now best known for his early work in genetics and for coining the word *eugenic.* In his lifetime he made significant contributions to geography, meteorology, psychology, statistics, and anthropology, as well as genetics.

Mohandas K. Gandhi (1869–1948) was a leader of the anticolonial movement in India who used nonviolence as a means of bringing about social change. He had been influenced by Henry David Thoreau, and he inspired Martin Luther King, Jr.

Roger Garaudy (b. 1913) is a French Marxist philosopher who was raised a Roman Catholic but converted to Islam in 1982. In 1995 he published a book denying the Holocaust and was tried and fined by a French court.

Bill Gates (b. 1955) is one of the founders and the Chairman of Microsoft and a trustee of the Bill and Melinda Gates Foundation with his wife Melinda Gates and Warren Buffett.

Melinda Gates (b. 1964) is a trustee of the Bill and Melinda Gates Foundation with her husband Bill Gates and Warren Buffett.

Clifford Geertz (1926–2006) was Professor Emeritus in the School of Social Science at the Institute for Advanced Study, Princeton, New Jersey.

Henry George (1839–1897) was an American economic theorist who developed a theory based on land taxation, known as the *single tax,* as a means of redistributing wealth.

Elbridge Gerry (1744–1814) was a Massachusetts politician who is best known for his manipulation of the boundaries of voting districts, called *gerrymandering.*

Anthony Giddens (b. 1938) is a theorist and advocate of "third way politics."

Charlotte Perkins Gilman (1860–1935) was a feminist writer, lecturer, and activist. She is best known for her novel *Herland* (1915).

William Godwin (1756–1836) was the earliest British anarchist theorist.

Joseph Goebbels (1897–1945) was Germany's minister for propaganda and national enlightenment under Adolf Hitler.

Emma Goldman (1869–1940) was known as "Red Emma" and was a leading anarchist, lecturer, popularizer of the arts, and agitator for birth control, women's rights, and free speech.

Albert [Arnold] Gore, Jr. (b. 1948) was the forty-fifth vice president of the United States. He served in the U.S. House of Representatives from 1977 to 1985 and was elected to the Senate from Tennessee in 1985, serving until 1993. He lost the 2000 presidential election to George W. Bush, even though he won the popular vote. Since then he has been an environmental activist and shared the 2007 Nobel Peace Prize with the United Nation's Intergovernmental Panel on Climate Change. His film *An Inconvenient Truth,* on global warming, won the Academy Award for a documentary film in 2007.

André Gorz (1923–2007) was a French social theorist. Gorz was a pseudonym, the name by which he was best known. He was born as Gerhard Hirsch, changed his name to Gérard Horst in 1930, and used Michel Bosquet as a pseudonym for his work as a journalist in the 1950s and 1960s.

Antonio Gramsci (1891–1937) was an Italian social theorist and is considered one of the most original Marxist theorists.

T[homas] H[ill] Green (1836–1882) was a professor of philosophy at Oxford University.

Alan Greenspan (b. 1926) served as chairman of the Federal Reserve, a position he held from 1988 to 2006. He is generally considered the most powerful unelected official in Washington, D.C.

Angelina E. Grimké (1805–1879) was an abolitionist and women's rights pioneer.

Sarah Moore Grimké (1792–1873) was an abolitionist and women's rights pioneer.

Gustavo Gutíerrez (b. 1928) is a Peruvian theologian, one of the founders of Liberation Theology, and was a professor at the Pontifical University of Peru. He is currently John Cardinal O'Hara Professor of Theology at the University of Notre Dame in the United States.

Jürgen Habermas (b. 1929) is one of the most important contemporary thinkers influenced by Marxism and the Frankfurt School. He is now probably most important as a theorist of deliberative democracy. He is Professor Emeritus of Philosophy, University of Frankfurt.

Michael Hardt (b. 1961) is Professor of Literature and Italian in the Department of Romance Studies at Duke University.

Michael Harrington (1928–1989) was cochair of the Democratic Socialists of America and a professor of political science at Queens College of the City University of New York.

H[erbert] L[ionel] A[dolphus] Hart (1907–1992) was the major theorist of legal positivism and author of the influential *The Concept of Law* (1961).

Nancy C. M. Hartsock (b. 1943) is a professor of political science and women's studies at the University of Washington in Seattle.

Friedrich August von Hayek (1899–1992) was one of the most important conservative thinkers of the twentieth century. His *The Road to Serfdom* (1944) was one of the most important defenses of free markets.

William Least Heat-Moon is the pseudonym of William Trogdon (b. 1939), the author of *Blue Highways* (1982), *PrairyErth* (1991), and *River-Horse* (1999). The name *Heat-Moon* is often seen without the hyphen.

Georg Wilhelm Friedrich Hegel (1770–1831) was the most important German philosopher of the nineteenth century.

Ammon Hennacy (1893–1970) was an important American anarchist.

Johann Gottfried von Herder (1744–1803) was a German philosopher, clergyman, and literary critic.

Julia "Butterfly" Hill (b. 1974) sat in a tree she called Luna for 738 days to protest logging. She was inducted into the Ecology Hall of Fame, continues as an environmental and political activist, and founded the organization Circle of Life.

Adolf Hitler (1889–1945) was founder and leader of the National German Workers' Party, chancellor (1933–1945), and head of state (1934–1945) of Germany. He was the leading figure of the Nazi movement and is still venerated by Nazis and neo-Nazis everywhere.

Thomas Hobbes (1588–1679) was one of the most important of the social contract theorists.

bell hooks was born Gloria Watkins (1952), but under the pen name hooks, she has written a number of important works on African-American feminism.

Dwight N. Hopkins is Professor of Theology at the University of Chicago Divinity School.

Max Horkheimer (1895–1973) was the director of the Institute for Social Research in Frankfurt, Germany, and developed the philosophical basis for critical theory.

Hubert H. Humphrey (1911–1978) was Democratic Senator from Minnesota (1949–1964 and 1971–1978) and was vice president from 1964 to 1968. He was the Democratic nominee for president in 1968.

Ivan Illich (1926–2002) was the Austrian-born cofounder of the Center for Intercultural Documentation (CIDOC) in Cuernavaca, Mexico. He was a radical priest who wrote extensively about contemporary society.

Ada María Isasi-Díaz (b. 1943) is a former Roman Catholic nun, a political refugee from Cuba, and the founder and primary exponent of Mujerista Theology, which addresses the concerns of Latina women.

Thomas Jefferson (1743–1826) was the third president of the United States from 1801 to 1809. Of all the things he accomplished, Jefferson thought his three most important actions were writing the Declaration of Independence and the Virginia Act for Establishing Religious Freedom and founding the University of Virginia.

Pope John Paul II (b. Karol Joseph Wojtyla, 1920–2005) was the first pope from Poland, elevated to the papacy in 1978.

Lyndon Baines Johnson (1908–1973) was president from 1963 to 1969. He presided over a period of great change in U.S. social policy, particularly the beginnings of the extension of civil rights to African Americans and the war on poverty. He is still best known for his failure to solve the Vietnam crisis.

Theodore Kaczynski (b. 1942) is the Unabomber, who assembled and mailed bombs that injured or killed individuals who worked in the fields of technology and industry. He published a manifesto calling for a return to a less technology-based life and direct action to achieve that goal. He is currently serving time in prison for his actions.

Franz Kafka (1883–1924) was a Jewish Czech author who wrote in German. He was born in Prague, which was then part of Austria. He is best known for his stories and novels depicting individuals in difficult situations.

Daniel Kahneman (b. 1934) is Professor of Psychology and Public Affairs at Princeton University. He was awarded the Nobel Prize in Economics in 2002.

John Fitzgerald Kennedy (1917–1963) was the thirty-fifth President of the United States, from 1961 to 1963, and the first Roman Catholic to be elected to that office.

John Maynard Keynes (1883–1946) was an English economist who argued for the use of government spending to stimulate the economy.

Ayatollah Ruhollah Khomeini (1903?–1989) was the religious leader of Iran after the Shiite overthrow of the Shah. He was one of the intellectual fathers of Islamic revivalism.

Rev. Dr. Martin Luther King (1929–1968) was a leader of the U.S. civil rights movement and won the Nobel Peace Prize in 1964.

Russell Kirk (1918–1994) was an important modern conservative. His *The Conservative Mind* (1953) provided an intellectual basis for modern conservatism. He founded the journals *Modern Age* in 1957 and *University Bookman* in 1960; both served as outlets for conservative writing.

Irving Kristol (b. 1920) is generally considered to have been the founder of U.S. neoconservatism. He was active on the far Left as an undergraduate and is now the John M. Olin Distinguished Fellow at the American Enterprise Institute, a conservative think tank. He founded the journals *The Public Interest* in 1965 and *The National Interest* in 1985.

Prince Pyotr [Peter] Kropotkin (1842–1921) was born into the Russian aristocracy but became the most important anarchist thinker of all time.

Will Kymlicka is Canada Research Chair in Political Philosophy, Queen's University, Canada, and one of the foremost theorists of multiculturalism.

Ernesto Laclau (b. 1935) is a professor of government at the University of Essex in the United Kingdom.

Emma Lazarus (1849–1887) was an American poet and essayist best known for her poem "The New Colossus," which appears on a plaque on the Statue of Liberty.

Ursula K. Le Guin (b. 1929) is a major science fiction, fantasy, and children's author whose novel *The Dispossessed* (1974) is a contribution to anarchist theory.

V. I. Lenin (b. Vladimir Ilyich Ulyanov, 1870–1924) was the leader of the Russian Revolution of 1917 and ruled the Soviet Union from the revolution to his death.

Aldo Leopold (1886–1949) was the author of *A Sand County Almanac* (1949) and an early environmentalist.

Abraham Lincoln (1809–1865) was the sixteenth president of the United States from 1861 to 1865.

John Locke (1632–1704) was an important British philosopher and political thinker. His most important works were *Essay Concerning Human Understanding* (1689), and in political thought, *Two Treatises of Government* (published in 1690 but written earlier). The U.S. Declaration of Independence was based on the *Second Treatise of Government.*

James Ephraim Lovelock (b. 1919) is an environmental theorist who originated the Gaia hypothesis. He is currently a Visiting Honorary Fellow at Green College, University of Oxford.

Ned Ludd [or Lud] provided the name for the Luddites. Possibly a mythical figure, he is credited with breaking up machinery for weaving around 1799 because he believed the machines would take over his job.

György Lukács (1885–1971) was a Hungarian philosopher and literary critic whose theoretical work, particularly *Geschichte und Klassenbewusstsein* (*History and Class Consciousness,* 1923) led to a revival of Marxist thought.

Rosa Luxemburg (c. 1870–1919) was a Polish Marxist revolutionary who opposed both Lenin's centralism and Bernstein's gradualism.

Jean-François Lyotard (1924–1998) was a French philosopher best known for his exposition of postmodernism.

Wangari Maathai (b. 1940) won the Nobel Peace Prize in 2004. She founded the Green Belt Movement, a grassroots development organization that mobilized poor women to plant over 30 million trees and also provides education on family planning and nutrition. She is the first woman from Africa to receive the Nobel Peace Prize.

Catharine A. MacKinnon (b. 1946) is Professor of Law, University of Michigan, and the most important feminist legal theorist.

James Madison (1751–1836) was secretary of state (1801–1809) during the presidency of Thomas Jefferson and was the fourth president of the United States, from 1809 to 1817. Madison is now mostly remembered as one of the authors of *The Federalist Papers* (1787–1788) and as a major contributor to the drafting of the U.S. Constitution.

Errico Malatesta (1850–1932) was a leading Italian anarchist theorist.

Malcolm X (b. Malcolm Little, 1925–1965) was a leader of the Nation of Islam but split from it to form the Organization of Afro-American Unity shortly before his assassination.

Nelson Rolihlahla Mandela (b. 1918) was the symbol of the campaign by the African National Congress (ANC) against apartheid, or racial separation, in South Africa. Imprisoned from 1964 to 1990, upon his release he was elected president of the ANC and then served as president of South Africa from 1994 to 1999.

Karl Mannheim (1893–1947) was a Hungarian-born sociologist active in Germany until he fled the Nazis in 1933. He is best known as the major theorist of the sociology of knowledge.

Mao Zedong (1893–1976) was the long-time leader of the People's Republic of China.

Herbert Marcuse (1898–1979) was a member of the Frankfurt School who stayed in the United States after the school returned to Germany following World War II. He was a major influence on the New Left.

Karl Marx (1818–1883) was the founder of communism.

Abu alA'la al-Mawdudi (1903–1979) of Pakistan was one of the intellectual founders of Islamic revivalism.

George McKay (b. 1950) is professor of cultural studies at the University of Central Lancashire, England.

Timothy McVeigh (1968–2001) was executed for bombing the Alfred P. Murrah Federal Office Building in Oklahoma City.

Dimitri Anatolyevich Medvedev (b. 1965) was elected President of the Russian Federation in 2008.

Lester Milbrath (1925–2007) was Professor Emeritus of Political Science and Sociology, State University of New York–Buffalo. Formerly he was the Director of the Research Program in Environment and Society in Buffalo.

Angela Miles (b. 1946) is Professor in the Department of Adult Education and Counseling Psychology at the Ontario Institute for Studies in Education in Toronto and is Associate Director of the Transformative Learning Centre.

John Stuart Mill (1806–1873) was the most influential philosopher in the English-speaking world in the nineteenth century. He is best known today for his essay *On Liberty* (1859).

David Miller (b. 1946) is Official Fellow of Politics at Nuffield College, Oxford University, England, and an important political theorist.

Warith Deen Mohammad (b. Wallace Dean Muhammad, 1933) became the leader of the Nation of Islam after the death of his father, Elijah Muhammad. But he rejected his father's racial message, renamed the organization the American Muslim Mission, and took it into the mainstream of Islam.

Charles de Secondat, baron de La Brède et de Montesquieu (1689–1755), better known as Montesquieu, was a French political thinker whose book *De l'esprit des lois (The Spirit of the Laws*, 1748) influenced the writers of the U.S. Constitution, particularly his advocacy of a separation of powers.

Cherríe Moraga (b. 1952) is a Chicana feminist author and playwright.

Evo Morales (b. 1959) was elected the socialist President of Bolivia in 2006.

J[ohn] P[ierpont] Morgan (1837–1913) was an American banker and financier.

William Morris (1834–1896) was the leader of the British arts and crafts movement whom some label as an anarchist theorist. He considered himself a Marxist.

Johann Most (1846–1906) was a German immigrant to the United States who advocated "propaganda by the deed" and published bomb-making manuals.

Chantal Mouffe (b. 1943) is Quinton Hogg Senior Research Fellow at the Centre for the Study of Democracy at the University of Westminster in London.

Muhammad (570–632) was the founder of Islam.

Elijah Muhammad (b. Elijah Poole, 1897–1975) was the spiritual leader of the Nation of Islam.

John Muir (1838–1914) was born in Scotland but spent his life in the United States as a naturalist and advocate for the preservation of wilderness. In particular, he was instrumental in getting Congress to pass the bill that established a national park to protect the Yosemite Valley. He was one of the founders and the first president of the Sierra Club.

Benito Mussolini (1883–1945) was the founder of the fascist movement and head of the Fascist Party in Italy.

Ralph Nader (b. 1934) was a leader for automobile safety and on various environmental and safety issues before becoming the presidential candidate of the Green Party in the 2000 U.S. election. He ran as an independent candidate in the 2004 and 2008 presidential elections.

Arne Naess (b. 1912) is a Norwegian philosopher who coined the term *Deep Ecology.*

Gamal Abdel Nasser (1918–1970) was the leader of the Egyptian revolution and head of the country for many years.

Sergei Nechaev (1847–1882) was an advocate of terrorism and the inspiration for the insane revolutionary in Fyodor Dostoevsky's *The Possessed* (1871).

Antonio Negri (b. 1933) was a professor of political science at the University of Padua. He was arrested in connection with terrorist activities in Italy in the seventies, spent some years in exile in France, and is currently serving his sentence in Rome. Many believe that his arrest and conviction were without basis.

Jawaharlal Nehru (1889–1964) was a leader of the anticolonial movement in India and prime minister of India from 1947 to 1964.

A. S. Neill (1883–1973) was a pioneering educator who founded the Summerhill School based on democratic ideals.

Richard Milhous Nixon (1913–1994) was president of the United States from 1969 to 1974, the only president forced to resign from office to avoid impeachment. He presided over the largest expansion of social welfare programs in U.S. history, ended the war in Vietnam, and reestablished political relations with the People's Republic of China.

Kwame Nkrumah (1909–1972) was the leader of Ghana from 1957, when it gained independence, to 1966.

Robert Nozick (1938–2002) was a professor of philosophy at Harvard University and author of *Anarchy, State, and Utopia* (1974), the best exposition of anarcho-capitalism.

U Nu (1907–1995) was a leader of Burmese independence, the first prime minister of Burma (1948–1962), and as U Thant, secretary-general of the United Nations (1961–1971).

Julius K. Nyerere (1922–1999) was the first president of Tanganyika and then of Tanzania.

Susan Moller Okin (1947–2004) was Martha Sutton Weeks Professor of Ethics in Society in the Department of Political Science at Stanford University. At the time of her death, she was the Marta S. Horner Distinguished Visiting Professor at the Radcliffe Institute for Advanced Study.

Robert Owen (1771–1858) was a British utopian socialist who founded the New Harmony community in Indiana.

Thomas Paine (1737–1809) was a political agitator, revolutionist, and political theorist.

Olof Palme (1927–1986) was a Swedish leader of European democratic socialists.

Christobel Pankhurst (1880–1958) was a daughter of Emmeline Pankhurst and was active in the British suffrage movement.

Emmeline Pankhurst (1858–1928) was a leader of the British suffrage movement.

Sylvia Pankhurst (1882–1960) was a daughter of Emmeline Pankhurst and a leader of the British suffrage movement.

Anton Pannekoek (1873–1960) was the Dutch founder of Council Communism.

William L[uther] Pierce (1933–2002) was the leader of the National Alliance.

Augusto Pinochet (1915–2006) was head of the military government that ruled Chile from 1973 to 1990. In power he suppressed the opposition, leaving at least 3,000 Chileans dead. He is credited with reviving the Chilean economy, but an investigation for corruption begun before his death continues today.

Plato (c. 427?–347 B.CE.) was the founder of social philosophy in the West.

Richard Allen Posner (b. 1939) is a judge on the U.S Court of Appeals, Seventh Circuit, and a Senior Lecturer in Law at the University of Chicago Law School.

Pierre-Joseph Proudhon (1809–1865) was a leading French anarchist theorist.

Vladimir Putin (b. 1952) was the president of the Russian Federation from 2000 to 2008, when, according to the Russian constitution, he had to retire, at which point his chosen successor appointed him Prime Minister. He was a colonel in the KGB (the Soviet equivalent of the U.S. Central Intelligence Agency) until 1990. In 1999 Boris Yeltsin (1931–2007) appointed him prime minister, and later that year, when Yeltsin stepped down, Yeltsin appointed Putin president.

Robert D. Putnam (b. 1941) is the Peter and Isabel Malkin Professor of Public Policy at Harvard University and the author of *Bowling Alone: The Collapse and Revival of American Community* (2000).

Sayyid Qutb (1906–1966) was an Egyptian Sunni Muslim leader and one of the intellectual founders of Islamic revivalism. He was jailed from 1954 to 1964 and executed for his opposition to Egypt's leaders.

Thomas Rainborough [or Rainborowe] (1610–1648) was one of the leaders of the army who sided with the Levellers in the English Civil War.

Tariq Ramadan (b. 1962) is a philosopher who advocates anchoring Islamic principles in the culture of western Europe. He a Professor of Islamic Studies in the Faculty of Theology at the University of Oxford, England and a Visiting Professor at Erasmus University, Rotterdam, The Netherlands. Ramadan is also a Senior Research Fellow at St. Antony's College, Oxford; Doshisha University, Kyoto, Japan; and the Lokahi Centre, London.

Ayn Rand (1905–1982) was a novelist, lecturer, and essayist who influenced the growth of libertarianism and minimalism in the United States.

Marcus G. Raskin (1934–2002) was cofounder of the Institute for Policy Studies.

Walter Rauschenbusch (1861–1918) was a Baptist minister and one of the leading theorists of the Social Gospel movement.

John Rawls (1921–2002) was a professor of philosophy at Harvard University and has been the major liberal theorist of the twentieth century.

Élisée Réclus (1830–1905) was a Belgian geographer and an anarchist theorist.

Ernest Renan (1823–1892) was a French philologist and historian.

Paul Ricoeur (1913–2005) was a French philosopher who taught for many years at the University of Chicago. He published *Lectures on Ideology and Utopia* in 1986 but is best known for his works on the meaning of life.

John G[lover] Roberts, Jr. (b. 1955) is the current Chief Justice of the U.S. Supreme Court.

George Lincoln Rockwell (1918–1967) was the leader of the American Nazi Party until his assassination.

Llewellyn H. Rockwell (b. 1944) is the Founder and President of the Ludwig von Mises Center in Auburn, Alabama.

John Roemer (b. 1945) is the Elizabeth S. and A. Varick Stout Professor of Political Science and Economics at Yale University.

Murray Rothbard (1926–1995) was a leading American anarcho-capitalist.

Jean-Jacques Rousseau (1712–1778) is the best-known French political philosopher.

Claude-Henri Saint-Simon (1760–1825) was a French utopian socialist.

Margaret Sanger (1883–1966) was an early advocate of birth control and women's rights.

Ziauddin Sardar (b. 1951) is an Islamic liberal theorist. He is Editor of *Futures* and Visiting Professor in the School of Art of City University, London.

Jean-Paul Sartre (1905–1980) was a French novelist and philosopher.

Albert Sauvy (1898–1990) was a French demographer who coined the term *Third World*.

Phyllis Schlafly (b. 1924) is a leading advocate of conservatism and the best-known conservative antifeminist. She established her conservative credentials with the book *Choice Not An Echo* in 1964 and founded the Eagle Forum in 1972 to oppose the Equal Rights Amendment

Sarah Scott (1723–1795) was a British writer now considered an early feminist.

Amartya Sen (b. 1933) is Lamont University Professor, Harvard University, and Adjunct Professor of Population and International Health, Harvard University, and a Fellow of Trinity College, Cambridge University. He won the Nobel Prize in Economics in 1998.

Léopold Sédar Senghor (1906–2001) was a leader of the anticolonial movement in Senegal and the leader of the country after independence. He became known as a significant poet in French.

George Sessions (b. 1938) is one of the primary theorists of Deep Ecology. He is the former Chair of the Philosophy Department and Professor of Philosophy at Sierra College, Rocklin, California.

Charles M[onroe] Sheldon (1857–1946) was a Kansas minister and author of *In His Steps* (1896–97).

Luíz Ignácio Lula da Silva (b. 1945) was elected president of Brazil in 2002.

Peter Singer (b. 1946) is the Ira W. DeCamp Professor of Bioethics at the University Center for Human Values, Princeton University. He is the author of *Animal Liberation: A New Ethics for Our Treatment of Animals* (1975) and is credited with beginning the modern animal rights movement.

Ellen Johnson Sirleaf (b. 1938) is the first democratically elected woman leader of an African country.

Adam Smith (1723–1790) is best known as the author of *The Wealth of Nations: An Inquiry into the Nature and Causes of the Wealth of Nations* (1776).

Georges Sorel (1847–1922) was a French journalist and political theorist.

George Soros (b. György Schwartz, 1930) is a Hungarian born financial speculator and head of Soros Fund Management and the Open Society Institute.

Herbert Spencer (1820–1903) was an English philosopher and the major proponent of social Darwinism.

Lysander Spooner (1808–1887) was a lawyer, abolitionist, and an early American anarcho-capitalist.

Joseph Stalin (b. Iosif Vissarionovich Dzhugashvili, 1879–1953) was the leader of the Soviet Union after Lenin.

Elizabeth Cady Stanton (1815–1902) was one of the founders of the first women's rights conventions in 1848 in Seneca Falls, New York, and a leader of the nineteenth-century women's rights movement.

Manfred B. Steger (b. 1961) is Professor of Global Studies, Academic Director of the Globalism Institute; Program Director in the Global Cities Institute at RMIT University, Melbourne, Australia; and a Senior Research Fellow at the Globalization Research Center in Honolulu, Hawaii.

George E. Stiglitz (b. 1943) is now thought of as an antiglobalization campaigner, but he supports globalization, just not the way it is taking place. He is University Professor in the Business School, the Department of Economics, and the School of International and Public Affairs at Columbia University. He was a Senior Vice President and Chief Economist for the World Bank, and he shared the Nobel Prize in Economics in 2001.

Max Stirner (b. Johann Kasper Schmidt, 1806–1856) was the founder of individualist anarchism.

Mahmoud Mohamed Taha (1909–1985) was a Sudanese politician and theologian who argued for a radical rereading of the *Qur'an* based on the historical circumstances of its writing.

Charles Taylor (b. 1931) is Board of Trustees Professor of Law and Philosophy at Northwestern University and Professor Emeritus of Political Science and Philosophy at McGill University. He was formerly Chicele Professor of Moral Philosophy at Oxford University. He won the Templeton Prize For Progress toward Research or Discoveries about Spiritual Realities in 2007.

Harriet Taylor (1807–1858) wrote about women's rights and was the wife of John Stuart Mill, whom she influenced to write on the subject.

William Thompson (1775–1833) wrote on socialism and women's rights, the latter material in collaboration with Anna Doyle Wheeler.

Henry David Thoreau (1817–1862) was a naturalist, writer, and advocate of civil disobedience.

James Tobin (1918–2002) won the Nobel Prize in Economics in 1981. He proposed a worldwide tax on foreign exchange trading and bond trading that became known as the "Tobin Tax."

Leo Tolstoi (1828–1910) was a famous Russian novelist who is also known as an anarchist theorist.

Camilo Torres (1929–1966) was a priest who joined the National Liberation Army (ELN) of Columbia and died in combat.

Sojourner Truth (b. Isabella Baumfree, 1797–1883) was born a slave and became a noted lecturer and abolitionist.

Benjamin R. Tucker (1854–1939) was one of the most important American anarchist theorists.

Unabomber See *Theodore Kaczynski.*

Theo van Gogh (1957–2004) was a Dutch filmmaker who made a film depicting violence against women in Muslim countries and was murdered by a young Muslim man.

Tabare Vazquez (b. 1940) was elected president of Uruguay in 2004.

Amina Wadud (b. 1952) is an African-American Muslim convert who led a mixed-gender congregation in prayer March 18, 2005, and has continued to do so throughout the world. She retired from Virginia Commonwealth University and is now Visiting Scholar at the Starr King School of the Ministry in Berkeley, California.

Wilhelm Richard Wagner (1813–1883) is best known for his operas expressing Teutonic mythology.

Muhammad bin Abd al-Wahhab (1702–1791) was the founder of the Wahhabist sect of Islam, whose descendants unified the Saudi kingdom. He encouraged people to abandon polytheism and worship Allah alone. The sect is more accurately known as *Salafism.*

Alice Walker (b. 1944) is an African-American author who is best known for her novel *The Color Purple* (1982).

Colin Ward (b. 1924) was one of the editors of the anarchist weekly *Freedom* from 1947 to 1960. He founded *Anarchy* and edited it from 1961 to 1970. An architect, teacher, lecturer, and freelance writer, Ward significantly advanced anarchist theory in the second half of the twentieth century.

Josiah Warren (c. 1798–1874) was an early American anarchist theorist.

Anna Doyle Wheeler (1785–1848) was an early English socialist feminist and collaborated with William Thompson on many projects, particularly on *Appeal of One Half of the Human Race, Women, Against the Pretensions of the Other Half, Men* (1825).

Rowan Williams (b. 1950) is the Archbishop of Canterbury and has been the titular head of the Anglican Church since 2002.

Mary Wollstonecraft (1759–1797) was one of the earliest feminist theorists.

George Woodcock (1912–1995) was a British anarchist theorist who settled in Canada.

Frances Wright (1795–1852) was a lecturer and writer concerned with women's rights, slavery, and the plight of workers.

Boris Yeltsin (1931–2007) was appointed President of Russia in 1990 and then elected in 1991, the first popularly elected President. He advocated greater democracy and economic reforms and withstood a number of attempts to remove him from office. He resigned on December 31, 1999.

Muhammad Yunus (b. 1940) is the founder of the Grameen Bank and was awarded the Nobel Peace Prize in 2006.

Index